The Haunted House
on Film

ALSO BY PAUL MEEHAN
AND FROM MCFARLAND

*The Ghost of One's Self: Doppelgangers in Mystery,
Horror and Science Fiction Films* (2017)

The Vampire in Science Fiction Film and Literature (2014)

Horror Noir: Where Cinema's Dark Sisters Meet (2011)

Cinema of the Psychic Realm: A Critical Survey (2009)

*Tech-Noir: The Fusion of Science Fiction and
Film Noir* (2008; paperback 2018)

The Haunted House on Film

An Historical Analysis

PAUL MEEHAN

McFarland & Company, Inc., Publishers
Jefferson, North Carolina

ISBN (print) 978-1-4766-7458-2
ISBN (ebook) 978-1-4766-3820-1

LIBRARY OF CONGRESS AND BRITISH LIBRARY
CATALOGUING DATA ARE AVAILABLE

© 2020 Paul Meehan. All rights reserved

No part of this book may be reproduced or transmitted in any form or by any means, electronic or mechanical, including photocopying or recording, or by any information storage and retrieval system, without permission in writing from the publisher.

Front cover images © 2020 Shutterstock

Printed in the United States of America

*McFarland & Company, Inc., Publishers
Box 611, Jefferson, North Carolina 28640
www.mcfarlandpub.com*

Table of Contents

Preface: A Haunted House Near You	1
Introduction: Houses of Horror	5
One. No Ghosts Allowed: Mystery House Films of the Silent and Early Sound Period (and Beyond)	19
Two. Haunting Comedy: Dark Laughter in a Haunted House	36
Three. Love Amongst the Ruins: Haunted Romance	65
Four. The Classics	82
Five. A Haunting We Will Go: 1940s–1980s	111
Six. "Based on a True Story"	139
Seven. Haunted Houses for a New Millennium	158
Conclusion: The Haunted Screen	198
Filmography	203
Chapter Notes	211
Bibliography	212
Index	213

Preface: A Haunted House Near You

There's a house that's believed to be haunted in most every neighborhood in America. It's usually a run-down dwelling or abandoned home that attracts kids looking for ghostly thrills. In my old neighborhood in Brooklyn there was a house where an elderly woman lived that we kids called the "Witches House," a place that hadn't been painted in many years and had a dilapidated look. The eccentric old lady who lived there alone reportedly never left the house and had all her food and other goods delivered to her door. She was doubtless just an old woman who no longer had the wherewithal to keep the place up, but our childish imaginations transformed her into an evil witch, and her house into a haunt. On Halloween the braver boys would dare to ring the doorbell and run away, but the "witch" within never put in an appearance.

In his nonfiction book on the horror genre *Danse Macabre*, famed writer Stephen King recounts an anecdote about an abandoned place in his childhood hometown of Durham, Maine, called the Marsten House. King relates how, when he was ten years old, he and another boy snuck into the ramshackle mansion to explore the deserted dwelling, which contained decrepit furniture, a badly out of tune piano, stacks of moldering magazines and other pieces of junk. Not content to confine themselves to the ground floor, the two boys decided to explore the upstairs rooms, but unbeknownst to them King's older brother and cousin had followed them into the house. King and his companion were promptly scared out of their wits when the kids downstairs began to play eerie chords on the old piano, much to the amusement of the older boys. While it was just a prank, King and his friend were permanently spooked and never returned to the Marsten House.

When I moved to the Richmond District in the western part of San Francisco during the 1990s, I discovered that about three blocks from where I live was another ruined house with a much more sinister reputation. At 6114 California Street, nestled between two modern apartment buildings, lay the ruins of a weird, medieval-looking house painted entirely in black. It reminded me of the mad inventor Rotwang's anachronistic dwelling lying in the middle of the futuristic city in Fritz Lang's 1927 sci-fi classic *Metropolis*. The decrepit house was surrounded by a chain link fence, while busted-up furniture and other refuse littered the front yard. I would later learn that the creepy old place was called the "Black House" or the "Devil's House" because it had been the abode of one Anton LaVey, founder and high priest of the Church of Satan.

LaVey grew up in Marin County and reportedly quit school at 16 to join the Clyde Beatty Circus, where he performed as a lion tamer and magician. A showman and huckster at heart, LaVey hit his stride in San Francisco during the psychedelic 1960s when he fell in with a group of weird characters who inhabited another strange abode, the Westerfeld House, a Victorian mansion in the city's Haight-Ashbury district. At the time, the notorious writer and experimental filmmaker Kenneth Anger was renting the mansion, where he shot a short film entitled *Invocation of My Demon Brother* which featured a musical soundtrack by Mick Jagger. Playing the role of Lucifer in the film was Bobby Beausoleil, who would later join the homicidal Manson family cult and would commit the murder of music teacher Gary Hinman on Manson's orders. Anger moved out of the Westerfeld in 1967, but occult rituals continued to be performed over the years, and when the mansion was sold in 1986 the new owner had monks from the Hartford Street Zen Center perform a cleansing and blessing for the house, which seems to have exorcised any residual dark forces lingering therein.

In 1966 LaVey founded the Church of Satan and moved his operation to the house at 6114 California Street, where he authored his demonic manifesto, *The Satanic Bible*. He painted the house black and began conducting satanic rituals inside that soon brought him notoriety and made him a minor celebrity. Sporting a shaven head, a devilish beard and black robes, he cut a diabolic figure as he rubbed elbows with Hollywood luminaries like Sammy Davis, Jr., and Jayne Mansfield and initiated them into the church. Dubbed the "Black Pope" by the media, he claimed to have been hired as a "technical advisor" for director Roman Polanski's 1968 horror hit *Rosemary's Baby*, and even to have played the role of the devil in a key scene, but this cannot be verified. Ceremonies conducted at the Black House were chiefly of the orgiastic variety, but some rituals reportedly involved cadaver body parts obtained from a local coroner. In spite of its dark reputation, however, no acts of murder or mayhem were ever associated with the Black House, and the Satanists were considered just another far-out, but harmless, hippie cult.

LaVey's dark star began to wane after the infamous "Helter Skelter" murder spree perpetrated by Charles Manson and his demented family in Los Angeles in 1969. Roman Polanski's wife Sharon Tate was murdered, along with coffee heiress Abigail Folger, Hollywood hair stylist Jay Sebring, Steven Parent, Wojciech Frykowski, Leno LaBianca, Rosemary LaBianca, and Sharon Tate's unborn son posthumously named Paul in a brutal homicide committed by Manson's followers. As Sebring was a member of the Church and LaVey also had connections with Polanski and Manson Family members Bobby Beausoleil and Susan Atkins, LaVey and the Church suffered from guilt by association and went into a steep decline. LaVey continued to conduct the rites of Lucifer in the Black House, but the cult faded into irrelevance during succeeding decades.

The Black Pope died in 1997 and the house fell into ruin, becoming the dilapidated wreck I would become familiar with. The tiny single-family home, which had been built in 1905, was bulldozed in 2001 and replaced by an unremarkable two-and-a-half story condo built in 2008. The city retired the 6114 California Street address, and today no one would know that the Church of Satan had ever existed there. But the Black House was not the only haunt in my neighborhood.

My friend Toby (not his real name) lives in a third story walk-up apartment in the Richmond District located a few blocks from Golden Gate Park. Toby and I played together in the house band in a local club for a couple of years, and his apartment is a gathering place for musicians who like to get together for informal jam sessions. It's a well-worn but spacious place with excellent acoustics for recording. Doing some research, I found that the house was built in 1910, just four years after the devastating 1906 San Francisco earthquake.

From time to time Toby would tell us that his apartment was haunted. He would talk about how the ghost (which he perceived as being female) would call out his name at night and made loud, clamorous noises. He also said that he got in trouble with one of the other tenants who thought that another person was living in the apartment with him. None of us thought very much about any of this, as the ghost had never put in an appearance during our many visits.

All this was to change during a jam session one afternoon in Toby's living room, where I was playing synthesizer, Toby was on amplified harmonica and another musician, Chuck, was playing alto sax and the session was being recorded on a Tascam DR-05 digital recorder. We had been playing for several hours and were tired and trying to get our rhythm in sync when a strange, anomalous sound was heard in the room. It was a loud, raucous tapping sound that seemed to come from somewhere in front of me and appeared to be trying to play in sync with what we were playing. When we were through jamming, I played the recording back and noted that the anomalous sound was curiously flat and lacked what is called "room tone" or "room reverb" and seemed to be entirely artificial.

On another occasion the session was over and the musicians were packing up their instruments. It was early evening and I happened to be alone in the apartment when I suddenly had the eerie sensation that someone, or something, was watching me. I looked around, half expecting to see a dark form emerging from the shadows, but I didn't see anything. Needless to say, I got out of there as fast as I could. Since then, I've thought about convincing Toby to let me stay overnight at his place, but I'm not sure I have the nerve.

My strange experiences at Toby's haunted house got me to thinking about movies on this theme, and after doing some research I discovered that books on this important subgenre of the horror film were practically non-existent. While these ghostly tales have a long and illustrious pedigree in the literatures of England, Japan and America, it is only in the last two decades that the haunted house film has attained a measure of critical acclaim and mass popularity.

Surprisingly, when one looks back at the history of these films, they do not all fall into the horror category, but are equally at home in the comedy, mystery and romance genres. And it turns out that ghosts are not the only inhabitants of these haunts, which are also tenanted by gangsters, psycho-killers, vampires, poltergeists, criminal masterminds, gorillas, monsters and djinns. Enter here into a haunted realm bound only by the borders of imagination.

Introduction: Houses of Horror

Since ancient times, legends about haunted houses have both fascinated and terrified humankind. The haunted house is a liminal realm, a twilight locus between two realities where, as one of the characters in the film *The Others* (2001) explains, "the world of the dead gets mixed up with the world of the living." Its rooms and corridors reek of death and decay and harbor ghastly beings and dreadful secrets. It is an accursed place where ghosts and other terrors walk.

Yet as frightening as haunted houses are, they are also a source of entertainment for those who get a thrill out of being scared out of their wits by the supernatural, or the illusion thereof. Allegedly real-life haunted houses such as the Winchester Mystery House in San Jose, California, the Lemp Mansion in St. Louis, Missouri, and the House of the Seven Gables in Salem, Massachusetts, are tourist attractions, and some even offer overnight stays for would-be ghostbusters to catch a glimpse of a spook or record evidence of one on digital media. There are also highly successful theme parks and so-called "haunted attractions" or "haunts" such as Disney's Haunted Mansion that simulate ghostly encounters inside a haunted house.

The concept of the haunted house has provided inspiration for many classic Gothic romances and modern horror tales. It has also inspired many of the most memorable films in the horror genre, including *The Old Dark House*, *The Uninvited*, *Psycho*, *The Innocents*, *The Haunting*, *Rosemary's Baby*, *The Shining*, *The Amityville Horror*, *The Exorcist* and *Poltergeist*. In the 21st century, the haunted house film is more popular than ever before in crowd pleasers and critically acclaimed cinema fare such as *The Devil's Backbone*, *The Others*, *The House Next Door*, *The Grudge*, *1408*, *The Woman in Black* and *Crimson Peak*, among others.

The haunted house phenomenon stretches back into antiquity. The first recorded instance was chronicled by the Roman writer Pliny the Younger (61–112 CE) in a letter to his patron Lucias Sura describing a haunted house in the city of Athens. The place remained uninhabited until the philosopher Athenodorus (74 BCE–7 CE) rented it at a reduced rate. The house was haunted by the ghost of an old man bound in chains that appeared to the philosopher during the first night of his residence. Athenodorus followed the apparition into the building's courtyard, where he noted that it disappeared at a certain spot. The next day he had the spot dug up, whereupon the skeleton of the old man wrapped in chains was discovered. The remains were exhumed and given a proper burial, and the ghost never bothered the philosopher again.

This story contains several features that would characterize the haunted house tale for centuries to come. First, the haunted property is offered for rent at a reduced rate due to the presence of a ghost. Second, the living resident of the house was obliged to discover the underlying mystery behind the haunt. Third, once this reason was ascertained, the ghost could be placated and exorcized and the situation resolved.

Plutarch (46–120 CE), a Greek historian of the Roman period, relates a story about a haunted bath house in his classic work *Lives of the Noble Greeks and Romans*. These events took place sometime during the Roman occupation of Greece during the first century CE, in the author's hometown of Chaeronea, located in the province of Boeotia. The story centers on a handsome but impetuous youth in the town named Damon Peripoltas. A Roman legionary captain became passionately fond of the young man, but when the captain's gifts and entreaties were rebuffed by the lad, the soldier threatened him with violence. In response, Damon and a number of his companions murdered the captain and fled into the surrounding wilderness to escape punishment and became a band of outlaws and brigands.

The town magistrates pronounced a death sentence upon Damon for the crime, but were unable to enforce it, and the outlaws remained in the countryside looting and pillaging until a plan was devised. Word went out to Damon that the murder had been forgiven, and that he had been awarded a position in the town government. Lured out of the woods by this ruse, Damon was set upon and killed in the town's bath house. In the aftermath of the killing, strange apparitions were seen and eerie groans heard inside the Chaeronean baths. The haunted building was walled up, but Plutarch reports that spectral forms and terrible cries continued to be heard by people in the neighborhood. Once again, a building becomes haunted by the victim of a violent crime that is committed within its confines.

Another take on the haunted house theme from the Roman era appears in the work of the comic playwright Plautus (254–184 BCE) in his play entitled *Mostellaria*, which loosely translates from Latin as "The Haunted House." Like Pliny's story it is set in Athens, where a dissolute young man named Philoaches has borrowed a large sum of money to purchase the freedom of Philematium, the slave girl he is in love with. As he and his friends attend to their debaucheries, his father Theuropides unexpectedly returns from overseas and demands an accounting for the loan. In order to cover up his master's indiscretions, the slave Tranio greets Theuropides before he can enter his house and forbids him from entering because the house is haunted. Tranio explains that Philoaches has used the loan to purchase the house next door because their family can no longer live in the haunted house. A series of comic misadventures ensues as the play proceeds to a happy ending. While *Mostellaria* is a work of comic fiction, it does indicate that the ancient Romans were well acquainted with the concept of the haunted house. The play also demonstrates the comedic possibilities of the theme.

Apart from myth and legend, the existence of haunted houses has long been debated in various law courts. In a case brought before a French court in 1575, the plaintiff, M. Gilles Bolacre, had rented a house in the city of Tours and after moving in claimed to have been plagued by paranormal disturbances. In light of this, Bolacre sued the owner before the local tribunal to obtain a declaration that the lease was null and void. The declaration was granted, but the lessor of the house later appealed to a higher court in Paris, where the matter was argued a second time and the voiding of the lease was eventually upheld once more.

In modern real estate law, a property is said to have a *stigma* if buyers or tenants avoid it for reasons unrelated to its physical features or condition. A stigma is attributed to events that have previously transpired on the property, including natural death, criminal activity, suicide and murder. Examples of stigmatized real estate include the Los Angeles house where Sharon Tate and several others were murdered by members of the Manson family in 1969, which could not be sold and was eventually torn down, and the home in Amityville, Long Island, where the DeFeo family was murdered in 1974 that would become the locale for the popular 1979 horror film *The Amityville Horror*.

Another reason for the stigmatization of a property is if the house is reputed to be haunted. The most well-known example of a paranormally stigmatized house was a home in Nyack, New York, that was the subject of a 1991 court case entitled *Stambovsky v. Ackley*. The property was a waterfront Victorian owned by Helen Ackley, who claimed that it was haunted by three ghosts who lived during the 1700s (which was odd because the house was not built until 1890). Ms. Ackley and her family related that they heard phantom footsteps, heard doors slamming by themselves and saw apparitions of the spirits in the home, and their stories were reported in local papers and *Reader's Digest*. When Ms. Ackley sold the house to out of towner Jeffrey Stambovsky, however, no mention was made of the haunting, and the buyer filed an action requesting rescission of sale and for damages and false representation by Ackley and the realty company. The New York State Supreme Court initially ruled against the plaintiff on the basis of the doctrine of *caveat emptor* (let the buyer beware), but an appeals court later reversed the trial court's decision, ruling that the seller had an obligation to disclose that the house had a reputation for being haunted, as it potentially affected the home's valuation. The court held that as a matter of law, the house was haunted, while taking no stance on the paranormal reality of the haunting, and *Stambovsky v. Ackley* has come to be called the "Ghostbusters ruling."

The basic narrative elements of the "traditional" haunting have remained remarkably consistent down through the centuries. One of the most recent credible accounts of a haunted house appears in the 1978 nonfiction account *Night Stalks the Mansion* by Constance Westbie and Harold Cameron. In this memoir Harold Cameron recounts the ordeal of the Cameron family after they moved into an historic country manor in a suburb of Philadelphia that was being offered at a bargain rate by a real estate company. Soon after moving in, the family was subjected to nocturnal visitations by two ghosts who were heard walking around the property but were never seen. They also experienced strange disturbances, anomalous noxious odors and other ghostly phenomena. Looking into the history of the house, Cameron eventually discovered that it had been owned by a prominent doctor and his wife in the mid–19th century whose fourteen-year-old daughter had been raped and strangled by a slave in 1864. The slave had been hunted down and lynched and the mother of the girl subsequently hanged herself in despair. Cameron believed that these were the two unquiet spirits who haunted the mansion. Bound by a stringent rental agreement, the Camerons were obligated to remain in the house for two years and promptly left when their lease expired.

Night Stalks the Mansion, an allegedly true account of a haunting, shares many of the same story elements as cinematic treatments of the theme. A family moves into an old house that they buy or rent for a ridiculously low price. After moving in they start experiencing unexplained phenomena that threaten the family's stability. The history of the house is researched, whereupon it is discovered to be the site where a hideously violent crime has been committed. These narrative elements occur in many haunted house films, including *The Uninvited, Burnt Offerings, The Amityville Horror, Darkness, The Haunting in Connecticut* and *The Disappointments Room*, among others.

Parapsychologists have advanced a theory that explains the haunted house phenomenon not in terms of ghosts but as being a kind of recording or photograph of a horrific event imprinted upon the physical space of the house. Sometimes referred to as the "mental imprint manifestation" theory, it is explained by the early psychic investigator Oliver Lodge thusly: "Take for example a haunted house ... wherein some one room is the scene of a ghostly representation of some long past tragedy ... the original tragedy has been literally *photographed* on its material surroundings, nay, even on the ether itself, by reason of the emotion felt by those who enacted it; and thenceforth ... an hallucinatory effect is experienced corresponding to such an impression."[1] According to this theory these dire events have been recorded on the material space of the house and are played back over and over again in a process analogous to cinema. Horrormeister Stephen King was familiar with this parapsychological concept and used it as the basis for the hauntings in his popular novel *The Shining*.

Poltergeists constitute a different type of manifestation from the traditional haunted house. The word translates from German as "noisy ghost," and the phenomenon creates what might be termed a temporary haunted house. While traditional hauntings can go on for decades or even centuries, the poltergeist is relatively short-lived, usually lasting for weeks or months before slowly petering out. While a haunting is confined to a specific place, the poltergeist attaches itself to a person, usually a child just entering puberty, who is referred to as the "focus" of the phenomenon. The "noisy ghost" produces effects that are much more dramatic than a haunting, including the movement of heavy objects like furniture, the teleportation of material objects (called *apports*) and other inexplicable goings-on. Some paranormal researchers theorize that these effects are evidence of psychokinetic powers on the part of the focus person, while others believe that they are caused by spirits or demonic entities. Poltergeist-infested domiciles are more common than traditional haunted houses. UCLA parapsychologist Barry Taff estimates that only 5 percent of the haunting cases he investigated were genuine haunted houses, while the rest were poltergeist manifestations.

Poltergeist outbreaks have provided entertainment for the masses for centuries. In London in 1762 a poltergeist infestation dubbed the "Cock Lane Ghost" drew crowds of onlookers from all over the city hoping to catch a glimpse of the phenomenon, while the so-called "Bell Witch" case that began in 1817 in Tennessee achieved a similar notoriety and attracted curiosity-seekers from far and wide, including President Andrew Jackson. In the age of cinema poltergeists have provided entertainment for the masses in films such as *The Entity, An American Haunting, Paranormal Activity, The Conjuring 2* and, of course, *Poltergeist* and its sequels.

Because Protestant religious dogma did not admit the existence of ghosts, poltergeist outbreaks were thought to be the work of demonic forces rather than departed spirits. This notion is most apparent in William Friedkin's fright classic *The Exorcist*, and it has worked its way into the *Paranormal Activity* and *Conjuring* series of films. Devil worship is also associated with haunted houses in *Seven Footprints to Satan, The Black Cat* and *Rosemary's Baby*.

Another phenomenon associated with haunted house tales is mediumship. The quasi-religion of Spiritualism, which arose during the early 19th century, claimed that psychically talented "mediums" could pierce the veil of death and communicate with the departed. Because they were supposedly sensitive to the occult realm, mediums are frequently brought into haunted houses by paranormal investigators to sense the presence of ghosts and to conduct séances to divine the spirit's motives for the haunt. Mediums and psychic "sensitives" are a staple of haunted house narratives, and they are prominently featured in horror movie fare such as *The Haunting, The Legend of Hell House, Poltergeist, The Haunting of Julia, The Shining, Beetlejuice, The Others* and *The Haunting in Connecticut*. The most prominent example of psychic ghostbusters in contemporary cinema, however, are the self-styled demonologists Ed and Lorraine Warren who appear in the *Conjuring* series of films.

Aside from real-life accounts of hauntings, the fictional haunted house narrative was spawned in the gothic literary tradition that began in the late 18th century. Horace Walpole's 1764 romance *The Castle of Otronto* is considered the first gothic novel. Set in the 16th century, it is a tale involving a mad nobleman, a damsel in distress, secret passageways, a painting that comes to life and ghosts of a gigantic variety set against the backdrop of the titular haunted castle. Anne Radcliffe's *The Mysteries of Udolpho* (1794) followed in a similar vein, ensconcing its heroine in the mysterious castle of Udolpho, but in this case all of the ghostly goings-on are revealed to have a prosaic explanation.

The great German fantasist E.T.A. Hoffmann's 1817 novel *Das Majorat* is another seminal work of gothic fiction. The story takes place inside the ancestral home of the Roderich baronial line, a crumbling castle located on the desolate shores of the Baltic. The elder Baron Roderich reputedly dabbled in astrology and witchcraft, and the family and their home have become accursed as a result of these supernatural delvings. There is also the matter of a treasure hidden in a secret vault somewhere in the bowels of the castle. *Das Majorat* tells a complex story that unfolds over several generations. Its gothic castle is haunted by the ghost of a murdered servant and is the scene of a number of tragic events and unnatural deaths set against a backdrop of astrology and somnambulism.

Edgar Allan Poe's 1845 story "The Fall of the House of Usher" is a classic of gothic fiction that is familiar to modern readers. The last heir of an accursed line of nobles, the decadent Roderick Usher inhabits a decaying mansion located in the middle of a blighted landscape. The house is scarred with a great crack in the middle of its walls that threatens to rupture its structural integrity. While there are no ghosts in evidence, Poe gives us non-supernatural thrills in the form of congenital madness, hyperesthesia, catalepsy, premature burial and resurrection. The house itself is a haunted presence that broods over the doings of the doomed characters before dissolving into its final ruin. Poe's story has been filmed several times, most notably by director Roger Corman in the first of a series of lavish Poe adaptations.

The novels of the Brontë sisters would take gothic fiction in a new direction. Charlotte Brontë's 1847 novel *Wuthering Heights* chronicles the unholy love between Catherine Earnshaw and the tumultuous character Heathcliff, a violent and sadistic man, set against the backdrop of Wuthering Heights, a rough-hewn estate located in the middle of desolate moors. When Catherine dies, Heathcliff is haunted by her ghost and is eventually driven to madness and suicide. This tale of obsession, love and death has become a literary classic and has been filmed several times, most notably in the classic 1939 version featuring Laurence Olivier and Merle Oberon in the starring roles.

Her sister Emily's novel *Jane Eyre*, published in the same year, likewise established many of the conventions of what would come to be called the "female gothic." The book's eponymous heroine gains a position as governess for the wealthy but mercurial Mr. Rochester at his ancestral manor, Thornfield Hall. Thornfield is a pleasant enough place, except for a rookery and a wing of the house that is kept locked and from which maniacal laughter sometimes emanates. Rochester proposes marriage, and on the night before the wedding Jane awakens to find a spectral woman examining her bridal outfit and faints when the woman approaches her. The next day she learns that the woman is Rochester's first wife, who had gone mad and has been kept locked up in the secret wing of the manor for years. The wedding is called off as a consequence and Jane flees from Thornfield, which is later burned to the ground by the crazy spouse, the first in a long line of gothic pyromaniacs. *Jane Eyre* was brought to the big screen in a 1944 prestige production starring Joan Fontaine and Orson Welles.

Set against the background of the Salem witch trials in 17th century Massachusetts, Nathaniel Hawthorne's novel *The House of the Seven Gables* (1851) is the saga of the aristocratic Pyncheon family who suffer under a curse upon their house. It started during the witch trials, when the family patriarch, Colonel Pyncheon, seized land owned by the humble carpenter Matthew Maule by having him tried and executed for witchcraft. As the noose is drawn around his neck, Maule curses the colonel by crying out, "God will give him blood to drink!" Pyncheon hires Maule's son to build the titular mansion, and the junior Maule avenges his father by hiding a valuable map that deeds large swathes of land to the family. Soon after the house is completed, the colonel is found dead inside it under mysterious circumstances, leading to speculation that Maule was indeed a witch who has cursed the Pyncheon family. For generations afterward his heirs become obsessed with finding the lost document, even to the point of murdering each other over it. While the house is reputedly haunted, there are no ghosts in evidence and Hawthorne's tale is really a parable about greed and how the dead hand of the past reaches out to stifle the present. The book was filmed in 1940 and starred George Sanders. The real House of the Seven Gables is currently a tourist attraction in Salem, although all of the events depicted in the novel are entirely fictitious.

By the middle of the 19th century all the conventions of the gothic genre had been established. The action takes place within the confines of a mysterious mansion or castle that is thought to be haunted. There are secret passageways, hidden rooms containing insane relatives and sometimes lost treasures. The houses are inhabited by ghosts or their owners are afflicted by a supernatural family curse. In the female gothic variant, the accursed dwelling place serves as a backdrop for a tumultuous romance. The house is sometimes destroyed by a fire or other disastrous event by the end of the tale.

During the Victorian era the haunted house narrative went in new directions. The acclaimed novelist Henry James' *The Turn of the Screw* (1898) is widely considered by critics to be the finest ghost story in the English language. The novel is told in the first person by a governess (the character has no name) who is hired by a wealthy Londoner to look after his nephew and niece in his isolated country estate at Bly. At first the children seem normal, but she soon perceives that they are being haunted by the ghosts of the previous governess and the former groundskeeper, who have died under mysterious circumstances. The governess strives to unravel the enigmas at Bly and save the children from the baleful influence of the spirits. Although James never claimed that his novel was based on a true event, the writer noted in his diary that he had heard a ghost story during a dinner with the archbishop of Canterbury about a couple of young children on an isolated estate who were haunted by the ghosts of two servants. James simply added the character of the governess and concocted *The Turn of the Screw*. The novel has formed the basis for several stage and screen adaptations, most notably Jack Clayton's masterful version *The Innocents* (1961).

Bram Stoker's *Dracula* (1898), one of the most famous horror novels of all time, popularized the legend of the vampire and has provided inspiration for countless stage productions and films. The novel's first three chapters are set in Count Dracula's castle in Transylvania where the protagonist, Jonathan Harker, is held prisoner by the evil count. Castle Dracula is an eerie domain of decay and death where undead creatures of the night lurk and escape is impossible (Harker does indeed exit the castle, but the reader is never told how). Dracula leaves Transylvania and travels to England, where he takes up residence in another haunted ruin, Carfax Abbey. While *Dracula* is not generally considered a haunted house story, the first three chapters of the book are arguably the most nightmarish and effective. Castle Dracula would be vividly brought to life in the monumental set design for Todd Browning's 1931 version starring Bela Lugosi.

During the 20th century, American horror writer H.P. Lovecraft dealt with the haunted house theme in a number of his key works. His 1924 short story "The Rats in the Walls" takes place in Exham Priory, a ruined edifice in England that is being restored by the current heir of the Delaporte family. The priory is described as having been built employing "an architecture involving Gothic towers resting on a Saxon or Romanesque substructure, whose foundation in turn was of a still earlier order.... Roman, and even Druidic or native Cymric, if legends speak truly."[2] While the house is being rebuilt, Delaporte hears the scurrying of armies of phantom rats behind the walls and eventually discovers a ruined pagan temple beneath its foundations, along with the skeletons of a half-human race nurtured by a demonic force. In another story, "The Dreams in the Witch House" (1933), a mathematics student named Gilman, who is living in an aged boarding house that dates back to the era of the witch trials, is subjected to disturbing dreams in which the ghost of a witch, her familiar and an entity who is perhaps the devil torment him before causing his untimely death. The "Witch House" was reportedly based on the forbidding Grimshaw House in Salem, although the house in the story was located in the fictional town of Arkham, Massachusetts.

Lovecraft's novella *The Shunned House* (1937) is the author's most developed treatment of the theme. The narrative takes place in Lovecraft's native Providence, where the unnamed narrator and his uncle, Dr. Elihu Whipple, become fascinated with an abandoned 18th century colonial with an evil reputation. Several members of the house's former owners, the Harris family, have died in the accursed place. Dr. Whipple and his nephew are drawn to explore the house and employ 20th century devices such as flamethrowers, a Crookes tube, gas masks and sulfuric acid to bear upon the haunt, with predictably dire results, until the forces of chaos are exorcised. Lovecraft based the house on a "hellish place" he had once observed in Elizabeth, New Jersey, and the Babbit house in Providence. *The Shunned House* was filmed as a feature in Italy in 2003 under the title *La Casa Sfuggita* and again as a 12-minute short in 2012.

Shirley Jackson's *The Haunting of Hill House* (1959) is considered one of the classics of American horror fiction. Hill House, a New England mansion with an evil reputation built in the 19th century, is the subject of a professor who is conducting a paranormal experiment designed to prove the existence of haunted houses. The book's protagonist, however, is Eleanor, a vulnerable young woman with psychic abilities who is brought into the experiment in order to release the house's supernatural energies. Unfortunately, the professor's plan works all too well as fearful unseen presences stalk the investigators through its dark spaces leaving no doubts about the reality of the phenomenon. Ms. Jackson's deft psychological characterizations and spooky atmospherics combine to craft one of the most memorable ghost stories in all of literature. The haunted Hill House was reputedly inspired by two real structures, one a ruined house she had seen from a train in New York City's Harlem neighborhood, the other a photograph of a house in California that she later learned was built by her own great-grandfather. The novel was lensed by veteran director Robert Wise as *The Haunting*, itself one of the classics of haunted house cinema.

Rosemary's Baby (1967) by novelist Ira Levin offered a novel take on the haunted house concept, namely a haunted apartment building right in the middle of New York. The book's heroine, Rosemary Woods, a naïve, shallow young woman, and her husband Guy move into a creepy old apartment building on Manhattan's Upper West Side. The complex is the den of a coven of witches who seduce the immoral Guy and make him agree to have his wife bear Satan's child. Bewitched by the cult, Rosemary slowly apprehends the truth but is powerless to stop the witches from carrying out their evil plan. Levin's novel was brought to the big screen in a hit movie written and directed by Roman Polanski in 1968. Exteriors for the film were shot at New York's gothic Dakota Apartments, where John Lennon would be shot to death some years later.

Peter Straub is arguably the finest writer of ghost fiction in contemporary America. In his novel *Julia* (1975) young mother Julia Lofting is devastated by the loss of her daughter Kate in a freak accident. Unable to cope with her grief and her overbearing husband Magnus, she opts to buy her own house and live there alone. She settles into an old house in London that has an evil history where she is haunted by the ghost of a previous tenant, a sadistic little girl named Kate. Or is Magnus trying to gaslight her in order to have her declared insane and get his hands on her money? Straub keeps the reader guessing until the very last page. *Julia* was filmed as *The Haunting of Julia* in 1976 starring Mia Farrow and Kier Dullea.

Stephen King's novel *The Shining* (1977) took place in a haunted hotel in the mountains of Colorado, where failed writer Jack Torrance has taken a job looking after the Overlook Hotel during the winter off-season with his wife and young son. Alone and snowbound in the isolated hotel, Jack and his family slowly come under the sway of the hotel's undead guests and come apart at the seams. Master filmmaker Stanley Kubrick turned King's novel into a hit movie starring Jack Nicholson in 1980. The hotel in the book is called the Overlook, but King conceived the novel after staying at the Stanley Hotel in Estes Park, Colorado. The movie, however, was filmed at the Timberline Lodge in Oregon.

The House Next Door (1977) by Anne Rivers Siddons offered a brand-new conception of the haunted house. The novel's protagonist is Colquitt Kennedy, who lives in an upscale Atlanta neighborhood with her husband. A brilliant but eccentric architect is hired to construct a contemporary-styled house on a vacant lot next door. Upon completion, the structure proves to be an aesthetic marvel, but it brings madness and death to whoever lives in it, and even those who live in its vicinity. By the end of the novel the Kennedys find themselves in mortal danger from the evil forces contained inside the house. *The House Next Door* was adapted as a telefilm for cable's Lifetime Channel in 2003.

These classic works solidly established the literary and filmic haunted house tale as a sub-genre of the ghost story. These haunted motifs have continued in more recent novels by talented writers such as *The Woman in Black* by Susan Hill, *House of Leaves* by Mark Z. Danielewski, *Rose Red* by Stephen King, *Nazareth Hill* by Ramsey Campbell, *House of Bones* by Graham Masterson, *A Winter Haunting* by Dan Simmons and *The Unseen* by Alexandra Sokoloff.

The narrative structure of the haunted house tale had thus been set forth by these works of literature, many of which were adapted for the cinema and became classics of the horror movie genre. There is, however, another inspiration for haunted house films provided by purportedly true stories about haunts, poltergeists and demonic infestations. The most well-known example is *The Amityville Horror* (1979), a popular hit allegedly based on "a true story." Other examples of films allegedly inspired by true life paranormal cases would include *The Entity* (1982), *An American Haunting* (2005), *The Haunting in Connecticut* (2009) and *The Conjuring 2* (2015). Some of these films adhere closely to the facts of these events, while others greatly dramatize or even falsify accounts of their parapsychological material. In addition, real-life hauntings and supernatural goings-on have inspired fictional works such as Henry James' *The Turn of the Screw* and William Peter Blatty's *The Exorcist*.

In the cinema, the default iconography for the haunted house is the standard "old dark house" replete with mold, cobwebs and a history of violence and madness such as the houses appearing in *Wuthering Heights*, *House of Usher*, *The Woman in Black* and *Crimson Peak*. It can also be a stately old manor hiding ghastly secrets, as in *House of the Seven Gables*, *Jane Eyre*, *Rebecca*, *The Haunting*, *The Innocents*, *The Legend of Hell House*, *The Changeling* and *Dark Shadows*, or a gothic haunted castle as in *Dracula* or *The Haunted Palace*. It can also take the form of a haunted hotel (*The Shining*, *1408*), an apartment (*Rosemary's Baby*, *The Tenant*, *Dark Water*) or an orphanage (*The Devil's Backbone*, *House of Voices*). It can also be a seemingly normal modern house as in *The Amityville Horror*, *Poltergeist* or *The Grudge*.

The haunted house can also be depicted in non-traditional forms such as the Bauhaus-inspired mansion in *The Black Cat* (1934) or the Ennis House, designed by Frank Lloyd Wright which was used in exterior shots for *House on Haunted Hill* (1958) and resembles a Mayan temple. The haunt in *The House Next Door* is a contemporary-styled architectural marvel, while the spook house in *Thirteen Ghosts* (2001) is a clockwork structure of glass and steel. *Elephant Walk* featured a palatial "bungalow," a mansion built in native style in Ceylon, while Gull Cottage in *The Ghost and Mrs. Muir* is a cozy English domicile.

Cinema's haunted places, like real-life hauntings, usually have their origins in deeds of violence or hubris. The murder of a family by one of its members turns an ordinary house into a haunt in *The Amityville Horror* and *The Grudge*. The ghost of a murdered child inhabits haunted domains in *The Devil's Backbone* and *The Changeling*. A family curse may afflict a dwelling, as in *House of the Seven Gables*, *Dragonwyck* or *House of Usher*. Practicing witchcraft or the occult can make a house a portal to Hell in films such as *The Exorcist* or *The Haunting in Connecticut*. Some houses are doomed because they have been constructed in an accursed locale. The suburban home in *Poltergeist* is erected atop a cemetery where the bodies still lie in the ground underneath. The futuristic structure in *The Black Cat* is built upon the ruins of Fort Marmarusk, a scene of mass suffering, death and betrayal during the First World War. The palatial estate in *Elephant Walk* is deliberately placed in the migratory path of elephants, so as to defy nature. Sometimes the house is deliberately built to conjure spooks or demons, as in *Thirteen Ghosts* or *Darkness*. The purest form of the haunted house, however, is the house that is born bad from the beginning without any prior history, such as the haunts in *The Haunting* and *The House Next Door*.

The haunted house in film is a claustrophobic prison in which both the living and the dead are entrapped. The ghosts in these films are frequently bound to a location due to a curse and are forbidden to leave due to rules governing the afterlife. The ghostly couple in *Beetlejuice*, for instance, are unable to leave their former home, as it is surrounded by a surrealistic desert inhabited by gigantic sandworms. The haunted house in *The Others* is surrounded by seemingly endless layers of fog from which the ghosts cannot find their way. Likewise, the team of psychic researchers in *The Haunting* are locked inside the Hill House estate every evening, while the denizens of *The House on Haunted Hill* are hoping to collect $25,000 (upped to a cool $1,000,000 in the sequel) if they spend a night imprisoned within a haunted house. A more frequently used plot device confines the occupants inside their house due to a mortgage or rental contract.

Hollywood did not warm to the supernatural haunted house melodrama until the mid–1940s. During the silent film era, German cinema invented and perfected the horror film with a series of genre entries such as *The Student of Prague, The Cabinet of Dr. Caligari,* and *Nosferatu* that reflected the pessimism, financial depression and decadence of German society in the post–World War I period. By contrast, America was going through the high times of the Roaring Twenties. As a result, haunted houses in American films of the period eschewed the supernatural in favor of comedies starring silent film comedians Harold Lloyd in *Haunted Spooks* (1920) and *The Haunted House* (1921) with Buster Keaton, or else featured houses haunted by grotesque criminals in *The Bat* (1926), *The Cat and the Canary* (1927) and *The Terror* (1928).

During the 1930s the horror genre was dominated by the supernatural creatures spawned at Universal Studios. Dracula, Frankenstein and the Mummy supplanted the more traditional terrors of ghosts and haunted houses, and the reign of the Universal monsters would last until the end of the horror movie cycle in the mid–1940s. *House of Frankenstein* (1944) and *House of Dracula* (1945) were enacted in spooky environs that substituted these creatures for ghosts. The first serious Hollywood film featuring supernatural ghosts in a haunted house was Paramount's *The Uninvited* (1944). The haunted house comedy continued to be popular during this period in the Bob Hope vehicles *The Cat and the Canary* (1939) and *The Ghost Breakers* (1940) and the Abbott and Costello features *Hold That Ghost* (1941) and *The Time of Their Lives* (1946). The female gothic version of the haunted house was represented in film versions of the classics *Wuthering Heights* (1939), *Rebecca* (1940) and *Jane Eyre* (1944).

Haunted house movies were gone from the scene for most of the atomic 1950s, the supernatural melodrama having largely given way to the novelty of science fiction horror. Alien invaders, mutants and giant bugs had more resonance for the times than the antiquated notion of ghosts. During the 1960s, however, the haunted house film made a big comeback with some of the finest films of the sub-genre, including Alfred Hitchcock's *Psycho* (1960), Roger Corman's *House of Usher* (1960), Jack Clayton's *The Innocents* (1961), Robert Wise's *The Haunting* (1963) and Roman Polanski's *Rosemary's Baby* (1968). *Psycho* and *Rosemary's Baby* were enormous popular hits, while *House of Usher* ushered in the new era of the color horror film as well as being the first haunted house movie in color.

The 1970s produced William Friedkin's *The Exorcist* (1973), considered one of the great horror films of all time, as well as a number of above average movies on the theme such as *The Legend of Hell House* (1973) and *The Tenant* (1976). But the haunted house film really took off with the release of *The Amityville Horror* in 1979 and *Poltergeist* in 1982. The success of these films would lead to the first haunted house movie franchises as they spawned, and are still spawning, a seemingly endless series of sequels and remakes. Stanley Kubrick's screen adaptation of Stephen King's popular horror novel *The Shining* (1980) was a box-office hit, while newbie director Tim Burton offered up a surrealistic take on the afterlife and the haunted house in the comedy *Beetlejuice* (1988).

At the turn of the 21st century the haunted house movie rose to new heights of popularity, beginning with remakes of *The Haunting* (1999), *House on Haunted Hill* (1999) and *Thirteen Ghosts* (2001). This was followed by strong entries such as *The Others* (2001), *The Devil's Backbone* (2001) and *The House Next Door* (2002). As the millennium progressed, haunted house franchises blossomed in the wake of crowd pleasers like *The Grudge* (2004), *Paranormal Activity* (2007), *The Haunting in Connecticut* (2009) and *The Conjuring* (2013). Other memorable haunts included those in *The Woman in Black* (2012) and *Crimson Peak* (2015).

In an age of big-budget blockbusters and special effects-laden spectaculars, haunted house films can be made cheaply and without elaborate and expensive effects or name stars. A case in point is *Paranormal Activity*, a film purporting to be found footage of a poltergeist infestation that was made for peanuts yet scored big at the box office. The haunted house film relies mainly on atmospherics and acting to achieve its effects. Many modestly budgeted films dispense with sets and soundstages altogether in favor of utilizing a creepy old house as a location. These cost factors serve to make the haunted house film economically viable.

Before the advent of cinema, theatrical productions sought to simulate the terrors of the haunted house. Devices like the magic lantern and the camera obscura were utilized to create the illusion of hauntings. In 1797 a Frenchman named Etienne Gaspard Robertson staged a spook show he called a "Fantasmagorie" in the crypt of an abandoned convent in Paris. He used a powerful projector set up behind a waxed gauze screen to create the illusion of ghosts and skeletons leaping out at the audience. Musical instruments such as the glass harmonica were utilized to create an unearthly soundtrack that accompanied the visuals. Around the same time a German showman named Johann Schropfer staged séance-like shows in Leipzig in which specters were conjured in a smoke-filled room by means of an invention he called a *Gespenstermacher*, or "ghost maker," a device that projected images onto the smoke.

These types of shows came to be called "Phantasmagoria," and they soon became popular all over Europe. The most sensational of these employed an illusion called "Pepper's Ghost" after its inventor, John Henry Pepper. The effect involved placing an actor in a hidden pit and projecting his image onto a sheet of glass on the stage to produce the illusion of a ghost appearing and disappearing. Pepper's Ghost was first employed in 1862 in a play on the London stage entitled *The Haunted Man* that was written by Charles Dickens and became a sensation.

The Phantasmagoria in turn led to the invention of spook house rides and haunted attractions. First of these was the Orton and Spooner Ghost House which opened in London in 1915 and featured steam-powered ghostly thrills. As the century progressed haunted attractions began to spring up all over America, particularly around Halloween. In 1969 the Haunted Mansion attraction opened in Disneyland and set a standard for spook house rides. By 1995 there were reportedly 3,500 to 5,000 haunted attractions, sometimes called "haunts," operating in the United States alone. The popularity of the Haunted Mansion prompted Disney to duplicate the ride at the Magic Kingdom in Orlando, Florida, and later Mansions were opened in Disney parks in Tokyo, Paris and Hong Kong. Other notable haunts include the Scare House in Pittsburgh, Pennsylvania, Ghostly Manor in Sandusky, Ohio, Trauma Towers in Blackpool, England, and the Daiba School Horror in Tokyo, Japan.

Updating the technologies of previous centuries, these post–Millennial haunts employ a wide variety of techniques to induce fear in their audiences, including animatronic creatures that breathe fire and shoot machine guns, intense lighting effects, mazes, fog machines and other devices designed to disorient and confuse. Some haunts feature actors that can interact with visitors while staging scenes of violence and terror. The Terror Behind the Walls attraction in Philadelphia employs actors who walk around on stilts or drop down from nowhere on bungee cords. In addition to these commercial ventures, Christian groups operate "Hell Houses" at Halloween that portray the hellish consequences of acts they consider sinful, like abortion, alcoholism, drug abuse and homosexuality.

Another aspect of haunted house entertainment consists of tourist attractions at allegedly real haunted locales where curiosity seekers can book tours or overnight stays hoping to catch a glimpse of a ghost. Examples include the Lemp Mansion in St. Louis, where several members of the Lemp family committed suicide, the former ocean liner the *Queen Mary*, said to be haunted by the spirits of long-departed passengers and the Stanley Hotel in Colorado where Stephen King conceived *The Shining* after experiencing nightmares during an overnight stay. These attractions have become a cottage industry in America, and this phenomenon was satirized in the 2007 movie *1408*, which was based on a King short story.

The past several years have seen a proliferation of reality TV shows on cable channels that highlight the history and investigation of prominent haunted hotspots in the United States. The lineup includes *Ghost Hunters, Ghost Brothers, Ghost Whisperer, Ghost Adventures, The Haunted, Haunted Casefiles, Most Haunted USA, Paranormal Files, Paranormal Witness, Paranormal Lockdown,* and on and on and on. Many of these shows feature would-be ghostbusters trolling through these haunts with exotic technological devices such as electromagnetic field readers, infrared cameras, motion sensors and digital audio recorders hoping to record evidence of paranormal activity. Ghost hunting equipment has become another profitable cottage industry due to the popularity of these shows.

The haunted house tale is timeless and has held a fascination for the human mind for millennia. It shows no signs of slowing down in the high-tech 21st century. It preys on our fears of the familiar suddenly turned terrifying. Stephen King has written, "Your house is the place where you're supposed to be able to unbutton your armor and put your shield away. Our homes are the places where we allow ourselves the ultimate vulnerability: they are the places where we take off our clothes and go to sleep with no guard on watch."[3] And Anne Rivers Siddons, author of *The House Next Door*, reflects, "To a woman, her house …

is kingdom, responsibility, comfort, total world to her ... to most of us, whether or not we are aware of it. It is an extension of ourselves; it tolls in answer to one of the most basic chords mankind will ever hear. My shelter. My earth. My second skin. Mine. So basic is it that the desecration of it, the corruption, as it were, by something alien takes on a peculiar bone-deep horror and disgust."[4]

These spaces where we live and dream are sacred refuges for our memories, indeed for our very existences, and intrusions upon them by supernatural entities constitute an especially intimate type of unease and fear that has endured, and will endure, for all time. So let us now meet these terrors that shatter our everyday domesticity, our complacency and our very reality within those haunted spaces in the night, in the dark.

Chapter One

No Ghosts Allowed

*Mystery House Films of the Silent
and Early Sound Period (and Beyond)*

Cinema was independently invented in the last decade of the 19th century in Europe and America. In France, the Lumière brothers were film pioneers who first exhibited and popularized this new creative medium to Parisians in 1895. Their films were simple documentaries that depicted everyday scenes such as a train arriving at a station, but the novelty of photographs that moved proved to be a popular new form of entertainment that drew large audiences.

Among the admirers of this novel invention was a stage magician named George Méliès, who also wished to explore the new medium. He purchased a film camera and set up the first movie studio in the Paris suburb of Montreuil, a facility that was equipped with theatrical devices such as trapdoors, scrim curtains, along with glass walls and ceilings. During one shooting session the camera jammed and was restarted, and when the film was later projected he discovered that objects within the frame had disappeared, and the concept of cinematic special effects was born. The magician instantly grasped the implications of manipulating reality using camera trickery, and his films would employ novel techniques such as fades and dissolves, slow and accelerated motion to conjure new vistas of the fantastic.

The 1896 Méliès production *The Haunted Castle* (*Le Chateau Hante*) provided the first depiction of a haunted house in screen history. In this hand-colored three-minute short, a bat flying through the haunted castle transforms into the figure of Mephistopheles, who proceeds to make several objects appear and disappear. Next, two cavaliers enter the house and are subjected to a number of pranks played upon them by the devil including the conjuring of four specters, until one of them uses a crucifix to make the Evil One vanish. Because of the bat transformation scene, *The Haunted Castle* is sometimes considered the first vampire film as well.

Another early French film of the period was *The House of Ghosts* (*La Maison Ensorcelée*, 1908), directed by Segundo de Chamon, in which two men and a woman enter a haunted house and encounter its ghostly inhabitants. A painting comes to life, turning into a hideous revenant, a ghost in a sheet appears, and there are slapstick antics as chairs beneath the actors vanish, spilling them onto their bottoms. The visitors watch in disbelief as unseen hands hold a knife that slices a sausage and a loaf of bread and neatly fold table napkins before their meal in an elaborate stop-motion sequence that simulates poltergeist activity.

Finally, the room itself begins to tilt back and forth, sending furniture sliding to and fro across the floor.

These films showcased the power of the cinema to depict supernatural effects. Ghosts and devils appear and disappear and objects vanish or move by themselves. The special effects in *The House of Ghosts* in particular are quite elaborate and sophisticated. Both films treat the subject of the haunted house whimsically, and their cinema trickery is designed to inspire wonder rather than fear. Interested parties can currently view both of these pioneering efforts on YouTube.

A number of early films featured the haunted house motif. In the Danish film *Der Graa Dame* (1909) an heir must disguise himself as a specter in order to claim his inheritance and utilizes secret passages and trapdoors in a gothic mansion to appear and disappear. *The Haunted Bedroom* (1913) concerned a ghost who has hidden money away for his sister's dowry and must communicate its whereabouts to his living sibling. The American film *The Ghost Breaker* (1914), co-directed by the great Cecil B. DeMille, was a comic treatment of the theme in which crooks masquerade as spooks in order to pilfer loot from an old Spanish castle, while in the British film *The Haunting of Cecil P. Gould* (1915) an English heiress sells her family mansion to an American millionaire, then disguises herself as a ghost in an effort to scare the new owner away from her former property.

The first serious treatment of the haunted house theme, however, would emerge from the haunted screens of the postwar German cinema, whose "shudder films" became popular after the international success of Robert Weine's expressionist classic *The Cabinet of Dr. Caligari* (1920). *Caligari*, with its nightmarish imagery, imbued Germany's haunted screen with a true taste of the supernatural. F.W. Murnau's *Nosferatu* (1922), a rogue adaptation of Bram Stoker's seminal vampire novel *Dracula*, utilized exterior shots of Orova Castle in northern Slovakia to picture the vampire's forbidding haunted abode in the film's early scenes.

A year earlier Murnau had directed *The Haunted Castle* (*Der Schloss Vogelod*, 1921) which, despite its title, was an Agatha Christie–like drawing room murder mystery. Unlike *Nosferatu* it was shot almost entirely in interiors. The titular Castle Vogelod was a neat and trim dwelling, with none of the cobwebs or gothic detritus usually found in a haunted palace. The only horrific scene in the film is a nightmare sequence in which a clawed, hairy hand reaches through a window into the dreamer's bedroom, wraps itself around his head and starts to draw him out of the room, whereupon he awakens. In some ways *The Haunted Castle* was the precursor to the American "mystery house" films of the late 1920s. All that was missing was the obligatory masked criminal.

Over in America the horror movies of the 1920s were dominated by the films featuring actor Lon Chaney, Sr. The so-called "Man of a Thousand Faces" captivated screen audiences using elaborate makeup to portray a succession of grotesque characters, most famously in *The Hunchback of Notre Dame* (1923) and *The Phantom of the Opera* (1925). None of these films, however, dealt with the supernatural, ghosts or haunted houses. Even the vampire he played in *London After Midnight* (1927) turned out to be merely a detective in disguise. The American psyche of the time rejected the supernatural and consigned spirits and spooks to the realm of comedy. But the haunted house, albeit with no ghosts allowed, was poised to flower on American movie screens.

The impetus was provided by a genre of mystery/comedy plays that became popular on the Broadway stage. Chief among these was Mary Roberts Rinehart and Avery Hopwood's *The Bat*, which opened in 1920 and ran for a record breaking 867 performances. Other crowd-pleasers included John Willard's *The Cat and the Canary*, and, on the London stage, Edgar Wallace's *The Terror*. All of these plays featured a group of unfortunates confined to an old dark house where they are menaced by a masked killer, and all of them wound up being adapted for the screen.

D.W. Griffith, the acclaimed director of the celluloid classics *The Birth of a Nation* (1915) and *Intolerance* (1916), was first out of the box with his production of *One Exciting Night* (1922). Griffith had attempted to purchase the movie rights to *The Bat*, but when the cost proved prohibitive, he decided to write his own treatment of the "mystery house" theme. The movie takes place at the Fairfax Mansion in Louisville, where the family heir John Fairfax (Henry Hull) has returned to his ancestral home after many years studying abroad. While attending a lawn party with his aunt (Grace Griswald), he falls in love with a girl he meets there named Agnes Harrington (Carol Dempster). Unfortunately for Fairfax, Agnes' mother (Margaret Dale) is insisting that she marry the wealthy J. Wilson Rockmayne (Morgan Wallace) because she has lost her fortune due to bad investments and is being blackmailed by Rockmayne, who has knowledge of a theft she committed during a desperate moment of weakness. Rockmayne, an oily character sporting a mustache and a monocle, is not exactly Agnes' idea of a husband, but she feels obliged to follow her mother's orders.

Unknown to Fairfax, bootlegger Clary Johnson (Herbert Such) has been using the mansion to stash his booze. Upon learning of the heir's return, Johnson removes the illegal hooch from the Fairfax estate and hides his profits, a half million bucks in cash, in a trunk, but is shot to death by a mysterious individual during the process. The shootout alerts the police, causing the assailant to flee, leaving the money behind. After the corpse is removed a servant, seeing the trunk and thinking it may contain valuables, decides to remove it to an undisclosed location. A title informs us, "Built by an eccentric forebear, the house is reputed to be full of mysterious panels and passages," as the servant is shown concealing the trunk with the loot behind a hidden panel.

Fairfax has invited the guests from the garden party to his mansion "for the fishing season," and when they arrive, they find a crime scene and a detective (Frank Sheridan) investigating Johnson's homicide and looking for his ill-gotten gains. After questioning the guests, the policeman leaves, and as night falls on the mansion Fairfax drives the male guests back to their hotel, leaving his aunt, Agnes and her mother alone in the house. Then a strange figure is shown slinking through the darkened corridors of the house, a man wearing a black cape, a black hat and a mask that obscures the bottom half of his face. When Fairfax returns with a guest (Charles B. Mack), the guest is stabbed to death by the mystery man and the police return to investigate the double murder. The killer is unmasked in the final reel as a tremendous storm engulfs the mansion in the film's melodramatic climax.

One Exciting Night failed to excite movie audiences of the time, and proved to be a financial failure for Griffith. The screenplay, derived from a story by Irene Sinclair, is unfocused and overly complex, containing many extraneous scenes, such as a sub-plot involving a maid and a servant designed to provide comic relief. Griffith cast his girlfriend Carol Dempster in the lead role as damsel in distress, but she fails to generate much electricity on the screen. Her co-star Henry Hull, who had played the lead role in the Broadway production of *The Cat and the Canary*, fares a bit better but struggles against the plodding material of this would-be thriller. Hull would go on to horror movie fame playing the titular lycanthrope in Universal's *The Werewolf of London* (1935). The director reportedly ballooned the film's budget considerably while shooting the complex storm sequence for the climax, and even included some actual footage of a hurricane he had previously shot.

Griffith, who had directed the first feature-length American horror film, the Edgar Allan Poe adaptation *The Avenging Conscience* in 1914, does little to conjure up a haunted house *mise en scene* for the proceedings. Filmed at Griffith's studio in Mamaronek, Long Island, the mansion's interior scenes have a bit of spooky ambience but fail to deliver horror movie chills despite a title that warns of "strange stories of ghostly apparitions about this house." Nevertheless, *One Exciting Night* was the first of the "old dark house" thrillers that would employ a formula consisting of equal parts of mystery, comedy and drama. The film's obligatory masked menace, clad in a slouch hat, cape and scarf may have inspired the pulp magazine character The Shadow, who would become popular in later decades.

The Mary Roberts Rinehart/Avery Hopwood hit play *The Bat* was brought to the screen in 1926 under the direction of Roland West. Advertised as a "Comedy/Mystery/Drama," *The Bat* begins with the daring theft of the fabulous Favre Emeralds right under the noses of the police by the eponymous criminal, who wears a grotesque bat mask to conceal his identity. For his next caper the Bat plans to rob the Oakdale Bank, but is beaten to the punch by another masked criminal, who makes off with $200,000 in cash stuffed in a travelling bag. The Bat follows the robber to the mansion of Courtleigh Fleming, the president of the bank who is recently deceased.

Courtleigh Mansion is currently being rented by dowager Cornelia Van Gorder (Emily Fitzroy), who reads in the newspaper that bank clerk Brooks Bailey (Jack Pickford) has been accused of the bank robbery. Later that day Van Gorder's niece Dale Ogden (Jewel Carmen) arrives at the mansion with Bailey, who is pretending to be a gardener, but Van Gorder easily sees through the ruse, and Dale reveals that they are engaged to be married, and that he has come to the mansion in an effort to clear his name. Under the circumstances, Van Gorder allows him to stay until the situation is sorted out.

Soon the Bat is seen lurking around the premises, along with a second mysterious cloaked figure wearing a hat and scarf that conceal his features. The complex plot revolves around a missing piece of the blueprint of the mansion that indicates the location of a secret room. The missing piece is in the possession of the deceased Courtleigh's nephew, Richard Fleming (Arthur Housman), but when he is shot to death Dale retrieves the paper, but soon loses track of it. Police detective Moletti (Tullio Carminati) and physician Dr. H.E. Wells (Robert McKim) are called to investigate, while Van Gorder brings gun-toting private investigator Anderson (Eddie Gribbon) in on the case.

For most of the movie the eccentric characters chase the Bat and the second mystery man around the mansion, and it turns out that the stolen money has been stashed in the hidden room on the blueprint. The mystery man is shown to be the former owner of the house, Courtleigh Fleming (Charles Herzinger), who has faked his death and stolen the money from his own bank. After many travails, the Bat, who has also been after the stolen loot, is unmasked and his identity revealed.

Director Roland West does a remarkable job of "opening up" the stage production into the medium of cinema with his deft use of chiaroscuro and extreme long shots. The

Emily Fitzroy (top), Jewel Carmen (left) and Tullio Carminati are featured on this lobby card for Roland West's mystery house thriller *The Bat* (1926).

film's shadowy atmospherics, devised by cinematographer Arthur Edeson, were obviously influenced by contemporaneous German expressionism. With his elongated ears and wicked fangs, the masked Bat presents a figure of terror and dread that is highly effective. The master criminal is shown clambering over rooftops and creeping through darkened corridors like a specter, but is also a flesh and blood menace. A fine supporting cast of eccentric characters provides dramatic and comic uplift, including Louise Fazenda as Lizzie the maid, who screams her way through much of the movie, Sojin Kamiyama as a sinister Japanese butler and red herring and Eddie Gribon as the pistol packin' private eye. Jewel Carmen portrays a charming ingénue as Miss Dale, while Emily Fitzroy's Van Gorder knits her way through the night of murder and mayhem without dropping a stitch. All in all, it's a balanced blend of comedy, horror and mystery that served to establish the formula for the "old dark house" thriller.

The Fleming Mansion is constructed as a series of monumental sets that contain zones of light and shadow falling across a maze of stairways and corridors, a hidden room and a "haunted ballroom" that one character refers to as "the happy home of the heebie-jeebies." These sets were designed by ace production designer William Cameron Menzies, whose film credits would later include *Gone with the Wind* (1939), *The Thief of Baghdad* (1940) and *Around the World in 80 Days* (1956). The vastness of the structure tends to overwhelm the actors in some of the extreme long shots, which also emulate the proscenium of the stage at times. There are several shots of the mansion surrounded by twisted trees and flying bats that adopt the iconography of the haunted house. The Bat provided an inspiration for Bob Kane's dark superhero Batman, who would come along during the next decade and would adopt the character's signature bat symbol as part of his costume. The film would be remade twice, once in a sound version, *The Bat Whispers* (1930), and again as *The Bat* in 1959 starring Vincent Price.

The following year saw the release of the film version of John Willard's 1922 theatrical hit *The Cat and the Canary* (1927). "Coming to you direct from B'way," ad copy for the film exclaimed, "New York's smashing stage success that has thrilled thousands!" The director was German émigré Paul Leni, who had lensed the expressionist classic *Waxworks* (1924), the first wax museum horror thriller. Leni would bring a touch of Teutonic Caligarism to the Hollywood screen for the first time.

The film begins with an expressionist flourish as a monstrous hairy hand sweeps away some thick cobwebs to reveal the movie's title. This is followed by a fantastic wide shot of ailing millionaire Cyrus West surrounded by enormous medicine bottles and giant phantom cats representing West's predatory relatives who are after his fortune. As the old man expires, the action shifts to West's estate at Clifton Castle on the Hudson, "the grotesque mansion of an eccentric millionaire," that indeed resembles a medieval castle. On this night, twenty years after Cyrus' death, attorney Roger Crosby (Tully Marshall) is due to read West's will to his assembled relatives and potential heirs, including his niece Annabelle West (Laura La Plante), Paul Jones (Creighton Hale), Charles Wilder (Roger Crosby) and Aunt Susan (Flora Finch). Also present is the housekeeper, Mammy Pleasant (Martha Mattox), a creepy middle-aged woman who insists that the house is haunted by the ghost of Cyrus West.

Heiress Annabelle West (Laura La Plante) is stalked by a sadistic masked criminal in Paul Leni's *The Cat and the Canary* **(1927).**

The interior of Clifton Castle indeed has the ambience of a haunted house. Curtains billow in the wind as the camera travels down a long hallway, chairs are draped in shrouded coverings that seem like seated figures, and deep shadows seem to lurk in every corner. The will is read in one of the dreary rooms at midnight, where it is revealed that Annabelle is heir to the estate. There is a proviso, however, which states that if the primary heir is shown to be insane, a secondary heir will inherit everything. The lawyer Crosby will not reveal the identity of the second heir which is inscribed on a letter kept on his person, and Annabelle is also given a sealed envelope that she must open before she goes to sleep in Cyrus West's bedroom that night. In addition, the heiress is due to be examined by a doctor who will certify her sanity or lack thereof.

Just then a gruff-looking individual in a guard's uniform arrives. The Guard (George Siegmann) informs them that he is searching the grounds for a lunatic who has escaped from a nearby asylum and has been tracked to the estate. The madman is called the Cat because "he's a maniac who thinks he's a cat and tears his victims like they were canaries," and the guests are warned not to leave the house. Soon afterward Annabelle and Crosby are holding a confidential meeting during which he is to reveal the identity of the secondary heir, but in the middle of the conversation a secret panel opens up and a mysterious figure with clawed hands, presumably the Cat, grabs the lawyer and drags him into the darkness before he can transmit the information. Screaming in fear, she runs downstairs to join the others, who have doubts about what happened.

Retiring to the old man's bedroom, Annabelle opens the letter and finds it contains a clue to the location of the lost West Diamonds inside the room. She finds a diamond necklace inside a secret panel and decides to wear it to bed, but as she sleeps another secret panel opens and a hairy, claw-like hand emerges from the wall and snatches the necklace from around her throat. She screams and runs downstairs to join the others, but once more no one will believe her story. It becomes obvious to the audience (but not to the characters) that the second heir is trying to gaslight Annabelle in order to inherit the estate when she is declared mentally unstable. The plot thickens as Crosby's dead body is discovered behind another secret panel.

Only Paul believes her stories, but when he attempts to retrieve the letter containing the identity of the second heir from Crosby's pocket, he finds that the corpse is missing. He locates the secret panel and slips into a hidden passage inside the wall where he encounters the Cat, a grotesque figure cloaked in black with bulging eyes and hideous fangs. They fight and Paul is knocked unconscious and the Cat stalks Annabelle, who is saved by the fortuitous arrival of the police. The Cat is unmasked and the identity of the murdering second heir is revealed, and the Guard admits he was an actor who was hired to perpetrate the plot. In the aftermath, Paul and Annabelle fall in love and the film ends on a happy note.

Adapted from the stage play by scenarist Robert F. Hill, *The Cat and the Canary* adheres to the familiar "mystery house" formula, lumping comedy, mystery and melodrama together into an uneven whole. There is the usual confederacy of suspects, a supposedly haunted mansion, a murder, a damsel in distress, a hidden treasure, secret passageways and a master criminal sporting a grotesque disguise. Laura La Plante carries much of the film with her performance as the menaced heroine, while Creighton Hale and Flora Finch provide comic relief. One of the most riveting performances is Martha Mattox's portrayal of the grim housekeeper Mammy Pleasant that prefigures Judith Anderson's similar role in Alfred

Hitchcock's *Rebecca* (1940). One of the film's major flaws, however, is the makeup for the Cat, which consists of an operatic slouch hat and cape along with one bulging eye and a pair of ridiculous-looking fangs that suffers greatly in comparison with the frightening mask worn by the title character in *The Bat*.

Fortunately, director Paul Leni brings a heady dose of German expressionism to the proceedings. He utilizes moving camera, optical superimpositions and extended dissolves, unusual lighting and compositions to create a mood of mystery and horror that elevates the film far above the formulaic mediocrity of other mystery house thrillers of the period. The opening sequence showing Cyrus West surrounded by giant medicine bottles and huge snarling cats conveys expository information to the viewer in symbolic form instead of simply using titles. The exterior of Clifton Castle resembles a medieval gothic structure, while the interiors are bleak, cheerless, and shadow-haunted, an environment that often seems dreamlike and nightmarish. Leni's compositions are frequently oriented toward the vertical, which gives them an unsettling, uncanny quality. All in all, Leni's tour de force is arguably the most memorable depiction of a haunted house that had appeared on the screen up until this point.

Leni would go on to shoot *The Man who Laughs* (1927), a blend of historical epic and horror about a man whose face is deliberately disfigured into a grotesque mask of mirth that was based on a Victor Hugo novel and starred German actor Conrad Veidt. His next film *The Last Warning* (1928) was a mystery melodrama set in an abandoned theater, but was much inferior to his first old dark house effort. *The Cat and the Canary* would be remade as *The Cat Creeps* in 1930, and again under its own title in 1939 as a vehicle for comedian Bob Hope. Unfortunately, Paul Leni died of blood poisoning in 1929 and a talented film career was tragically cut short. The film's commercial success helped establish Universal Studios and producer Carl Laemmle as the leading purveyors of horror films in Hollywood.

The success of the Warner Brothers production *The Jazz Singer* (1927) ushered in the age of talking pictures and brought the era of the silent film to a close. Warner's proprietary "Vitaphone" movie sound system consisted

The spooky Clifton Castle on the Hudson is featured in this poster for *The Cat and the Canary* (1927).

of an oversized phonograph record that provided a soundtrack to accompany the projected film. Most of *The Jazz Singer* was shot silent, with only the musical numbers and a few dialogue scenes with sound, but this novelty created an immediate popular sensation. To capitalize on this trend, the Warner's subsidiary First National Pictures rushed a trio of mystery house movies into theaters with partial soundtracks consisting of ghostly sound effects, limited dialogue and even musical numbers. "See it! Hear it!" the ads shrieked. "Spooks speak spooky!"

Émigré Danish director Benjamin Christensen, best known for his infamous documentary *Witchcraft Through the Ages* (*Haxan*, 1920), directed all three films in the mystery house sub-genre. All three were written by Christensen and featured dialogue titles written by mystery author Cornell Woolrich under the pseudonym of William Irish. Based on a play by Owen Stevens, *The Haunted House* (1928) starred Thelma Todd, Chester Conklin and Flora Finch in a standard Old Dark House thriller in which the heirs of a deceased millionaire search for a fortune in bonds hidden somewhere in a supposedly haunted Connecticut mansion. Eva Southern plays a mysterious somnambulist who sings the film's musical theme, "Love's Old Sweet Song," while sleepwalking through the spook house, accompanied by the sound of a wailing wind and a howling dog. There are the requisite hidden passages, clutching hands, concealed panels and a mysterious villain in black, all played mostly for laughs with never a ghost in sight. Like many movies of the period, *The*

Thelma Todd is menaced by one of the spectral denizens of director Benjamin Christensen's lost film *The Haunted House* (1928).

Haunted House is a lost film, having been routinely destroyed by the studio like many others over safety concerns about flammable nitrate film stock. All that is left is the soundtrack, dutifully preserved on a Vitaphone disc.

The second film in the series, *Seven Footprints to Satan* (1929), was based on a popular fantasy novel by A. Merritt. Creighton Hale from *The Cat and the Canary* stars as playboy millionaire James Kirkham, and Thelma Todd co-stars as his fiancé Eve Martin. As the film opens, Eve requests Kirkham's assistance selling her family heirlooms, including the fabulous Romanoff Emerald at an auction, but a melee breaks out during the proceedings, causing the couple to exit the auction house through a side door. They duck into a waiting limo, but find out too late that it is not Eve's car as the chauffeur drives them to a strange house where they are kidnapped at gunpoint and held captive.

They soon learn that the mansion is the domain of a cult of devil worshippers and is inhabited by an incredibly strange group of people, including a seductive Lady in Black (Laksa Winters), a surly dwarf (Angelo Rossitto), a swami (Kamiyama Sojin), a demented cripple called "The Spider" (Ivan Christy), the werewolf-like Professor Moriarty (William V. Mong) and even a gorilla ("the beast of Satan"). Lurking in the wings is Satan himself, a figure of dread clad in a robe and hood like an evil cleric from the Spanish Inquisition. The couple undergoes various ordeals as they are terrorized by these creepy characters and the Romanoff Emerald is taken from them by force. They witness a number of bizarre and horrific tableaux, including a naked woman being whipped, another young woman (played by a sixteen-year-old Loretta Young in her screen debut) being carried off for human sacrifice and orgiastic rites attended by men in tuxedos and scantily-clad women.

In the climactic scene, Eve and Kirkham are taken to Satan's chamber, where the Evil One sits enthroned on a dais surrounded by his acolytes. Eve is selected to be the next sacrificial victim, but Kirkham offers himself up in her place. In order to spare her life, Kirkham must undergo an ordeal that involves ascending seven stairsteps leading up to the throne. Each step is adorned with an illuminated number from 1 to 7, and he must be careful to tread only on the proper steps or Eve's life will be forfeit. As Kirkham successfully completes the ordeal, the people in the room suddenly get up and leave *en masse* as the film comes to an unexpected and rather unsatisfying denouement.

Unlike Christensen's other two haunted house entries, *Seven Footprints to Satan* is still in existence and is one of the most bizarre films of the period. It was one of a number of Hollywood movies from the 1920s, such as *Puritan Passions* (1923), *Dante's Inferno* (1924) and *The Sorrows of Satan* (1925) that featured the devil as a character. Creighton Hale makes an unlikely hero type and Thelma Todd acts properly horrified by the strange goings-on, but it's really a directorial tour-de-force that highlights Christensen's use of shadowy lighting, production design and architecture to achieve its effect. The rambling narrative structure, composed of unrelated and confusing scenes, give the film the ambience of a nightmare. This spook house is tenanted by some of the most unusual and eccentric *dramatis personae* this side of a freak show.

Christensen's *House of Horror* (1929) also starred Chester Conklin and Thelma Todd. The story concerns Conklin and his spinster sister, played by Louise Fazenda who are lured away from a general store they jointly operate in Ohio by a mysterious individual (William Mong) to visit the New York mansion of their reclusive and miserly uncle Abner (Emile Chautard). The old dark house is filled to the rafters with all manner of antiques that have been collected over a lifetime by the eccentric uncle. Once ensconced in the creepy old place they are joined by four strangers who join them in searching through the horror house for a missing diamond as the usual spooky goings-on ensue. Like *The Haunted House*, *House of Horror* is also a lost film whose sound track has survived on a Vitaphone disc.

Warner's follow up to *The Jazz Singer* was another musical *The Lights of New York* (1927), Hollywood's first all talking motion picture. This was followed by *The Terror* (1928), the first all talking horror film. Based on a long running London stage play by mystery writer Edgar Wallace, the film was yet another mystery house thriller. This one takes place at Monkhall, an old English country manor that has been converted into an inn operated by Doctor Redmayne (Alec B. Francis) and his daughter Olga (May McAvoy). A homicidal master criminal known only as the Terror is thought to be lurking in the vicinity of the inn, and a number of oddball characters are guests who are attempting to collar the arch-fiend. These include Mrs. Elvery (Louise Fazenda) a spiritualist who conducts séances to glean information from the spirit world, Scotland Yard detective Ferdinand Fane (Edward Everett Horton), and two convicts released from prison to catch the terror, Joe Connors (Matthew Betz) and Soapy Marks (Otto Hoffman). The Terror is depicted wearing a black robe with a cowl that hides his features until his identity is revealed in the final reel.

Offering the usual blend of horror, mystery and comedy in an old dark house setting, *The Terror* is another lost film whose soundtrack has been preserved on a Vitaphone disc. By all accounts the novelty of sound was severely overworked, with all manner of ghostly sound effects constantly intruding upon the action. Women shrieked, doors slammed, the wind moaned and the Terror played spooky tunes on a hidden pipe organ like the Phantom of the Opera. Actor Conrad Nagel, wearing an operatic cape and a domino mask, read screen credits to the audience and announced the time and location of each scene. Edward Everett Horton, best known for playing light comedy roles, is oddly cast as a Scotland Yard alienist, while leading lady May McAvoy lisped badly while delivering her dialogue. Director Roy del Ruth reportedly failed to deliver an effective thriller, as contemporary critics dismissed *The Terror* as being stagebound, slow-paced and monotonous.

With the coming of sound, studios began to offer new versions of their silent-era hits. Universal's first all-talking horror film was a remake of *The Cat and Canary* retitled *The Cat Creeps* (1930). The screenplay by Gladys Lehman hewed closely to the plot of both the stage play and the previous *Cat* movie while Helen Twelvetrees took over the central role of Annabelle West. It was the last film directed by Rupert Julian, best known as the director of the silent version of *The Phantom of the Opera* (1925) starring Lon Chaney, Sr. It was simultaneously filmed in an English-language and a Spanish-language version, the latter starring Lupe Tovar, who would also star in Universal's Spanish-language version of *Dracula* released in the following year. Alas, both versions of *The Cat Creeps* are presently residing somewhere in the limbo of lost films.

Director Roland West remade his silent version of *The Bat* for United Artists as *The Bat Whispers* (1930). The retread followed the same plotline as the earlier film (and the stage play) in which a group of eccentric characters hunt for a stolen fortune in an old dark house while being stalked by the nefarious Bat. Grayce Hampton took over the role of dowager Cornelia Van Gorder, while Una Merkel played her niece, Dale. Chester Morris, who would go on to play screen sleuth Boston Blackie in a series of mystery films beginning in the 1930s, took over the part of Detective Anderson.

The film was shot in an experimental 65mm widescreen format called Magnifilm, an early precursor of Cinemascope. Director West also experimented with suspending the camera on overhead cables, on an electrically controlled dolly, on elevators and a moving crane. Because the 65mm format required a great deal more light than standard 35mm film, enhanced lighting had to be employed to achieve proper exposure, which caused problems for the actors who had to endure the excessive heat and light caused by the extra illumination. Elaborate miniature sets were constructed to depict the dark city environment as a backdrop for the Bat's criminal exploits. West shot the movie only at night between 6 p.m. and 4 a.m., reportedly to keep studio execs from interfering with his filmmaking process.

Unfortunately, all of these expensive and elaborate cinematic techniques failed to score at the box office. The exquisite miniature photography, which conjures a Gotham City–like urban landscape, is used mainly in the early scenes. Once the narrative moves to the confining interiors of the Fleming mansion the action slows to a crawl due to the constraints of filming with sound, where the actors could not stray far from the fixed position of the microphone that recorded the dialogue. This immobility serves to accentuate the theatrical nature of the original material and makes it seem like a filmed performance of the stage play, as most of the time the actors are filmed in static medium shots. The mansion interiors lack the monumental quality of the sets designed for *The Bat* by William Cameron Menzies, and are merely dark and confining. The Bat's wonderfully frightening makeup in the earlier version was abandoned in favor of a more conventional mask and a costume that sports a pair of bat wing-like appendages.

The widescreen Magnifilm format also worked against the success of *The Bat Whispers*, as very few theaters were equipped with projectors that could show the film. Exhibitors were reluctant to shell out money to convert to the new format at the same time as they were forced to upgrade their theaters for sound. As a result, most theaters showed prints of the film in standard 35mm format, which negated the widescreen advantages of West's original concept. Moreover, audiences had tired of the mystery

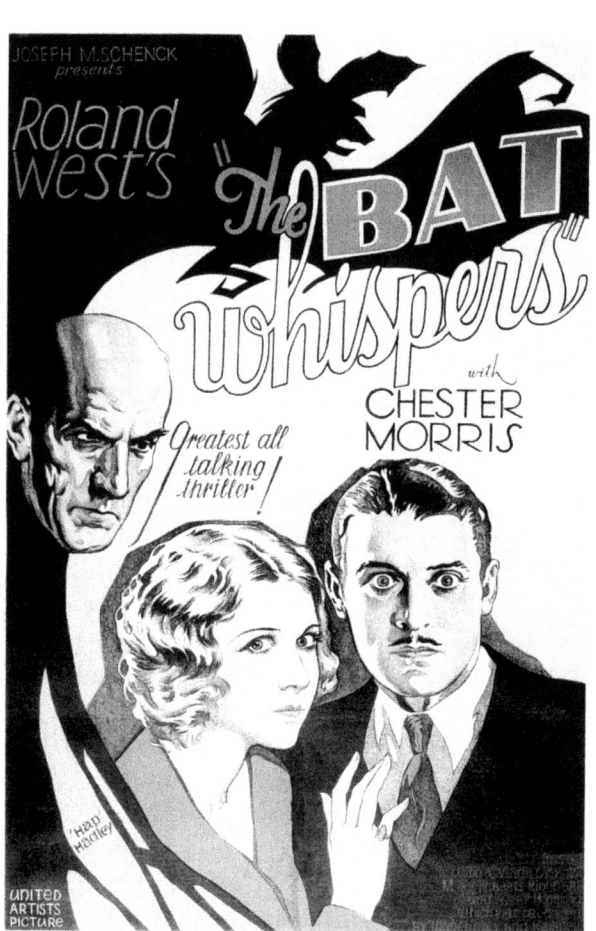

Chester Morris (right), Una Merkel and Gustav von Seyffertitz are featured in this poster for Roland West's sound remake *The Bat Whispers* (1930).

house format, which had become clichéd, and were entranced by a new approach to the horror film that had emerged in Hollywood.

The year 1931 saw the release of Universal's *Dracula* and *Frankenstein*, films that embraced the supernatural and offered a much scarier venue to thrill movie audiences. British director James Whale had invested *Frankenstein* with macabre Germanic horror combined with a hefty dose of mordant wit. Whale's next project was *The Old Dark House* (1932), which was based on a satirical novel by J.B. Priestly and featured newly-minted horror star Boris Karloff, who had portrayed the monster in *Frankenstein*, along with a distinguished British cast.

The film begins on a dark and stormy night in rural Wales, where washed out roads cause a group of sodden wayfarers to take emergency refuge in the creepy old mansion of the Femm family. These unfortunates include Phillip Waverton (Raymond Massey) and his wife Margaret (Gloria Stuart), Roger Penderel (Melvyn Douglas), Sir William Porterhouse (Charles Laughton) and his girlfriend Gladys Perkins (Lilian Bond). The orphans of the storm are not prepared for what they encounter inside the old dark house. The Fenn family is an eccentric bunch, a self-described "benighted household" that includes prissy alcoholic Horace (Ernest Thesiger), his fanatically religious sister Rebecca (Eva Moore) and their hulking mute butler Morgan (Boris Karloff).

(Bottom, left to right) Eva Moore, Raymond Massey, Melvyn Douglas, Lilian Bond, Charles Laughton and Gloria Stuart face off against a glowering Boris Karloff in James Whale's *The Old Dark House* (1932).

After initially enjoying the hospitality of the Femms, things begin to get dicey. The storm causes the electricity to conk out, leaving the shadowy abode in even deeper darkness. While looking for a lamp in an upstairs bedroom, Phillip and Margaret discover the bedridden patriarch of the Femm clan, 102-year-old Sir Roderick (Elspeth Dudgeon), who tells them about the madness that has touched the lives of the Femm family in the "unlucky house." He informs them that his eldest son, Seth, is a dangerous pyromaniac who is kept in a locked room in the attic before falling into a deathlike sleep.

As the night progresses, Morgan gets drunk, goes on a rampage and lets Seth out of his room. The most dangerous and psychotic member of the family, Seth (Brember Willis) lights the draperies in one room on fire as Penderel struggles to subdue him. Seth is killed during the struggle and Penderel barely manages to survive and is nursed back to health by Gladys, with whom he has struck up a romantic relationship. The next day dawns bright and clear and the guests take leave of their erstwhile hosts as if nothing peculiar has occurred.

The Old Dark House features dark atmospherics provided by cinematographer Arthur Edeson, pithy dialogue by scenarists Benn W. Levy and R.C. Sherriff, sparkling performances by a distinguished British cast, and crisp direction by James Whale. Ernest Thesiger, who would go on to play the screwball scientist Dr. Praetorius in Whale's sequel *The Bride of Frankenstein* (1935), steals most of the scenes he's in as the manic Horace Femm, while the great Karloff provides mute menace as the "uncivilized brute" Morgan. Most bizarrely, the part of the elderly patriarch Sir Roderick Femm is played by a woman, Elspeth Dudgeon, whose high-pitched voice is eerily unsettling. Whale paints this house of madness in deep chiaroscuro and frequently shoots the actors in tight close-ups with their faces framed in darkness as the lightning flashes and the thunder booms in the background.

The film departs from the usual mystery house formula in several important respects. First of all, it dispenses with the masked homicidal arch-fiend whose identity is the primary mystery in the plot. Second, there is no treasure or fabulous jewel to serve as a magnet for said criminal, and third, it relies on satire rather than drawing room comedy for its quota of comic relief. *The Old Dark House* moves away from the realm of mystery and harks back to the classic gothic novel, with a pyromaniac relative locked away in a secret room (à la *Jane Eyre*) and an ancient house bearing a family curse. The presence of Karloff and his association with the monster in *Frankenstein* places the film in continuity with the horror films that would soon be coming out of Universal Studios. Thought to be a lost film for many decades, cult director Curtis Harrington was instrumental in locating a print in the Universal vault in 1968 and arranging to have it restored and exhibited. In 1963, shlock director William Castle lensed a silly comic remake starring comedian Tom Poston and British actor Robert Morley.

Universal followed up with a more standard mystery house thriller entitled *The Secret of the Blue Room* (1933). After the same overture from *Swan Lake* used in *Dracula* two years earlier plays over the opening credits, the story begins within the imposing castle of the Von Helldorf estate, where Baron Robert Von Helldorf (Lionel Atwill) is holding a party for his daughter Irene (*The Old Dark House*'s Gloria Stuart) on her 21st birthday. Also at the party are Irene's three suitors, Tommy Brandt (William Janny), Frank Faber (Onslow Stevens) and Captain Walter Brink (Paul Lukas). During the party Tommy urges the Baron to recount the sinister legend of the castle's guest room, also known as the Blue Room.

The Baron relates how the room has been kept locked for the last twenty years after a series of mysterious events took place there that resulted in three deaths. In the first instance, the Baron's sister was found dead after an overnight stay in the Blue Room and her body discovered floating in the castle's moat the next day. Four months later the Baron's best friend was found shot to death at 1 a.m. inside the room and no murder weapon was ever found. Subsequently, a detective who tried to unravel the mystery stayed the night and was discovered dead from fright the next day, his face frozen into an expression of sheer terror. In order to prove his bravery to Irene, Tommy proposes that all three men spend "a night with the ghost" in the room, and volunteers to be the first of the suitors to do so.

On the surface the Blue Room itself does not seem forbidding, and even contains a piano for the musically inclined, but the door locks from the inside and there is no other way out. When the room is opened the next day,

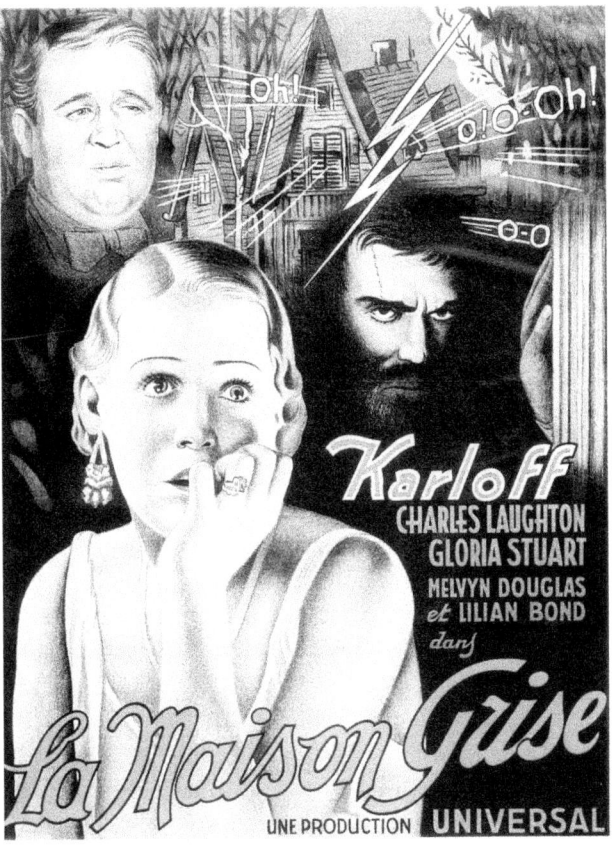

Gloria Stuart, Charles Laughton and "Karloff" are depicted in this French poster for *The Old Dark House* **(1932).**

however, Tommy is missing and is presumed dead as the Baron instructs his servants to search the moat for the body, which is not discovered. The next night, when it is Frank's turn in the room, he brings a gun along but is shot while playing the piano at exactly 1 a.m., and the Baron and Captain Brink determine that he was not slain by his own pistol.

Because they now have an unambiguous homicide on their hands, the Baron calls in Police Commissioner Forster (Edward Arnold) to investigate. The commissioner's detectives uncover some minor mysteries, such as the identity of a man who has been skulking around the estate, but fail to solve the enigma of the Blue Room. Finally, Captain Brink insists that he take his turn within the Blue Room, and he and the commissioner devise a plot to catch the murderer. That night at 1 a.m. a secret panel in the wall of the room opens, a hand holding a gun emerges and fires at the sleeping form of Brink. Fortunately, the assailant has only shot at a dummy of Brink, who chases the killer through the hidden door into a maze of secret passageways underneath the house. A shootout ensues in which the murderer is finally apprehended and his identity revealed.

Director Kurt Neumann crafts an effective mystery house thriller on a shoestring budget, reportedly incurring the least expensive production costs for a Universal movie that year. The film's fine cast includes horror star Lionel Atwill, continental leading man

Paul Lukas, the dignified Gloria Stuart and character actor Edward Arnold, all of whom acquit themselves admirably. The screenplay by William Hurlbut from a story by Erich Philippi, is derivative but original enough to be entertaining, although the killer's identity is pretty obvious to the audience, and the mysterious events occurring in the Blue Room twenty years earlier are never explained or even touched upon. Cinematographer Charles Stumar's moving camera swoops through the castle's rooms and secret passageways to create tension, while Stanley Fleischer's production designs reportedly reused the sets from *The Old Dark House* by disguising them with weird hanging tapestries and appropriately spooky statuary. Director Neumann would go on to lens classic science fiction favorites of the 1950s such as *Kronos* (1957) and *The Fly* (1958).

From independent production company Mayfair Studios came yet another mystery house programmer, *The Monster Walks* (1933). After the visage of a gorilla appears superimposed over the opening credits, the film begins with a shot of the dead body of Dr. Phillip Earlton laid out in his bedroom at the Earlton estate. The newly-deceased corpse was formerly a mad scientist type who conducted experiments on an ape named Yogi, who is kept in a cage in the basement. On that dark and stormy night Phillip's daughter Ruth Earlton (Vera Reynolds) and her fiancé, Dr. Ted Clayton (Rex Lease), arrive at the old house for the reading of her father's will by attorney Herbert Wilkes (Sidney Bracey). Also present are Ruth's uncle Robert (Sheldon Lewis), a cripple who is confined to a wheelchair, servants "Tanty" Krug (Martha Mattox), her son Hanns (Mischa Auer) and Ruth's African American chauffeur Exodus (Willie Best).

When the will is read, Ruth is revealed as the sole heir, but if she should die Robert will inherit all of the estate and the Krugs are to be paid a paltry $50 a month. As the storm has made the local roads unpassable, Ruth, Ted, Wilkes and Exodus are obliged to spend the night in the mad savant's lair, but between the presence of the corpse upstairs and the piercing screams of the ape in the cellar (actually an adult chimpanzee), the guests are understandably edgy. Later that night a hairy hand emerges from a secret panel in Ruth's room and attempts to strangle her. When Mrs. Krug stays in Ruth's room to comfort her, the hirsute paw comes forth once more and strangles the housekeeper to death instead. Is the homicide the work of Yogi the ape, or is there a plot afoot to murder Ruth for her inheritance hatched by Robert and a disgruntled Hanns?

The film includes most of the familiar mystery house plot elements, including the reading of a last will and testament containing a codicil that puts a young woman heiress in danger, a group of sinister characters confined to an old dark house during a thunderstorm, an oddball cast member who provides comic relief, and of course, the obligatory clutching hand. Director Frank Stayer moves the action along at a snail's pace, shooting in uninteresting medium shots and providing little in the way of murky atmosphere. Most of the cast members turn in lackluster performances, with the exception of Martha Mattox, who had played a similar role as a housekeeper in Paul Leni's *The Cat and the Canary*, and African American comedian Willie Best, who manages to generate a few laughs despite the outrageous racism of the film's script. Best would go on to play opposite comic Bob Hope in one of the great haunted house comedies, *The Ghost Breakers* (1940), to be discussed in the next chapter, Where the film departs from the standard mystery house formula is in using an ape in place of a mysterious criminal as the film's obligatory menace. Homicidal simians had previously appeared in Universal's *The Unholy Three* (1930) and *The Murders in the Rue Morgue* (1932), and would become a fixture of haunted house comedies in later decades.

By the mid–1930s movie audiences had tired of the mystery house formula. The sequel to *The Terror*, entitled *Return of the Terror* (1934), failed to impress movie-goers and critics alike, despite the efforts of an interesting cast that included Mary Astor, Frank McHugh, Irving Pichel and J. Carrol Naish. Audiences seeking ghastly thrills were more likely to be attracted to Universal's stable of newly-minted creatures, an ever-expanding roster that included Dracula, Frankenstein, the Mummy and the Invisible Man. Other studios had jumped on the horror bandwagon as well and were busy churning out their own brands of terror, such as Paramount's *Dr. Jekyll and Mr. Hyde* (1931), *Island of Lost Souls* (1933) and *Supernatural* (1933), MGM's *Freaks* (1932) and *The Mask of Fu Manchu* (1932) and Warner's *Svengali* (1931), *Doctor X* (1932) and *Mystery of the Wax Museum* (1933). The Bat, the Cat and the Terror simply couldn't compete with these cinema monstrosities, and so faded into obscurity.

Later decades saw a slight resurgence of the form in a number of oddball retreads. *The Bat* was remade in 1958 and starred Agnes Morehead as Cornelia Van Gorder and featured Vincent Price in the role of a sinister physician, Dr. Wells. In this iteration, the Bat is depicted wearing a black mask that covers his entire face, clawed gloves and a fedora. The Fleming mansion is not a very memorable old dark house, and overall it's pretty dull stuff in comparison to the two earlier versions despite the efforts of screen vets Morehead and Price and writer/director Crane Wilbur. Shlockmeister William Castle went to England to produce and direct a disappointing remake of *The Old Dark House* (1963) that starred American comedian Tom Poston and British thesp Robert Morley. *The Cat and the Canary* fared better, but was also played for comedy in a 1939 version starring Bob Hope, Paulette Goddard, Gale Sondegaard and George Zucco, and a 1978 British comic remake with Carol Lynley, Wilfred Hyde-White and Honor Blackman.

An advertising blurb for *The Terror* colorfully describes the horrors and attractions of the mystery house sub-genre thus: "Black shrouded death hovers throughout the picture while the audience shudders and shivers. Flickering lights, ghostly shadows, strange murders, knives flashing in dark places, shrieks and screams, guns blazing out of darkness, dead bodies falling, appalling situations ... and, throughout, spine chilling touches of human comedy!" This meld of murder mystery, horror and comedy had its origins in theatrical productions on the Broadway and London stage and enjoyed a brief fluorescence during the late silent and early sound period, but were quickly superseded by the more intense terrors of the 1930s horror cycle. Nevertheless, the mystery house formula produced three classics of the early horror film, Paul Leni's *The Cat and the Canary*, Roland West's *The Bat* and James Whale's *The Old Dark House*.

Yet no ghosts were allowed to inhabit these forbidding old houses, as movie audiences preferred the novel vampires, monsters and mad doctors spawned by Hollywood studios. The concept of ghosts was anathema to Protestant America, who preferred to steer clear of spiritual matters concerning the afterlife. The only spooks haunting houses were to be found in comic treatments of the theme, where these apparitions were permitted, but played for laughs instead of chills.

Chapter Two

Haunting Comedy
Dark Laughter in a Haunted House

It's hardly surprising that haunted houses and comedy sometimes go together. Laughter can serve to take the edge off of supernatural dread, and ghosts are fantastic characters who can perpetrate all manner of comic antics. The meld of haunted houses and humor can be traced back to the Roman playwright Plautus' farce *Mostellaria* (discussed in the Introduction), and was evident in the early French haunted house films *The Haunted Castle* and *The House of Ghosts*. The mystery house films of the 20s and 30s always contained characters and sub-plots that provided a healthy dose of comic relief. Comedic treatments of the haunted house theme began in earnest in the 1920s and have persisted to the present day, and have showcased the efforts of major screen comedians such as Buster Keaton, Harold Lloyd, Abbott and Costello, Bob Hope, Don Knotts, Gene Wilder, Eddie Murphy and Johnny Depp.

The first significant Hollywood haunted house comedy was *The Ghost Breaker* (1914). The film was co-directed by Cecil B. DeMille and Oscar P. Apfel and based on a 1909 stage play of the same name by Paul Dickey and Charles W. Goddard. Silent film star H.B. Warner plays Warren Jarvis, the titular ghost breaker, an aristocratic Kentuckian who is persuaded to come to the aid of Princess Maria Theresa (Rita Stanwood) in unraveling the riddle of her inheritance, the secret of which is contained within a locket. Jarvis and his faithful African American valet Rusty Snow (John Burton) accompany the Princess back to her spooky ancestral castle in Spain to uncover its secrets, but are stymied by the efforts of the Duke D'Alva (Horace B. Carpenter), who has arranged a series of phony ghosts to "haunt" the castle with the hope of discovering the fortune himself.

The film was remade in 1922 under the direction of Alfred E. Green starring Wallace Reid as Jarvis, Lila Lee as the Princess Maria, Walter Hiers as Rusty Snow and Arthur Carew as the Duke D'Alva. Both films are now lost, but it was remade a third time as *The Ghost Breakers* (1940) starring Bob Hope and a fourth as *Scared Stiff* (1953) with Dean Martin and Jerry Lewis. In both sound remakes the location of the haunted estate was moved from Spain to the Caribbean. *The Ghost Breaker* introduced the unfortunate and offensive racial stereotype of the superstitious African American whose exaggerated fear of ghosts is intended to provide comic relief. To add insult to injury, in both silent versions the role of Rusty Snow was played by a Caucasian actor in blackface.

Haunted Spooks (1920) featured silent film star Harold Lloyd as a character referred to only as "The Boy," a loser at love who is so distraught about losing the girl of his dreams that he unsuccessfully tries to commit suicide in a number of amusing scenes. Fortunately, he runs into a lawyer (William Gillespie) who convinces him to marry his niece Mildred (Mildred Davis, a.k.a. "The Girl"). Mildred is set to inherit a large estate in the deep South from a deceased relative, but the will stipulates that she must be married and live in the house for an entire year with her husband. A marriage is quickly arranged and as the bride and groom drive to the property, Mildred's conniving uncle (Wallace Howe) makes plans to scare the couple away from the supposedly haunted house using phony spooks so that he can claim the estate for himself.

Once they arrive at the mansion, the house's African American servants tell them tall tales about the "ghastly grinning ghosts" who are said to walk its halls. Sure enough, figures in white sheets are seen roaming about the house, but these are the uncle's hirelings tricked out to fool the credulous. Other apparitions soon appear, such as a small table that appears to move by itself and a pair of pants walking around without a top that causes Lloyd's hair to comically stand on end, but these turn out to be caused by the antics of a young boy. In the end the "ghosts" are exorcised and the happy couple goes off to share marital bliss together.

Lloyd's inventive comedy style enlivens *Haunted Spooks*, the humor being generated by his fearful reactions to the faux ghosts. It should be noted that only the second half of the film is set in the haunted house, but this is consistent with the two-act structure of the comedy shorts of the period. Once again there are no real specters in evidence, and the apparitions are merely part of a plot motivated by greed designed to secure the property perpetrated by the crooked uncle. Lloyd was injured during the filming when he posed with a prop bomb that exploded in his hand during a publicity photo shoot, causing the loss of two of his fingers, burns to his face and temporary blindness, but he soon recovered and returned to filming wearing a five-fingered prosthetic glove to hide his deformity.

Silent film star Buster Keaton was the next comedian to venture into a haunt in the short *The Haunted House* (1921). Keaton plays a hapless bank clerk who gets mixed up in a robbery perpetrated by the bank's manager and is mistaken for one of the crooks. Running from the law, he takes refuge in an old dark house that is reputedly haunted that the police won't enter. Unknown to Buster, a group of counterfeiters has been using the house as a hideout and have installed a number of trick devices inside. They also go about in scary costumes in order to bolster the house's haunted reputation. Unknown to

Silent film comedian Harold Lloyd ("the Boy") and Mildred Davis ("the Girl") appear in this French poster for Lloyd's comic short *Haunted Spooks* (1925).

either Buster or the counterfeiters, however, a theatrical troupe fleeing a mob of angry patrons after a disastrous performance of *Faust* has also hidden themselves in the house still wearing their stage costumes.

A series of comic misadventures ensues as Buster encounters apparitions such as ghosts clad in white sheets, skeleton men and Mephistopheles himself inside the haunted house that leave him scared stiff. He has even more problems with a trick staircase that keeps turning into a slide and dumping him on his rump. Eventually the cops are able to collar the crooks, but on his way to jail the gang's leader manages to knock Keaton on the head, sending him into a dream in which he is ascending the trick stairs, which are fantastically transformed into a stairway to heaven.

Keaton's comic genius imbues *The Haunted House* with all manner of ingenious sight gags, the most outlandish of which is a scene in which two of the skeleton men assemble a man's body out of component parts who then, via the magic of the cinema, comes to life and walks away. Buster's signature deadpan delivery keeps the humor flowing through a series of mock supernatural encounters that utilize elaborate costumes, camera trickery and mechanical gags. The film adheres to the two-act structure used in silent shorts, so that only the second half of the film takes place inside the haunted house. As in *The Ghost Breaker* and *Haunted Spooks*, there are no real ghosts within the haunt, only people in costumes pretending to be spirits in order to scare the protagonists away from a piece of real estate as part of a criminal scheme.

As the haunted house comedy short faded in the early 1920s, it would be supplanted by the mystery house feature-length films, beginning with *One Exciting Night* in 1922. The two forms had a lot of themes in common such as colorful crooks searching for a treasure hidden inside an old mansion, mysterious figures in disguise aiming to scare its inhabitants into leaving the house or otherwise intimidate them, high spirited humor and a complete absence of supernatural ghosts. Change was in the air, however, in later decades.

The only case of a migrating haunt in screen history occurs in the British comic satire *The Ghost Goes West* (1936). The story begins in 18th century Scotland, during one of its many wars of independence waged against England. As the Scottish troops assemble for battle, a feud between the Glourie and MacClaggan clans arises, during which Murdoch Glourie (Robert Donat) is accused of cowardice. Murdoch, who is more interested in dallying with the lassies than fighting, dies an ignominious death while hiding from the MacClaggans and is condemned by his father to haunt the halls of Castle Glourie until he can restore his clan's honor by humiliating a MacClaggan.

Two hundred years later, the last descendent of the Glourie clan, Donald (also Donat), is deeply in debt and obliged to sell the castle to brash American grocery store magnate Mr. Martin (Eugene Pallette). While staying at the castle, Martin's daughter Peggy (Jean Parker) encounters Murdoch's ghost, who is clad in traditional highlander garb, and mistakes him for his double, Donald. The ghost turns his considerable charms on Peggy, causing romantic sparks to fly between Peggy and Donald.

Martin intends to dismantle the castle stone by stone and transport it to the United States to be reconstructed as part of a publicity campaign for his business, and enlists Donald to supervise the work. Castle Glourie is taken apart and loaded on board the cargo hold of an ocean liner for its trip over the pond, and Murdoch's ghost goes along with it. When his apparition appears in front of the passengers during a costume party, it causes a sensation that creates headlines for American newspapers and even gets debated in the U.S. Congress.

Once the castle has been reassembled in Sunnymeade, Florida, Martin installs modern conveniences such as electricity and radios, and even puts gondolas in the moat. A gala opening night is arranged for Castle Glourie, complete with searchlights like a Hollywood film premiere, and the ghost, who is supposed to appear at midnight, is set to be the star of the show. Not everyone is convinced that the apparition will materialize, however. Chief among the skeptics is Martin's business rival Ed Bigelow (Ralph Bunker), who doesn't believe in spooks and boasts of his own Scottish heritage as the last of the MacLaggans. Upon hearing this, Murdoch's ghost manifests and goes after Bigelow, forcing the terrified businessman to grovel and admit to the superiority of clan Glourie to the MacLaggans. Murdoch's curse is lifted as his soul departs for heaven while Donald and Janet head towards inevitable matrimony.

This was acclaimed French director Rene Clair's first English-language effort, and he delivers a sparkling supernatural romantic comedy that prefigures his later work in the similarly-themed *I Married a Witch* (1942). Clair balances the fantastic, romantic and comedic elements of the story and forms them into a flawless whole. British actor Robert Donat, who had starred in Alfred Hitchcock's breezy thriller *The Thirty-Nine Steps* (1935), is in fine form in his dual role as Murdoch and Donald Glourie, and is especially charming while playing the ghost. American comedian Eugene Pallette provides additional laughs while ingénue Jean Parker is perky and pleasant as the female lead. Production values by the famed Alexander Korda are excellent, while the screenplay by Robert E. Sherwood has affinities with Oscar Wilde's satire *The Canterville Ghost*, which would be directed in 1944 by fellow Frenchman Jules Dassin.

The notion of moving a haunted house and its ghostly occupant from one continent to another is a novel and intriguing idea. The supernatural beliefs of the Old World are transplanted to the New in a manner analogous to the transplantation of European mythologies into Hollywood during the 1930s horror movie cycle. In contrast to the faux phantoms of the mystery house films and the silent-era American haunted house comedies, *The Ghost Goes West* featured the very first instance of a paranormal ghost inhabiting a haunted house in a feature film.

Several haunted house comedies of the 1930s and 40s devolved from the mystery house movie plot formula that had begun in the late 20s with *The Cat and the Canary* and *The Bat*. By the late 30s this type of film had become overly clichéd, so filmmakers sought to tweak the formula. The mystery house thrillers had always had a comedic element, which was now brought to the forefront at the expense of the mystery and horror aspects. *The Gorilla* (1939) was based on a 1925 Broadway play by Ralph Spence that had previously been lensed in 1927 and 1930 that was now adapted as a vehicle for the comedic talents of the Ritz Brothers.

The film unfolds in a stately mansion in upscale Westchester New York owned by the wealthy Walter Stevens (horror veteran Lionel Atwill), who has received a death threat from a psycho killer known only as "The Gorilla." During a telephone conversation with an unknown party it is revealed that Stevens is deeply in debt to the tune of a quarter of a million dollars and is being pressured to pay up. Also on hand in the mansion are Stevens' servants, butler Peters (horror icon Bela Lugosi) and perpetually terrified maid Kitty (Patsy Kelly).

On that conveniently dark and stormy night Stevens' niece Norma Denby (Anita Louise) and her fiancé Jack Marsden (Edward Norris) arrive from Paris and announce they are planning to wed tomorrow. Stevens discusses the disposition of his brother's will with his niece, explaining that they are both to inherit half of the family fortune, but in the event that one of them dies, the survivor will inherit the entire package. He also tells them about the death threat, but not to worry, as he has hired three private detectives from Acme Investigators to protect him. The three gumshoes, Mulligan (Al Ritz), Harrigan (Harry Ritz) and Garrity (Jimmy Ritz) promptly arrive on the scene to prevent the Gorilla from carrying out his murderous scheme, but at the stroke of midnight the lights go out and Stevens disappears.

The rest of the film consists of the trio of bumbling detectives demonstrating their talent for incompetence as they search for their missing employer through the many rooms and secret passageways of the old dark house. To add to the general chaos, a real gorilla from a nearby carnival is brought onto the premises and wreaks havoc through the house before being subdued, and a mysterious stranger (Joseph Calleia), who claims to be a Securities and Exchange Commission agent arrives to go snooping around looking for incriminating documents. Kitty the maid screams her head off, Peter the Butler slinks around looking sinister, and the three inept private eyes stagger from one inane vaudeville routine to another until Stevens is discovered bound up inside a hidden room and the Gorilla is revealed to be the SEC guy who is promptly remanded to the nearest jail.

This film follows the standard mystery house plotline at first. It features a young woman whose inheritance of a fortune places her in danger, a stalwart fiancé, an old, dark house honeycombed with secret passages, a sinister servant, the inevitable clutching hand and a psychotic criminal who assumes the persona of an animal. All of this is pushed into the background upon the arrival of the Ritz Brothers, whose zany routines move the film completely into the realm of comedy. While the comedians may have been popular in their heyday, modern audiences are less inclined toward their style of mirth making, for unlike contemporaneous comic trios such as the Three Stooges or the Marx Brothers, the Ritz's shtick was to have all three of the brothers copy each other's actions and mannerisms in unison, a technique that doesn't have the same comedic impact today. Kitty the maid, played by Patsy Kelly (who, decades later, would later have a small part in *Rosemary's Baby*), is supposed to provide additional comedy but her gravel-voiced delivery merely grates on the nerves. Horror stars Lionel Atwill and Bela Lugosi play it straight but are peripheral to the main action, and future film noir heavy Joseph Calleia is slick and sinister as the bogus SEC investigator. Veteran director Alan Dwan serves up some spooky atmospherics inside the film's shadowy mansion during the early scenes, but the complicated screenplay by Rian James and Sid Silvers soon gets lost in a maze of too many sub-plots and red herrings. Taking its cue from the 1933 thriller *The Monster Walks*, the characters are not menaced by supernatural ghosts, but by a savage flesh-and-blood gorilla.

The third screen version of *The Cat and the Canary*, released in 1939, would be a seminal work in the history of horror comedy. Designed as a vehicle for radio comic Bob Hope, the film took the basic narrative framework of the earlier versions but amped up the comedic element and changed the locale of the haunted mansion from the banks of the Hudson River to the Louisiana bayou country. The plot centers around a group of oddball characters who have gathered in the old dark house of an eccentric millionaire to witness the reading

Two. Haunting Comedy

of the dead man's will by an attorney Mr. Crosby (George Zucco), to ascertain who is heir to the estate. This motley crew of relatives consists of Charles Wilder (Douglas Montgomery), Fred Blythe (John Beal), Aunt Susan (Elizabeth Patterson) and cousin Cicily (Nydia Westman). Hope portrays radio actor Wally Campbell ("your favorite and mine"), who is paired with co-star Joyce Norman (Paulette Goddard), and presiding over the proceedings is spooky housekeeper Miss Lu (Gale Sondergaard).

Following the familiar plotline, Joyce is revealed as heiress to the estate, but the will stipulates that she must live on the property for thirty days without losing her sanity, otherwise everything will revert to a secondary heir listed on a letter in Crosby's possession. This arrangement, of course, gives the other family members a motive to gaslight or even murder Joyce to gain the inheritance. At this point a guard (John Wray) appears to inform them that a homicidal madman called the Cat has escaped from a nearby loony bin and is prowling around the bayou. Later that night Crosby is drawn into a secret panel by the Cat and disappears, along with the letter identifying the second heir.

The usual hi-jinx follow as Wally and Joyce discover a fabulous diamond necklace, which is promptly stolen by the Cat's clutching hand that appears from behind a secret panel in the wall. Crosby's dead body is discovered when it falls out from behind another panel in the library. In the climax, Joyce enters a maze of secret passageways behind one

(Top, left to right) Elizabeth Patterson, Gale Sondergaard, Nydia Westman and (bottom, left to right) John Beal, Bob Hope, Douglas Montgomery and Paulette Goddard are pictured in this lobby card for the 1939 remake of *The Cat and the Canary*.

of the panels and is trapped there, where she is stalked by the Cat. Wally manages to find his way inside the maze and goes to her rescue, confronting the Cat and preventing Joyce from being killed. Once again, the escaped madman story proves to be a ruse perpetrated by the second heir, whose identity is finally revealed.

While Paul Leni's 1927 silent version of *The Cat and the Canary* was influenced by the dark shadows of German expressionism, the 1939 sound remake adapts some of the conventions of a 30s-era radio melodrama as Hope, basically playing himself, inflicts his brand of radio comedy upon the proceedings. Women scream, gunshots ring out and doors creak open in typical radio sound effects fashion. Hope's aggressive performance dominates the film, the character's cowardice in the face of danger providing the bulk of the film's humor. "I always joke when I'm scared," Wally explains nervously, "even my goosebumps have goosebumps." Co-star Paulette Goddard is charming and attractive, knows how to express fright convincingly, and her onscreen chemistry with Hope is a big factor in making the film work. Horror stalwarts George Zucco and Gale Sondegaard use their screen personas to provide some spooky ambience, while supporting player Nydia Westman dishes out additional comedy in her role as the nerved-out Cicily. Elizabeth Patterson reprised her role as Aunt Susan from the 1930 remake *The Cat Creeps*.

As this version of *Cat* emphasizes laughs over chills, there's not much in the way of horror content until the final minutes of the film. Relocating the haunted mansion to the Louisiana bayou country, director Elliot Nugent makes good use of the swampy scenery, complete with gators, croaking frogs, Spanish moss, grim-looking Seminoles and watery lighting effects. The antebellum southern gothic haunt would be replicated decades later in the Eddie Murphy horror comedy *The Haunted Mansion* (2003). In comparison with the ghostly, castle-like mansion in the 1927 version, the haunted house in the remake is merely rundown and decrepit. The inimitable Gale Sondegaard provides much of the film's spooky atmospherics as the mediumistic Miss Lu, who is seemingly in touch with the house's ghosts, and who utters memorable lines of dialogue such as "I'm never lonely, I've got my friends" and "The house is full of murmurs." When the house lights periodically dim (something that is never explained in the film), she quips, "sometimes they get into the machinery."

The remake of *The Cat and the Canary* was a popular success that served to make the haunted house comedy economically viable, and a raft of similarly-themed movies starring period comedians followed. The first of these reunited Bob Hope and Paulette Goddard in a remake of another silent comedy, *The Ghost Breakers* (1940). Once again Hope plays a radio personality, Larry Lawrence, who runs afoul of a mobster after running an embarrassing piece on the hoodlum on his New York radio show. Forced to leave town in a hurry, he stows away inside a clothes trunk belonging to Mary Carter (Paulette Goddard) and is taken to a ship bound for Havana, where Mary has just inherited some property. Once the ruse is discovered, Larry books his own passage on the ship, along with his faithful African American family retainer, Alex (Willie Best).

Mary has inherited a mansion, the "Castillo Maldito," a forbidding abode located on an island off the coast of Cuba that is reputedly haunted. Upon their arrival in Havana, Mary is beset by aggressive lawyer Mr. Parada (Paul Lukas), who warns her about the Castillo's evil reputation and offers to purchase the property for an undisclosed buyer. She also crosses paths with Geoff Montgomery (Richard Carlson), an American who seems to know a lot about local voodoo practices. Larry Tags along as a "ghostbreaker," a self-styled exorcist who will rid her of her spook problem. "I take family skeletons out of closets and dust them off," he explains.

That night Larry, Alex and Mary travel to the island haunt, where they encounter a witchy-woman (Virginia Brissac) and her zombie son (Noble Johnson) while exploring the imposing gothic ruin. A large painting of the family matriarch Maria Ysobel Sebastian, who is a ringer for Mary, hangs prominently in the manor's main hall. Wandering through the Castillo's family crypt, Larry and Alex witness what appears to be the glowing specter of the former lord of the manor, Don Santiago, arise from his coffin, walk about, and then return, but when they open the coffin lid, they discover nothing but a skeleton. The Ghostbreakers are confounded by these seemingly supernatural events, as well as the presence of Parada, Montgomery and Cubano gangster Francisco Mederos (Anthony Quinn), who are caught sneaking around the premises. Their interest becomes clear when it is revealed that there is a valuable silver mine located beneath the Castillo. In the end Mary wrests her inheritance from the villains, and the ghost of Don Santiago turns out to have been a real spook.

Once again Hope and Goddard are in fine comedic and romantic form in this lively and scary haunted house comedy. Director George Marshall keeps the action and the laughs flowing smoothly from Walter De Leon's screenplay. Superb production values and art direction transform the original silent film material into one of the most acclaimed horror comedies in screen history. The principals are aided and abetted by the efforts of movie heavies Paul Lukas, Richard Carlson and Anthony Quinn that build the suspense. Special praise must be accorded to African American comedian Willie Best, who must struggle through a number of offensively racist jokes while playing Hope's valet. In the process, however, West has some of the funniest dialogue as he delivers the punch lines provided by Hope, who sometimes acts as the straight man in the exchanges. Another African American actor, Noble Johnson, provides much of the film's tangible menace playing a creepy, bald-headed zombie.

Moving the film's haunt from Spain to Cuba allowed the scenarist to introduce voodoo and zombies into the mix, although these are actually part of the culture of Haiti, not Cuba. Plot elements of the mystery house formula are evident, such as an heiress in peril, a hidden treasure, and a gaggle of fortune-hunting crooks. The big difference, however, is that the supernatural beings are real instead of being a con-

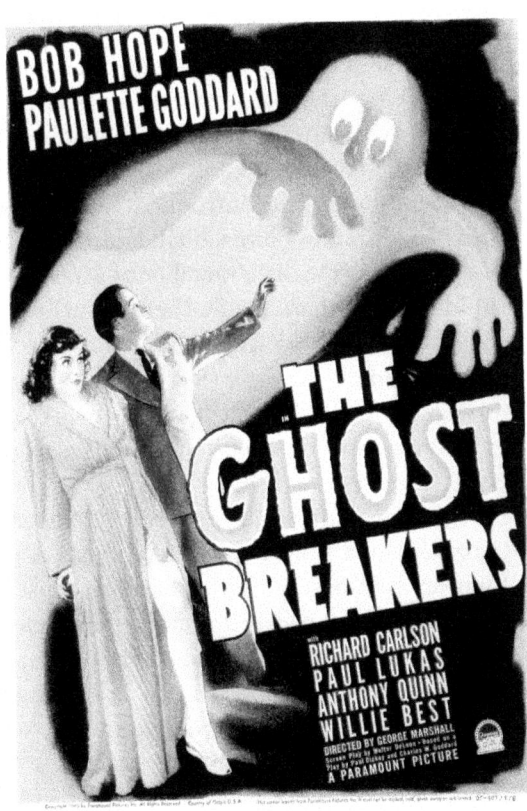

Bob Hope and Paulette Goddard are spook busters in this poster for the supernatural comedy *The Ghost Breakers* (1940).

trivance to steal money, an angle that adds an edge of fright to the comedy. Castillo Maldido is a marvelously conceived haunted gothic castle, with its main set sporting high-vaulted ceilings and an enormous grand staircase presided over by a large, brooding portrait of Mary's ancestor (and doppelganger) Maria Ysobel. In one of the film's most memorable scenes, Mary dresses herself up like the lady in the picture and descends the staircase like a ghost.

While the notion of "ghost breaking" is not taken seriously in the film, being used merely as a ruse by Larry, a trailer for the movie depicts Hope sitting in the offices of "Ghostbreakers, Inc." surrounded by ringing telephones soliciting his psychic exterminating services. This bit clearly foreshadows a similar outfit in the same line of business decades later in the comedy hit *Ghostbusters* (1984). *The Ghost Breakers* was remade yet again as *Scared Stiff* (1953) that starred Dean Martin in the Hope role and Jerry Lewis playing the Willie Best part that was lensed by the same director, George Marshall.

The Ghost Breakers turned out to be an even bigger critical and box-office success for Paramount than *The Cat and the Canary*, and other studios took notice of the trend and followed suit with haunted house comedies of their own. Chief among these was Universal's comedy team of Bud Abbott and Lou Costello in *Hold That Ghost* (1941). As the film opens, Chuck Murray (Bud) and Ferdinand "Ferdie" Jones (Lou) are gas station attendants when gangster "Moose" Matson (William B. Davidson) pulls up to have his car serviced. While they are working on the auto, Chuck and Ferdie are trapped inside when the cops show up and Moose speeds away to avoid arrest. A shootout ensues during which Moose is killed, and the boys later learn from the hoodlum's lawyer that Matson's will contains an odd stipulation that whoever is with him at the time of his death will inherit his now deserted tavern, the Forrester's Club.

Moose's attorney introduces them to bus driver Charlie Smith (Marc Lawrence), who has been hired to drive Chuck and Ferdie to the inn for an inspection tour. Unknown to them, Smith is really a member of Matson's gang who is looking for Moose's stash of cash hidden somewhere inside the club, which was really a clandestine gambling joint. The bogus bus driver takes the boys out to the club, along with a trio of other passengers, radio actress Camille Brewster (Joan Davis), Dr. Jackson (Richard Carlson from *The Ghost Breakers*) and waitress Norma Lind (Evelyn Ankers). When the bus pulls up at the club during a heavy rainstorm, Charlie promptly drives off and strands the passengers at the remote inn.

Strange things happen during the stormy night that seem to indicate that the former gambling den is now a haunted house. A ghostly figure wearing a sheet is seen, a candle appears to move by itself, Charlie's corpse is discovered at several locations and Ferdie's bedroom keeps converting itself into a gaming room complete with roulette wheels and dice tables. It turns out that all of these "supernatural" events are being caused by gangsters who are seeking the hidden loot and trying to scare the guests away from the property, but their plot is foiled and Ferdie manages to find Matson's fortune hidden inside a stuffed moose's head. The boys use the money to buy a nightclub where they hire Ted Lewis and the Andrews Sisters, who perform their song "Aurora" in their inimitable fashion.

Widely considered by critics to be one of the very best efforts of the comedy team, *Hold That Ghost* shines with the comic wit of scenarists Robert Lees, Fred Rinaldo and John Grant, and the brisk direction of veteran Arthur Lubin. Bud and Lou are at the very top of their form as they bumble through the haunt pursued by ganefs and ghosts alike. Additional laughs are provided by future TV comedienne Joan Davis, who shows a special chemistry with Costello in their scenes together. The "moving candle" bit, in which Lou hyperventilates in terror while watching a candle moving by itself was so funny it was reused in *Abbott & Costello Meet Frankenstein* several years later. Future sci-fi/horror star Richard Carlson and Universal scream queen Evelyn Ankers play it straight, and Shemp Howard of the Three Stooges has a bit part as a soda jerk, while the musical number performed by the Andrews Sisters at the end of the film is a real hoot.

Once more a haunted house is devoid of ghosts and instead is infested by crooks looking for a hidden treasure and trying to scare the house's rightful owners away by impersonating spooks. The radio connection is again apparent, as the Joan Davis character is a radio actress who is employed primarily for her ability to scream, a talent that she demonstrates at several points during the film. As if to emphasize this connection, Abbott and Costello would later perform a live version of the movie on the radio program *Hollywood Premiere*. The comedy duo's first brush with the supernatural would prove to be a lucrative genre meld that would result in an extended series of horror comedies as Bud and Lou met Frankenstein, the Invisible Man, Dr. Jekyll and Mr. Hyde and the Mummy, and they would later star in another haunted house comedy, *The Time of Their Lives* (1946).

That same year Universal released a film that fell somewhere between the mystery house and horror comedy sub-genres, *The Black Cat* (1941). As the movie begins, Henrietta Winslow (Cecilia Loftus), matriarch of the Winslow clan, is reportedly near death, and her relatives have gathered at the estate in anticipation of the reading of her will. These worthies include her niece Myrna (Gladys Cooper), Myrna's husband Montague (Basil Rathbone), her stepson Richard (Alan Ladd) and granddaughter Elaine (Anne Gwynne). Also at the mansion are two sinister-looking servants, the housekeeper Abagail (Gale Sondegaard) and groundskeeper Eduardo Vigos (Bela Lugosi). Two more unusual characters are drawn to the Winslow estate that night by rumors of Henrietta's demise, real estate agent Gil Smith (Broderick Crawford) and antiques dealer Mr. Penny (Hugh Herbert), who are looking to make a deal to purchase the house and its furniture from the heirs.

Unfortunately for the greedy heirs, reports of Henrietta's death have been greatly exaggerated. The wheelchair-bound old lady has made a recovery and suddenly appears among them to announce the terms of her will. Her blood relatives are to inherit six-figure sums, but Montague is distressed by the paltry sum he has been awarded because he is deep in debt. The bulk of the estate, however, including the Winslow house, are to be given to her young granddaughter Elaine, who she considers the least predaceous of her relatives. Henrietta will never sell the house while she is alive because she is a cat worshipper who has built a shrine to her felines in a separate building on the property, a temple/crypt that contains a crematorium and the ashen remains of her furry friends stored in jars. The crematorium is large enough to accommodate a human body, and she has given instructions that upon her death, her body is to be cremated and her ashes will join those of her beloved pets.

Henrietta narrowly avoids being poisoned by some milk that has been tampered with that accidentally kills one of her cats instead. When she brings the poor kitty to the shrine to be cremated, an unknown assailant enters through a secret passage and stabs her to death with a pair of knitting needles. Now that she is actually deceased, the family gathers for the disposition of the estate once more, only to find out that an additional clause in the will states that nobody will inherit anything until Abagail is dead and all of Henrietta's cats have used up their nine lives. Predictably, Abagail is found hanged and Myrna is almost murdered in the same fashion. Gil pursues the killer, whose identity is finally disclosed and who turns out to be one of the cast members that the audience would least suspect.

Director Albert S. Rogell, together with ace cinematographer Stanley Cortez, imbue *The Black Cat* with gobs of murky atmosphere in typical Universal horror movie fashion, but the screenplay, "suggested by" the Edgar Allan Poe story, has nothing to do with the author's work. Horror stars Basil Rathbone and the inimitable Gale Sondergaard lend a spooky touch to the proceedings, while Bela Lugosi has a throwaway red herring role and is reduced to slinking around the set trying to look sinister. While the mystery house ambience of the film works well, the comedy element is much less effective. Broderick Crawford, the actual star of the film, blusters his way through his role as a dunderheaded real estate agent, while his cohort Penny, played by comedian Hugh Herbert, delivers his dialogue with an annoying "hoo-hoo-hoo" verbal mannerism that quickly becomes irritating. Even Sondegaard and Lugosi are pressed into service in a misguided attempt to provide comedy.

The fog-shrouded Winslow House is a typical haunted manor in the old dark house tradition, but the cat shrine, adorned with rows of urns containing feline remains and dominated by a sleek ebon statue of a black cat, is especially eerie. A live black cat, said to be an "omen of death," stalks about the house and is ultimately responsible for the demise of the film's murderer. The plot is basically a reprise of *The Cat and the Canary* that contains an unusual inheritance, an heiress in peril, secret passages, a clutching hand, and a gaggle of predatory relatives under suspicion of murder. The Hugh Herbert character wanders around the house breaking furniture and tinkering with various mechanisms in scenes that tend to minimize the spooky ambience of the haunt. The film should not be confused with the 1934 Universal horror movie with the same title, to be discussed in a later chapter.

Over at the poverty row Monogram Studios another comedy team was poised to embark on a career of spook busting. This was the East Side Kids, who would later morph into the Bowery Boys, a gang of lovable waifs from the slums that included core members Leo Gorcey, Huntz Hall and Bobby Jordan. In *Spooks Run Wild* (1941), the boys are on the way to summer camp when they wind up at the supposedly haunted Billings House, which they discover is inhabited by a mysterious, vampire-like figure named Nardo (Bela Lugosi) and his dwarfish assistant Luigi (Angelo Rossitto). After a series of comic misadventures, the boys suss out a real killer (Dennis Moore) and discover that Nardo is merely a stage magician.

Ghosts on the Loose (1943) begins with the wedding of Huntz Hall's sister Betty (Ava Gardner) and Jack (Rick Vallin), who have purchased a home for a suspiciously low price because it is located next to a supposedly haunted house. When the East Side Kids get the couple's address wrong and enter the haunt next door, they encounter a series of ghostly occurrences, which turn out to be engineered by a Nazi spy ring headed by Emil (Lugosi again) who are hiding out in the house and are trying to scare people away from their operation. The boys battle with the spies and subdue them as the police arrive along with the newlyweds. In *Spook Busters* (1946), the gang has just graduated from pest control school and accepts an extermination job at yet another haunted house, where they encounter the usual ghostly shenanigans. This time, however, they discover that the supposed paranormal activity is being caused by a mad scientist (Douglass Dumbrille), who is conducting illegal experiments in the building's basement. Upon encountering the boys, the savant conceives the inane idea of transplanting Huntz Hall's brain into the body of a gorilla. This is one of a number of films that feature a gorilla as the menace lurking within a haunted house.

Gonzo comedians Ole Olsen and Chic Johnson, whose zany antics enlivened screen romps such as *Hellzapoppin* (1941) and *Crazy House* (1943), went into the spook busting business with *Ghost Catchers* (1944). As the film opens, Colonel Brekenridge Marshall (Walter Catlett) has moved from Georgia to a New York townhouse with his two daughters, Melinda (Gloria Jean) and Susannah (Martha O'Driscoll), only to find that the place is haunted by the tap-dancing ghost of one Wilbur Duffington, a socialite who drank too much brandy one night in 1900 and fell out of a high window. The sisters seek help from Ole and Chic, who operate a nightclub next door and attempt to exorcise Duffington's ghost by throwing a raucous jitterbug party. This tactic seems to work at first, but when the noises return the comics uncover a gang of criminals looking to find valuables hidden in the mansion who want to frighten the Colonel and his daughters off the property. The histrionic comedy style of Olsen and Johnson will not please every taste, but the film also features horror stars Lon Chaney, Jr., and Tor Johnson, as well as composer/songster Mel Torme in bit parts. As in *The Ghost Breakers*, the haunt is inhabited by a real spook in addition to the usual gang of crooks.

Ghost Crazy (a.k.a. *Crazy Knights*, 1944) featured another wacko comedy team having a jaunt in a haunt. This one is composed of future stooge Shemp Howard, Billy Gilbert and "Slapsie" Maxie Rosenbloom, who all play themselves. Gilbert and Shemp are travelling performers who have a carnival act called "Barney, the Gorilla with a Human Mind," in which Shemp puts on an ape suit to impersonate a real gorilla to fool the audience while doing tricks. Barney, Shemp and Gilbert eventually link up with Maxie in a supposedly haunted mansion where the gorilla gets loose while Shemp dons the monkey suit, leading to a series of predictable consequences. *Ghost Crazy* presents another bizarre instance of a gorilla instead of a ghost being the scary creature inside a haunted house.

The acclaimed British actor Charles Laughton portrayed the titular character in MGM's lavish production of *The Canterville Ghost* (1944). Based on a satiric novella by Oscar Wilde about an American family who move into a haunted English castle and turn the tables on its ghost, the film was updated to the World War II era. Backstory on the haunt begins in 1634 Britain, where the cowardly Sir Simon de Canterville (Laughton) defiles his family's honor by running away from a duel. Hiding himself inside an alcove in the ancestral castle, his father, Lord Canterville (Reginald Owen) orders the room bricked up to punish his son for disgracing the family name, and curses Sir Simon to haunt the castle until one of his descendants will perform an act of bravery and clear the Canterville family name.

Cut to wartime Britain in 1943, where a troop of American rangers has been billeted in the castle, which is now owned by the six-year-old Lady Jessica de Canterville (Margaret O'Brien) and considered the most haunted house in England. Sir Simon's ghost promptly appears each night to terrorize the troopers with frightening apparitions until one of the soldiers, Cuffy Williams (Robert Young), manages to scare the ghost by donning a sheet and gas mask. Cuffy strikes up a friendship with Lady Jessica and the two befriend the ghost when a birthmark reveals that Cuffy is a descendant of the Canterville line. Sir Simon gives Cuffy the Canterville family signet ring to wear while committing an act of bravery that will free him from his curse. Unfortunately, Cuffy fails to engage the enemy during his first combat experience and is ordered to be transferred to a support unit, dashing Sir Simon's hope for release from the curse through an act of family bravery.

Before the transfer is completed, however, Cuffy is alone in the castle while the rest of his unit is on maneuvers nearby, and a German plane drops a parachute bomb on the castle. The bomb is live but fails to explode, and Cuffy realizes that if it goes off it will kill the entire company. He then attaches the parachute and bomb to a jeep and, putting himself in danger, manages to drive the jeep into a ravine where the bomb explodes harmlessly. Having saved the company from annihilation, his superior officers allow him to rejoin his unit, and his act of courage breaks the family curse and frees Sir Simon from being earthbound, allowing the Canterville Ghost to joyously ascend into heaven.

Oscar Wilde's whimsical story about an American family that moves into an English castle and turns the tables on its cowardly ghost is updated into the World War II era by screenwriter Edwin Blum, who also manages to inject an element of wartime propaganda into the plot. Director Jules Dassin handles the comedy, supernatural thrills and war sequences smoothly and melds them all into a pleasing unity, and optical special effects superimpositions are used to great effect. Laughton is superb as the titular ghost of Sir Simon, cutting a buffoonish figure in his 17th century costume while performing such antics as materializing holding his own severed head or squirming around on top of the bomb as it is driven toward destruction. Much of the comedy derives from the ghost's hereditary cowardice as Sir Simon is harassed by the mocking G.I.s. Robert Young brings his amiable screen persona to the role of Cuffy Williams, and Margaret O'Brien is cute as a button as the Lady Jessica. Additional comedy is provided by cast members Rags Ragland, Una O'Connor and Mike Mazurki.

As previously noted, the film shares several plot elements with Rene Clair's *The Ghost Goes West* (1936), including a British haunted castle, a ghost condemned by a family patriarch to haunt it due to an act of cowardice, the ghost's eventual redemption and a culture clash between Europe and America. The haunted Canterville Castle is an eerie domain of angles and shadows, as this abode of "the most fearful of all English phantoms," is rendered in exquisite detail by MGM's prestige set design and art direction.

Bud Abbott and Lou Costello starred in another haunted house comedy, *The Time of Their Lives* (1946), only this time the haunt was inhabited by real ghosts. The film begins in the year 1780, during the fifth year of the Revolutionary War. Lou plays master tinker Horatio Prim, who wants to marry his sweetheart Nora O'Leary (Anne Gillis), a servant working at the estate of the wealthy Thomas Danbury (Jess Barker). Toward this end he is carrying a letter of recommendation from George Washington that he plans to show to Danbury in order to gain his permission for their marriage. Horatio gives the letter to Nora for safekeeping from Danbury's valet Cuthbert Greenway (Bud), who is also seeking her hand.

Danbury, it turns out, is a traitor to the revolution, and when Nora accidentally overhears him plotting in collusion with Benedict Arnold, he seizes her and hides the letter inside a hidden compartment in a clock on the mantelpiece. Danbury's fiancé Melody Allen (Marjorie Reynolds) also gets wind of the plot and gets Horatio to aid her in warning General Washington, but when the general's troops arrive, Melody and Horatio are mistakenly shot as traitors. The mansion is burned to the ground and the two bodies are dumped in a well on the estate. A plaque is placed atop the well that reads, "here were buried two traitors," who are cursed to remain on the estate forever unless their innocence be proven. The earthbound spirits of Horatio and Melody are confined to the Danbury estate and cannot move beyond its borders.

The Danbury manor is rebuilt during the 1940s by Sheldon Gage (John Shelton), who furnishes the house with some of the original furniture that had escaped the fire. He invites his fiancé June Prescott (Lynne Baggett), her aunt Millie (Binnie Barnes) and his psychiatrist Dr. Ralph Greenway (played by Bud, who is a descendant of Cuthbert) to spend the night at the newly-restored colonial mansion. Also present is the housekeeper Emily (Gale Sondegaard once again), a self-styled psychic who claims that the house is haunted. She turns out to be right, as Horatio and Melody are all too eager to perform their ghostly pranks on the guests. Invisible to the living, they tinkle on a harpsichord, turn the radio up to full blast, while Melody dons a pair of silk stockings and runs up the main stairway as a pair of disembodied legs.

Looking for a way to exorcise the spooks, Emily leads the others in a séance, where she channels the voice of Danbury's disembodied spirit, who reveals the identity of the ghosts and the hidden location of Horatio's letter. When they check the compartment inside the clock, however, they discover that the letter is not there. It turns out that the clock is just a facsimile, and that the original item is currently residing in a New York museum. Seeking to make amends for the misdeeds of his ancestor Cuthbert, Greenway volunteers to obtain the letter, but is forced to steal the clock from the museum instead. He returns to the estate with the police in hot pursuit and barely manages to retrieve the letter from inside the clock. Their honor restored, the ghosts are freed from their curse and ascend into heaven.

One of the comic duos more unusual efforts, *The Time of Their Lives* separates Bud and Lou so that the usual interplay between Bud the straight man and Lou the funny man is minimized. Instead, Lou is paired with Marjorie Reynolds while Bud seems to be acting in a different movie altogether. While the comic antics of the cast are amusing and entertaining, a lingering shot of Melody's and Horatio's corpses lying at the bottom of the well injects a note of morbidity into the proceedings that is jarring and works against the film's lighthearted tone. The scene in which Emily becomes possessed during the séance and speaks in the voice of the dead Tom Danbury also strikes an eerie note. Gale Sondegaard plays the same housekeeper/psychic medium character that she had portrayed in *The Cat and the Canary* and *The Black Cat*, prompting Binnie Barnes to ask her, "Didn't I see you in *Rebecca*?" a reference to a similar part played by Judith Anderson in Hitchcock's thriller. Director Charles Barton turns out a slick, funny programmer that makes effective use of special effects, and Barton would go on to direct Bud and Lou in their most memorable horror comedy, *Abbott and Costello Meet Frankenstein* (1948).

The restored, pristine colonial-era manor in the film is a far cry from being a cobwebby gothic haunt. In actuality, the ghosts haunt the well for over a hundred and fifty years between the burning of the original house and its resurrection. Part of the comedy arises from Horatio and Melody encountering 20th century inventions such as radio. As in *The Ghost Goes West* and *The Canterville Ghost*, the spirits of the protagonists are cursed to remain earthbound at the site of their demise due to an act of betrayal or cowardice in the face of an enemy, and are only admitted into heaven when they prove themselves worthy.

The 1940 Bob Hope/Paulette Goddard haunted house comedy *The Ghost Breakers* was remade as a vehicle for the comedy team of Dean Martin and Jerry Lewis as *Scared Stiff* (1953). The remake follows the plot of the 1940 version closely as crooner Larry Todd (Martin) and his sidekick Myron Mertz (Lewis) run afoul of some New York gangsters and sail for Cuba with Mary Carroll (Lizbeth Scott), who has inherited a haunted castle on an island off the coast. Once again crooks are looking for hidden treasure on the property and the threesome encounter a real ghost and a zombie while exploring the spook house. In the end the crooks are vanquished, the treasure discovered and Dino gets the girl.

Lensed by the same director, George Marshall, the film is much inferior to the 1940 version both in terms of its comedy and horror content. Martin and Lewis lack the comedic chemistry of Bob Hope and Willie Best, and the haunted castle is played much more for laughs than spooky chills. The first (but not the last) haunted house musical comedy effort, the film is marred by cornball musical numbers performed by Dino and Brazilian songstress Carmen Miranda (a.k.a. "the Lady in the Tutti-Fruiti Hat") that are a severe drag on the action. The film takes almost 90 minutes to get Dean and Jerry into the haunt, and once there the action moves swiftly toward the denouement. One interesting facet of the film occurs when Larry describes himself to one of the crooks as a "ghostbuster." "You heard of

Dean Martin (left), Lizbeth Scott and Jerry Lewis romp through a haunted Cuban castle in *Scared Stiff* **(1953).**

trust busters, bronco busters and gang busters," he explains. "I'm a ghostbuster, so watch it, buster." Hope, along with his cohort Bing Crosby, appear in a gag cameo at the end of the film with their heads atop skeleton bodies.

Producer/director William Castle was busy grinding out schlocky, gimmick-laden horror flicks during the 1950s and 60s. For his haunted house opus *Thirteen Ghosts* (1960), he devised a technique called "Illusion-O," which involved filming the spooky sequences using red and blue filters (in a black and white film). Audiences were given a cardboard "ghost viewer" with blue and red cellophane strips; in order to see the ghosts, one looked through the red strip, if not, one could use the blue strip to avoid seeing them.

The plot revolves around the Zorba family that includes father Cyrus (Donald Woods), mother Hilda (Rosemary DeCamp), daughter Medea (Jo Morrow) and young son Buck (Charles Herbert), who are struggling to make do with Cyrus' paltry salary as a paleontologist when they are informed that Cyrus has inherited the house belonging to Cyrus' uncle, Dr. Plato Zorba, who is recently deceased. Uncle Plato's house is an aging ramshackle structure, but they decide to move in in spite of a stipulation in the will that the family must continue to live there or ownership will be transferred to the state. It turns out that the house is haunted by eleven ghosts that Plato, who was an occultist, has "collected" and installed in the house. In addition, Plato himself died in the house, bringing the roster of spooks up to twelve. Also part of the mix is Plato's creepy housekeeper Elaine Zacharias (played by Margaret Hamilton, who portrayed the wicked witch in *The Wizard of Oz*).

Plato's personal attorney Benjamin Rush (Martin Milner) knows that his client liquidated all of his assets shortly before his death and suspects that the money is stashed somewhere in the house and is determined to find it before the Zorba family does. While exploring the house, Buck discovers a case containing a pair of special glasses that enable him to see the ghosts. These "terrifying" specters include a flaming skeleton, a chef with a meat cleaver, a ghostly lion and its headless tamer, a wailing woman and other bizarre revenants. As if this ghostly cavalcade isn't enough, Rush dons a ghastly outfit and pretends to be a spook in an attempt to scare the Zorbas out of the house so he can locate the hidden money.

A strange book written by Plato in Latin is found by Cyrus and, once translated by a colleague at the museum, explains the ghost catcher's occult theories. According to the book, a thirteenth ghost is needed within the house in order to exorcise all the undead spirits. In the meantime, Buck discovers a clue about the location of the money, and Rush decides to murder the boy so he cannot reveal it. When he tries to smother Buck in a trick bed with a descending canopy, the ghosts come to the boy's aid and dispatch Rush instead. Upon his death Rush becomes the thirteenth ghost, the spirits in the house are exorcised, and the film ends with the Zorba family counting out a big pile of uncle Zorba's money.

While it's ostensibly a horror flick, *13 Ghosts* is much more in the realm of juvenile comedy and depicts some of the least scary spooks in screen history. In addition, the technological breakthrough of Illusion-O manages to render the goofy apparitions only partly visible. Still, it's a fun kiddie romp that deliberately tones down the chills in favor of a sitcom-like approach involving a 60s-era nuclear family who find themselves in a fantastic situation. Castle makes effective use of the Los Angeles Museum of Natural History, where paleontologist Cyrus is shown lecturing visitors amid the giant skeletons of extinct mammals. A cast of B-list actors turn in adequate performances and witchy-woman Margaret

Hamilton plays the standard housekeeper/medium role that Gale Sondegaard was usually assigned. Like many haunted house movies, *13 Ghosts* includes a subplot involving a criminal who is searching for a fortune hidden inside the house and impersonating a ghost in order to scare the tenants away. Producer/director Castle appears as himself in a jocular prelude to the film introducing the audience to the use of the "ghost viewer" device. The film was remade in 2001 under the title *Thirteen Ghosts* (sometimes rendered as *Thir13een Ghosts*) as a straight-up horror flick.

Nerved out TV comedian Don Knotts, best known as Andy Griffith's goofball sidekick on *The Andy Griffith Show*, starred as the title character in the haunted house comedy *The Ghost and Mr. Chicken* (1966). Knotts plays Luther Heggs, a typesetter for the newspaper the *Rachael Courier Express* in Rachael, Kansas, who yearns to move up to becoming a news reporter for the paper. He gets his chance when he is assigned to spend the night at the local haunt, the Simmons Mansion, and write an article about his experience. The place is reputedly haunted by the ghost of old man Simmons, who stabbed his wife in the throat and then jumped from a window to his death 20 years earlier. The mansion is scheduled to be torn down by the Simmons family heir Nick Simmons (Philip Ober) as part of a real estate deal.

Luther is assigned to stay at the house on the 20th anniversary of the murder/suicide, and the cowardly newspaperman is soon freaked out by the strange goings-on at the mansion. The bloodstained pipe organ begins playing by itself, and a painting of Mrs. Simmons is discovered to be bleeding from a pair of scissors imbedded in the portrait's neck. Fleeing in terror from the haunt, Luther pens a lurid account of his experiences that cause an uproar in the town. Nick Simmons sues the paper for libel, but the ladies of the town's Psychic Occult Society and Luther's girlfriend Alma (Joan Stalery) come to Luther's defense. The judge deems the evidence presented at the trial to be inconclusive, and orders all interested parties to return to the mansion at midnight in order to prove or disprove the reality of the haunting.

When the judge, jury and curious bystanders enter the house at midnight, they find nothing amiss, leading the judge to declare that the paranormal activities are all the result of Luther's overactive imagination. The crowd exits the mansion, except for Alma, who stays behind hoping to find evidence to the contrary. As a despondent Luther starts to walk home, he hears the organ playing once more and re-enters the mansion, where he encounters his friend Mr. Kelsey (Liam Redmond), the janitor at the *Courier Express*. Mr. Kelsey informs him that he was the former gardener at the Simmons Mansion and that he is the one responsible for the faux haunting. Furthermore, he knows that it was Nick Simmons who murdered his aunt and uncle in order to inherit the estate, and his plan to raze the mansion is an effort to conceal any evidence of the crime. When they hear Alma screaming, they follow the sound to find her being held hostage by Nick, whereupon "Mr. Chicken" suddenly finds his courage and subdues Nick. In the aftermath Luther is vindicated, Nick is arrested, and Luther and Alma get married.

The film's comedy relies solely on Don Knotts' nervous, cowardly shtick, and his appeal is clearly a matter of personal taste. By today's standards, *The Ghost and Mr. Chicken* comes off as juvenile and corny, while the haunted house angle is not played for thrills. Like *Thirteen Ghosts*, it has the ambience of an extended episode of a TV sitcom. Scenes inside the Simmons Mansion were reportedly filmed in the set used for the comedy series *The Mun-*

Comedian Don Knotts is frightened by his own mirror image inside a haunted house in *The Ghost and Mr. Chicken* (1966).

sters on the Universal Studios backlot. The screenplay by James Fritzell and Everett Greenbaum contains a number of logical holes, and Alan Rafkin's direction is not particularly memorable. Once again the haunting turns out not to be a supernatural occurrence, but instead is connected to a murder and a criminal scheme to obtain a fortune.

One of the more bizarre takes on the haunted house film was the Woolner Brothers production of *Hillbillys in a Haunted House* (1967), which showcased a musical jaunt into a haunt. As the film opens, three country singers, Woody Weatherby (Ferlin Husky), Jeepers (Don Bowman) and Boots Malone (Joi Lansing) are motoring to Nashville in their convertible to perform at a C&W jamboree in Nashville when a sudden rainstorm forces them to take shelter in the deserted Beauregard Mansion. Little do they know that a group of spies, Dr. Himmil (John Carradine), Gregor (Basil Rathbone), Maximillian (Lon Chaney, Jr.) and Madame Wong (Linda Ho) have set up their hi-tech headquarters in the mansion's cellar. For inexplicable reasons the spies also keep a gorilla named Anatole (George Barrows) caged up in the facility. The spy ring has been tasked to steal a secret formula for rocket fuel from a nearby missile installation, and make use of mechanical spooks and skeletons to frighten people away.

While the three hillbillies wander around the decrepit house exploring and performing musical numbers, the spies put their plan into action but fail to obtain the formula. Their bungling effort clues secret agent man Jim Meadows (Richard Webb), who works for an outfit called MOTHER (an acronym for Master Organization to Halt Enemy Resistance) to the plot. As Meadows comes snooping around the Beauregard place, Anatole manages to get out of his cage, kidnaps Boots, and takes her into the spies' secret den. Woody and Jeepers join forces with Meadows as they search for Boots and eventually find their way into the hidden basement. During the ensuing gunfight the real ghost of confederate General Beauregard materializes and orders the spies to leave his house, and Anatole gets out of his cage once more and dispatches Dr. Himmil. The spy ring is brought to justice by the MOTHER agent, and the three singers continue on to Nashville, where they perform at the jamboree.

This one's got it all: spies, country music, phony ghosts, a real ghost and even a gorilla. Another example of a haunted house musical comedy, *Hillbillys in a Haunted House* is neither funny nor scary, and the music will only appeal to aficionados of the country and western idiom. Songs performed include "We're On Our Way to Nashville," "Living in a Trance" and "The Minute You're Gone," and the last ten minutes of the film consists of musical numbers sung at the Jamboree. Country star Ferlin Husky isn't much of an actor, but Don Bowman provides some comic relief and Joi Lansing is easy on the eyes. Outside of the music, the film's primary appeal lies in the interplay between horror stalwarts Lon Chaney, Jr., John Carradine and Basil Rathbone (in his final screen appearance). The daffy screenplay by Duke Yelton tries to tie in all these disparate elements and doesn't come close to succeeding, while veteran director Jean Yarbrough, who had lensed a number of Universal horror classics in the 1940s, struggles hopelessly with this inane material.

For some reason, the haunted house comedy was non-existent between the late 1960s and the mid–1980s. It re-emerged in the post–*Star Wars* era of special effects with *House* (1986). The film's protagonist is author Roger Cobb (William Katt), a Vietnam vet who is struggling with post-traumatic stress disorder in connection with his war experiences. In addition, he is haunted by the abduction of his little boy Jimmy (Eric Silver), who is presumed dead, and the subsequent dissolution of his marriage. Roger, under pressure to produce another novel, moves back into his family home where his aunt Elizabeth (Susan French) hanged herself years earlier, and where he hopes to find the solitude that will overcome his writer's block.

Soon after moving into the house Roger is assailed by ghostly apparitions and other paranormal phenomena. He is attacked by levitating garden tools, a hag-like female creature, a winged goblin and the ghost of Aunt Elizabeth who tells him, "This house knows everything about you." His chief tormentor, however, is the zombie-like ghost of his Army buddy Big Ben (Richard Moll), who blames Roger for abandoning him to be captured and killed by the Viet Cong and is out for revenge. In addition to his supernatural woes, he is also forced to contend with the boorish antics of his next-door neighbor Harold Gorton (George Wendt), who claims to be Roger's biggest fan and constantly intrudes on his activities. Harold joins Roger in his struggle with the paranormal forces inside the haunt until Roger is able to confront and exorcise his personal demons, and in the end be reunited with his wife and son.

House is a wild thrill ride dominated by the special effects creations of James Cummins and Mark Sullivan, who employ elaborate puppetry and stop-motion animation to conjure a bevy of creepy ghoulies and ghosties, although some of these look a little creaky by 21st century f/x standards. Acting-wise, it's basically a two-man show, with William Katt playing the straight man and the portly George Wendt (best known as "Norm" from the TV sitcom *Cheers*) providing the brunt of the comedy. But *House* places its accent more on horror than comedy as the unfortunate Roger deals with apparitions that are hallucinatory reflections of bogey men haunting him from his past. The zombie-like Big Ben, a reflection of his guilt over his wartime experiences, is the most fearsome specter of them all, and represents the central force behind Roger's supernatural woes.

Exteriors of the haunted house were shot on an estate called Mills View, a Victorian-style structure built in 1887 in Monrovia, California that has a slight resemblance to the spooky house used in *Psycho*. Director Steve Miner shoots the interior scenes using low-key lighting that lend the film a properly dark atmosphere for the ghastly goings-on. *House* inspired a four-movie haunted house franchise in three sequels, *House II: The Second Story* (1987), *The Horror Show* (1989) and *House IV: Home Deadly Home* (1991), all of which had little or nothing to do with the original movie.

The husband and wife comedy team of Gene Wilder and Gilda Radner co-starred in *Haunted Honeymoon* (1986), a film that harkened back to the mystery house thrillers of previous decades and was set during the heyday of radio in the 1930s. Wilder plays Larry Abbot, an actor on the radio program "Manhattan Murder Theater" who is due to marry his fiancé and fellow radio star Vickie Pearle (Radner) in a few weeks, but has come down with a bad case of verbal jitters, a condition that threatens his future as a radio actor and might even make it impossible to take his marriage vows. Larry's uncle, Dr. Paul Abbot (Paul L. Smith), proposes to cure him of his panic attacks by giving him a good scare. Accordingly, Larry and Vickie travel to the Abbot family home, a gothic mansion in upstate Stormville, New York, to tie the knot.

Meanwhile, at the Stormville estate, Larry's middle-aged Aunt Kate (played by portly comedian Dom DeLuise in drag), has changed her will to make Larry the sole heir to the family fortune. This does not sit well with other members of the Abbot family, who now have a motive for eliminating him to claim the inheritance. On arriving at the mansion, Vickie is introduced to Larry's eccentric relatives, a motley crew that includes his cousin Charles (Jonathan Pryce), his uncle Francis (Peter Vaughn), the cross-dressing Francis, Jr. (Roger Ashton-Griffiths) and the stage magician Montego the Magnificent (Jim Carter), as well as the estate's Karloffesque butler Pfister (Bryan Pringle). To make matters worse, at dinner Aunt Kate reveals that one of the assembled family members is a werewolf. A series of frenetic comedy scenes ensues as Larry is menaced by the lycanthrope, a ghost and a mysterious figure who is out to murder him.

This embarrassingly unfunny attempt at haunted house humor was written and directed by Wilder, and despite a talented cast the laughs fail to materialize. Some of the more memorable scenes include a werewolf smoking a cigarette, Wilder attempting to make love to the corpse of a transvestite, and an awful song and dance rendition of the old standard "Balling the Jack" performed by DeLuise and Radner. Wilder was apparently trying to copy the hyperbolic comedy style of the Mel Brooks movies he had starred in, *The Producers*, *Blazing Saddles* and *Young Frankenstein*, but fails utterly. In her final film role before dying of ovarian cancer in 1989, *Saturday Night Live* alumnus Gilda Radner gives it her all, but appears painfully gaunt and haggard. Wilder does pay homage to Paul Leni's 1927 mystery house classic *The Cat and the Canary* during scenes that take place in a narrow corridor lined with windows and billowing curtains. The radio connection recalls 1940s-era haunted

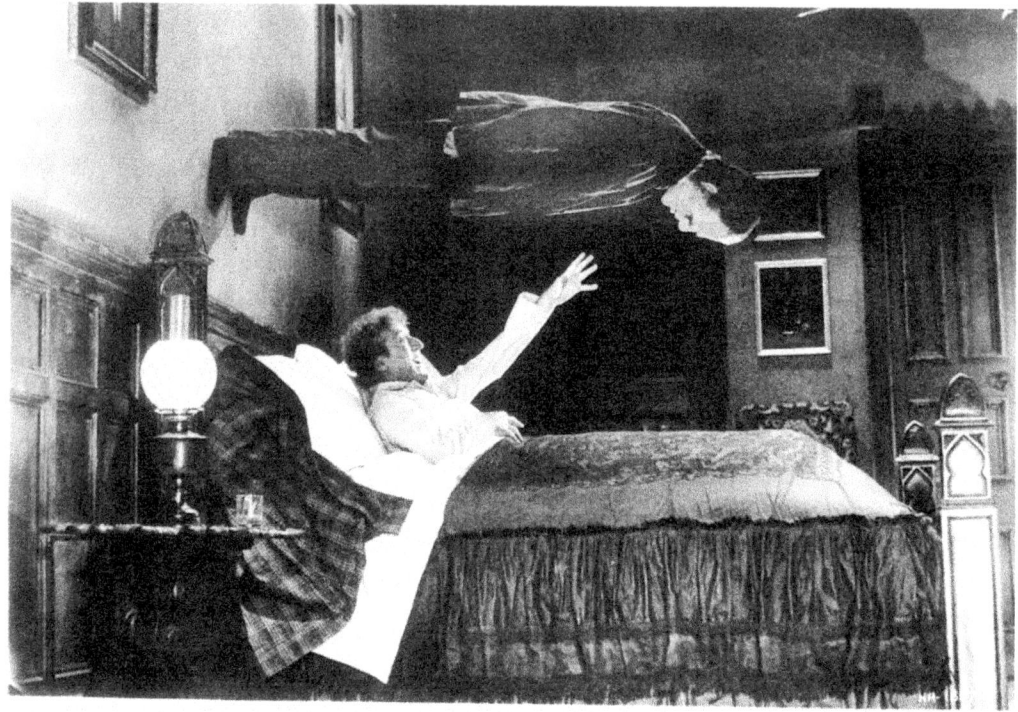

Larry Abbot (Gene Wilder) encounters a ghostly manifestation (Bryan Pringle) while on his *Haunted Honeymoon* (1986).

house comedies like *Hold That Ghost* and *The Ghost Breakers*. Exterior shots of the Abbot estate were filmed at Knebworth House, a famous mansion in Hertfordshire, England that was also used as a spook house location for such horror/fantasy fare as *Horror Hospital* (1973), *Lair of the White Worm* (1988) and *Batman* (1989).

The most acclaimed haunted house comedy of them all is surely Tim Burton's madcap netherworld tour *Beetlejuice* (1988), a film that depicted a haunting from the ghost's point of view. The two ghosts involved are Barbara and Adam Maitland (Geena Davis and Alec Baldwin), a Connecticut married couple who die unexpectedly in a car accident and return home to realize that they are ghosts and their house has been sold to new owners, the Deetz family from New York. These include husband Charles (Jeffrey Jones), a real estate broker, mother Delia (Catherine O'Hara), a flaky sculptor and goth daughter Lydia (Winona Ryder), who is so "strange and unusual" that she has the mediumistic ability to see the ghosts.

The Maitlands are none too pleased with the prospect of sharing their home with these interlopers, but when they try to leave, they find the house is now situated in the middle of a desert wilderness populated by giant sandworms from which they are unable to escape. They also discover a mysterious book entitled *Handbook for the Recently Deceased*, a guidebook to the afterlife. Using the *Handbook*, they are able to enter a netherworld bureaucracy where strict rules are imposed on the departed. Their "case worker," Juno

(Sylvia Sydney), informs them that they must remain in their house for 125 years, and if they want the Deetz family to leave, they will be obliged to scare them away themselves. Unfortunately, the mild-mannered Maitlands are not cut out for the haunting business, and only cause Lydia to become aware of their presence and befriend them. When the Deetzes hold a dinner party, the ghosts possess Charles, Delia and the other guests and force them to dance to calypso music, but this only inspires Charles to want to turn the house into a haunted theme park.

In their desperation the Maitlands consider using the services of Betelgeuse (Michael Keaton), a self-styled "bio-exorcist," to scare away the interlopers, but are put off by the ghost's crazed demeanor. In the meantime, Delia's interior designer Otho (Glenn Shadix) gets hold of the *Handbook* and attempts to summon the Maitlands during a séance designed to convince Charles' boss Maxie Dean (Robert Goulet) that the ghosts are real in order to obtain funding for the proposed haunted attraction. Otho's amateur attempt at magic goes awry, however, causing the Maitlands to turn into decaying corpses, and in desperation Lydia summons Betelgeuse from the netherworld to aid them, on the condition that she will marry him. All hell breaks loose as Betelgeuse wreaks havoc on the living and the dead alike and summons a monstrous preacher (Tony Cox) to unite him with Lydia in unholy matrimony. Lydia is saved from a fate worse than death by Barbara, who uses one of the giant sandworms to send Betelgeuse back to oblivion before the ceremony is completed, and in the aftermath the Maitlands and the Deetzes learn to share their mutual home in harmony.

Beetlejuice was Tim Burton's second feature film effort, but the novice director's morbid imagination crafted what is perhaps the funniest (and weirdest) horror comedy of all time. The film's humor far outweighs its ghastliness, however, as the psychedelic visions of the afterlife come off as being existentially disturbing rather than terrifying. Burton was working with a marvelously inventive screenplay by Michael McDowell, Larry Wilson and Warren Skaaren that proved to be the perfect vehicle for his talents.

Self-proclaimed "bio-exorcist" Betelgeuse (Michael Keaton) sits astride the house haunted by Barbara and Adam Maitland (Geena Davis and Alec Baldwin) in this poster for Tim Burton's horror-comedy hit *Beetlejuice* (1988).

Betelgeuse (Michael Keaton) prepares to commit unholy matrimony with Lydia (Winona Ryder) in *Beetlejuice* **(1988).**

Betelgeuse was reportedly a more terrifying, even demonic figure in the first drafts of the script, but later rewrites transformed him into a more humorous character. Michael Keaton delivers a high-powered, knockout performance as the title character, a.k.a. "the ghost with the most," and is supported by the comedic talents of an all-star cast consisting of Jeffrey Jones, Geena Davis, Winona Ryder, Alec Baldwin, Catherine O'Hara, Sylvia Sydney and Glen Shadix. The production is also enlivened by the rousing musical score of Danny Elfman as well as the playful calypso tunes of Harry Belafonte.

Reportedly shot with an extremely modest budget of only $15 million, the film was a runaway box-office hit. Eschewing expensive special effects, Burton resorts to unusual lighting effects to create a spectral mood, expressionistic set design and elaborate costuming and makeup (the film won an Academy Award in this category) to enliven the haunt and create a ghastly mood. The New England haunted house is stately on the outside but creepy on the inside, with several pathways that lead directly to the netherworld, and it presents a completely different environment to the ghosts than it does to the living. For example, the ghosts experience the passage of time much differently than the humans do. As in many haunted house tales, the spooks are trapped inside the house, but the script does not explore the reason why the Maitlands are condemned to remain in the haunt for more than a century. As in *High Spirits*, there is a sub-plot in which the owner plans to exploit the house as a tourist attraction. The titular character's name, "Betelgeuse," is derived from the name of a star in the constellation of Orion, and Burton would later return to the haunted house theme in *Dark Shadows* (2012).

A haunted castle in Ireland provided the locale for the horror comedy *High Spirits* (1989), in which Peter O'Toole stars as Peter Plunkett, the owner of Castle Plunkett, a rundown castle that he has converted into a bed and breakfast. Plunkett's business venture is deeply in debt and the property is only three weeks away from being foreclosed by an American businessman who plans to dismantle the castle and ship it to Malibu to be converted into a theme park. To prevent this, Plunkett devises a plan to turn the castle into "the most haunted place in the Emerald Isle" and proposes to use his staff to impersonate ghosts. The first bus bearing American tourists that arrives at Castle Plunkett for the haunted house tour includes estranged married couple Jack and Sharon Crawford (Steve Guttenberg and Beverly D'Angelo), priestly acolyte Brother Tony (Peter Gallagher), and Malcolm (Martin Ferrero) a ghostbuster from the Duke University parapsychology lab who is there to investigate the haunt.

The guests easily see through the ruse and dismiss the faux ghosts, but that night Jack witnesses the materialization of two real ghosts, Martin Brogan (Liam Neeson) and Mary Plunkett (Daryl Hannah), who are stuck in a time loop reenacting Martin's murder of Mary on their wedding night 200 years ago. When Jack intercedes between the two ghosts the loop is broken, and Mary forms a living-dead attachment to him. As Jack begins to fall in

Peter Plunkett (Peter O'Toole) confers with his ghostly family members in the ancestral crypt in *High Spirits* (1989).

love with Mary's forlorn ghost, Martin starts to woo Jack's wife Sharon and the two soon become living/dead lovers. What follows is a supernatural bedroom farce as the castle's bevy of ghosts begins to act upon the libidos of the guests, propelling them into a variety of erotic situations. The oddball ending has the two couples, Mary and Jack and Martin and Sharon, united with each other in a strange reversal of life and death.

Writer/director Neil Jordan, who would go on to lens the Oscar-winning drama *The Crying Game* (1992), rushes the action along at a madcap pace, while the phenomenal Peter O'Toole delivers a hilarious, scenery-chewing performance that recalls a similar role he played as a Christ-obsessed wacko in *The Ruling Class* (1972). Romantic leads Daryl Hannah and Steve Guttenberg share a fine screen chemistry, while future action star Liam Neeson exudes charisma as a lusty Irish ghost. Martin Ferrero, best known as the "bloodsucking lawyer" who gets eaten by the T. Rex in *Jurassic Park*, provides additional comedy as a goofball psychic investigator. The film displays an erotic edge in its portrayal of carnal and romantic relationships between the living and the dead, but there are complications. As Steve explains to Mary, "You're a ghost, I'm an American, it could never work out," but by the end of the film these situations are resolved happily on All Hallows Eve, when the spirits become flesh for a short time. Jordan's screenplay references *The Ghost Goes West* in the plot elements wherin an impoverished European aristocrat is being compelled to sell a Celtic castle to an American businessman who intends to transport the castle to America and make it into a theme park. *High Spirits* contains some beautiful Irish music and scenery, and the Castle Plunkett exteriors were filmed on location at Dromore Castle in County Limerick, Ireland.

Unlike Tim Burton's *Beetlejuice*, Disney Studios relied heavily on special effects for *The Haunted Mansion* (2003), a vehicle for comedian Eddie Murphy that was a spin-off of a popular Disney theme park attraction. Murphy plays Jim Evers, an aggressive New Orleans real estate agent who has carved out time from his busy schedule to take his family on a vacation. At the last minute, however, his wife Sara (Marsha Thomason) gets a phone call concerning a hot property for sale and Jim decides to check it out on the way to the vacation spot. Driving out of town with his wife, his daughter Megan (Aree Davis) and son Michael (Marc John Jeffries), they travel out to the Gracey estate, a decrepit antebellum mansion located deep in Louisiana bayou country. As Jim confers with the mansion's owner, Edward Gracey (Nathaniel Parker), about the deal, a storm blows up which floods the local roads, stranding the Evers family at the estate where they are invited to spend the night. The family is then introduced to the estate's servants, an eccentric group that includes the menacing butler Ramsley (Terence Stamp) and subordinate retainers Ezra (Wallace Shawn) and Emma (Dina Waters).

That night the children encounter a floating blue orb that leads them to a room containing the antique portrait of a woman who is a ringer for Sara. The servants reveal that the picture represents Elizabeth Henshaw, a mixed-race woman who poisoned herself on the night of her wedding to Edward Gracey's grandfather, who subsequently hanged himself in despair. While Sara is beguiled by Gracey, Jim and the kids consult Madame Leota (Jennifer Tilly), a talking head ensconced in a crystal ball who tells them that everyone in the mansion is a ghost cursed to remain earthbound because of the tragic suicides, and that Gracey's ghost is planning to "marry" Sara, who he sees as the reincarnation of Elizabeth. Madame Leota guides Jim and the children through the estate's cemetery, where they find a letter from Elizabeth stating that she loved Gracey and was poisoned by Ramsley, who disapproved of the interracial marriage. Before the marriage ceremony is completed, Jim manages to present the incriminating letter to Gracey, whereupon a spectral dragon materializes to drag Ramsley to the netherworld and Gracey is reunited with the spirit of Elizabeth in the afterlife. The curse is lifted, the ghosts are exorcised and Jim winds up with the deed to the formerly haunted mansion.

This handsome Disney production is an example of the studio's standard kiddie fare, a genre that tends to put a damper on Eddie Murphy's often outrageous comedic style. While it's fun family viewing, *The Haunted Mansion* doesn't come off as being either funny or scary. The film's elaborate special effects, however, do manage to conjure up a pleasant mood of fantasy. With a budget of $90 million, a troop of animated suits of armor, a ballroom full of dancing ghosts, along with an assortment of ghastly ghouls are brought to vivid life on the screen. Scenarist David Berenbaum was obliged to construct a movie plot around the bare bones of an amusement park ride and lifts narrative elements from older films. The haunt in the middle of a bayou recalls a similar antebellum mansion in the 1939 version of *The Cat and the Canary*, while the portrait of a dead woman that resembles the features of a living doppelganger appears in 1940's *The Ghost Breakers*. The film's climax, in which a ghost is poised to marry a living woman while an evil ghost is transported to damnation by a serpentine creature, seems to have been lifted from *Beetlejuice*. One of the most elaborate haunted houses in film history, the titular haunted mansion was constructed on Sable Ranch in Santa Clarita, California, a "movie ranch" used for large-scale set constructions, where the mansion set's basic structure was augmented by computer-generated add-ons that gave it a closer resemblance to the Disneyland ride.

Ramsley (Terence Stamp, left) greets Eddie Murphy, Marsha Thomason, Marc John Jeffries and Aree Davis inside *The Haunted Mansion* (2003).

During the 1960s, TV producer Dan Curtis hit on the idea of combining a daytime soap opera with elements of gothic romance. The result was *Dark Shadows*, a show that starred actor Jonathan Frid as Barnabas Collins, an aristocratic New England vampire who inhabited the gothic estate of Collinwood Mansion in Collinsport, Maine. Surprisingly, the genre meld proved to be a runaway hit and became one of the most popular shows on daytime television. Decades later, director Tim Burton conceived of producing a feature film version, *Dark Shadows* (2012), starring the quirky thespian Johnny Depp.

The film version begins in the year 1760 as the wealthy Collins family settles in Maine, where they establish the fishing village of Collinsport and build the palatial Collinwood Mansion. Sixteen years later the scion of the clan, Barnabas Collins (Depp) falls in love with a young lady named Josette du Pres (Bella Heathcote), thereby incurring the wrath of Angelique Bouchard, a servant at the estate who is also in love with him. Angelique is a witch who employs her magical powers to bring about the downfall of the Collins clan by killing off Barnabas' parents, bewitching Josette to leap to her death from a high cliff and changing Barnabas into a vampire who is buried alive by the townsfolk of Collinsport.

Cut to the year 1972, where a young woman named Victoria Winters (also played by Bella Heathcote) travels to Collinsport to accept a job as a governess for a troubled child of the modern-day Collins family. When she arrives at the mansion, she is introduced to the eccentric Collins household, including the strong-willed family matriarch Elizabeth (Michelle Pfeiffer) and her nephew David (Gully McGrath), who is suffering from PTSD after the recent drowning death of his mother. Other oddball family members include David's father Roger (Jonny Lee Miller), Elizabeth's teenage daughter Carolyn (Chloe Grace Montez) and weirdo psychiatrist Julia Hoffman (Helena Bonham Carter), who is treating the boy's illness. David claims that his mother's ghost visits him at the mansion and is reassured that the new governess seems to have an open mind about the subject. What the family doesn't know is that Victoria is a psychic who can see dead people, and that very night she is visited by the specter of her doppelganger Josette.

On that same night a group of construction workers accidentally excavate Barnabas' coffin and unleash the undead vampire, who brutally slakes his thirst on the blood of the entire crew. Making his way to Collingwood, he introduces himself to Elizabeth, who recognizes him from a portrait in the mansion and soon ascertains that he is a vampire. When he reveals the secret location of a cache of family riches, she allows him to stay at the estate provided he does not harm any of the family members. The next day he is introduced to Victoria and is stunned by her resemblance to Josette and falls in love with her.

The family's newfound wealth allows them to revive their flagging fishing business in Collinsport, which alerts the sorceress Angelique, who is still alive and operates a rival fishery, to the fact that Barnabas has returned. Still in love with Barnabas, she tries to seduce him but he resists her advances, causing enmity between the two supernatural beings. The rest of the film is occupied with the struggle between vampire and witch, a contest in which Angelique has the upper hand. In the climax, the entire Collins family must use their unique powers to defend Collinwood against her witchery, a battle in which she is ultimately defeated. Afterward Barnabas saves Victoria, who is still under Angelique's spell, from sharing Josette's fate in a death dive into the sea by turning her into a vampire, whereupon the two are united in undead bliss.

In his second haunted house opus, Burton crafts a handsome production using elaborate special effects and exquisite art direction that befits the director's status as an A-list filmmaker. Johnny Depp's wacky performance as Barnabas Collins dominates the film with his vampiric antics that are alternately comical and horrifying. Much of the film's comedy derives from Barnabas' struggle to cope with the 20th century world as he is confounded by troll dolls, lava lamps and other mystifying artifacts. In the funniest scene in the film, Depp rails against images of singer Karen Carpenter on the family's TV, not understanding the nature of television. "What sorcery is this?" he exclaims. "Reveal yourself, tiny songstress!" In like fashion, he also thinks that the McDonald's golden arches represent the devil's horns of Mephistopheles. Depp is supported by the spirited performances of other cast members, most notably those of Michelle Pfeiffer, Eva Green, Bella Heathcote and Helena Bonham Carter. On the minus side, the screenplay by Seth Grahame-Smith is convoluted with too many sub-plots that cause the pacing to slow and the film to run on longer than necessary. In contrast to Burton's whimsical approach in *Beetlejuice*, *Dark Shadows* contains several scenes of brutality in which Barnabas puts his fangs to a number of innocent victims in typical horror movie fashion. Like the earlier film, it also features a young woman who has the ability to see ghosts.

"Not every family has a house like this," quoth Barnabas, extolling the virtues of Collinwood Mansion. "Have you ever seen such majesty? The perfect marriage of European elegance and American enterprise." Collinwood, as realized by production designer Rick Heinrichs, is indeed a splendid ancestral abode. The exterior of the edifice sports a castle-like turret and gothic spires, while the interior is dominated by a huge central hall, a massive central staircase and an enormous chandelier. There are 200 rooms in the mansion, the great majority of which are empty circa 1972, causing voices to echo through its vast empty spaces. The house is adorned with elaborate statuary representing marine themes such as eels, seahorses and merfolk, some of which become animated by the witch to attack the Collinses during the climactic battle. In addition to Barnabas the vampire, it turns out that Collinwood is also haunted by two ghosts and a werewolf.

The haunted house has been a fertile field for comedy from the silent era into the 21st century and has engaged the talents of some of the finest comic

Vampire Barnabas Collins (Johnny Depp) poses in front of his ancestral estate, Collinwood Mansion, in this poster for Tim Burton's *Dark Shadows* (2012).

talents in film. These include Harold Lloyd (*Haunted Spooks*), Buster Keaton (*The Haunted House*), Bob Hope (*The Cat and the Canary, The Ghost Breakers*), Abbott and Costello (*Hold That Ghost, The Time of Their Lives*), Charles Laughton (*The Canterville Ghost*), Jerry Lewis (*Scared Stiff*), Don Knotts (*The Ghost and Mr. Chicken*), Gene Wilder (*Haunted Honeymoon*), Peter O'Toole (*High Spirits*), Michael Keaton (*Beetlejuice*), Eddie Murphy (*The Haunted Mansion*) and Johnny Depp (*Dark Shadows*). Honorable mentions go to less exalted comedians and comedy teams such as the Bowery Boys (*Spooks Run Wild*, etc.), Olson and Johnson (*Ghost Catchers*), the Ritz Brothers (*The Gorilla*) and Shemp Howard (*Ghost Crazy*). At the same time these films also drew upon the talents of well-known horror movie actors such as George Zucco, Gale Sondegaard, John Carradine, Basil Rathbone, Lon Chaney, Jr., and Bela Lugosi to leaven the laughter with a measure of spooky chills.

Like the mystery house films, many haunted house comedies dispensed with ghosts in favor of mobsters, hoaxers, mad scientists and even gorillas. But while American mystery and horror films shied away from the notion of supernatural spooks, houses haunted by real ghosts first appeared in comedies such as *The Ghost Goes West* and *The Canterville Ghost*. In later decades haunted house comedies would be populated by all manner of paranormal beings, including not only ghosts but vampires, werewolves and zombies as well. A little bit of terror and a little bit of laughter, it seems, will always be a potent mix.

Chapter Three

Love Amongst the Ruins
Haunted Romance

In addition to the old dark house mysteries and comedy haunts, there was another type of film that dealt with the theme of accursed houses. This was the gothic romance, a type of film that combined elements of the so-called "woman's picture" with the haunted house thriller. The conventions of the gothic romance form, sometimes referred to as the "female gothic," were established in the mid–19th century in Charlotte Brontë's *Wuthering Heights* and Emily Brontë's *Jane Eyre*. Both of these novels featured conflict arising from unlikely romances between persons of the upper and lower classes, cursed marriages, and domineering male figures. More importantly, both were set against the backdrop of eerie old houses.

As the Brontës' novels were brought to the big screen they inspired the production of similarly-themed gothic romances for Hollywood audiences. These films tended to share a number of plot elements. The protagonist was usually a young woman of the lower classes who becomes romantically involved with a wealthy, dominating man. One other constant in these films was a haunted piece of real estate such as Manderly in *Rebecca*, Thornton Hall in *Jane Eyre* and Gull Cottage in *The Ghost and Mrs. Muir*. The haunted house was such an essential feature of the gothic romance that many of the films took their titles from the name of the haunt, such as *Wuthering Heights*, *Dragonwyck*, *Elephant Walk* and *Crimson Peak*. One feature of many of these houses was a secret room that concealed a ghost or a hidden character. Ghosts inhabiting these houses could be psychological in nature, or they could be real spirits with whom a romantic relationship was possible. These films tended to be based on well-respected literary properties, and many of them were prestige productions helmed by acclaimed Hollywood directors that featured A-list stars.

The first gothic romance film was Samuel L. Goldwyn's production of Charlotte Brontë's *Wuthering Heights*, which was lensed for MGM by veteran director William Wyler and released in 1939. As the film opens, a weary traveler named Lockwood (Miles Mander) struggles through a snowstorm on the Yorkshire moors to seek refuge at Wuthering Heights, "a house as bleak and desolate as the waste around it." Inside the dark and forbidding abode, Lockwood receives a chilly welcome and is grudgingly granted shelter by the overbearing master of the house, Heathcliff (Laurence Olivier). His guest is assigned to a dusty, long unused bridal chamber with a window that is partially open to the elements, but when Lockwood attempts to close the shutters he sees a woman out in the snowstorm who is calling Heathcliff's name and who clutches his hand in an icy grip. When Heathcliff is informed about the strange occurrence, he becomes highly excited and runs out into the storm, whereupon his housekeeper Ellen (Flora Robson) proceeds to relate the history of the Earnshaw family in flashback.

Forty years earlier the Earnshaw patriarch (Cecil Kellaway) brings a young Heathcliff home with him to live at Wuthering Heights. At first the young orphan is treated as one of the family, but when Earnshaw dies, he is relegated to the status of stable boy by Earnshaw's envious son Hindley (Hugh Williams). Cathy (Merle Oberon), however, is simpatico with Heathcliff and enters into a quasi-romantic relationship with him as the couple roams over the moors together, but the young woman is also attracted to the aristocratic high life of the neighboring Linton family. When Edgar Linton (David Niven) asks her to marry him, she is torn between his offer and her passion for Heathcliff and discusses her dilemma with Ellen. Unknown to them, Heathcliff is listening to their conversation and, thinking that she prefers Linton runs away from Wuthering Heights.

Her choice being made for her, Cathy marries Linton and settles down to a placid married life until Heathcliff returns several years later. He has made a fortune in America and been transformed into a gentleman, but at the same time has been consumed by bitterness and seeks to revenge himself on the Earnshaw family. With his newfound wealth he has bought Wuthering Heights from Hindley, who has become a drunken reprobate and is heavily in debt. In order to spite Cathy, he marries Linton's sister Isabella (Geraldine Fitzgerald), who has foolishly fallen in love with him. Devastated by this turn of events, Cathy becomes gravely ill, and when Heathcliff hears of this he rushes to her bedside as Linton goes to fetch the doctor. The lovers have their last moments together as Cathy dies of a broken heart in his arms. After she expires, Heathcliff urges her to come back from the dead to haunt him. "Catherine Earnshaw," he extols, "may you not rest as long as I live on. I killed you. Haunt me then! Haunt your murderer! I know that ghosts have wandered on the earth. Be with me always!" His soliloquy ends with the famous lines "I cannot live without my life! I cannot die without my soul!"

The film then flashes forward to the framing story as Ellen finishes telling the tale to Lockwood. Suddenly the family physician, Dr. Kenneth (Donald Crisp) arrives and tells them that he has seen Heathcliff walking through the snowstorm with his arm around a woman. This sight caused the doctor's horse to throw him, and as he continued on foot, he discovered Heathcliff's corpse lying in the snow with only his footprints showing. Ellen knows that he has finally joined Cathy in the afterlife, and a final shot shows the ghosts of Heathcliff and Cathy walking together on the moors as the lovers are united in death.

This handsome Goldwyn production does full justice to the Brontë novel, although the screenplay by Ben Hecht and Charles MacArthur only covers sixteen of the book's thirty-four chapters. This abbreviation, however, serves to condense the narrative into a more concentrated dramatic whole. Director Wyler crafts a beautifully realized blend of costume picture, romantic drama and female gothic, although the more supernatural aspects of the story are played down or take place off screen. When Lockwood has his encounter with Cathy's spirit, for instance, the audience does not see the ghost or the spectral hand that grasps at him at the window, but the apparition is merely related to Heathcliff and Ellen. Likewise, at the film's conclusion the viewer is not treated to Dr. Kenneth's vision of the ghosts of Cathy and Heathcliff walking together through the snowstorm. The film might have been more powerful had these sights been seen onscreen instead of merely being talked about.

Sir Laurence Olivier poses as Heathcliff in this publicity still for William Wyler's adaptation of Charlotte Brontë's *Wuthering Heights* (1939).

Principals Laurence Olivier and Merle Oberon both turn in memorable performances despite reportedly not getting along well on the set. The film was nominated for eight Academy Awards, including Best Picture, and an Oscar nod went to Olivier for Best Actor, but it only won in the Best Cinematography category for director of photography Gregg Toland. Toland was reportedly the first d.p. to shoot with the Mitchell Camera Corporation's BNC camera which would thereafter become the industry standard for Hollywood studios, and the talented cinematographer would go on to shoot the acclaimed visuals for Orson Welles' masterwork *Citizen Kane*. The physical structure of the Wuthering Heights homestead, as rendered by art director James Basevi, is a perfectly realized envisioning of the unlucky dwelling as depicted in the novel, and is shown as a cheerless, confining hovel located in the middle of a barren heath. It appears in its most haunted aspect during the film's early scenes in which Toland employs low-key lighting setups to capture the spooky ambience of a haunt. Scenes depicting the forbidding Yorkshire moors were shot on location at Wildwood Regional Park in California. *Wuthering Heights* explores the dynamics of a necrophiliac relationship between a living person and a ghost that can only be resolved when the doomed lovers are united in the afterlife, with the unhappy house as the locus of the tragic affair.

The gothic romance received a boost with the publication of Daphne Du Maurier's 1938 mystery thriller *Rebecca*, a work that updated the female gothic genre into a 20th century milieu. The novel was such a monster hit that its adaptation for the big screen was inevitable. The task fell to the acclaimed producer David O. Selznick, who in turn brought the equally acclaimed British director Alfred Hitchcock to Hollywood to make his first film in America. Hitchcock, in turn, assembled a fine cast of English thespians to act in this prestige production. Du Maurier's chief innovation to the female gothic formula was to transform the gothic novel's ghost from supernatural being to psychological construct. The theme of the haunted house remained, however, in the form of the stately British manor called Manderley.

Like Du Maurier's novel, Hitchcock's *Rebecca* (1940) begins with an eerie dream sequence in which the voice of the film's nameless heroine (Joan Fontaine) describes the onscreen action. "Last night I dreamed I went to Manderley again," her voice solemnly intones as the disembodied dreamer's eye drifts through the estate's front gate and up the fog-bound drive to the dark, imposing edifice of the de Winter ancestral mansion. "Time could not mar the perfect symmetry of its walls," the narrator continues, but "I looked upon a desolate shell." Manderley now lies in ruins, but as moonlight plays over the gothic mansion, ghostly lights seem to gleam in the windows for a moment. As a cloud passes over the moon, however, the illusion quickly fades and the dreamer laments that she can never return to Manderley again.

The rest of the film unrolls in flashback as Maxim de Winter (Laurence Olivier) and the story's heroine (Fontaine), have their first meeting, during which she interrupts Maxim as he is about to hurl himself off a cliff in Monte Carlo. This leads to a whirlwind romance between Max, a member of the landed English gentry, and the shy young woman, who is a mere servant, but despite the difference in their stations Maxim marries her and takes her back to Manderley, his imposing estate on the rugged Cornwall coast. The bride is intimidated by her newly elevated status and her many duties as the lady of the house, and she feels a strong antipathy toward Mrs. Danvers (Judith Anderson), the mansion's severe, black-clad chief housekeeper.

As she tries to settle into the routine of being the second Mrs. De Winter, she becomes aware of another presence at Manderley, that of Maxim's dead wife, Rebecca, who drowned in a boating accident a year earlier. The first Mrs. De Winter's accouterments are everywhere in the form of clothing, furniture and monogrammed items. In addition, Rebecca's bedroom, "the most beautiful room in the house," is lovingly maintained as a kind of shrine to the dead woman by Mrs. Danvers and kept locked. The suffocating presence of Rebecca's unseen persona threatens to overwhelm the young wife, who feels that Maxim can never truly love her while he is obsessed with his first wife's memory. The evil Mrs. Danvers, who harbors a strange necrophiliac passion for Rebecca, preys upon the young woman's vulnerabilities and insecurities, and nearly succeeds in making her commit suicide out of despair.

When Rebecca's boat and her skeleton are accidentally discovered by a diver, an inquest is convened because it appears that the boat was deliberately scuttled and there is evidence of foul play. Max, who might be accused of murdering Rebecca, confesses all to his wife, revealing that she was a cruel, promiscuous woman who he hated. One night he confronted her in a beach cottage where she used to conduct trysts with her lovers and they had a fierce argument when she announced she was pregnant with another man's child. In a fit of rage, he hit her and accidentally killed her, then placed her body in the boat and sank it. During the inquest her former lover Jack Favell (George Sanders) surfaces with a letter Rebecca wrote on the day of her death that seems to indicate that she was pregnant and he was the father. As the hearing progresses, however, Rebecca's doctor is sought out and reveals that she was not pregnant, but instead was suffering from a terminal illness. Her death is ruled a suicide and Max is freed from suspicion of murder, but as Max and his wife are driving home, they find Manderley in flames, having been set afire out of spite by Mrs. Danvers, who perishes in the fiery conflagration that also exorcises the ghost of Rebecca.

Hitchcock is at the top of his form directing this popular and critically acclaimed gothic thriller in his first Hollywood outing. It was nominated for eleven Academy Awards, including Olivier as Best Actor and Fontaine as Best Actress, and wound up winning Best Picture and Best Cinematography for director of photography George Barnes, although Hitch was passed over in the Best Director category. Hitch elicits fine performances from a distinguished British cast, including Laurence Olivier, Joan Fontaine, George Sanders and Judith Anderson, who was nominated for a Best Supporting Actress Oscar for her performance as the witchy Mrs. Danvers, a seminal role that would later be echoed by actresses such as Gale Sondergaard and Margaret Hamilton. Hitchcock's visuals utilize fog, shadows and rain to build a mood of mystery and suspense, while George Barnes' camera swoops through the haunted corridors of Manderley. The famed "Selznick touch" imbues this prestige effort with stately British elegance and exquisite production values.

Because of the novel's popularity, producer Selznick insisted that the screenplay adaptation by playwright Robert E. Sherwood and Joan Harrison conform strictly to the book's narrative. The main peculiarity of both the novel and the film is that the young woman who is the story's central character has no name. She was reportedly referred to simply as "I" (i.e., the narrator) in the film's shooting script. *Rebecca* was a modern-day ghost story in which the ghost is not a supernatural specter, but instead is psychological in nature. Dramatic tensions arise from the conflict between the two Mrs. De Winters, one a weak personality and the other a flamboyantly charismatic persona; one living, the other dead. Rebecca's ghost is kept alive by Maxim's guilty conscience, by the perverse necrophiliac yearnings of Mrs. Danvers, and by the dead woman's imprint upon Manderley itself.

Manderley is an overarching presence that enfolds the characters in its spectral gothic web. Exterior long shots of the mansion were filmed using a miniature, while interiors were

The second Mrs. De Winter (Joan Fontaine) dresses up in a costume favored by the first Mrs. De Winter in *Rebecca* (1940).

constructed on the sound stages Selznick had previously used for *Gone with the Wind* a year earlier. Their construction was the work of production designer Lyle R. Wheeler, with an uncredited assist from William Cameron Menzies. Daphne Du Maurier reportedly based Manderley on a similar venerable estate in Cornwall named Menabilly, an ivy-covered manor where she had lived for many years.

Three. Love Amongst the Ruins

After the critical and popular acclaim afforded to the gothic romances *Wuthering Heights* and *Rebecca*, the next major literary work to be adapted for the big screen would be Emily Brontë's *Jane Eyre* (1944). The title character is an orphan child who suffers humiliations at the hands of her aunt Mrs. Reed (Agnes Morehead), then is remanded to a strict girl's school operated by Mr. Brockelhurst (Henry Daniell). Upon reaching maturity, Jane (Joan Fontaine) accepts a job as a governess at Thornfield Hall, the estate of the wealthy Edward Rochester (Orson Welles). Arriving at the gloomy, castle-like country mansion, Jane meets with the housekeeper Mrs. Fairfax (Edith Barrett), and Rochester's charming young ward Adele (Margaret O'Brien). As Jane settles into her duties looking after Adele at Thornfield, she notices that there is a secluded part of the mansion presided over by an enigmatic servant named Grace Poole (Ethel Griffies).

One night as Jane is walking on the foggy moors alone, she encounters the master of the house for the first time as Mr. Rochester comes galloping through the dark and is thrown from his horse when he unexpectedly encounters her. After their chance meeting, she has an audience with her employer, who is proud, sardonic and harsh and treats her with diffidence as a mere servant. Later that night Jane is awakened in her bed by the sound of strange laughter and footsteps, and when she gets up to investigate, she finds Rochester's bed in flames. She manages to rescue him from the burning bed, but has no clue as to who or what might have started the fire.

Some months later Rochester invites a group of his upper-class peers to stay at Thornfield. Among them is Blanche Ingram (Hillary Brooke), a cultured beauty that everyone expects will marry Rochester. One evening during their stay a mysterious man named Richard Mason (John Abbott) arrives from Spanish Town, Jamaica, for a private meeting with Rochester. In the middle of the night the guests are awakened by a blood-curdling scream coming from the hidden wing of the house. Rochester assures everyone that this is just one of the servants having a nightmare, but secretly calls Jane to attend to Mason, who has suffered a grievous wound, while he calls a doctor to Thornfield. As Jane staunches Mason's flow of blood, she hears an unknown person shaking the door to the secret wing, along with more eerie laughter and sounds of weeping. Rochester arrives with the physician, and Mason is quickly patched up and sent on his way.

It turns out that Rochester does not intend to marry Blanche, who he considers a gold digger, and when the guests depart, he asks Jane to marry him instead. Jane is ecstatic, but on the day of their wedding Mason reappears to assert that Rochester has a living wife, his sister Bertha, who is a congenital lunatic kept in seclusion at Thornfield for many years. After calling off the wedding, Rochester invites everyone back to Thornfield for a glimpse of the raving madwoman, who has been responsible for all the strange goings-on at the mansion. A devastated Jane flees back to her aunt's to recuperate, but one night during a storm she hears Rochester's anguished voice calling to her and decides to return to Thornfield. She finds the estate in ruins, and learns from Mrs. Fairfax that the crazy wife escaped from her confinement and set the house afire, and that Rochester vainly tried to rescue her from the flames and was blinded in the process. The movie ends happily as Jane and Rochester are reunited and are finally free to wed, and their love eventually leads to the restoration of his sight.

The plot of the movie version adheres fairly closely to the novel, although as with *Wuthering Heights* a number of chapters have been condensed or excised. Adapted for the screen by Aldous Huxley (best known for his dystopian novel *Brave New World*), John Houseman and the film's director Robert Stevenson, the 1944 version still stands as the most acclaimed iteration of Emily Brontë's classic work. British expatriate Stevenson wrings passionate performances from principals Orson Welles and *Rebecca*'s Joan Fontaine, and imbues the production with both dark atmosphere and dignity. He shoots in extreme long shots, tight close-ups and employs low-key lighting techniques to build a mood of mystery and dread, aided by ace cinematographer George Barnes, who had won an Oscar for his gothic camerawork on *Rebecca*. Many scenes take place amid wind and storm, staging that externalizes the tempestuous passions of the lovers. Stevenson would go on to work for the Walt Disney studios and would eventually direct the children's classic *Mary Poppins* (1964). A distinguished cast, including Henry Daniell, Agnes Morehead, John Sutton and Sara Allgood deliver solid supporting performances, while child actress Margaret O'Brien, who would also appear in *The Canterville Ghost* in that same year, is pleasant and charming. Another child actress, Elizabeth Taylor, appears in a small, yet tragic role, and would go on to become a major star. Composer Bernard Hermann contributed a stirring romantic score that presages his work for some of Hitchcock's most exciting thrillers. This confluence of talent served to make *Jane Eyre* into one of the most memorable gothic thrillers of the 1940s.

There are many similarities with the plot of *Rebecca*, including a romance between a lower-class woman and an upper-class man who is consumed with guilt about his previous marriage, an accursed palatial estate containing a secret room, and the mansion being burned down by an insane character at the film's conclusion. *Rebecca*'s imperious Maxim de Winter would seem to be in a direct line of succession from the equally dominating Edward Rochester, and it's not a stretch to think that Daphne Du Maurier might have drawn upon these themes from Emily Brontë's classic novel. *Jayne Eyre*'s Thornfield Hall, however, bears little resemblance to the elegant Manderley, instead resembling a medieval castle with towers and walls of fitted stonework. Thornfield is dark, gloomy and cavernous, making the characters appear to be swallowed up in its shadows in several scenes. Although there is no ghost *per se*, it is haunted by a pyromaniac madwoman whose very existence represents a terrible family secret. Rochester's crazy wife is never actually seen by the audience, but her presence is suggested by the sound of footsteps in the dark, her eerie laughter and a hidden force trying to break through a locked door.

Brontë's novel had undergone a more sinister adaptation during the previous year in *I Walked with a Zombie* (1943), a product of RKO's horror film unit headed up by Val Lewton. The lurid, "audience tested" title had been forced upon him by the studio heads, but the literate Lewton decided he would turn this B-movie thriller into "*Jane Eyre* in the West Indies." Working with veteran scenarist Curt Siodmak, who had scripted several of the classic Universal horror programmers, Lewton fashioned a contemporary gothic romance with supernatural overtones inspired by Brontë's work. Lensed by the acclaimed French émigré director Jacques Tourneur, the film would turn out to be one of the most exquisite and haunting horror films of the period.

The "I" of the title is nurse Betsy Connell (Frances Dee), who accepts a job caring for the wife of sugar plantation owner Paul Holland (Tom Conway) on the Caribbean island of San Sebastian. Arriving at Fort Holland, the family's estate on the tropical isle, she is unaware of the nature of her patient's true condition until she encounters Jessica Holland (Christine Gordon) wandering through the plantation grounds like a wraith in a white, flowing dress. Jessica is suffering from a mysterious affliction of the brain that renders her mindless, and she is kept confined in a tower on the estate. Paul informs Betsy that Jessica's illness, thought to be the result of a virulent tropical fever, is considered incurable. During her stay at Fort Holland, Betsy becomes aware of a bitter enmity between Paul and his alcoholic half-brother Wesley Rand (James Ellison), and learns of a love triangle that formerly existed between the siblings and Jessica.

Even as Betsy begins to fall in love with Paul, she resolves to try and cure Jessica. When insulin treatments fail to help her, Betsy hears of "better doctors" among the voodoo practitioners of the island. Determined to try every avenue for a cure, she leads Jessica on an eerie journey through the sugar cane fields at night to reach the "Houmfort" where the voodoo ceremonies are conducted. On their way they meet Carrefour (Darby Jones), the towering zombie guardian of the Houmfort, who allows them to pass without incident. At the ceremony Betsy witnesses ecstatic voodoo drumming and the spirit possession of one of the celebrants, but when she consults the oracle of the god Damballah about Jessica's illness, she is ushered into a hut where she unexpectedly encounters Wesley's mother, Mrs. Rand (Edith Barrett), who is dispensing modern medical advice under the guise of native superstition. While she is otherwise occupied, the natives become fascinated with Jessica, who they believe is a living/dead zombie, and subject her to a series of ritual tests that seem to confirm this before Betsy takes charge and returns her to Fort Holland.

Jessica's presence at the Houmfort creates a stir among the local populace, who demand that she return to their enclave to undergo further rituals. When their demand is refused, the voodoo cultists attempt to use their magic to compel her, and when this fails Carrefour is sent to abduct her and nearly succeeds when Mrs. Rand suddenly appears and orders him away. Their next gambit is to compel the weak-minded Wesley to murder his former lover. Taking Jessica's body in his arms, Wesley is pursued by Carrefour and flees into the ocean where the zombie cannot follow. The doomed lovers are united in death as Wesley drowns in the surf, and in the aftermath Betsy and Paul are now free to wed.

Nurse Betsy Connell (Frances Dee, left) encounters her patient, the zombified Jessica Holland (Christine Gordon), in the Val Lewton production *I Walked with a Zombie* **(1943).**

True to his desire to transform a standard horror thriller into "*Jane Eyre* in the West Indies," Lewton and company succeed admirably. Both stories feature a humble young woman who travels to the crumbling estate of a melancholy wealthy man and falls in love with him. Their plans for matrimony are thwarted by the man's still-living wife, who is incurably mad, and the wife's demise ultimately leads to the union of the frustrated lovers. Here the source material is transformed into a new and entirely original idiom, and *I Walked with a Zombie* is widely considered by critics to be one of the most memorable horror films of the period. The sequence in which Betsy and Jessica traverse the sugar cane fields at night is especially eerie and effective. Note that there is a West Indian connection in *Jane Eyre*, as Mr. Rochester's lunatic wife Bertha hails from Spanish Town in Jamaica.

After *Jane Eyre*, 20th Century–Fox's next prestige gothic romance was *Dragonwyck* (1946), adapted from a popular novel by Anya Seton. Scripted by Joseph L. Mankiewicz, best known for his collaboration with Orson Welles on the director's classic drama *Citizen Kane* (1941), the studio decided to let Mankiewicz produce and direct for the first time as well. *Dragonwyck* would star glamor actress Gene Tierney and perennial heavy Vincent Price, who had appeared together in Otto Preminger's acclaimed film noir *Laura* (1944).

Dragonwyck begins at a farm in rural Greenwich, Connecticut in 1848, where the humble farmer's daughter Miranda Wells (Tierney) receives a letter from her wealthy distant relation Nicholas Van Ryn (Price) requesting that she travel to his palatial Hudson Valley estate named Dragonwyck to work as a governess for his daughter Katrina. After some misgivings expressed by her sternly religious father Ephraim (Walter Huston), Miranda is allowed to comply with the request. Nicholas is a *patroon*, an imperious landowner of Dutch descent who lords over the tenant farmers on his properties who must pay him rent, veneration and tribute.

Arriving at Dragonwyck, Miranda finds the vast mansion to be a dark, forbidding place inhabited by a group of weird family members. Nicholas' wife Johanna (Vivienne Osborne) is a self-obsessed glutton and hypochondriac, while their daughter Katrina (Connie Marshall) is an introverted child suffering from parental neglect. Lording over the household is the arrogant, aristocrat Nicholas, who seems to harbor strange secrets. Even the obligatory creepy servant Magda (Spring Byington) warns her, "You'll wish with all your heart you never came to Dragonwyck." Brooding over the strange household is a large portrait of the Van Ryn family matriarch, who committed suicide after bearing a son to Nicholas' great grandfather. The lady is said to sing and play the harpsichord on certain nights, although only those with Van Ryn blood can hear the ghostly music.

Johanna seems to be suffering from a series of minor ailments, for which she is being treated by local physician Dr. Jeff Turner (Glenn Langan). During an annual harvest festival, Nicholas dances with Miranda, showing their mutual attraction for everyone to see. That night Nicholas brings a bunch of his favorite oleander flowers into his wife's bedroom, and the next morning she is found dead, presumably from one of her illnesses. Miranda learns that Nicholas despised and rejected his wife because she was unable to have more children after Katrina's birth and therefore could not bear him a son and heir. After an indecently short time, however, Nicholas proposes marriage and Miranda accepts.

As his new wife Miranda, comes to know her husband as a vain and godless man who does not feel bound by conventional morality. In the meantime, the peasant farmers who

Nicholas Van Ryn (Vincent Price) woos his cousin Miranda Wells (Gene Tierney) in Joseph L. Mankiewicz's gothic romance *Dragonwyck* (1946).

work Nicholas' lands are questioning the validity of the semi-feudal *patroon* system and are on the brink of revolt. As these events are unfolding, Miranda gives birth to a son, but the baby dies soon after from a heart defect and the loss causes Nicholas to have an emotional breakdown when he learns that Miranda, like his first wife, cannot bear him more children. He begins to spend more and more time alone in Dragonwyck's private tower room where, he jokes, he is "hiding an insane twin brother." When Miranda finally penetrates her husband's inner sanctum, she is shocked to learn that he has become a drug addict and appears to be mentally unbalanced. As Nicholas plots his next move, Miranda's maid Peggy (Jessica Tandy) confides her suspicions that he may try to murder his wife to Dr. Turner, who figures out that Nicholas' "favorite oleander" flowers are poisonous and had been used to murder Johanna. He arrives at Dragonwyck in time to rescue Miranda from the poison flowers, and Nicholas receives street justice when he is shot to death during a confrontation with the rebellious farmers.

Executive-produced by 20th Century–Fox mogul Daryl F. Zanuck, *Dragonwyck* was another A-list gothic romance with high-end production values and major stars. Triple-threat producer/writer/director Mankiewicz manages to wear all these hats successfully, although some critics feel that the historical portion of the narrative dealing with the uprising against the *patroon* system during the Anti-Rent Wars of 1839–1846 worked against the gothic mood of the film. There's plenty of dark atmosphere in evidence, however, as the characters play out their fates inside the stately but gloomy manor. Gene Tierney is intense and glamorous in her portrayal of the film's central character, while Price oozes gothic menace in a role that presages his nefarious portrayals in Roger Corman's series of Edgar Allan Poe adaptations beginning with *House of Usher* (1960). Walter Houston, Glenn Langan and Jessica Tandy (in her screen debut) also turn in solid performances in their supporting roles.

Note that the haunt in *Dragonwyck* lies in the same Hudson Valley location as the similar castle-like structure in the silent 1927 version of *The Cat and the Canary*. The film's plot, derived from Anya Seton's novel, contains many of the conventions of earlier gothics, such as the lower-class female protagonist who marries above her station, an imperious, demanding male foil, a ghostly ancestor whose portrait broods over the action and a hidden room concealing a terrible secret. The manor suffers under a family curse, but "the blackness in that house," as one character puts it, is entirely due to Nicholas' obsession with having an heir, which even overrides his erotic attraction to the lovely Miranda as he descends into a maelstrom of madness and drug addiction.

Tierney and Mankiewicz would join forces in the following year to produce another love story set against the background of a haunted house, *The Ghost and Mrs. Muir* (1947). Once again, the protagonist is a strong-willed woman, Lucy Muir (Tierney), a widow who feels the need to change her life and moves from London to the seaside village of Whitecliff in the early 1900s. She is attracted to a cozy house called Gull Cottage despite its reputation for being haunted by its former owner, a sea captain who reputedly committed suicide there and whose portrait still adorns the cottage's walls. Lucy, her young daughter Anna (Natalie Wood), and her maid Edna (Martha Huggin) move in, and it isn't long before the spirit of Captain Daniel Gregg (Rex Harrison) manifests itself.

Despite the formidable nature of the ghost, Lucy is nonplussed by his presence and refuses to move out of her new home. In time Lucy and the Captain are reconciled and learn to share the cottage in harmony together, and a soul-to-soul romantic relationship forms between them despite the ghost's non-corporeal state. She learns that he did not kill himself, but his death was an accident caused by a gas heater when he fell asleep. When Lucy begins to have financial problems, Captain Gregg comes to her aid by dictating his autobiography, entitled *Blood and Swash*, "the unvarnished story of a seaman's life," which is accepted by publisher Mr. Coombe (Robert Coote) and sells well enough to provide her with a steady income.

The ghost of Captain Gregg (Rex Harrison) falls in love with widow Lucy Muir (Gene Tierney) in *The Ghost and Mrs. Muir* (1947).

On her initial visit to the publisher in London she had met a fellow author, Miles Fairley (George Sanders), who writes syrupy children's books under the pseudonym "Uncle Neddy." The unctuous Miles helped introduce her to Mr. Coombe, and in the aftermath, she has become attracted to him. Realizing that his intimate but morbid relationship with Lucy must not continue, Captain Gregg resolves to end it and return her to a life among the living. While she is sleeping, he makes her forget their love and think it was all a dream before vanishing out to sea.

Lucy's relationship with Fairley continues during visits he makes to Whitecliff until one day while she is visiting the publisher in London she decides to pay him a surprise visit. Obtaining Uncle Neddy's address from an office clerk, she goes to his house and is horrified to discover that he is already married and has two children. Stunned by this terrible betrayal, she returns to Whitecliff a broken woman and becomes a recluse. Lucy spends the rest of her life in Gull Cottage attended by Martha until she is old and infirm. One foggy night when she is feeling poorly, she dies as she rests in her bedroom chair, whereupon the Captain appears to lead her out of the cottage and into a misty afterlife as the lovers are finally united.

Mankiewicz delivers a charming, comic, yet ultimately poignant story of an unlikely love relationship between the living and the dead. Screenwriter Phillip Dunne does a masterful job adapting the novel by R.A. Dick (the pseudonym of author Josephine Aimee Campbell Leslie). Gene Tierney is a beautiful and dignified screen presence as the soulful, sorrowful Lucy Muir and is perfectly cast opposite the distinguished British actor Rex Harrison, who plays the titular ghost with a shipload of maritime bluster. Rounding out the cast is George Sanders, who reprises the oily, ne'er do well character he portrayed in *Rebecca*. Cinematographer Charles Lang shoots inside the haunt in exquisite chiaroscuro, and composer Bernard Hermann delivers a hauntingly romantic score.

The Ghost and Mrs. Muir is not a gothic romance, although it contains an independent-minded female protagonist who falls in love with a domineering male, a mysterious house and a ghost. It is instead an example of what has been called *film blanc*, films with a positive outlook that sometimes employ supernatural characters and miraculous events. Examples include Hollywood chestnuts such as *It's a Wonderful Life*, *The Bishop's Wife* and *Here Comes Mr. Jordan*. Like the female gothics, however, *Ghost* is a romantic story set against the background of a haunted house. While Gull Cottage is a more humble haunt than the palatial mansions in the female gothics, like *Rebecca*'s Manderley it overlooks the rugged English coast that symbolizes eternity. The cottage was actually constructed on the California coastline near Palos Verdes in the Big Sur area. All of the filmic elements combine to create a beautifully produced screen classic. The film inspired a television sitcom that ran on NBC (and later on ABC) for three seasons between 1968 and 1970.

The gothic romance film faded from movie screens in the late 1940s and would never again gain the popularity of the 1939–1946 period, but they were about to mutate into new forms with the coming of widescreen and technicolor extravaganzas meant to compete with the burgeoning popularity of television. Paramount's *Elephant Walk* (1954) was a love story set in an exotic locale that utilized many of the conventions of the gothic romance, including a haunted family estate.

In postwar London, an English girl named Ruth (Elizabeth Taylor) is wooed by a wealthy colonial tea planter named John Wiley (Peter Finch), who marries her after a whirlwind courtship and whisks her off to his lavish plantation house in Ceylon. The palatial "bungalow," built in native style, is named Elephant Walk because John's father deliberately built it in the migratory path of a local herd of elephants that used to traverse it on their way to their watering hole. As John is driving his new bride to the estate, their path is blocked by a bull elephant, who challenges them before being shooed away by gunfire.

Ruth is unable to easily transition to her new life in the alien environment of Elephant Walk. Her husband seems distant and more inclined to pal around with a gang of British expatriate hangers-on who are all too eager to drink his liquor and enjoy his hospitality. In addition, she has a strained relationship with the estate's chief retainer, a stern native man named Appuhamy (Abraham Sofaer). Worst of all, she becomes aware that everyone at Elephant Walk is under the spell of John's dead father, Tom Wiley, who is referred to with reverence as the "Guv'nor" or the "Old Gentleman." Appuhamy in particular is in the thrall of the Guv'nor's ghost, speaking to the dead man at his grave, which is located right outside Ruth's window, and maintaining the old gentleman's room just the way it was on the day of his death. This secret room is kept locked, and Ruth is not allowed in.

Isolated and alone, she finds a kindred spirit in her husband's plantation manager, Dick Carver (Dana Andrews), with whom she strikes up a platonic relationship, but despite her husband's arrogant neglect, this never progresses into a full-blown love affair. The herd of wild elephants keeps menacing the bungalow, but they are always repulsed by the servants and a system of protective walls. Nevertheless, a feeling of doom seems to hang over the place. Ruth manages to obtain the key to the Guv'nor's secret room and explores the mysterious shrine that includes a full-length portrait of the dead man, along with many of his belongings. Soon afterward, she witnesses a bizarre ritual celebrating the Old Master's birthday, in which presents are distributed around the father's grave in a kind of "black Christmas."

Things come to a head when a severe drought and an outbreak of cholera plague Elephant Walk. Ruth shows her mettle by becoming indispensable to the efforts to contain the epidemic, an effort that serves to bring her closer to her husband. She confronts him about the unhealthy influence of his father, stating, "He's ruling you from beyond his grave." The dead man's spell is finally broken when the thirst-crazed elephants descend upon the bungalow and the maddened herd of pachyderms rampages through Elephant Walk and Appuhamy is killed. John rescues Ruth from the stampede and they watch as the mansion goes up in flames and the Guv'nor's ghost, represented by his burning portrait, is exorcised in the cleansing fires.

Lensed by veteran director William Dieterle on location in Ceylon, *Elephant Walk* is part travelogue and part gothic romance that is enlivened by its lush cinematography, its exotic locale and the luminous screen presence of a young Elizabeth Taylor. The main problem with the film is that its title implies its conclusion, clueing the audience to the climax during which the angry elephants get to stalk through Elephant Walk. It's a handsome production that builds to a spectacular, though hardly unexpected, ending, but the dramatic interplay between the characters tends to bog down amid the tropical spectacle.

If *I Walked with a Zombie* is *Jane Eyre* in the West Indies, then *Elephant Walk* is *Rebecca* in Ceylon. It was scripted by John Lee Mahin from a novel by Robert Standish (a.k.a. Digby George Geraghty), and the similarities to the earlier film are obvious. Both of them involve a lower-class woman protagonist who marries a wealthy man with a mysterious secret who

Ruth Wiley (Elizabeth Taylor) is aghast as a herd of thirst-maddened elephants rampage through her husband's palatial estate in *Elephant Walk* (1954).

installs her in a palatial home. Both feature an imposing servant who worships the spirit of a dead person whose memory is ritually preserved within a secret room, and in both films the manor houses are destroyed by fire. One big difference, however, is that Dieterle shoots in vibrant color and does not attempt to paint Elephant Walk in the shadows of the gothic romance. Likewise, the spirit of the deceased Guv'nor does not manifest itself as a ghostly, unseen presence as in *Rebecca*, but instead is conjured in a series of quasi-religious rituals performed by John, the expats and the natives. Still, *Elephant Walk* represents a strange and exotic take on the female gothic formula.

Many decades later the gothic romance would be revisited in 21st century fashion by the acclaimed Mexican-American director Guillermo del Toro in *Crimson Peak* (2015). Set in Buffalo New York around the turn of the century, the heroine of the piece is Edith Cushing (Mia Wasikowska), the daughter of wealthy businessman Carter Cushing (Jim Beaver). Fourteen years earlier, after the death of her mother, her mother's ghost had visited her to warn her to "beware of Crimson Peak." The adult Edith is a "young Jane Austin" who has written a lurid ghost story, but her horror novel remains unpublished. Her life changes when English baronet Sir Thomas Sharpe (Tom Hiddleston) and his sister Lucille (Jessica Chastain) visit Buffalo. Sir Thomas is seeking funding from Carter Cushing for his invention, a clay mining apparatus, but his request gets turned down by the family patriarch.

Romantic sparks begin to fly between Edith and the English nobleman over the objections of her father and her childhood friend, physician Alan McMichael (Charlie Hunnam), but when Mr. Cushing hires a private detective to dig up dirt on Sir Thomas, he is brutally murdered, leaving her an heiress who is free to marry the baronet.

Edith travels with Thomas and Lucille to the Sharpe ancestral estate in Cumberland, England named Crimson Peak because of the blood-colored clay upon which their manor, Allerdale Hall, rests. The enormous, isolated manor is in a decrepit, decaying state due to the Sharpe family's declining fortunes. There is a hole in the roof of the main hall and the floor is slowly sinking into crimson clay. Oddly, Thomas is sexually cold toward her and fails to consummate their marriage, while Lucille is distant and seems to resent her presence. Edith begins to see strange apparitions in the dark, gloomy hallways that attempt to communicate with her, and she recalls the message from her mother's ghost to "beware of Crimson Peak."

One winter day Edith accompanies Thomas to a post office in the nearest town, where she intercepts a letter to Allerdale from an unknown person in Milan, Italy and hides it from Thomas. When a sudden blizzard strands them in town, they stay at a hotel overnight where the marriage is finally consummated, but upon returning to the manor Lucille is openly hostile to her for reasons Edith does not understand. Tapping into Edith's fortune, Thomas is able to build his clay mining contraption and spends much of his time working on his pet project, while Edith becomes afflicted with a wasting illness.

Snooping around the mansion, Edith finds evidence that reveals the grim truth: Thomas has previously married three wealthy women and poisoned them for their inheritances, and she is also being targeted for her money. She also discovers, to her horror and disgust, that the siblings are involved in an incestuous relationship with each other, and that when their mother found out Lucille murdered her. In the meantime, Dr. McMichael learns about the Sharpe's perfidious deeds from the detective Mr. Cushing had hired to investigate them. Before Edith is forced to sign over all her assets, McMichael arrives at the mansion to rescue her and a battle royal ensues in which Thomas and Lucille are slain and become ghosts and McMichael leads Edith away from the accursed haunt. An epilogue states that Edith has written a gothic novel entitled *Crimson Peak*.

Producer/writer/director del Toro's *Crimson Peak* took the gothic romance to a new level utilizing sophisticated special effects and a budget of $55 million. Along with co-scripter Matthew Robbins, del Toro deliberately created an homage to classic works of female gothic such as *Jane Eyre* and *Rebecca*, as well as woman-centric haunted house fear films like Robert Wise's *The Haunting* and Jack Clayton's *The Innocents* (to be discussed in the following chapter), although a 21st century sensibility also allowed them to employ explicit violence and previously forbidden themes like sexuality and incest. Period detail is superbly realized by production designer Tom Sanders, costumer Kate Hawley and cinematographer Dan Laustsen. Lead actress Mia Wasikowska carries much of the film with her sensitive portrayal of the strong-willed, yet vulnerable heroine, while Tom Hiddleston, best known for his role as the sinister deity Loki in Marvel's *Thor* series of movies, is by turns charming and sinister as the conflicted baronet Sharpe. Jessica Chastain, however, steals every scene she's in as the insidious, domineering Lucille.

One of the strongest characters in the film, however, is the haunt itself. The exquisite Allerdale Hall set is the most elaborate haunted mansion ever constructed for a gothic romance. The manor's enormous main hall was four stories high and was dominated by a huge central staircase leading to rooms and balconies on ascending levels that are accessible by an elevator. Colored in dark teal, highly saturated dark blues and greens and, of course, reds, these hues served to establish a mood of death, decay and mystery. Del Toro's well-known visual obsessions with steampunk mechanisms and insects is clearly in evidence in Thomas' clay mining contraption and mechanical dolls, and in a moth motif that permeates elements of the architecture and furniture of the house. There is even an entire room filled with fluttering black moths that recalls a similar habitat created by the moth-obsessed serial killer Buffalo Bill in *The Silence of the Lambs*.

Perhaps the only jarring note in *Crimson Peak* is in the portrayal of the mansion's ghosts. Del Toro's hi-tech CGI and motion capture specters lack subtlety and exist merely to warn Edith about the dangers of the house and do not menace her despite their fearsome appearance. They seem out of place in a narrative that hinges on a distinctly human brand of evil. Despite any faults, however, *Crimson Peak* represents the apex of the gothic romance genre and skillfully melds it with the conventions of the hardcore horror film. Del Toro had previously tackled the haunted house tale in *The Devil's Backbone* (2001) and would go on to win a Best Picture Oscar for his romantic fantasy *The Shape of Water* (2017).

For the most part, the gothic thrillers were costume romances, so-called "women's pictures" that concentrated on the travails of female protagonists in love relationships with dominating and sometimes evil husbands, and class warfare situations. Female gothics had their origins in literary classics and popular novels and their adaptations were, for the most part, glossy prestige productions with major stars and big budgets. These gothic thrillers were the work of some of Hollywood's most talented and acclaimed directors, a list that includes William Wyler, Alfred Hitchcock, Jacques Tourneur, Robert Stevenson, Joseph Mankiewicz, William Dieterle and, most recently, Guillermo del Toro. They starred A-list actors and actresses such as Laurence Olivier, Joan Fontaine, Orson Welles, Gene Tierney, Vincent Price and Elizabeth Taylor, and featured the work of some of Hollywood's most talented screenwriters, cinematographers and production designers.

All of these films featured some variety of haunted house, although, like the mystery house films and the haunted house comedies, scarifying ghosts were scarce. There were romantic ghosts in *Wuthering Heights* and *The Ghost and Mrs. Muir*, psychological ghosts in *Rebecca* and *Elephant Walk* and ghosts linked to insanity in *Jane Eyre* and *Dragonwyck*, but only *I Walked with a Zombie* strayed into supernatural horror territory during the period from 1939 to 1954. Undead revenants and psychic poltergeists would eventually come to haunt movie screens, however, and would provide a basis for some of the cinema's most memorable horror films.

Chapter Four

The Classics

During the 1930s and 1940s, Universal Studios was known as the "House of Horrors" because of its output of films in the horror genre. Beginning in 1931 with its productions of *Dracula* and *Frankenstein*, Universal cornered the market with a seemingly endless series of sequels featuring its stable of screen monsters, a list that included Dracula, Frankenstein, the Invisible Man, the Mummy, the Wolf Man, and a few lesser-known creatures of the night. Other studios quickly followed suit with their own entries into the horror movie market: Paramount with *Dr. Jekyll and Mr. Hyde* (1931) and *Island of Lost Souls* (1933), Warner Brothers with *Mystery of the Wax Museum* (1932) and *Doctor X* (1932) and MGM with *Freaks* (1932) and *Mark of the Vampire* (1936). The popularity of these films persisted until the year 1946, when the bottom of the horror market fell out after the end of World War II.

Yet all during this heyday of horror in the 1931–1946 period, there was only a single film that featured a supernatural ghost in a traditional haunted house narrative, namely Paramount's *The Uninvited* (1944). Part of the reason for this dearth of phantasms in the classic horror films was an American distaste for the idea of ghosts, who represented metaphysical notions of the afterlife, on religious grounds. Writing about *The Uninvited*, horror historian Carlos Clarens explains, "Paramount, perplexed by a story in which ghosts turned out to be not only real but evil ... advertised their film as, 'the story of a love that is out of this world.' The picture met with the success it merited, but failed to earn ghosts a place in the cinema comparable to the one they enjoy in literature. Horror films, especially in Hollywood, prefer to steer clear of spiritual matters."[1]

Instead of ghosts, the Universal horror movie paradigm revolved around the notion of the monster. Unlike ethereal spooks who merely wished to intimidate some haunted unfortunates from beyond the grave, the Universal ghouls were solid, real-world menaces who could strangle one, rip one's throat out or drain one's blood. They were not restricted to the confines of a haunted house, but were free to roam about at will, spreading death and mayhem throughout the countryside. Monsters were highly visual and violent, while ghosts were a more subtle quality. But even though ghosts were scarce on the Universal lot, there were a couple of memorable haunts that graced two of their most acclaimed horror films.

In the first three chapters of Bram Stoker's 1889 gothic novel *Dracula,* real estate agent Jonathan Harker travels to the vampire's castle in Transylvania in order to sell some property in England, but winds up being taken prisoner by the Count. Unable to leave, he wanders around the eerie abode during the day and fends off attacks of the Count's undead brides by night. During his confinement, he witnesses Dracula crawling up the sheer castle wall like a lizard, sees a live baby being fed to the brides, and watches the Count summon the wolves of the forest to dismember the infant's mother. The narrative abruptly shifts when Dracula leaves Harker behind in the castle and departs for England, where the rest of the story unfolds. Many critics and readers alike judge that the three opening chapters, which take place within the stifling confines of the decaying castle, are the most effective and frightening in the novel, and Stoker never explains how Harker manages to free himself in the book's later pages.

The 1931 Universal screen version, derived from a stage play, has Renfield (Dwight Frye) instead of Harker arrive at the castle to confer with Count Dracula (Bela Lugosi). Dracula creeps out of his coffin and descends the castle's enormous crumbling staircase to greet his guest. Dismayed by the dilapidated condition of the ruin, Renfield nonetheless follows through with the deal. He is conducted to a more hospitable room in the castle where the Count plies him with food and wine as the necessary documents are signed. Unfortunately for Renfield, Dracula has drugged the wine, and when he collapses into unconsciousness the Count feasts upon his blood, which serves to make the man his slave. The following evening Dracula departs for his newly purchased English property, Carfax Abbey, with Renfield in tow. As soon as the vampire reaches London, however, the movie reverts to its stage-bound origins and the action slows to a crawl.

Dracula's brides (Dorothy Tree, Geraldine Dvorak and Cornelia Thaw) converge upon a drugged Renfield (Dwight Frye) in *Dracula* (1931) amid one of the magnificent set designs of Charles D. Hall.

Like Stoker's novel, Universal's *Dracula* is most evocative in the scenes that take place within the Transylvanian castle. Exterior shots of Castle Dracula were painted on glass, a common technique used in the decades before the advent of green screens and computer-generated imagery. The castle's interior was an imposing gothic set crafted by production designer Charles D. Hall that filled the entire soundstage and was extended even further upward via the use of another glass painting. An enormous crumbling stairway, along with an eighteen-foot-wide spider web, dominated the set in which Dracula greets Renfield. The scenes in which the Count and his brides rise from their coffins takes place in the castle's cellar as rats and insects crawl amid the coffins. These scenes are enlivened by the fluid camerawork of the great German cinematographer Karl Freund, who had shot expressionist classics such as Fritz Lang's *Metropolis* and F.W. Murnau's *The Last Laugh* before emigrating to Hollywood.

Dracula was an enormous popular success that revolutionized the American horror film. The moldy, decaying castle inhabited by supernatural beings established a template for the gothic iconography of the Universal horrors that followed. While Castle Dracula was a spectacular haunt, only the first 18 minutes of the film take place in Transylvania, and from there on the film devolves into more prosaic settings until the final reel that takes place inside the ruins of Carfax Abbey. Unfortunately, the monumental castle set would never be equaled in any subsequent Universal production, although it was re-used for a brief scene in the sequel, *Dracula's Daughter* (1936). The Count constituted an undead menace, but his speedy departure from his gothic domain and his corporeal solidity were at odds with the basic conventions of the haunted house narrative.

Universal released James Whale's *Frankenstein* later that same year, and this second foray into the realm of horror was also a monster hit that propelled Boris Karloff, who had portrayed the monster, into stardom. The studio would pair Lugosi and Karloff in a number of horror films that were outside of the creature feature cycle. These films, including *The Raven* (1935), *The Invisible Ray* (1936) and *Black Friday* (1939) dispensed with monsters and the supernatural in favor of science fiction. The first Karloff/Lugosi joint venture, *The Black Cat* (1934), was by far their best and featured one of the most bizarre haunts in the history of horror.

The Black Cat opens on the Orient Express travelling through central Europe, where a young American couple on their honeymoon, Peter Alison (David Manners) and his wife Joan (Jacqueline Wells) are on their way to a vacation spot. They are joined by the charming but sinister Dr. Vitus Verdegast (Bela Lugosi), who confides that he has just been released from a Russian prison camp fifteen years after the end of the Great War. Continuing on their way in a bus during a thunderstorm with Verdegast and his brutal servant Thamal (Harry Cording), they are regaled with grim tales about the locale during the war, "the greatest graveyard in the world." When the bus crashes and the driver is killed and Joan injured, the party continues on to Verdegast's destination, the house of architect Hjalmar Poelzig, a futuristic mansion built atop the ruins of Fort Marmaros, the site of horrific slaughter during the conflict.

Arriving at the marvelous steel and glass edifice, they are greeted by Herr Poelzig (Boris Karloff), who extends his hospitality to the couple while Vergegast tends to Joan's injury, but unknown to the Alissons Verdegast has come on a mission of vengeance. Poelzig had commanded Marmaros during the war and sold out the fortress to the Russians, causing tens of thousands of troops to be killed or taken prisoner. Verdegast is also seeking his wife, not knowing if she is alive or dead, and it isn't long before he learns her fate when Poelzig conducts him deep into the cellar of the house, where her corpse is preserved inside a glass case, one of several kept as bizarre trophies by the mad architect. Poelzig tells Verdegast that she died two years after the end of the war, along with his daughter, but the girl, Karin (Lucille Lund), is really alive and is living in the house as Poelzig's wife.

As the vendetta between the two enemies remains unresolved, Poelzig, who is a devil worshipper, is preparing to conduct the rites of Satan during the "dark of the moon" and intends to use Joan as a human sacrifice. The Alisons are prevented from leaving and Peter is locked in a room while Joan is taken as an unwilling participant in the black mass being conducted by Poelzig and the other acolytes. But before the unholy rite can be consummated, Verdegast and Thamal man-

Satanic architect Hjalmar Poelzig (Boris Karloff, right) displays to Dr. Vitus Verdegast (Bela Lugosi) the mummified corpse of Verdegast's wife (Lorna Luft) in Edgar G. Ulmer's *The Black Cat* (1934).

age to free Joan and he discovers Karin is dead, murdered by Poelzig. Enraged, Verdegast subdues his enemy and proceeds to flay Poelzig alive as Peter escapes to rescue Joan. As the couple flees to safety, Vergegast activates dynamite charges buried in the foundation of Marmaros and destroys Poelzig's house of evil in a tremendous explosion.

One of the most unusual and perverse horror shows ever to come out of Universal, *The Black Cat* is a lurid compendium of torture, necrophilia and Satanism that turned out to be the studio's top-grossing film of the year. In their first pairing Lugosi has the more sympathetic role but is upstaged by Karloff, who appears in Luciferian makeup, complete with a pronounced widow's peak and pointed ears that truly make him resemble a devil's disciple. The Poelzig role was reportedly based on the real-life Satanist Aliester Crowley, a flamboyant celebrity who characterized himself as "the world's wickedest man." The screen chemistry between the two titans of terror was instrumental in making the movie work, although their rivalry was a continuing factor on the screen and off. While the movie's titles proclaimed that the film's plot was "suggested by the immortal Edgar Allan Poe classic," nothing remains of Poe besides the title, and the story was entirely the work of scenarist

Peter Ruric. Cinematographer John J. Mescall's fluid moving camera sweeps through the darkened, doom-laded corridors of the former Fort Marmaros, while musical director Heinz Roemheld employs themes from Bach, Beethoven, Tchaikovsky and other classical composers to great effect.

The film's success, however, was primarily due to its director, the German émigré filmmaker Edgar G. Ulmer, who had worked on a number of expressionist classics in his home country including set design for Paul Wegener's horror classic *The Golem* (1920). Working with Universal art director Charles D. Hall, who had constructed the monumental haunted castle sets for *Dracula*, Ulmer devised one of the most unusual haunts to appear in horror films. The exterior shots of Poelzig's futuristic mansion, perched atop a hill, resembles an evil-looking factory structure and was reportedly modeled on the Ennis-Brown House, a famous building designed by Frank Lloyd Wright in 1925 that would later be utilized for *House on Haunted Hill* (1958). Interiors, designed by Ulmer himself, were in the Bauhaus style of architecture, a German style that emphasized clean lines and square geometric spaces that was a total departure from the crumbling, cobwebby gothic haunts usually seen in horror flicks. While there are no ghosts in evidence or any overtly supernatural elements, this "Bauhaus of horror," with its concrete vaults containing the preserved corpses of Poelzig's sacrificial victims displayed like ghastly trophies, is uniquely eerie and disturbing. The doomed structure, cursed by wartime treachery and infected with an atmosphere of death and dread, is aptly described by Verdegast as "the masterpiece of construction built upon the ruins of the masterpiece of destruction."

As previously mentioned, the very first Hollywood movie to feature a supernatural ghost in a haunted house was *The Uninvited* (1944). Unbelievably, not a single horror film made by Universal's monster factory or any other major studio dealt with the classic ghost story during the 20s, 30s or Early 40s. Taking a cue from Val Lewton's tasteful RKO productions such as *I Walked with a Zombie*, Paramount sought to combine the thrills of the horror movie with the gothic appeal of a "woman's picture" such as *Rebecca* to reach as wide an audience as possible. Unlike the Universal horror programmers, which had descended into juvenile monster rallies such as *Frankenstein Meets the Wolf Man* (1943), Paramount's approach was to fashion a literate, intelligent tale of terror based on Dorothy MacArdle's novel *The Uneasy Freehold* with an A-list budget.

The Uninvited is set in 1937, where musician/composer Roderick "Rick" Fitzgerald (Ray Milland) and his sister Pamela (Ruth Hussey) are vacationing near the English village of Biddlecombe on the rugged coast of Cornwall when they come across a charming but empty seaside mansion named Windward House that the siblings take a fancy to. Inquiring after the property, they find that it is for sale at a below-market rate from the owner, Commander Beech (Donald Crisp). While signing the ownership paperwork they meet the commander's granddaughter, Stella Meredith (Gail Russell), who reveals details about the house's unhappy history. Her mother, Mary Meredith, had died by falling into the ocean when Stella was three years old, and her grandfather has forbidden her to return to the family home at Windward House.

Upon moving into their new digs, the Fitzgeralds soon become aware of certain peculiarities about the place. They detect a cold spot in a locked artist's garret room that Rick plans to turn into his music studio, watch as candles dim by themselves, smell a ghostly scent of mimosa, and become aware of a woman's phantom voice that weeps through the night until dawn. When romance blooms between Rick and Stella, she defies the commander and visits Windward House once more, but her presence only seems to potentiate the psychic forces within the haunt. A spirit entity appears to possess her as she runs from the house and nearly throws herself off the same cliff where her mother had plummeted to her death.

The Fitzgeralds consult village physician Dr. Scott (Alan Napier) concerning "ugly rumors about the place" and find out that Stella's father, John Meredith, was a painter who had an affair with his model, a Spanish gypsy named Carmel, much to the chagrin of his wife, Mary. The rivalry between the two women came to a head after Stella's birth, leading to the deadly incident in which Carmel stole the infant Stella, and when Mary pursued her, Carmel pushed her over the cliff. In the aftermath, Carmel suddenly became ill and died. A frightening apparition begins to manifest itself in the halls of Windward House, a ghostly woman's form that appears in the middle of a swirling mist. It is assumed to be the vengeful spirit of Carmel who wants to harm Stella out of pure spite.

A séance is held at Windward during which Stella becomes possessed and starts speaking Spanish, presumably in Carmel's voice, but Stella claims she is aware of another, benevolent presence that she believes to be her mother's ghost. This means that there are two ghosts in the haunt, one who wants to harm her and one who wants to protect her. The supernatural goings-on at Windward House raise the commander's concerns about Stella's well-being, causing him to remand her to a sanatorium under the care of the sinister Miss Holloway (Cornelia Otis Skinner). Puzzled by Stella's absence, the Fitzgeralds pay a visit to Miss Holloway's establishment, but she anticipates their coming and releases Stella before they arrive. Eventually the sordid truth is revealed: Carmel was Stella's mother and is trying to protect her child from beyond the grave, while Mary Meredith's ghost is the vengeful spirit that is trying to destroy her. Arriving back at the house before Mary's ghost can cause further harm, Rick explains her true parentage to Stella, which causes Carmel's ghost to leave the haunt and return to the afterlife. Rick then confronts Mary's angry phantasm and exorcises the evil spirit simply by scolding it and hurling a candelabrum at it.

British director Lewis Allen crafts a superior supernatural thriller that shows

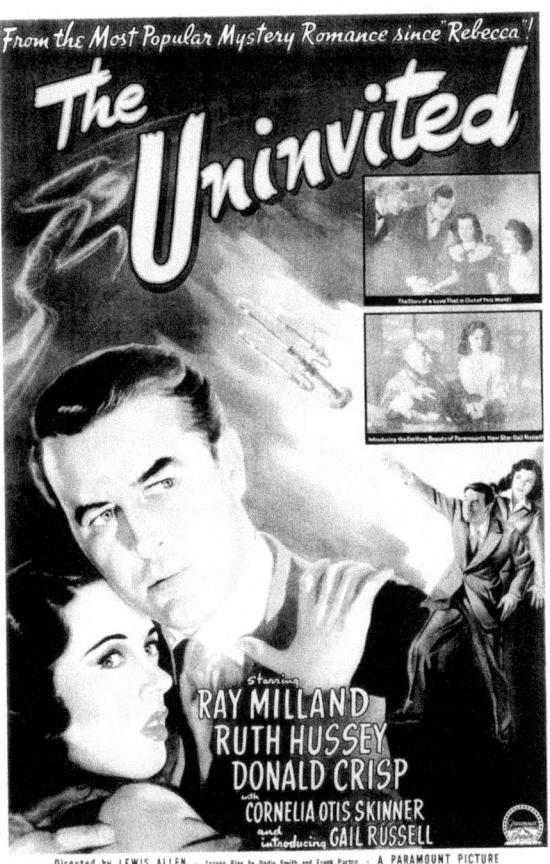

Ray Milland and Gail Russell are pictured in this poster for Hollywood's first supernatural haunted house thriller, Lewis Allen's *The Uninvited* (1944).

the influence of the RKO Lewton shockers in its intelligent approach to the material and its restrained but spooky atmospherics. The plot, devised by screenwriters Frank Partos and Dodie Smith from Dorothy MacArdle's novel, unfolds as a mystery story that unearths the identities and motivations of the ghosts as in many classic haunted house tales. Cinematographer Charles Lang was nominated for an Academy Award for his moody camerawork, and composer Victor Young's musical composition "Stella by Starlight" became a jazz standard. Ray Milland combines both strength and suavity in his role as Rick and Gail Russell projects both wide-eyed innocence and primal fear as Stella, while supporting players Ruth Hussey, Donald Crisp and Alan Napier add a touch of class to the proceedings. Apart from Milland's performance, the most memorable part in the film was played by Cornelia Otis Skinner, whose black-clad Miss Holloway character cuts a sinister figure that recalls Judith Anderson and Gale Sondegaard in earlier gothics, and Ms. Skinner would go on to have a career as an acclaimed novelist. On the minus side, the movie is often overly talky, and Milland's glib exorcism of the ghost at the film's climax is ludicrous and rings a false note.

The Uninvited stands as a milestone in the history of the supernatural haunted house film. Poster art advertised it as being "from the most popular mystery romance since *Rebecca*," and it is set in the same seaside Cornwall location as the earlier film, but unlike the psychological ghost in *Rebecca*, Windward House's phantom is highly visible and psychically affects its environment. The specter appears as a swirling, luminous woman's form that is vibrant and frightening and has no antecedent in horror cinema. This phantasm was devised by Paramount's veteran special effects specialist Farciot Edouart using optical superimpositions, and has been compared to the apparitions in *Raiders of the Lost Ark* (1981) and *Poltergeist* (1982). The depiction of ghosts onscreen is highly problematical and may partially explain the dearth of spirits in horror films during the classic horror cycle, as it's much less challenging to use makeup and costuming to create a werewolf, a mummy, or some other flesh and blood creature. Some filmmakers, such as Robert Wise in *The Haunting* (1963), would dispense with showing ghosts entirely, and there is still debate among horror film purists as to whether or not to show ghosts onscreen. In addition to the apparition, psychic phenomena such as "cold spots," olfactory and auditory effects that are associated with real-life haunted houses are depicted in the film. Although Windward House was supposedly located on the rugged coast of Cornwall, the film was actually shot in San Francisco, California, and Phoenix, Arizona.

The film was a popular and critical success and after its release it was the basis for two radio adaptations that featured Ray Milland. Cinema luminaries Martin Scorsese and Guillermo del Toro have cited *The Uninvited* as a seminal and important horror film. Yet despite this popularity and acclaim the supernatural haunted house thriller remained in limbo. During the following year Paramount released a non-sequel sequel entitled *The Unseen* (1945) that promised "menace more deadly than *The Uninvited*," but eschewed the supernatural in favor of conventional film noir mystery. It was lensed by the same director, Lewis Allen, and starred Gail Russell, but despite a screenplay co-written by noir icon Raymond Chandler, it proved to be nothing more than a mediocre mystery thriller.

The supernatural haunted house film languished for over a decade before undergoing a renaissance in the late 1950s. Earlier in the decade the horror genre had taken a detour into science fiction territory that loosed novel terrors upon movie screens, but the gothic thriller made a comeback on three separate fronts. First came England's Hammer Studios with their retreads of the classic Universal creatures in *The Curse of Frankenstein* (1957) and *Horror of Dracula* (1958). Around the same time a spate of gothic horror films were produced in Italy such as Mario Bava's *Black Sunday* (1960) and Ricardo Freda's *The Ghost* (1963). Third, director Roger Corman began turning out a series of color adaptations of the works of Edgar Allan Poe beginning with *House of Usher* (1960).

The film begins as Phillip Winthrop (Mark Damon) arrives at chez Usher, a forbidding, moldering mansion standing amid a foggy, blighted landscape located somewhere in New England. Winthrop has come from Boston seeking his fiancé, Madeleine Usher (Myrna Fahey), but her brother Roderick (Vincent Price) tries to prevent him from seeing her. Roderick suffers from a "morbid acuteness of the senses" that makes him ultra-sensitive to light, sound and other sensations. He claims that his sister is mortally ill and bedridden, but Madeleine quickly joins her fiancé, who wishes to take her to Boston and marry her, but Roderick insists that she suffers from mental illness because she is "obsessed with thoughts of death." Nonetheless, Phillip is determined to take Madeleine away from her accursed ancestral domain and refuses to leave without her.

The house of Usher is a diseased environment filled with cobwebs and rot that has an enormous crack running through its foundation. It seems to have a life of its own and attacks Phillip in a number of ways. A kettle boils over and sears his foot, a bannister loosens and nearly causes him to fall, and a chandelier descends from the ceiling and almost falls on him. "The house made those things happen," Roderick explains, and shows Phillip a series of lurid paintings of the Usher clan, a rogue's gallery of murderers, swindlers, harlots and thieves. "For hundreds of years," he tells Phillip, "foul thoughts and foul deeds have been committed within these walls—the house itself is evil!" Roderick makes it clear that the reason he opposes the marriage is to prevent Madeleine from having children and perpetuating the evil Usher bloodline.

Despite Roderick's misgivings, Phillip is more determined than ever to get Madeleine away from "this atmosphere of sickness and delusion," but as they are preparing to leave, she argues with her brother and suddenly falls into a deathly swoon. Heartbroken, Phillip mourns his fiancé and assists Roderick and his manservant Bristol (Harry Ellerbe) in carrying the coffin down to the Usher family crypt. The next day, as Phillip is about to leave, Bristol confides that Madeleine is prone to fits of catalepsy, a disease that induces a state indistinguishable from death, and that she may still be alive. Phillip rushes to the crypt only to find her coffin empty and bloody marks where she has clawed her way out. As he follows her trail of bloodstains through the murky passages, Madeleine, who has gone mad from her premature burial, attacks Roderick. During their struggle flames issue forth from the fireplace and spread throughout the house until it is entirely engulfed in fire. Roderick and Madeleine perish in the conflagration and Phillip escapes to witness the fiery end of the house of Usher and all its evil.

Producer/director Corman, who had lensed a number of low-budget horror, science fiction and other genre films aimed at a youth audience for American International Pictures, broke out of this milieu with this high-end production filmed in color and Cinemascope. Shooting in widescreen, anamorphic format and employing wide angle lenses, Corman made the modest sets appear much larger. Budgeted at a mere $200,000, the director creates a vivid atmosphere of gothic dread that is a worthy evocation of Poe's work. The fluid camerawork of ace cinematographer Floyd Crosby and the sumptuous set designs of Daniel Haller also contributed to the film's total effect. Screenwriter Richard Matheson (author of *I Am Legend* and *The Incredible Shrinking Man* as well as a number of episodes for TV's *The Twilight Zone*), expands Poe's rather brief story to feature length while being true to the original material. Horror superstar Vincent Price dominates the film with his performance as the decadent, aristocratic, platinum-haired Roderick Usher.

As in the best haunted house movies, the haunt itself is a major character. Like Hill House in *The Haunting*, the house is a living, evil entity that projects its malice into its human inhabitants. While phantoms do not directly stalk its halls, in a dream sequence Phillip is assailed by the ghosts of the Usher family that he recognizes from their portraits, and the house's physical attacks on his unwanted presence resemble poltergeist manifestations. The exterior of the house was rendered via a matte painting, and has a slightly two-dimensional appearance, while Daniel Haller's interiors are painted in dull browns and deep reds that connote gothic rot and decay to create one of the most vivid haunted houses, and the first haunt in a color film in the history of horror cinema. Footage of the flaming

Madeleine Usher (Myrna Fahey) is subjected to a premature burial in this poster for the first of Roger Corman's Poe adaptations, *House of Usher* (1960).

ceiling collapsing was highly dramatic and would be reused in several later films. *House of Usher* was a huge success, scoring among the five biggest box-office hits of 1960, and its seminal popularity ushered in a series of Corman Poe adaptations starring Vincent Price.

During that same year another horror film would be released that featured the most iconic haunt ever to appear in film. Alfred Hitchcock's *Psycho* (1960), a tale of lust, murder and psychological possession, took place against the backdrop of a spook house that was an integral part of the action. *Psycho* begins in Phoenix, Arizona where Marion Crane (Janet Leigh), disgruntled over her inability to marry her boyfriend Sam Loomis (John Gavin), steals $40,000 from her boss and skips town with the pilfered loot in a desperate scheme to start a new life somewhere with Sam. Driving aimlessly for days, a rainstorm forces her to seek lodging in the Bates Motel, operated by Norman Bates (Anthony Perkins), near a small town in Northern California. Overlooking the motel is a dark, foreboding gothic house inhabited by Norman's mother.

Phillip Winthrop (Mark Damon) and Madeleine Usher (Myrna Fahey) explore the darkened recesses of the *House of Usher* (1960).

After checking in, Marion shares a meal with Norman in the motel's office where they are surrounded by the stuffed birds created by Norman's taxidermy hobby. He appears to be a shy but charming young man who is dominated by his elderly mother, and the two engage in a pleasant conversation. After their chat Marion returns to her motel room where she is brutally murdered while taking a shower by what appears to be Mrs. Bates wielding a knife. In the aftermath of the murder, Norman cleans up all evidence of the crime and sinks her car, along with her body and the $40,000, into a nearby bog.

One week later, back in Phoenix, Marion's sister Lila (Vera Miles) is concerned about her sister's absence and contacts Sam, who is equally clueless about Marion's whereabouts. They are joined by another interested party, a private detective named Milton Arbogast (Martin Balsam), who has been hired to find Marion and the missing money. Arbogast checks every hotel and motel in the surrounding area and finally finds a clue at the Bates Motel near the small town of Fairvale in Northern California. The P.I. checks in with Sam and Lila by phone before trying to explore the Bates house, telling them he has seen a woman looking out of a window and wants to talk to her, but when he enters the house, he is stabbed to death by Norman's homicidal mother. After the second killing Norman hides a quarrelsome Mrs. Bates in the house's fruit cellar until things blow over.

When they don't hear back from Arbogast, Sam and Lila decide to investigate on their own and travel to Fairvale, where they check with the local sheriff (John MacIntire), who informs them that Norman and his mother led an isolated existence living in the Bates house together until about ten years ago, when Mrs. Bates became romantically involved with another man. Shortly thereafter, the lovers were found dead in bed together, poisoned in an apparent double suicide. When Lila protests that a woman was seen staring out of one of the house's windows, the Sheriff replies, "Well, if the woman up there is Mrs. Bates, then who's that woman buried out in Greenlawn cemetery?"

Returning to the motel, Sam and Lila decide to solve the mystery themselves and register at the motel as husband and wife. After checking into the same room where Marion had stayed, they find evidence that she had been there and Lila resolves to speak to Mrs. Bates. Sam distracts Norman in the motel office while Lila sneaks into the Bates house, but doesn't encounter Mrs. Bates until she finds the old woman seated on a chair in the fruit cellar. Attempting to speak to her, Lila discovers, to her horror, that it is only a grinning corpse that has been mummified by Norman's taxidermy skills. It is further revealed that Norman is a split personality who impersonated Mrs. Bates and wore her clothes while he committed the murders. Norman is taken into custody and a psychiatrist (Simon Oakland) expounds to Sam, Lila and the assembled law enforcement officers about Norman's dual personality and that he has now permanently become his mother. In the film's chilling epilogue, we see Norman sitting in a cell, speaking internal monologue in his mother's voice as his features dissolve into the dead woman's skull face.

Considered by critics to be Hitchcock's most powerful work, *Psycho* was a box-office smash and had a profound influence upon horror cinema. A raft of "slasher" films followed over the decades, from *The Texas Chainsaw Massacre* (1974) and *Halloween* (1976) to *Scream* (1996) and innumerable others. Hitch's directorial hand was never surer as he played the audience like a Stradivarius with a series of horrifyingly violent tableaux, although these scenes of mayhem are relatively tame by today's standards of blood and gore. The film's total effect was greatly enhanced by the brilliant editing of George Tomasini, the elegant storyboarding of Saul Bass and the screeching violins of composer Bernard Herrmann. Although its primarily a director's film, principals Janet Leigh, John Gavin, Vera Miles and Martin Balsam perform flawlessly, and Anthony Perkins' performance as the mother-obsessed psychopath is especially chilling. Joseph Stefano's masterful screenplay, derived from a novel by horror luminary Robert Bloch, was inspired by the real-life exploits of psycho Ed Gein, a murderer and grave robber who was fond of raiding the local cemetery to obtain body parts that he fashioned into horrid manikins made of human flesh.

One of the film's most eerie and enduring aspects is the Bates house itself, a brooding domain of terror that towers over the bland horizontal layout of the motel below and is a visual metaphor for the way that Mrs. Bates' dark personality dominates Norman's. The house was designed by art director Robert Clatworthy and production designer Joseph Hurley and was reportedly inspired by the 1925 painting "House by the Railroad" by artist Edward Hopper. This type of architecture was common in the Northern California locale where the film takes place, and is known as "California Gingerbread" or "California Gothic." While the exterior of the house appears old and decrepit, the interior sets were not rotting and cobwebby, but instead are clean and well-ordered because it is Mrs. Bates' house, not Norman's.

The Bates House set remained standing on the Universal backlot for years after the film's completion and has been moved and refurbished several times and later appeared in

Psycho killer Norman Bates (Anthony Perkins) poses in front of the iconic Bates house in this publicity still from *Psycho II* (1983).

a number of movies and television shows, from *Laramie* to *Murder She Wrote*. It was also re-used in the sequels *Psycho II* (1983), *Psycho III* (1986), *Psycho IV: The Beginning* (1990), as well as Gus Van Sant's 1998 color remake. Like *Rebecca*, *Psycho* is a modern gothic that features a haunted mansion, a ghost, and an insane relative concealed in a hidden room, and like *Rebecca* it is a psychological ghost story involving necrophilia and the possession of a weaker living personality by a more dominant dead persona. This is reflected in the relationship between mother's room, which is large and sumptuously furnished, and Norman's, which is small, cramped, and filled with toys and childish objects. The prestigious American Film Institute ranks *Psycho* as the 14th greatest movie of all time, and the Bates House is surely the most famous and iconic haunt in the history of the cinema.

Henry James' 1898 novella *The Turn of the Screw* is widely considered the greatest ghost story in the English language and was the basis for British director Jack Clayton's screen adaptation entitled *The Innocents* (1961). The film stars Deborah Kerr as Miss Giddens, a middle-aged woman who is hired as a governess by a wealthy London bachelor (Michael Redgrave) to look after his niece and nephew at Bly, his country estate. The children, Miles and Flora, were orphaned and left in his care, but he is "a very selfish fellow" who leads a bachelor lifestyle and has no desire to rear them. Accordingly, she is to have full authority over the children and is never to trouble him with any problems that may arise. He mentions that the previous governess, Miss Jessel, died unexpectedly a year ago and Miles was placed in a boarding school until a suitable replacement could be found.

Accepting the job, Miss Giddens travels to the sprawling estate at Bly and at first finds it a pleasant place where she bonds with her young charge Flora (Pamela Franklin) and the matronly housekeeper Mrs. Grose (Megs Jenkins). Oddly, Flora somehow knows that Miles is returning home before Miss Giddens receives a letter from the school to that effect for being a bad influence on the other students. When Miles (Martin Stephens) arrives at Bly he has no explanation for his dismissal, but the governess is charmed by the young boy's

The ghost of Peter Quint (Peter Wyngarde) haunts governess Miss Giddens (Deborah Kerr) in Jack Clayton's *The Innocents* (1961).

character, yet notes an odd precociousness in his mannerisms, which seem more adult than childlike. Once they are reunited, the siblings seem to drift off into their own shared separate reality.

One day Miss Giddens sees a strange man peering down at her from high atop the house's tower, but upon investigating finds only Miles tending to his flock of pigeons. Afterward, she finds a small photograph of the man who is identified as Peter Quint (Peter Wyngarde) by Mrs. Grose, who explains that he was the uncle's valet at Bly, but who is now dead. She further reveals that Quint and Miss Jessel were lovers, and that Quint was a wicked and sadistic man who abused her and may have corrupted the children. He died accidentally and afterward Miss Jessel drowned herself in the lake in grief. After hearing this, Miss Giddins begins to experience terrifying apparitions of the dead lovers; Quint appears outside a window and stares at her menacingly and Miss Jessel is seen standing in the reeds by the lake.

Miss Giddens comes to believe that the ghostly couple is trying to possess the children in order to continue their evil lives from beyond the grave, but Mrs. Grose is not so sure. The children's behavior becomes more bizarre as they exhibit cruelty to animals and Miles kisses the governess lasciviously on the lips. During a "performance" given by the children Miles recites a morbid poem about "my lord" who is "arisen" that includes the lines "What shall I say when his feet enter softly/leaving the marks of his grave on the floor?" Determined to exorcise the ghosts by forcing the children to confront them, when Miss Jessel's apparition appears at the lake once more she attempts to make Flora confess that she sees the phantom, but this only causes the child to go into a hysterical rage. Miss Giddens orders Mrs. Grose (who did not see the ghost) to remove Flora from Bly so she can be alone with Miles, but her second attempt at exorcism provokes a similar hysterical reaction in Miles that leads to tragic consequences for the boy.

Arguably the most exquisite and terrifying ghost story ever filmed, *The Innocents* draws the viewer into a claustrophobic vortex of fear punctuated by the appearances of Bly's two phantasms. Director Jack Clayton's pacing is superb, and he coaxes brilliant performances from the small cast of actors. As in *House of Usher*, the film was shot in Cinemascope and Clayton was obliged to compose the images in widescreen format. Working with his cinematographer Freddie Francis, colored gels and lenses painted black around the edges were used to conjure a feeling of extreme claustrophobia. Interior sets were very brightly lit in order to achieve enhanced depth of focus, a technique Greg Toland had used in *Citizen Kane*. Along with editor Jim Clark, Clayton employed elaborate overlapping dissolves in which multiple images fade into each other in a single shot which is particularly effective during an extended dream sequence. Natural sounds such as wind, rain and birdsongs are also used to subtly build auditory tension.

Much of the film's success can be ascribed to the riveting performances of a fine British cast. Acclaimed English actor Michael Redgrave projects a boorish selfishness while he manipulates the hapless Miss Giddens in the film's early scenes. Young Pamela Franklin imbues the role of Flora with equal measures of cruelty, otherworldliness and childish sweetness, while Megs Jenkins is perfectly cast as the stolid matron Mrs. Grose. The brunt of the film's acting burden is borne by Deborah Kerr, who masterfully carries the film with her measured performance as Miss Giddens, whose gradual descent into a web of supernatural terror is entirely believable. Her foil is provided by child actor Martin Stephens in a standout performance as the spirit-possessed Miles, whose dramatic interplay with Kerr provides most of the film's supernatural tension. Stephens had previously appeared in another sinister role as the leader of the human/alien hybrid children in *Village of the Damned* (1960).

The most serious problem with *The Innocents*, however, lies with its screenplay. Originally scripted by William Archibald from his 1950 stage adaptation of James' *The Turn of the Screw*, Clayton wished to expand the film's original concept from that of a ghostly haunting to that of a psychological thriller. Accordingly, Truman Capote was assigned to "Freudianize" the screenplay by rewriting it to make Bly's phantoms into figments of the governess' neurotic/erotic imagination. This unlikely scenario is belied by certain aspects of the plot. Why, for instance, does Miss Giddens hear a spectral voice calling Flora's name the moment she arrives at Bly, and how does Flora know that Miles is returning home before the notice of his dismissal arrives by post? And why does Miles recite his morbid verse about the ghost of Quint if he is not possessed? Psychologically, a person experiencing such vivid hallucinations would have to be severely schizophrenic or suffering from some severe physical illness. This focus on Miss Gidden's supposed sexual obsession with Quint (and Miles) would surely make the Victorian Henry James turn over in his grave.

Exterior shots of Bly were filmed at the Sheffield Park mansion in East Sussex, England, and interiors were lensed at Shepperton Studios in Surrey. The haunt is festooned with numerous mirrors, shadowy corridors and odd-looking statuary that grace the old dark house in which, as Flora says, "big rooms get bigger at night." Peter Wyngarde cuts a fearful figure as the ghost of Peter Quint, but somehow the apparitions of Miss Jessel (played by Clytie Jessop) are even more terrifying. Her ghost is seen in broad daylight, a forlorn figure dressed in black standing silently in the reeds out in the lake. These understated specters are more effective and believable than ghosts depicted via special effects in later films. As discussed in the introduction, James' ghostly tale was inspired by an allegedly true story related to him by the archbishop of Canterbury.

Director Robert Wise, who had begun his career directing the horror films *Curse of the Cat People* (1944) and *The Body Snatcher* (1945) for Val Lewton's RKO unit, returned to the genre with another high-class ghost story, *The Haunting* (1963). Based on acclaimed author Shirley Jackson's novel *The Haunting of Hill House*, the film begins with a montage of scenes depicting the tortured 90-year history of Hill House, a reputedly haunted mansion in a remote area of Massachusetts. Built by the wealthy religious fanatic Hugh Crain as his family estate, his first wife was killed in a carriage accident as she approached the house. Crain's second wife died in a fall down a flight of stairs under mysterious circumstances. When Crain died overseas the house was inherited by his daughter Abagail, who became a recluse confined to the house's nursery until she reached old age. The elderly Abagail hired a young woman as a caregiver, but she died calling for help while the caregiver was off dallying with her lover. The caregiver inherited the house, but went mad and hanged herself from the house's ornate spiral staircase.

The history of Hill House is being related by anthropologist Dr. John Markway (Richard Johnson) to its current owner, Mrs. Sanderson (Fay Compton), by way of explaining why he wants to rent the house from her. Dr. Markway is an expert on the supernatural who wishes to study the haunt in order to find "the key to another world." He proposes to conduct an experiment using a group of psychics he has selected in the hope that their mediumistic abilities will make them sensitive to the house's supernatural energies. Mrs. Sanderson agrees to the rental on the condition that her heir Luke be included to keep an eye on the proceedings.

Cut to the film's protagonist, Eleanor Vance (Julie Harris), a meek, middle-aged woman who leads a miserable existence living with her sister and her family in a tiny house. Upon receiving Dr. Markway's summons, she boldly steals the family's car and departs Boston for Hill House. A fantasy-prone individual, Eleanor imagines that she is embarking on a new life, but when she reaches her destination, she finds the haunt to be a dark forbidding place. Nevertheless, she enters Hill House and is soon joined by another member of the team, the witchy Theodora (Claire Bloom). The women are a study in contrasts: Theo is worldly and bohemian while Eleanor is shy and insecure. They are soon joined by young Turk Luke Sanderson (Russ Tamblyn) and Dr. Markway, who explains the nature of his experiment to them. Eleanor has been selected because of a poltergeist manifestation in her past, while Theo has been picked because of telepathic abilities which she has demonstrated in a laboratory setting.

It isn't long before the ghosts of Hill House come calling. At first only the two women are able to perceive the supernatural forces at work due to their psychic abilities. They are threatened one night by the terrifying sounds of something stalking through the halls and banging on the door to their room. On another occasion Eleanor hears voices and feels someone crushing her hand in a spectral grip. Soon the other members of the team begin to experience anomalous phenomena. So-called "cold spots" in the house are discovered by Markway in which the ambient temperature is far below normal, and the message "Help Eleanor come home" is found scrawled in chalk on one of the walls.

As Hill House exerts its influence on the investigators, its supernatural energies target the emotionally vulnerable Eleanor, who begins to feel "like a small creature swallowed by a monster." Tensions arise between Eleanor and Theo, who uses her telepathic abilities to goad the other woman by revealing her innermost thoughts about her romantic feelings concerning Dr. Markway. Eleanor's hopes are dashed, however, when Markway's wife Grace (Lois Maxwell) arrives at Hill House to join her husband. Lois is a skeptic who insists on spending the night in the nursery, "the black heart of the house." That night, as the team members try to sleep in the living room, the noisy spirit returns and this time it is heard by everyone. The ghost begins to pound on the parlor door, which bends outward unnaturally as it attempts to enter the room before stalking off to the nursery. When the noises abate the team enters the nursery only to find Mrs. Markway missing.

As the others frantically search for Markway's wife, Eleanor sinks further under the sway of the haunt. Unwilling to return to her dreary existence at her sister's, she begins to fantasize about staying at Hill House forever. She ascends the rickety spiral staircase in an apparent suicide attempt and is rescued by Markway but catches a glimpse of Grace's distraught face peering through a trapdoor. No longer willing to subject Eleanor to the destructive forces in the house, Markway orders her to leave immediately, but as she is driving away an invisible force takes control of the car and slams it into a tree, killing her instantly. In the aftermath, former skeptic Luke ruefully condemns Hill House, saying, "It should be burned down, and the ground sowed with salt."

Producer/director Robert Wise's faithful adaptation of Shirley Jackson's haunted house novel is a tour de force that stands as a milestone of supernatural horror. Working with

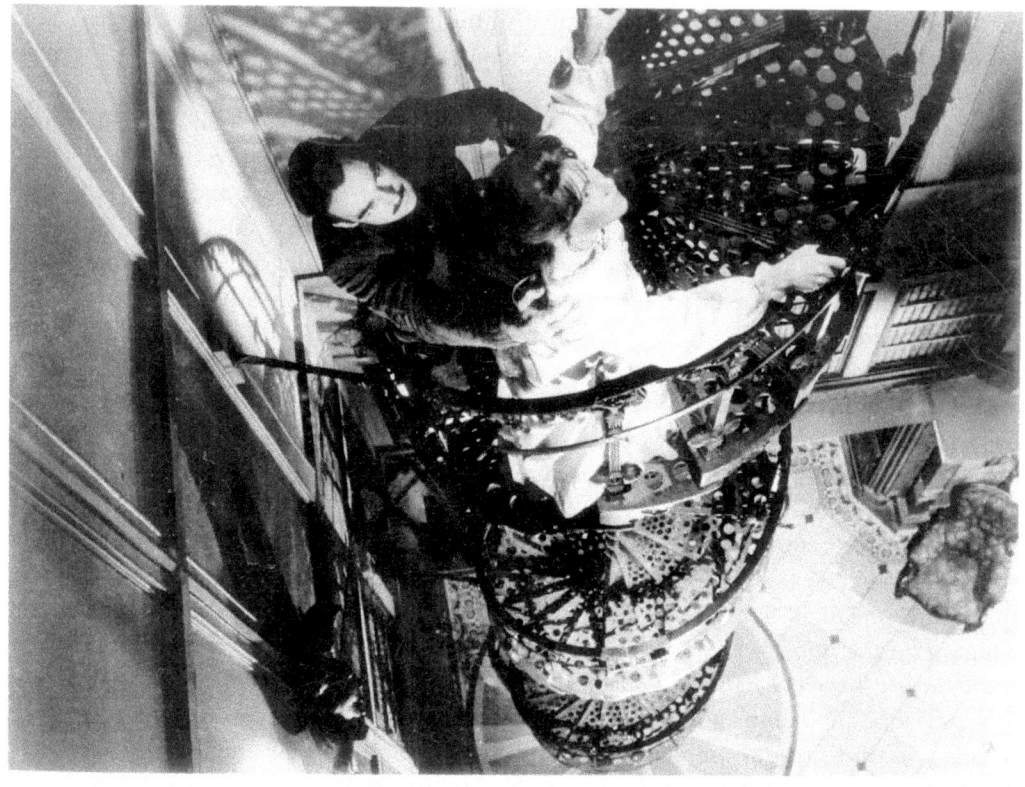

Dr. Markway (Richard Johnson) attempts to rescue psychic Eleanor Vance (Julie Harris) from Hill House's spiral staircase in Robert Wise's *The Haunting* (1963).

cinematographer David Boulton, Wise employed experimental techniques that were novel in a studio feature. Special infrared film was used to enhance the menacing stone structure of the Hill House exteriors. Like *House of Usher* and *The Innocents*, *The Haunting* was shot in widescreen Cinemascope format, and the haunt's interior spaces were further distorted by the use of a super wide angle 30mm Panavision lens that distorted the edges of the film frame and gave them a slightly rounded appearance, making them seem more confining and claustrophobic. High angles, low angles, subjective and hand-held camera techniques are all employed to great effect to achieve a sense of disorientation. Because the ghosts are not shown onscreen, elaborate sound effects such as disembodied voices and cacophonous banging are used to indicate their presence, and low-frequency abstract tones were used on the soundtrack to create a disquieting aural undertow. These many elements combine to create an eerie mood of uneasiness and dread that hangs over Hill House. Scenarist Nelson Gidding captures the fantastic essence of Shirley Jackson's novel and incorporates much of the author's elegant prose into the film's screenplay.

The spooky goings-on at the haunt provide a backdrop for the dramatic interplay between the characters, who are forced into close quarters with each other in the spook house. The main conflict is between the staid Eleanor and the worldly Theo, who is a lesbian and may want to seduce Eleanor. Theo uses her telepathic abilities to perceive Eleanor's weaknesses and exploit them mercilessly. Claire Bloom plays Theo with a catty wickedness, while Julie Harris' Eleanor is pitiful and ultimately suicidal. As the protagonist, Eleanor's fearful mental musings are conveyed to the audience via internal monologue as she descends into a maze of psychotic delusion. Harris was reportedly suffering through a bout of depression during filming and was alienated from Bloom, and this off-screen tension seems to have intensified their performances.

Like *House of Usher*, *The Haunting* is about a house that is "born bad" and carries a family curse more than it is about the haunt's ghostly inhabitants. Unlike the stereotypical haunted house tale, there is no mystery to clear up about the ghost's identities and motivations, and no exorcism of the house's evil forces in the final reel. Exteriors of Hill House were lensed at the gothic Ettington Park mansion in the village of Ettington, Warwickshire, in England. Interiors scenes were shot at MGM-British Studios, and the interior sets were built by art director Elliott Scott complete with ceilings, an unusual practice in set design as it limits vertical camera movement, but in this case the ceilings accentuated the claustrophobic nature of the rooms. Scott decorated the interiors with all manner of 19th century bric-a-brac, mirrors and odd statuary that clutter the film frame and further lend it a closed-in feeling. Hill House is a remarkable creation and still stands as one of the most memorable haunts in horror movie history.

The Haunting is often compared with *The Innocents* as to which is the more effective approach to the depiction of ghosts in the supernatural haunted house thriller. This dichotomy between the seen and the unseen is what horror writer Peter Straub refers to as the difference between "ghosts visible" and "ghosts invisible." In some actual cases of hauntings, ghosts appear as apparitions, while in others they are only manifested through sounds. Director Wise, taking his cue from the Val Lewton horror films of the 1940s such as *Cat People*, subscribed to the notion that an audience will be more frightened by what it does not see than what is actually shown, but this approach has its limitations. In his book on the horror genre *Danse Macabre*, Stephen King observes, "In a very real way, in spite of fine acting, fine direction, and the marvelous black and white photography of David Boulton, what we have in the Wise film ... is one of the world's few radio horror movies."[2] *The Haunting* opts for "ghosts invisible," and goes through great lengths never to show its phantoms, but as film is primarily a visual medium, it can be argued that the "ghosts visible" of *The Innocents* constitute a more effective way to convey terror to the audience.

The four years between 1960 and 1963 produced four all-time classics of the haunted house film, namely *House of Usher*, *Psycho*, *The Innocents* and *The Haunting*. These films are all milestones of horror cinema in a more general sense, and the Usher Mansion, the Bates House, Bly and Hill House were all unforgettable haunts that carved out a niche for the sub-genre after decades of fright films in which supernatural ghosts were anathema to Hollywood filmmakers.

A very different take on the haunted house was a New York City apartment building inhabited by a coven of devil worshippers in Roman Polanski's horror opus *Rosemary's Baby* (1968). The film opens with an establishing shot of the New York skyline, and as the credits roll the camera slowly pans across the rooftops of the city's Upper West Side until it glides over the medieval-looking gothic spires of the Dakota apartment complex (called the Bramford in the movie). A young couple, aspiring actor Guy Woodhouse (John Cassavetes) and his wife Rosemary (Mia Farrow) arrive at the Bramford to inspect a vacant apartment in the gloomy 19th century era complex. The building agent (Elisha Cook, Jr.) informs them that the previous tenant, an older woman, died suddenly, but Rosemary intuits that there is something not quite right about the place. For one thing, a heavy piece of furniture has been moved in front of an empty closet by the woman for no apparent reason.

Despite Rosemary's vague misgivings, they rent the apartment and move in. One night while doing the laundry in the building's creepy basement, she makes the acquaintance of Terry Gionoffrio (Angela Dorian), a pregnant runaway who has been taken in by the Castavets, an elderly couple who live on the same floor. Soon afterward, Terry takes a fatal fall out of one of the Bradford's windows and during the police investigation Rosemary meets Roman Castavet (Sidney Blackmer) and his wife Minnie (Ruth Gordon). The Castavets, who seem like an eccentric and meddlesome couple, insinuate themselves into the lives of Rosemary and Guy, but Rosemary begins to perceive that her husband has cozied up to the Castavets for reasons she cannot understand. She is also puzzled by weird chanting she hears coming through the thin walls from the Castavet's apartment next door.

Soon after establishing this unusual relationship with the odd couple, Guy unexpectedly gets a part in a play when the actor originally hired is suddenly stricken blind. Encouraged by this sudden boost to his career, Guy suggests that they try to have a baby, but on the night that they are attempting to conceive Minnie brings over a homemade desert that Guy aggressively insists she consume. Suspecting something, Rosemary only eats half of the confection, which contains a powerful soporific drug. Minnie's concoction puts her into a twilight state instead of full unconsciousness, and she remembers being lifted up and carried into the apartment next door, where the Castavets and other naked members of a Satanic cult are conducting a ritual. A figure approaches that at first resembles Guy but morphs into a scaly inhuman being that copulates with her before she blacks out. The next day Guy tries to convince her that her memory was just a dream she had after they made love, but Rosemary is not so sure.

Before long Rosemary discovers she is with child and the Castavets become intimately involved in her pregnancy, insisting she become the patient of eminent Park Avenue OB/GYN Dr. Sapperstein (Ralph Bellamy), who treats her with unusual herbs and formulas. As her suspicions deepen, Rosemary turns to a friend, an avuncular older man named Hutch (Maurice Evans), who is a writer and a man of learning. As he probes the identities of the Castavets, Hutch is killed in a hit and run accident but posthumously passes on the truth to Rosemary. The name Roman Castavet is an anagram for his true identity, Steven Marcato, the leader of an infamous devil cult at the Bramford.

Rosemary, who will soon give birth, knows that Guy is a member of the cult and suspects that they want her baby to use as a human sacrifice in a satanic ritual. She tries to run away but is caught by the cultists and goes into labor. Losing consciousness, she awakens in her bed and is told that her baby died, but becomes suspicious when she hears crying sounds coming from the Castavets' apartment. Taking a large kitchen knife, she gains egress through the secret passageway in her apartment closet to find Guy, the Castavets and other devil worshippers assembled around a black basinet adoring the demonic infant within in an obscene parody of the Christian Nativity. Although she is repulsed by the inhuman child, her maternal instincts eventually overcome her revulsion as she accepts the role of the mother of Rosemary's Baby.

Rosemary Woods (Mia Farrow) attempts to kill the child of Satan in Roman Polanski's *Rosemary's Baby* **(1968).**

This improbable tale, penned by popular novelist Ira Levin, was rendered into an incredibly faithful adaptation of the novel by director Polanski (in his first American film), who also scripted. Polanski's direction makes the unlikely plot work as he creates a mood of suspense and dread as the vulnerable Rosemary is trapped within a web of horror and betrayal in an intensely urban setting. The director allows the tension and unease to build slowly and subtly until the film's terrifying premise is fully realized. The narrative unfolds through Rosemary's subjective viewpoint as portrayed via a riveting performance by Mia Farrow, while John Cassavetes, best known for his roles in gritty crime melodramas, is perfectly cast as her sinister and duplicitous husband Guy. The distinguished British thespians Maurice Evans and Sydney Blackmer provide acting heft as the film's dueling gray eminences, while the inimitable Ruth Gordon steals many of the scenes she's in as the quirky and banal Satanist Minnie Castavet, a performance that earned her a Best Supporting Actress Oscar. Critical appreciation of the film has only grown over the years, and in retrospect it is widely considered one of the greatest horror films in the history of the genre.

Exteriors for the Bramford Apartments (which author Ira Levin named after *Dracula*'s author Bram Stoker) were shot on location at the Dakota Apartments on New York's Central Park West, where John Lennon of the Beatles was shot to death by Mark David Chapman in December 1980. The apartment building's interiors were shot in Paramount's Los Angeles studios, and were designed by art director Joel Schiller, production designer Richard Sylbert and set designer Robert Nelson. Polanski adeptly exploited the horrors of apartment living, as he had in his previous film, *Repulsion* and would do again in *The Tenant* (1976). Sounds waft through the paper-thin walls like ghostly voices from another realm, and the building's hallways are dark, drab and dingy. The story has several gothic elements, including the manipulation of an innocent woman by a wicked man, an evil abode with a secret passageway, a hidden room with a terrible secret, and a mysterious group with supernatural powers. Devil worshippers had previously infested haunted locales in *Seven Footprints to Satan* and *The Black Cat*.

Rosemary's Baby has a reputation as an accursed film due to a bizarre series of fatal misfortunes that befell several members of the production crew. In April of 1969, producer William Castle, director of *House on Haunted Hill* and *Thirteen Ghosts* and who had a cameo in the film, was taken to the hospital with severe kidney failure, reportedly crying out, "Rosemary, for God's sake, drop that knife" in a fit of toxic delirium before dying soon afterward. By a strange coincidence, the film's composer, Krzysztof Komeda, who was in the same hospital recovering from a head injury sustained during a motorcycle accident, would succumb to a blood clot in his brain by the end of the month. Most horribly, Polanski's wife, actress Sharon Tate, was brutally murdered while she was pregnant by members of Charles Manson's demented cult followers in Los Angeles a year after the film's release during their so-called "Helter Skelter" murder spree.

Just a few years later, the devil's minions would be hard at work once more in another classic of the horror film, *The Exorcist* (1972). The film opens with a prologue set in an archeological site in Iraq, where elderly priest Father Merrin (Max Von Sydow) receives intimations of a coming confrontation with the ancient evil of a Mesopotamian demon called Pazuzu. The action then shifts to a brownstone in Georgetown, a wealthy suburb of Washington, D.C., where movie star mom Chris MacNeil (Ellen Burstyn) is raising her daughter Regan (Linda Blair) as a single mother. For no apparent reason, Regan begins to exhibit strange, aberrant behavior and weird noises and other poltergeist activity start to manifest inside the house. Heavy pieces of furniture move around by themselves, while Regan's appearance alters into a livid mask of horror and she acquires preternatural abilities such as telepathy and superhuman strength. The child is subjected to a seemingly endless series of ordeals at the hands of doctors and specialists, but medical science is unable to ameliorate her condition.

As Regan descends into the horrors of full-blown demonic possession, the girl is implicated in the death of Chris' friend, film director Burke Dennings (Jack MacGowran), who was apparently hurled through one of the home's windows and down a steep flight of stairs to his death after being left alone with Regan. The murder is investigated by homicide detective Kinderman (Lee J. Cobb), who suspects Regan of the crime, and in desperation Chris appeals to Jesuit priest Damien Karras (Jason Miller) for permission to conduct an exorcism. At first the priest is skeptical, but he is soon convinced that the supernatural is at work after witnessing various anomalous phenomena, including telepathy, psychokinesis, reverse speech and frigid cold spots in Regan's room.

Armed with this evidence, Karras approaches the bishop of his diocese, who grants permission to conduct the exorcism and summons the more experienced Father Merrin to conduct the ceremony. All hell literally breaks loose as the two priests do battle with the demons for the body and soul of the child, and the exertion causes the ailing Father

Merrin to die from a heart attack. The embattled Karras continues on alone until he manages to make the demons leave Regan and possess him, whereupon he jumps out of the bedroom window to avoid harming the child and plummets down the same steep flight of stairs where Burke had died. In the aftermath, Regan is freed from all demonic influences and retains no memories of the event as the MacNeil family moves out of the accursed house.

The Exorcist would turn out to be one of the most popular and critically acclaimed horror films in the history of the genre. Director Friedkin delivers a cinematic tour de force that caused audiences to swoon and even undergo religious conversions. Friedkin utilizes some of the documentary filmmaking techniques he had used in *The French Connection* (1971) to impart a sense of realism about the proceedings, while at the same time conjuring a fantastic realm of demonic terror and darkness. Several scenes were shot at exterior locations in Georgetown and New York City to provide a realistic backdrop for the unnatural events occurring inside the MacNeil house. The film manages to exploit the physical "body horror" of Regan's affliction and combines it with the existential dread engendered by the supernatural horror film. Acting by principals Ellen Burstyn, Jason Miller, Linda Blair, Max Von Sydow and Lee J. Cobb is superb, and creates a dramatic framework that helps make the unusual situations of the narrative entirely believable. Ms. Burstyn in particular delivers an incredibly intense portrayal of a loving mother battling tooth and nail to save her innocent daughter from a force beyond her understanding.

As in *The Haunting*, an innovative use of sound was used to generate terror and suspense, such as the sounds of dogs growling and snarling at the end of the Iraq sequence, Regan's eerie "backwards speech" that translates into guttural grunts and animal howls when the tape is played in reverse and the loud asthmatic wheezing of the possessed girl. The film won an Oscar for Best Sound and was nominated for nine other awards, including Best Picture, Best Director, Best Actress and Best Supporting Actress, but its only other award was for Best Adapted Screenplay by William Peter Blatty, who scripted from his best-selling novel of the same name. As previously discussed, Blatty drew his inspiration from accounts of an actual case of possession and exorcism that had occurred in 1949 and centered around an adolescent boy named Roland Doe in a Maryland suburb of D.C. Church records, however, indicate that this was more likely a spectacular poltergeist manifestation rather than a bona fide case of demon possession, although the boy underwent the ritual of exorcism and was relieved of his affliction.

One of the most iconic images in the film was of Father Merrin arriving at the MacNeil residence at night amid shadows, swirling fog and a streetlight's eerie glow that was inspired by the 1954 painting "Empire of Light" by the French surrealist Rene Magritte. Exteriors of the "house of exorcism," an unremarkable red brick townhouse with white shutters, were shot on location in Georgetown, and the residence at 3600 Prospect Street has since become a tourist attraction for visitors to Washington. Interiors were filmed at the CECO studios in Manhattan, where set designer Jerry Wunderlich painted the walls a bilious, pale gray-green color that elicits a feeling of disquiet in the viewer. Much of the film takes place inside Regan MacNiel's tiny bedroom, including the climactic exorcism scenes, where the room is transformed into a battleground between the cosmic forces of good and evil. To depict a "cold spot" within the bedroom, the set was actually refrigerated so that the audience could see the actor's icy breaths. These cold spots (which also appear in *The Haunting*)

Father Merrin (Max Von Sydow) arrives at the MacNeil townhouse in Georgetown to confront demonic forces in *The Exorcist* (1972).

have been observed by parapsychologists studying haunted houses and poltergeist outbreaks and are thought to be caused by the ghostly entities absorbing heat energy from the environment in order to cause the movement of objects and other physical manifestations.

Like *Rosemary's Baby*, *The Exorcist* was plagued with a series of bizarre misfortunes and deaths of cast members. During shooting, a bird accidentally flew into a circuit box, causing the MacNeil set to burn down. Shortly after shooting was completed, Jack Mac-Gowran, who played Burke Dennings, and Vasiliki Mailros, who portrayed Father Karras' mother, both passed away. Ironically, both their characters also died in the movie, and Jason Miller's son was nearly killed in a motorcycle accident. The MacNeil house itself was destroyed (via special effects) during a violent earthquake unleashed by demonic forces at the conclusion of the inane sequel, *Exorcist II: The Heretic* (1977).

In late October of 1974, famed horror writer Stephen King and his wife spent a night at the Stanley Hotel in Estes Park, Colorado, located just outside the entrance to Rocky Mountain National Park. It was the last day of the season and most of the guests had left before the hotel was due to shut down for the winter. King reportedly had horrible nightmares and saw visions in the hotel mirrors, during his stay, and these experiences inspired him to write his 1977 novel *The Shining*, which was set in a haunted hotel abandoned during the off-season. The novel was a popular success, and the acclaimed filmmaker Stanley Kubrick, best known for his atomic satire *Dr. Strangelove* (1964) and his visionary science fiction classic *2001: A Space Odyssey* (1968), adapted the King novel for the screen in a big budget version of *The Shining* (1980).

The story centers around failed writer and recovering alcoholic Jack Torrance (Jack Nicholson), who accepts a job as the winter caretaker of the Overlook Hotel in an isolated location high in the Rockies. Manager Stuart Ullman (Barry Nelson) explains that the Overlook is snowed inn for weeks at a time during the winter months, and that a previous caretaker named Grady went crazy from cabin fever and murdered his family in the hotel. Despite any misgivings, Jack accepts the job, hoping that the severe isolation of his surroundings will allow him to complete a novel he is writing.

Jack moves his wife Wendy (Shelly Duvall) and his young son Danny (Danny Lloyd) to the Overlook on closing day, where Danny meets the hotel's charming head chef Dick Hallorann (Scatman Crothers), with whom he shares an instant telepathic bond. Hallorann explains that this psychic link is called "the shining," and that some of the hotel's rooms have a "shine" to them and should be avoided, especially room 237. Despite the luxury of the rest of the resort, the Torrances are installed in a drab, cramped apartment in the servants' quarters. The hotel closes and Hallorann departs for his winter digs in Florida as the Torrance family tries to adjust to their new surroundings inside the cavernous hotel.

Danny Torrance (Danny Lloyd) tells his mother Wendy (Shelly Duvall) about his ghostly encounters inside the Overlook Hotel in Stanley Kubrick's adaptation of Stephen King's horror novel *The Shining* (1980).

The snows arrive during the following month, causing the telephone lines to fail and rendering the Overlook incommunicado with the outside world except for a shortwave radio. Snowbound inside the vast structure, Danny's "shining" begins to reveal apparitions of the Overlook's ghostly inhabitants to him. While riding his tricycle through the hotel's seemingly endless corridors he encounters the ghosts of Grady's murdered twin daughters, who invite him to come and play with them. Then, while riding past the dread room 237, he finds the door ajar and enters, and is traumatized by seeing what he describes as a "crazy woman" in the room. When Jack investigates, he discovers a naked young woman in the bathtub who tries to seduce him before she transforms into the ghost of an old woman (Billie Gibson), who died in the room as he flees in disgust.

As the ghosts begin to manifest themselves more boldly, Jack comes under their sway, camping out in the hotel's grand ballroom where he is served by phantom bartender Lloyd (Joe Turkel) and goaded into violence by the ghost of Grady (Philip Stone), who appears to him as a men's room attendant. In the meantime, Hallorann has perceived that something is wrong at the Overlook through his telepathic link with Danny and departs Florida for Colorado. While he is enroute, Jack falls completely under the evil influences of the hotel's spooks and attacks his wife and child with intent to commit homicide. As he attacks his family, Wendy and Danny barricade themselves inside their apartment's bathroom and Jack starts to hack his way through the door with an axe. He is interrupted by Hallorann, who has ridden to their rescue on a rented snowcat only to be chopped down by Jack wielding the axe. While Jack is distracted, Danny slips outside through the bathroom window and is pursued through the hotel's hedge maze, and Wendy wanders through the haunted hotel where she encounters several ghostly apparitions. Danny craftily eludes his father, who freezes to death in the maze, and afterward Wendy and Danny flee the hotel in Hallorann's snowmobile. The film's final shot shows Jack's image in an old photograph grinning at the audience, indicating that he has become one more of the Overlook's ghosts.

Audiences awaited the coming of *The Shining* with bated breath as they looked forward to the melding of Stanley Kubrick's visionary genius and Stephen King's contemporary horror. Unfortunately, Kubrick, who reportedly was not overly familiar with the genre, produced a horror film that was by turns arty and ridiculous and scrupulously un-scary. A big problem is Jack Nicholson's over-the-top portrayal of Jack Torrance, who commences his scenery-chewing nuts-boy routine before the family car even arrives at the Overlook. Nicholson's performance so dominates the film that he leaves little room for the other actors to operate in. Kubrick, who adapted King's book along with co-scripter Diane Johnson, made many changes to the source material that fans were unhappy with. Among them was King himself, who called it a maddening, perverse and disappointing film. Some of the visuals were mystifying or downright comical such as a scene in which torrents of blood pour from a hotel elevator, Danny speaking as his alternate personality Tony croaking out the nonsense word "redrum" (spell it backwards) and a shot of Nicholson frozen like a human popsicle inside the hedge maze at the movie's conclusion. On the other hand, if you're not looking for haunted house thrills and chills, it's entertaining to watch Nicholson go bat guano crazy, chase Shelly Duvall around the place and deliver the film's most famous line, "Here's Johnny!"

In addition, *The Shining* depicts some of the most banal and least terrifying ghosts in horror film history. The apparition of the Grady twins, for instance, was copied from a well-known picture by acclaimed art photographer Diane Arbus that rendered the scene

Jack Torrance (Jack Nicholson, left) is served double shots of "redrum" by the Overlook's spectral bartender Lloyd (Joe Turkel) in *The Shining* (1980).

annoyingly self-referential. Shots of the naked old woman's ghost from room 237 are alternately revolting and comical. Grady's ghost, who is depicted as a cultured, uniformed men's room attendant rather than a madman who slaughtered his family, likewise fails to elicit shudders. Lloyd, the Overlook's spectral bartender, is perhaps the blandest ghost of all as he serves up double shots of "redrum" to Jack while making small talk.

Outside of Nicholson's histrionic performances, the next most memorable character in *The Shining* is the Overlook Hotel itself. Taking a cue from *The Haunting*, King's tale is set in an accursed place where an evil force dwells that reaches out to ensnare the living. Eleanor Vance and Jack Torrance are unstable individuals who are seduced and ultimately absorbed into the netherworlds of Hill House and the Overlook Hotel, where they wind up as one of a number of resident spooks. The Timberline Lodge, located on Mt. Hood in Oregon, provided the exterior locations for the Overlook, but the interiors of the hotel were shot entirely on soundstages at EMI Elmstree Studios in Hertfordshire, England. Set designer Roy Walker travelled all over America taking pictures of hotels that he passed on to Kubrick, and much of the Overlook's décor was based on that of the Ahwahnee Hotel in Yosemite National Park.

Kubrick wanted to create a filmic environment that was a departure from the familiar gothic haunt and instead fashioned his contemporary house of shadows into the vast spaces of an empty resort hotel. The characters are small figures in an interior landscape that are overwhelmed by the enormous architecture and endless labyrinthine corridors of the Overlook. Kubrick's massive sets included the "Gold Room," the Overlook's immense ballroom, the spacious "Colorado Lounge," the hotel's main foyer and a full-sized mock-up of the Timberline's façade. The director made extensive use of the newly-invented Stedicam, a device that enabled moving camera shots to be filmed without the use of cumbersome tracks and dollies. Critics have pointed out that the Overlook's interior architecture doesn't make sense. Like San Jose's Winchester Mystery House, there are doors and staircases that lead nowhere, windows in impossible locations and other confusing spatial discrepancies, and like the haunted house in the novel *House of Leaves*, the structure seems to be larger on the inside than on the outside. These discontinuities were deliberately made so as to create a disquieting sense of space in the viewer. In addition to its architecture, Kubrick also used garish institutional colors, such as the intense red décor used in the men's room scene. The Overlook was the most expensive, innovative and elaborate haunt ever conceived or constructed for a film, but unfortunately, not the most effective in generating supernatural terror. Steven Spielberg's science fiction thriller *Ready Player One* (2018) featured a re-creation of *The Shining*'s haunted hotel as a simulated environment inside a futuristic computer game.

The Stanley Hotel, where King had originally been inspired to write *The Shining*, has itself become a haunted attraction. Guests can stay in room 217, where King spent the night and conceived of the novel and perhaps catch a glimpse of a phantom or two. Although the hotel has no history of violence or other weirdness, some psychics and paranormal investigators claim they have detected spirits within its environs. In 1997, King supervised a made-for-TV remake of *The Shining* that was filmed at the Stanley, and the author would revisit the notion of the haunted hotel in a short story that was filmed as *1408* (2007).

As discussed in the Introduction, a poltergeist is a mischievous spook that is fond of causing extensive physical damage to a household it has infested. Unlike conventional hauntings, poltergeist manifestations are short-lived and are not confined to a specific location, but instead attach themselves to a particular person, who is referred to as a "focus," and is usually a young person around the age of puberty. Unlike hauntings that continue on for long periods of time, poltergeist outbreaks tend to last for only a few weeks, but they can cause spectacular physical effects involving fire, water, electricity and the disappearance and reappearance of solid objects, or *apports*. This ghostly phenomenon was the basis for the film *Poltergeist* (1982), a big budget extravaganza produced by Hollywood wunderkind Steven Spielberg and directed by horror filmmaker Tobe Hooper.

Set in a suburban swath of newly-built tract housing in the Southern California community of Cuesta Verde Estates, the story centers around the "typical American family" of Steven Freeling (Craig T. Nelson), his wife Diane (JoBeth Williams) and their children Dana (Dominique Dunne), Robbie (Oliver Robbins) and Carol Anne (Heather O'Rourke). Steven is a real estate salesman who was instrumental in the development of Cuesta Verde, while Diane is a stay-at-home mom who cares for the kids. The Family's suburban bliss is punctured when little Carol Anne starts communing with the "TV people," strange entities who dwell inside the Freeling's television set as the child proclaims, "They're here." Soon afterward weird physical phenomena assail the home as silverware bends, furniture moves by itself and anomalous electrical effects begin to plague the household. During a thunderstorm a tree seems to come alive and smashes its way into Robbie's room. Things really go bump in the night as Carol Anne, who has a mediumistic sensitivity to the spooks, gets transported into a phantom dimension where she can be heard but not seen.

Frantic to get their daughter back, the Freelings turn to UC Irvine parapsychologist Dr. Lesh (Beatrice Straight), who brings along her assistant ghostbusters Ryan (Richard Lawson) and Marty (Martin Casella). The paranormal researchers witness a maelstrom of objects swirling through the air in Carrie Anne's room, including a light bulb that screws itself into a lamp socket and a vinyl record being played by the pointed end of a child's compass. After setting up their scientific instruments to record the phenomena, Dr. Lesh advises the Freelings that the disturbances are being caused by a poltergeist rather than a traditional ghost in a haunted house. She also admits that science cannot help their situation and suggests they consult a medium who has "cleaned many houses."

The pint-sized "extraordinary clairvoyant" Tangina Barrons (Zelda Rubinstein) arrives at the house to proclaim that their daughter is still alive in some strange netherworld where she is being menaced by an entity called "The Beast." Under the psychic's direction, the Freelings discover a pathway into the other dimension and manage to bring Carol Anne back to our reality, whereupon Tangina proclaims, "This house is clean." At first it seems that their paranormal troubles are over, but Steven learns from his boss Mr. Teague (James Karin) that their house was built atop an ancient Indian burial ground, and that the bodies are still buried under the foundations of the home. Spending their last night in the house before moving out, the family is assaulted by the ghostly forces once more. Robbie is attacked by a grinning clown doll that comes to life and an earthquake opens up a pit in the yard and Diane falls in, where she is assailed by rotting corpses that spill out of their coffins. Steven arrives in time to rescue his family as they watch their home fold in upon itself and vanish into the other dimension.

The Freeling family (left to right) Oliver Robbins, Craig T. Nelson, JoBeth Williams and Dominique Dunne confront ghostly goings-on inside their suburban home in Tobe Hooper's *Poltergeist* (1982).

Released during the "Spielberg Summer" of 1982 that also saw the release of his mega-hit *E.T.*, *Poltergeist* proved to be popular with critics and audiences alike. There was, however, a dispute over whether Spielberg or the film's nominal director Tobe Hooper actually directed the film which was resolved in favor of Hooper by the Director's Guild, but the film seems to have more of a distinctly Spielbergian flavor. While it's well acted and directed, *Poltergeist*'s strong suit is the complex and expensive special effects provided by Industrial Light & Magic that serve to bring the spooks and ghoulies to vivid life in a way that had never been done before on the big screen. ILM made a tree come alive, showed a man tearing his face off, depicted a room full of objects floating in the air and conjured a ghostly "Beast" from another dimension. On the minus side the screenplay by Spielberg and Michael Grais tends toward the maudlin, and the notion of a little girl trapped in another dimension seems to have been cribbed from an episode of the TV series *The Twilight Zone* entitled "Little Girl Lost" that aired in 1962. The film was nominated for Academy Awards for Best Score, Best Sound and Best Visual Effects but did not win in any category.

Poltergeist has affinities with another contemporary haunted house movie, 1979's *The Amityville Horror* (to be discussed in Chapter Six). Both films featured an American family who move into what seems to be an ordinary house that turns out to be haunted and transforms into the portal to a hellish otherworld. In both films the reason for the haunting is that the houses were built atop an Indian burial ground. But while *Amityville* claimed to be based on a true story, *Poltergeist* dispensed with any pretense of parapsychological verisimilitude in favor of a completely fantastic premise that had little to do with real-life poltergeist manifestations. In one scene, however, chairs are moved and stacked up in a playful fashion, while another shows *apported* jewelry cascading through the home's downstairs ceiling from a room upstairs. Oddly, director Hooper claims to have experienced poltergeist activity as a teenager after the death of his father.

The film inspired two sequels, *Poltergeist II: The Other Side* (1986) and *Poltergeist III* (1988), as well as a lame 2015 remake directed by Gil Kenan. Like *Rosemary's Baby* and *The Exorcist*, the *Poltergeist* films have a reputation for being accursed because of deadly misfortunes that befell the cast members. Dominique Dunne, who portrayed the Freelings' teenage daughter Dana, was murdered by her live-in boyfriend in November of 1982, and Heather O'Rourke, who played little Carol Anne in all three movies, died of complications from a congenital birth defect shortly before the release of *Poltergeist III*. The so-called "*Poltergeist* Curse" was thought to be due to effects technicians reportedly using actual human remains in the scenes of rotting corpses popping out of their coffins during the film's gruesome climax.

These classics of the haunted house film represent the pinnacle of the filmmaker's art in creating ghostly environments that elicit chills from movie audiences. Adapted from the works of some of the masters of horror fiction such as Edgar Allan Poe, Henry James, Robert Bloch, Shirley Jackson and Stephen King, they were executed by some of filmdom's most talented directors, including Alfred Hitchcock, Stanley Kubrick, Robert Wise, Roger Corman, Edgar G. Ulmer, William Friedkin, Jack Clayton and Tobe Hooper. Windward House, the House of Usher, Bly, the Bates House, Hill House, the Dakota, the Overlook Hotel and the other haunts represent the most macabre realms and terrifying spaces ever seen on the big screen.

Chapter Five

A Haunting We Will Go: 1940s–1980s

Horror returned to movie screens during the 1950s, after a brief hiatus when the genre had been placed on hold at the end of the classic horror film cycle that ended in 1946. The early part of the decade was dominated by a new breed of fear film, science fiction horror. The advent of the atom bomb, advances in space flight, the perils of radiation and the curious phenomenon of flying saucers provided ample inspiration for screenwriters to create novel terrors such as mutants, giant bugs, saucer men, prehistoric reptiles and homicidal robots. Later in the decade, however, the supernatural horror movie made a comeback, along with the haunted house film, a trend that continued well into the 1960s with the coming of Hammer Films, American International Pictures, William Castle's productions and the work of the Italian gothic directors.

A harbinger of things to come was a modest British effort produced by the independent studio Gainsborough Pictures entitled *A Place of Our Own* (1945), starring the popular matinee idol of the time James Mason. Set in England in 1906, the story revolves around the retired middle-aged businessman Henry Smedhurst (Mason) and his wife Emilie (Barbara Mullen), who purchase a manor, Bellingham House, for a suspiciously low price (this is always a bad sign). The house has been vacant for the last 40 years, but the Smedhursts quickly settle in and Henry hires Annette Allenby (Margaret Lockwood), an amiable young woman, to be a female companion for his wife. When the Smedhursts give a housewarming party, however, they learn from the local guests that the Bellingham House has a dubious history. Four decades ago, its last resident, Miss Elizabeth Harkness, was found dead from poison in the house, and suspicions fell on her caretakers, Mr. and Mrs. Abbott, who inherited the estate, but the death was ultimately ruled a suicide. The Abbotts never lived in the house themselves, but left England for America and died during the journey when their ship sank.

The Smedhursts practically adopt the vivacious Annette as a surrogate daughter, and the young girl soon falls in love with the town physician, Dr. Robert Selbie (Dennis Price). Bellingham House, however, begins to have a strange effect on Annette. She goes into trance states that make her feel as if someone else has lived inside her body for a while. She begins speaking in another woman's voice and hears eerie music being played on the piano. Worst of all, her health starts to deteriorate and none of Dr. Selbie's remedies can help her. The staid Henry slowly comes to accept the supernatural truth that Annette has become possessed by the spirit of Elizabeth Harkness, who was a sickly invalid, and that if the ghost is not exorcised Annette will die.

Searching for answers, Henry contacts Police Constable Hargreaves (Gus McNaughton), who briefs him on aspects of the Harkness case. He identifies a physician named Dr. Marsham as the doctor who was treating Elizabeth and was rumored to be in love with her, but who moved away long ago. As Annette's health worsens, the Constable searches for and finally locates Dr. Marsham, who sets out for Bellingham by train with all due dispatch. Marsham (Ernest Thesinger), a strange, shadowy figure, arrives at the manor late at night and is immediately escorted through the darkened halls to Annette's bedchamber, where he insists on going in to see her alone. When the Smedhursts enter the room sometime later there is no trace of Dr. Marsham and Annette has been restored to health and rid of Elizabeth's spirit. Afterwards, the Constable informs Henry that Marsham had been found dead on the train as Henry realizes that it was Marsham's ghost who had come to visit Elizabeth one last time. The film ends on a happy note as Annette and Dr. Selbie prepare for their marriage.

Made just one year after 1944's *The Uninvited*, there are a number of plot similarities between the two works, including a couple who purchase an abandoned manor at a cut-rate price, and a young woman who is brought into the haunt and becomes possessed by its ghost. Adapted for the screen by scenarist Brock Williams from a novel by Sir Osbert Sitwell, *A Place of Our Own* is a genteel English ghost story that plays more like a drama than a horror film. Director Bernard Knowles does little to establish an eerie mood by using chiaroscuro lighting setups, unusual angles and other fear-inducing techniques, and instead opts for conventionally lit medium shots more appropriate to a dramatic presentation. The one exception occurs in the last few minutes of the film during Dr. Marsham's ghostly visitation. A fine cast of seasoned British actors sustain the viewer's interest, particularly the performances of star James Mason and Ernest Thesiger, who had appeared in the horror classic *The Old Dark House*.

The film hews closely to the standard haunted house formula in which a property with a dubious past is purchased at a reduced price, ghostly happenings occur that lead to an investigation into their underlying cause, and an action is taken that exorcises the earthbound spirit that resolves the situation. It also contains the theme of lovers who are eventually united in death. Bellingham House is not the typical decrepit gothic manse, but instead is depicted as a cozy British domicile. The haunt's resident ghost manifests itself not externally as an apparition, but via the possession of a living person, although the most effective sequence in the film involves Dr. Marsham's invasive visit from outside the house.

Another quirky British haunted house thriller was an omnibus horror film with the misleading title *Three Cases of Murder* (1954). Taking a page from the similarly-themed British thriller *Dead of Night* (1945), the film combined three separate segments by three different writers and directors. The second part, "You Killed Elizabeth," was a straight whodunit, and the third, "Lord Mountdrago," was about a man who can enter other people's dreams and starred Orson Welles. The first tale, however, was an unusual haunted house story about a haunt that exists inside a painting entitled "In the Picture."

The film begins with the sound of breaking glass inside an art gallery as a man wearing 19th century clothes suddenly appears in front of a painting. The man, referred to as "Mr. X" in the credits (played by Alan Badel), seats himself in front of the painting, which depicts a rutted road stretching through foggy ground to a grim-looking house in the distance in the middle of a desolate waste surrounded by withered trees. As Mr. X sits admiring the picture, which is simply entitled "Landscape—Artist Unknown," curator Mr. Jarvis (Hugh

Pryce) is leading a tour group through the gallery and notices the broken glass. After the group passes by, Jarvis starts up a conversation with Mr. X, and they converse about the "empty coldness" of the "masterpiece of the mysterious." Mr. X states his opinion that the painting's composition is out of balance, and needs to be corrected by showing a light in one of the windows. Jarvis comments that the glass protecting the picture has been broken several times before in an anomalous fashion. X invites Jarvis to examine the painting more closely, and as the camera's viewpoint moves slowly toward the picture, the two men are drawn inside of it. They travel down the path, through the fog, to the front door in a beautifully staged visual illusion.

On the inside, the house is a gothic realm filled with *objects d'art* that have been pilfered from the museum and is set at odd angles with a cold wind continually blowing. Jarvis is introduced to the other denizens of the haunt, a female called the Woman (Leueen Mac Grath) and the eccentric Mr. Snyder (Eddie Byrne), whose hobbies are butterfly collecting and taxidermy. It isn't long before Jarvis learns that the house inside the painting is a kind of purgatory, that all the inhabitants are ghosts, and that Mr. X is the artist who painted the picture. What X is after is a book of matches that Jarvis has brought with him that will enable him to complete the painting.

Unfortunately, Jarvis is out of matches, and Mr. X is forced to bargain with Snyder for a precious candle and a light. Jarvis accepts a drink of "punch" from the woman, and afterwards finds he is paralyzed. As the terror of his situation dawns on Jarvis, Mr. X offers him to Snyder as a taxidermy project for his "trophy room." While Snyder takes Jarvis' measurements, Mr. X prepares to light the candle and place it in the window. The viewpoint shifts to the outside of the house once more as Jarvis' death scream is heard and a light appears in one of the windows. Next, we see Mr. X breaking the glass from inside the painting and materializing in the museum gallery once more. This time he strikes up a conversation with a young woman (Ann Hanslip), to whom he opines that the painting's composition is out of balance and needs a "delicate statue" to be placed in one of the windows. The two begin their journey into the picture and it is implied that Mr. X will claim another victim in his never-ending quest to complete the painting.

This little gem of a short film is built around an intriguing and entirely original conception of a haunt that exists entirely inside an accursed work of art and is inhabited by dead souls. Lensed by British director Wendy Toye from an original screenplay by Donald Wilson, "In the Picture" which runs for about 30 minutes, has the feeling of an episode of the classic TV series *The Twilight Zone*. The transition scene in which the actors magically enter the painting is brilliantly executed by cinematographer Georges Perinal. Director Toye renders the interior of the haunted house using tilted angles and dramatic lighting to create a domain of fear and claustrophobia in this limbo of the lost. A fine British cast brings the unusual story to life, and the performances of Alan Badel (who appears in all three segments of the film) as the sinister spirit Mr. X, and Hugh Pryce as the hapless Jarvis, are particularly effective.

Producer/director William Castle, who fancied himself a junior-league Alfred Hitchcock, churned out a series of gimmick-laden horror thrillers during the 1950s and 60s. One of his better efforts was *House on Haunted Hill* (1958), starring Vincent Price, Hollywood's premier horror star of the period. Price plays eccentric millionaire Fredrick Loren, who invites five strangers to attend a "party" at what the house's owner, Watson Pritchard (Elisha

Cook, Jr.), describes as "the only really haunted house in the world." In addition to Pritchard, the other attendees include psychiatrist Dr. David Trent (Alan Marshal), gossip columnist Ruth Bridges (Julie Mitchum), test pilot Lance Schroeder (Richard Long) and secretary Nora Manning (Carol Craig). Also in attendance is Loren's wife Annabelle (Carol Ohmart), for whom the "haunted house party" is being thrown. "There'll be food and drink and ghosts, and perhaps even a few murders," Loren quips to the audience. It soon becomes apparent that there is bad blood between Loren and Annabelle, as two of his former wives have died under mysterious circumstances.

The guests arrive for the party during the nighttime at the unusual-looking structure in a line of cars that resembles a funeral procession. Once they are assembled, Loren explains that he is offering each of them $10,000 if they opt to remain in the house all night. At the stroke of midnight, the house will be locked down until dawn, and none of the guests will be able to leave. Loren has prepared seven miniature coffins, one for each of them, containing a .45 automatic for self-defense. Pritchard takes the guests on a tour of the haunt, explaining that seven people have been murdered in the house, and shows them the wine cellar, which contains a pit filled with acid used by a previous tenant to dispose of a body.

Spooky happenings soon assail the guests but center around Nora. She finds a severed head inside a travelling case, discovers Annabelle's corpse hanging by its neck, and, most horribly, watches as Anabelle's ghost materializes outside her window and wraps her rope around Nora's ankles. It is eventually revealed that Annabelle has faked her death and is colluding with Dr. Trent to gaslight Nora with the goal of having her kill Loren. Their plan succeeds when Nora finds herself in the wine cellar and sees Loren approaching her with his gun drawn and shoots him dead with her own automatic before fleeing the scene. Trent arrives to throw Loren's body into the acid vat, but the lights go out and the sounds of a struggle are heard, followed by a splash. When Annabelle goes down to the wine cellar to check on Trent, she is instead confronted by a skeleton that emerges from the vat and taunts her in Loren's voice. Terrified, she accidentally falls into the acid, whereupon Loren emerges holding a stringed contraption he used to manipulate the skeleton. As the other guests arrive on the scene to check out Nora's story, Loren explains that he was

Vincent Price (lower right) presides over the spooky goings-on at "the only really haunted house in the world" in this poster for William Castle's *House on Haunted Hill* (1958).

playing a game of murder with his wife and Trent, and is now ready to let justice decide his fate. Pritchard, however, observes that there are now two more ghosts inhabiting the House on Haunted Hill.

While it's clearly aimed at a juvenile and drive-in audience, Castle's spook show has plenty of gothic atmosphere and even a few genuine shocks, including a scene in which Nora unexpectedly encounters a frightening old hag who turns out to be Mrs. Slydes (Leona Anderson), one of the house's caretakers. Mrs. Slydes does not appear to walk, but instead seems to glide across the floor in a ghostly fashion. The screenplay by Robb White harks back to the mystery house movies of the 20s and 30s, complete with a clutching hand and secret passageways, and the film is as much a murder mystery as a haunted house chiller. Vincent Price, at the height of his horror movie career, is wonderfully sinister as the demented millionaire, while Carol Ohmart matches his villainy with her performance as his cold, homicidal wife. Veteran character actor Elisha Cook, Jr., adds a quirky touch as the house's resident ghost whisperer who ends the film with the dire words "They'll be coming for me—soon they'll be coming for you."

Exteriors of the haunt were shot at the Ennis House, a photogenic structure built by acclaimed architect Frank Lloyd Wright in 1924 that has been used for a number of films over the years, including Ridley Scott's *Blade Runner* (1982). The building's horizontal architecture was inspired by Pre-Columbian Mayan architecture, and also provided the design template for the futuristic mausoleum in *The Black Cat* (1934). The interiors were more conventionally gothic, replete with cobwebs, odd bric-a-brac and assorted statuary. Oddly, poster art for the film featured an illustration of a four-story building in the Romanesque style. While no actual ghosts make an appearance, the sounds of spooky moans and rattling chains on the soundtrack suggest their presence. As was his wont, Castle paired every one of his films with a promotional gimmick, which in this case was something called "Emergo," an effect that consisted of a plastic skeleton rigged to sail over the heads of the audience by an elaborate system of ropes and pulleys. Like many of Castle's gimmicks, it was only deployed in a small number of venues and proved to be of dubious value in eliciting horror movie thrills.

Another haunted house gimmick was used in the cheapie Howco International production of *Terror in the Haunted House* (a.k.a. *My World Dies Screaming*, 1958). It was advertised as being "The First Picture In ... Psycho-Rama! The Fourth Dimension!" The film's protagonist is Sheila Justin (Cathy O'Donnell), newly married to her husband Philip (Gerald Mohr), who is undergoing psychiatric treatment in Switzerland. Sheila is suffering from recurring nightmares about a creepy old house she has never seen, "a moldering tombstone to a world that died." The film opens with a dream sequence that borrows from the opening of *Rebecca* as Sheila's viewpoint drifts through the old house as her voice over narrates her fearful reactions.

Sheila is set to relocate back to America with her new husband, but when they arrive at the property he has rented in Florida, she is horrified to find that it is the same house she has been dreaming about. They are stuck at the remote place when their car stops running, and are regaled with stories about the previous owners of the house, "the Mad Tierneys," by the property's eccentric caretaker Jonah (John Qualen). Sheila struggles to keep her sanity as she endures a series of strange goings-on at the dilapidated house, as all the time her husband seems curiously detached from the proceedings. Is the house haunted?

Or is Philip trying to gaslight her? The answer to these dire mysteries involves an axe murder, amnesia, a family curse and psychological manipulation as the complex plot unravels.

Lurid poster art for the film displayed a skeletal figure grasping a screaming woman, but no such scene occurs in this talky, low-budget programmer. Director William S. Edwards moves the action along at a snail's pace, and the screenplay by Robert C. Dennis is overly complicated, and while the plot takes some unexpected turns, the promised horrors are smothered by the pedestrian filmmaking. The director fails completely at establishing a mood of tension and suspense using low-key lighting, unusual angles or other tried-and-true techniques, while scenes that supposedly take place after dark are amateurishly shot in unconvincing "day for night" setups. Principals Cathy O'Donnell and Gerald Mohr struggle valiantly with the material, and Ms. O'Donnell gets to do a lot of screaming. The film was shot in a decrepit old house in Florida, and while it has a slight whiff of southern gothic it in no way conjures up a supernatural haunt. The promised thrills of "Psych-O-Rama" involved the use of subliminal cuts in which evil-looking faces would appear on the screen for a brief 1/50 of a second as the film was projected. Decades later the same technique would be used in *The Exorcist*, where images of a demon's face would appear subliminally during certain scenes.

The title of an Edgar Allan Poe poem and horror writer H.P. Lovecraft's novella "The Case of Charles Dexter Ward" provided the basis for another entry in Roger Corman's Poe series, *The Haunted Palace* (1963), starring the inevitable Vincent Price in a dual role. The film begins in 1765, in the perpetually fog-bound Massachusetts seaport of Arkham, where sorcerer Joseph Curwen (Price) is conducting weird rituals in the cellar of his imposing palace that involve kidnapping young women and offering them as sexual sacrifices to a nameless "thing" that resides within a pit in his dungeon. When Arkham maiden Hester Tillinghast (Cathie Merchant) goes missing, her fiancé, Ezra Weeden (Leo Gordon) leads the townsfolk in storming "the home of Satan himself" to rescue her. Arriving before the unholy rite can be consummated, the villagers haul Curwen out of his dungeon, tie him to a tree and burn him alive. As the flames engulf him, the warlock pronounces a curse upon Arkham and vows revenge from beyond the grave.

Over a century later, in 1875, Curwen's descendent Charles Dexter Ward (Price) returns to Arkham with his wife Anne (Debra Paget) to take up residence in the palace. Ward becomes fascinated with a painting of Curwen and gradually becomes possessed by the spirit of his ancestor. This process is hastened by the palace's caretaker Simon Orne (Lon Chaney, Jr.) and henchman Jabez Hutchinson (Milton Parsons), who encourage the emergence of Curwen's personality. Before long Ward's psyche has been subsumed by that of Curwen, and the resurrected warlock is up to his old tricks, including attempting to bring Hester back to life via black magic. Ward/Curwen uses spells from the dread grimoire the *Necronomicon*, which is now in his possession, to summon the Elder Gods to the haunted palace and to mate Anne with the unspeakable Thing in the dungeon.

Curwen, who is now in control, exacts his revenge on the descendants of the Arkhamites who executed him by burning some of them to death. This doesn't sit well with the villagers, who have come to realize that the sorcerer has returned from the dead. As Curwen prepares to offer Anne to the Thing, the angry townsfolk invade the palace with torches and pitchforks in the time-honored horror movie fashion, and prevent the unholy ceremony from taking place. A fire breaks out and quickly spreads, and when it destroys the painting of Curwen, Ward assumes control of himself. He helps to rescue Anne, but

Sorcerer Charles Dexter Ward (Vincent Price) invokes spells to conjure an ancient evil as his wife Anne (Debra Paget) looks on in Roger Corman's Poe/Lovecraft meld *The Haunted Palace* (1963).

while they watch the haunted palace burn down it becomes unclear as to whether Ward has completely escaped Curwen's influence.

The Haunted Palace was a departure from the AIP Corman Poe adaptation formula in that it incorporated the work of the early 20th century horror writer H.P. Lovecraft, whose work centered around the theme of wizards who wished to summon alien "Elder Gods" into our reality. Corman commissioned writer Charles Beaumont, best known as one of the main writers on the paranormal TV series *The Twilight Zone*, to adapt Lovecraft's novella *The Case of Charles Dexter Ward* for the big screen. Beaumont took nothing but the title from Poe's poem, and accordingly, Corman shot in a more starkly lit, more realistic style than he had used in his previous Poe efforts. It's a field day for the scenery-chewing hambone Vincent Price, who exudes eldritch villainy while chanting evil spells in Latin. Ailing fellow horror star Lon Chaney, Jr., delivers one of the better performances of his later career, while Debra Paget provides the requisite glamor and vulnerability as she is menaced by the nameless Thing in the Pit. Cinematographer Floyd Crosby, who had been Corman's cameraman since *House of Usher* (1960), imbues the fog and stone of the haunted palace with wide swaths of murky atmosphere, while composer Ronald Stein contributes an aggressively melodramatic horror movie score.

The film's gothic haunt is described by one of the characters as "a madman's palace brought over stone by stone" from an undisclosed European location to America. As designed by art director Daniel Haller, it's a maze of cobwebby stone stairways and passages with an elaborate wooden latticework leading down to the dungeon and the infamous pit. The exterior of the palace, shown briefly in a few shots, is rendered using matte work and resembles a medieval castle or fortress, although it seems unlikely that this solid stone structure would catch fire and burn as easily as it does in the film's climactic conflagration.

The popular success of Corman's Poe movies prompted United Artists to try to steal some of AIP's thunder by producing a series of similarly-themed horror films based on the works of other 19th century writers that also starred Vincent Price. Producer/screenwriter Robert E. Kent adapted Guy de Maupassant's *Diary of a Madman* for the screen in 1963, and in that same year produced *Twice Told Tales*, a three-part anthology film based on stories by Nathaniel Hawthorne. In "Dr. Heidegger's Experiment," a rejuvenation formula that can revive the dead is discovered, with dire results, while "Rappaccini's Daughter" features a scientist who experiments with poisons on his own daughter. The third episode was a rather loose adaptation of Hawthorne's 1851 novel *The House of the Seven Gables*. Hawthorne's novel had previously been lensed in a feature film version in 1940, which, ironically, also starred Vincent Price. The 1940 iteration was stripped of its gothic nuance and played as a straight drama, but Kent's version infused Hawthorne's novel with a heady dose of supernatural ambience.

The episode begins with a voice-over narration that explicates the house's history, dating back to the 1691 Salem witch trials, "a time of horror and blood" that "left a mark on the house that was not to be forgotten for 150 years." The Pyncheon family, who have always owned the house, are suffering under a curse inflicted on them by the manor's original owner, Matthew Maulle, who was cheated out of the property and is buried in the building's cellar. As the main narrative commences, Gerald Pyncheon (Vincent Price) returns to his ancestral home after a 17-year absence and brings his wife Alice (Beverley Garland) along with him. Gerald's sister Hannah (Jacqueline de Wit), who has resided in the house for years and is a student of the occult, warns the couple about the house's evil reputation, but Gerald will not be dissuaded. He has returned to search for a hidden vault containing valuable deeds that Maulle was alleged to have hidden in the house back in the 17th century.

Soon after they arrive Alice becomes bewitched by the house and begins to witness ghostly phenomena, including a levitated necklace that contains a cameo painting of a woman who bears a strange resemblance to herself. She hears a voice calling the name "Nora" and sees an apparition of Matthew Maulle (Floyd Simmons) who seems to be trying to communicate something. In the meantime, Gerald summons Matthew's descendant, Jonathan Maulle (Richard Denning), to the house in a vain attempt to find information on the location of the vault, but as Jonathan is leaving the house he encounters Alice, for whom he feels a strange attraction. Jonathan tells her that the woman in the cameo is Nora Holbrook, who was engaged to Matthew but was also hung during the Witch Trials, and that she must be Nora's descendant.

Ghostly phenomena begin to assail the haunt. A harpsichord plays by itself and the portrait of the family patriarch begins to drip blood from its painted lips. Alice begins to wander through the house aimlessly in a trance, and when she descends into the cellar Gerald follows her and comprehends that Maulle's remains must be buried beneath a panel in the floor. Using an axe, Gerald pries the panel loose to discover Maulle's skeleton lying in a pit, but, oddly, it is missing an arm. He also finds a map indicating that the hidden vault is concealed behind the patriarch's painting in the study. Maddened by greed, Gerald brutally murders Hannah with an axe so as not to share the treasure with her, and throws an unconscious Alice into the pit next to the skeleton. When he opens the vault, however, Maulle's missing skeletal arm reaches out to strangle him to death and the house itself is convulsed in an earthquake. Great cracks open in the walls and ceilings and blood drips forth from the openings as Jonathan, alerted to danger by a psychic link with Alice, arrives fortuitously to rescue her and the House of the Seven Gables is utterly destroyed by the tremblor.

Hawthorne's novel contains no overtly supernatural elements, but instead is a parable about the sin of avarice that dooms several generations of the Pyncheon family as they are cursed by their own greed. Robert E. Kent's screenplay reconstructs the novel as a straightforward haunted house story, complete with apparitions, poltergeist phenomena, witchery, an earthquake and gallons of gushing blood. Director Sidney Salkow does a workmanlike job with this lurid material, but overall, it's pretty dull stuff despite the murder, mayhem and spooky goings-on that pepper the plot. Price projects his usual sinister screen persona as the amoral and murderous Gerald Pyncheon, but the inimitable Beverly Garland, who

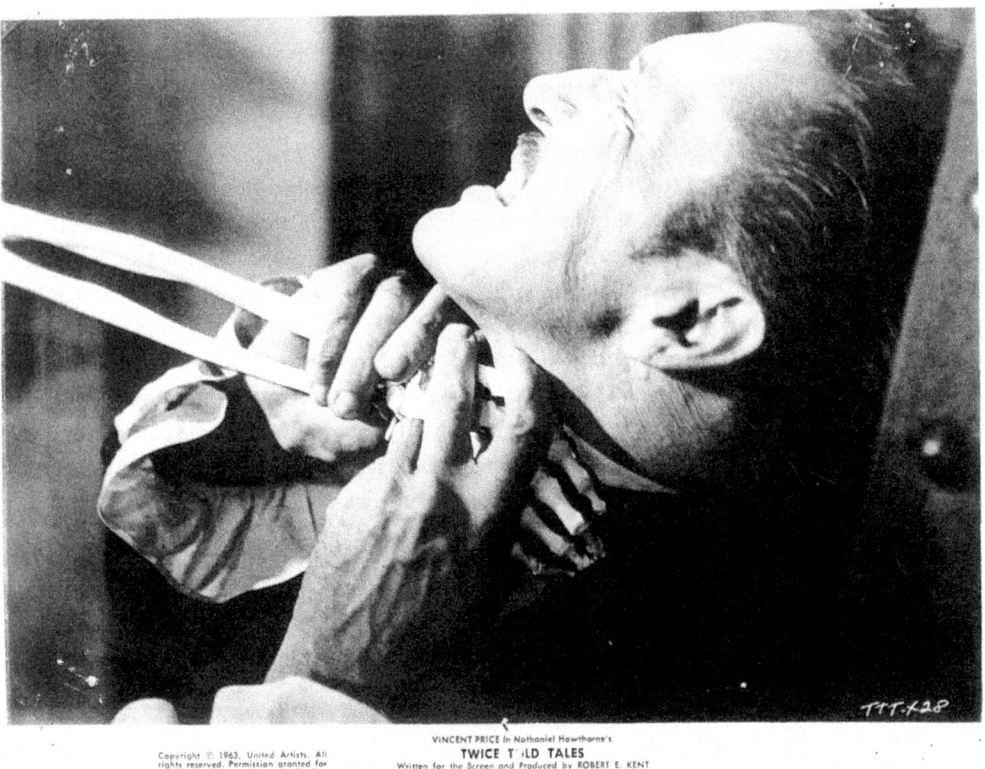

Gerald Pyncheon (Vincent Price) is strangled by a skeletal arm in the "House of the Seven Gables" segment of *Twice Told Tales* **(1963).**

had starred in some of Roger Corman's most memorable sci-fi horror flicks such as *It Conquered the World* (1956) and *Not of this Earth* (1957), steals the movie as the mediumistic Alice. Jacqueline de Wit also does a nice turn portraying the haunt's requisite middle-aged witchy woman Hannah Pyncheon.

A great many liberties were taken with the plot of Hawthorne's novel in order to make it emulate the AIP Corman/Poe product. The film is packed full of histrionic devices such as bleeding walls, a ghostly apparition, cold spots, poltergeist manifestations, and a strangulating skeletal hand, none of which appear in the book. Likewise, the Alice Pyncheon character has been transformed into a ghost whisperer who seems to potentiate the haunt's spectral happenings. Most obvious of all, the film's climax, in which the house is demolished by a freak cataclysm, was made to resemble Corman's *House of Usher*, despite the fact that the real House of the Seven Gables is still standing and is now a haunted attraction in Salem. Exteriors of the house are clearly a less than convincing scale model, while the darkened, cramped interiors were the work of production designer Franz Bachelin and set director Charles Thompson. As in many haunted house narratives, a cursed family portrait and a doppelganger figure in the plot.

While the Hammer horrors and the AIP Poe flicks led the gothic revival, it was ultimately a group of Italian filmmakers that perfected the form. Directors like Riccardo Freda and Mario Bava brought a Continental artistic sensibility to the gothic thriller and were able to translate the fear-drenched chiaroscuro ambience of the black and white horror film into a color milieu in a way that Hammer and AIP, using their more lurid approach to the medium, could not. Freda's *The Horrible Dr. Hitchcock* (1962) was a disturbing story concerning the titular physician, who has an erotic obsession with necrophilia. The film co-starred the queen of the scream queens, British actress Barbara Steele, whose large, expressive eyes were perfect for projecting primal fear onto an audience. Steele and the Dr. Hitchcock character returned in Freda's quasi-sequel, *The Ghost* (*Lo Spettro*, 1963).

The film takes place in a manor house in 1910 Scotland and opens with a séance during which the medium and resident housekeeper Catherine Wood (Harriet Medin) proclaims, in a spooky voice, "The black sign of death is on this house." Presiding over the séance is Dr. John Hitchcock (Elio Jotta), who is now paralyzed and confined to a wheelchair. Hitchcock is a student of the occult who is undergoing experimental treatments for his condition administered by Dr. Charles Livingstone (Peter Baldwin) involving the ingestion of multiple poisons. Unbeknownst to Hitchcock, Livingstone is carrying on an affair with Hitchcock's wife Margaret (Barbara Steele), and the two are secretly planning to murder him for the property and money in his estate.

The couple carries out their heinous plan, killing Hitchcock with one of the poisons used in the treatment. No one suspects foul play due to Hitchcock's ill health, but when the doctor's safe containing jewels and valuable documents cannot be opened due to a missing key, Margaret's inheritance is put on hold. As they search for the key, they are subjected to a series of ghostly phenomena. Hitchcock's wheelchair comes hurtling down the stairs from an upper room, Catherine speaks in a mediumistic trance in the dead man's voice, and objects start moving around by themselves. Then Catherine reveals that Dr. Hitchcock always kept the key to the safe in a pocket of the jacket he was buried in. Desperate, Margaret and Livingstone retrieve the key from her husband's decaying body in the family vault, but when the safe is opened the jewels and documents are missing.

At her wit's end, Margaret begins to suspect that her lover is trying to cheat her as the spooky phenomena ramp up. Blood drips from the ceiling of one of the rooms and, most frighteningly, Margaret witnesses an apparition of her husband's ghost in her bedroom and shoots it, but the bullets have no effect. Then Hitchcock's ghostly voice tells her that the jewels and documents are hidden underneath his coffin, and when she returns to the crypt, she finds them there. The lovers quarrel when Margaret thinks Livingstone is trying to steal all the treasure for himself and kills him with his own scalpel. Soon afterward, Catherine is found dead and Margaret is confronted by the apparition of her husband once more. Is Dr. Hitchcock really a ghost, or is he involved in a plot to gaslight his unfaithful wife? And who will survive in a game of mystery, madness and death?

The Ghost is a neat little horror thriller in which, thanks to an ingenious screenplay devised by Freda and Oreste Biancoli, the viewer is kept guessing at the outcome of these mysterious situations up until the last frame of film. Freda's grasp of the gothic material is sure as his fluid camera, manned

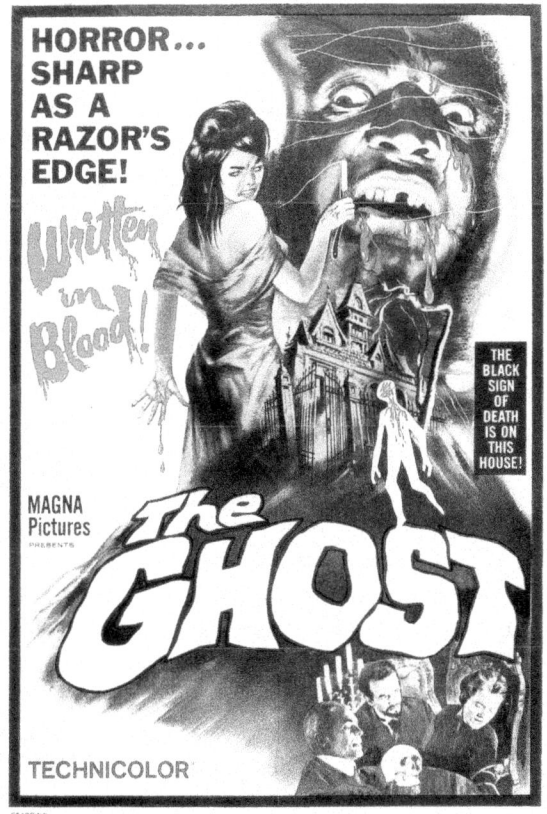

Barbara Steele presides over a house of evil in this poster for Ricardo Freda's *The Ghost* (1963).

by cinematographer Raffaele Masciocchi, drifts through the looming shadows of the haunted castle. This accomplishment is all the more impressive in that Freda reportedly shot *The Ghost* in a mere twelve days. Horror historian Carlos Clarens, discussing Freda's cinematic style, states that his films "are strictly Continental affairs, and most successful where their Anglo-Saxon counterparts fail: in the invocation of mood through color and décor, and in a visual sophistication that reveals the director's earlier occupation as an art critic."[1] The film's haunt, set in a Scottish castle, is barely glimpsed from its exterior. The castle's interior, however, is properly gloomy and claustrophobic and honeycombed with vaults and secret passages, as well as the requisite ghostly portrait of Dr. Hitchcock.

Freda's cameraman and assistant director on several of his productions was Mario Bava, who would go on to glory as one of the great horror directors of all time. Beginning with his gothic masterwork *Black Sunday* (1960) and its follow-up *Black Sabbath* (1963), Bava's work gained international popularity and cemented his reputation as one of the cinematic masters of the macabre. One of Bava's lesser-known works, bearing the ludicrous English language title *Kill, Baby, Kill* (a.k.a. *Operation Fear*, 1966), is one of the director's finest films, but it has fallen into an undeserved obscurity.

Kill, Baby, Kill opens in the remote Carpathian village of Karmingen, where a woman named Irena Hollander (Mirella Panfili) has written to authorities that someone is trying to murder her. When she turns up dead under mysterious circumstances, coroner Dr. Paul Eswai (Giacomo Rossi-Stuart) is dispatched to the village to conduct an inquest. Arriving at Karmingen Eswai confers with Inspector Kruger (Piero Lulli) and the town's burgomeister, Karl (Luciano Catenacci), who tell him that the superstitious townsfolk are foundering in the grip of supernatural fear over a number of deaths that have occurred there recently. As the trio launches their investigation, Eswai meets a young woman, Monica Schuftan (Erika Blanc), who has arrived at the village to visit the graves of her parents, and agrees to act as a witness to the autopsy. While conducting the procedure, Eswai discovers a silver coin that has been placed in the heart of Irena Hollander's corpse as a charm against witchcraft.

While Inspector Kruger departs for the Villa Graps, where Irena had worked as a maid, to question the baroness, Eswai is attacked by two of the townspeople who do not approve of his mission. He is rescued by the sudden appearance of the village witch, Ruth (Fabienne Dali), who frightens the thugs away. As Eswai continues on to the Villa Graps, Ruth is on her way to perform a protective ritual for Nadienne (Micaela Esdra) the daughter of the local innkeeper, who has come under the town's curse. The village is being haunted by the ghost of the baroness' seven-year-old daughter, Melissa Graps (Valerio Valeri), who has selected Nadienne as her next victim. Whoever sees the apparition of the white-clad child is forced to commit suicide while the ghost utters her eerie childish laughter. Alas, the witch's charms are of no use as Melissa's ghost appears at Nadienne's window and compels her to impale herself upon the sharp point of a candelabra.

In the meantime, Eswai arrives at the Villa Graps to link up with Inspector Kruger and question the baroness. From the outside, the villa is an imposing multistory structure, but inside it is a dark, crumbling gothic ruin. The interior contains an enormous winding staircase, walls with fading murals. suits of armor overgrown with cobwebs and a corridor lined with candleholders in the shape of human arms. He meets with the Baroness Graps (Giana Vivaldi), the only inhabitant of the villa, who lives in a large, sumptuous suite on an upper floor. The baroness, who has an air of oddness about her, is evasive and tells him nothing, claiming to have no knowledge of Kruger's visit. On his way out of the villa, Eswai encounters Melissa's ghost, who giggles and throws a phantom ball near him before running away.

That evening Monica has a delirious nightmare while she is asleep at the village inn, and when she awakens, she finds one of Melissa's dolls on her bed. Returning from the villa, Eswai discovers that Kruger is dead, the latest victim of the curse. The doctor and Monica confer with Karl, who reveals that Monica is actually the daughter of the baroness and Melissa's sister, but after they leave the ghost appears to the burgomaster and forces him to commit suicide. Armed with this knowledge, Monica and Eswai return to the villa once more but get trapped inside. They become separated, and Eswai gets lost within the seemingly endless rooms of the villa before meeting up with his own doppelganger and losing consciousness. He awakens in Ruth's witch's house, where he finds Karl's corpse lying on a table. Ruth explains that she and Karl were lovers, and that she is now going to avenge Karl's death.

Back at the villa, the baroness tells the captive Monica about her sister's fate and the origin of Karmingen's curse. Melissa was trampled to death by horses during a town festival while trying to retrieve her ball, and the villagers just watched her die without offering any assistance. Her sister's ghost then materializes and proceeds to chase Monica through the villa and down the huge spiral staircase. In the meantime, Ruth arrives to confront the baroness, who she knows is a medium that summoned Melissa's ghost back from the dead to take revenge upon the villagers. The witch and the medium engage in a mortal struggle in which both are killed, causing the child's ghost to de-materialize as Eswai arrives to rescue Monica.

Bava's unique directorial chops transform *Kill, Baby, Kill* into a superb gothic thriller that invokes a terrifying mood of nightmare and delirium. Shot largely on location in the medieval town of Calcata, the characters often seem hopelessly lost within its crumbling edifices and narrow alleyways. Bava employs avant-garde cinematic techniques such as shock zoom-ins and the visual smearing of images, an effect created by shooting through a piece of distorted glass, a method that was invented by Bava's father, veteran cinematographer Eugenio Bava. Monica's dream sequence in particular employs a series of frighteningly distorted images superimposed over each other in a montage of slow-motion dissolves that recalls a similar sequence created for *The Innocents*. The film's color palette consists primarily of bilious greens, ethereal blues and washed-out ochres that contribute greatly to the overall ghastly ambience.

While Giocomo Rossi-Stuart and Erika Blanc do a fine job as the nominal hero and heroine, the film's real stars are its unusual female characters. Fabiano Dali plays Ruth the village witch with an air of otherworldly detachment and Giana Vivaldi projects bitter ire and supernatural menace as the mediumistic Baroness Graps. The most memorable performance of all, however, is given by Valerio Valeri as the spectral child Melissa Graps, whose pale apparitional appearance provides the film's most fearful imagery. The acclaimed Italian director Federico Fellini would pay homage to the character by featuring a similar phantom girl in "Toby Dammit," his segment of the Edgar Allan Poe anthology film *Spirits of the Dead* (1968).

The exteriors of the Villa Graps were shot at an abandoned building in the town of Calcata, whose crumbling façade is the very image of a gothic ruin, while interiors were filmed in the Titanus Appia

The ghost of Melissa Graps (Valerio Valeri, top left) haunts Monica Schuftan (Erika Blanc) in this Italian poster for Mario Bava's *Kill, Baby, Kill* (a.k.a. *Operation Fear*, 1966).

Studios in Rome. The spaces inside the villa have a dreamlike quality, including the enormous spiral staircase that seems to revolve during one sequence like a huge hypnotic eye, and the baroness' lair, which is replete with billowing curtains and antique furniture dominated by an ornate four-poster bed in the middle of the room. Bava's background as a painter and cinematographer imbues the colors and compositions of the gothic haunt with an eerie, spectral quality that has the vividness of a hallucination. The film's silly title has served to relegate it to an undeserved obscurity, and it's a shame that it wasn't released under its Italian title *Operazione Paura*, which translates as *Operation Fear*. Directors Martin Scorsese and David Lynch have admittedly been influenced by this classic haunted house thriller.

Italian director Antonio Margheriti, although on a less exalted level than Freda and Bava, was nevertheless a competent filmmaker who worked in a variety of genres. His gothic thriller *Castle of Blood* (a.k.a. *Danse Macabre*, 1964) offered a quirky take on the haunted house theme. The film is set in England during the middle of the 19th century, where visiting horror writer Edgar Allan Poe (played by Silvio Tranquilli) is holding forth on the reality of the supernatural to his companion, Lord Thomas Blackwood (Umberto Raho) on All Hallows Eve in a London pub, where they are confronted by journalist Alan Foster (Georges Riviere), who forcefully expresses his skepticism concerning the reality of the uncanny. In response, Lord Blackwood tells the interloper that he owns a nearby castle that is reputed to be haunted, and makes a bet with Foster that he cannot spend the entire night inside the haunt. Even though all of the others who have accepted the challenge have died in the attempt, Foster accepts the wager.

Once he is ensconced in Blackwood's crumbling country manse Foster explores the dark, forbidding place, where he encounters the beautiful and mysterious Elisabeth Blackwood (Barbara Steele), the Lord's younger sister, with whom he instantly falls in love. Before he can consummate his romantic tryst, however, he is interrupted by another Blackwood family member, Julia (Margarete Robsahm), who appears to be Elisabeth's rival. Foster comes to suspect that the women are not living souls but undead phantoms, and his fears are confirmed when he meets Dr. Carmus (Arturo Dominici), another mysterious denizen of Castle Blackwood. Carmus reveals that all of the people in the castle, including himself, are ghosts who are condemned to re-enact the last five minutes of their lives every year on All Hallows Eve. Furthermore, the ghosts in the castle require the blood of a living victim for sustenance in order to continue their nebulous existence inside the haunt, which Foster will provide for them unless he can escape from the castle by dawn.

Foster is forced to watch the re-enactment of a multiple murder in which Elisabeth is forced to kill her lover (Giovanni Cianfriglia) and Julia in a wild altercation and other scenes of spectral mayhem. As the night progresses toward dawn the ghosts pursue the terrified Foster through the secret passageways and moldering catacombs of Castle Blackwood guided by the ghost of Elisabeth, who is intent on helping him escape. He manages to make it as far as the front gate as the sun rises, only to be accidentally killed when he becomes impaled on one of the gate's iron spikes. The next morning Blackwood and Poe arrive at the castle to find Foster's corpse propped up in a standing position at the front gate, whereupon Blackwood glibly extracts the wager money from the dead body while Poe remarks that the incident will provide the material for another one of his ghastly tales.

An intriguing work of 60s-era Italian gothic cinema, *Castle of Blood* is a stylish, well-

Barbara Steele and Georges Riviere enter into a living/dead love affair in *Castle of Blood* (1964).

paced effort from director Margheriti that is very much in the vein of the atmospheric horror films of Freda and Bava. It is marred, however, by a flawed screenplay by Gianni Grimaldi and Bruno Corbucci that is fragmented, episodic and frequently confusing as the film's hapless protagonist is drawn into one mysterious and baffling situation after another. Despite this, Margheriti conveys a disturbing sense of claustrophobia as Foster becomes trapped inside the confining web of the haunted castle while being pursued by its ghosts. The inimitable Barbara Steele emphatically conveys fear, desire and pain in her striking portrayal of the spectral Elisabeth, while Georges Riviere and Arturo Dominici offer strong supporting performances.

The oddest aspect of the movie is the filmmaker's attempt to portray it as a work written by Edgar Allan Poe. An opening credit states that the plot was based on a Poe story entitled "Danse Macabre," which also served as an alternate title for the film, but Poe never authored a story with that title, which is actually the name of an eerie waltz by the French composer Camille Saint-Saëns. Poe also appears as a character in the film's framing story who was supposedly inspired by the bizarre events to incorporate them into one of his horror tales, a notion that is likewise bogus. Castle Blackwood is a typical gothic haunt, replete with dusty crypts, shadowy hallways, forbidding chambers and phantoms dancing in the candlelight. As in many haunted house narratives, dramatic tension is generated by the protagonist being trapped inside, and while the film's ghosts are immaterial entities, the fact that they subsist on the blood of the living adds a vampiric element to the proceedings.

Taking a cue from Hammer Films, the British studio Amicus Productions specialized in making horror thrillers, but unlike Hammer's costume melodramas, the Amicus films were set in a 20th century milieu. Amicus' *The House that Dripped Blood* (1971) was an anthology horror film based on four short stories penned by Robert Bloch, the author of *Psycho*. Bloch adapted his stories for the screen and Hammer horror icons Peter Cushing and Christopher Lee were signed on to star in various segments of the omnibus film that are all linked to the titular haunt. In a framing story, Scotland Yard Inspector Holloway (John Bennett), assigned to investigate the disappearance of actor Paul Henderson, travels to the thespian's now-empty country manor and questions the town's real estate agent A.J. Stoker (John Bryans), who explains that four previous tenants of the house have been the victims of tragic circumstances. The four stories then unfold in flashback.

In the first episode, "Method for Murder," Charles Hillyer (Denholm Elliott), a writer of horror novels, and his wife Alice (Joanna Dunham) move into the house. Charles is struggling with writer's block while trying to complete his latest thriller about the psychopathic strangulation murderer Dominic. While toiling mightily over the novel, Charles begins to see visions of the leering Dominic (played by Tom Adams). Fearing for his sanity, the writer consults psychiatrist Dr. Andrews (Robert Lang), who explains that the Dominic character is an extension of the author's persona. Is Charles losing his mind, or has his murderous creation assumed a life of its own? Or is there some even more sinister game afoot?

The second weird tale, "Waxworks," stars horror veteran Peter Cushing as retired stockbroker Philip Grayson, who becomes obsessed with a sculpture depicting Salome holding the severed head of John the Baptist in a local wax museum because the wax figure's features have an uncanny resemblance to those of his deceased wife. The museum's oddball proprietor (Wolfe Morris) informs him that he modelled the figure's face on that of his own dead wife, who was an axe murderer. One day an old friend, Neville Rogers (Joss Ackland), shows up at the house and they pay a visit to the waxworks together, where Neville also becomes obsessed with the Salome figure. The crucial question becomes whose head will be the next to end up on the chopping block.

In the third story, "Sweets to the Sweet," Hammer alumnus Christopher Lee stars as widower John Reid, who moves into the house along with his young daughter Jane (Chloe Franks). John is emotionally distant with his daughter, and hires a young woman, Ann Norton (Nyree Dawn Porter), as a full-time tutor for the child. Under Ann's tutelage, Jane reveals herself to be an odd but innocent child, whose neuroses are seemingly exacerbated by her father's strict rules about having no toys or playmates. By the end of the story, however, the reasons for the child's harsh upbringing become horribly obvious.

Segment four, "The Cloak," relates the story of arrogant horror movie actor and avid occultist Paul Henderson (John Pertwee), who is in high dudgeon over the low-end production values of his latest film outing, a no-budget horror thriller entitled *Curse of the Bloodsuckers*. He finds a business card in his dressing room for a theatrical costume establishment, and goes there in search of a more convincing vampire cloak. The eccentric proprietor of the weird little shop, Theo von Hartmann (Geoffrey Bayldon), is all too glad to provide him with this bit of attire, but he soon learns that the cloak is much more authentic than he anticipated. British scream queen Ingrid Pitt appears as Henderson's vampiric co-star.

Back in the framing story, Inspector Holloway, who is still investigating Henderson's disappearance, returns to the house at night, only to learn the actor's horrific fate and comes under attack from the supernatural forces within the haunt. The film ends with realtor A.J. Stoker addressing the audience directly and explaining that the secret of the house is that "it reflects the personality of whoever lives in it and treats them accordingly."

The House That Dripped Blood is a fun haunted house romp enlivened by Peter Duffell's steadfast direction, a scary, yet witty screenplay by horrormeister Robert Bloch, and earnest performances by Hammer alums Peter Cushing, Christopher Lee and Ingrid Pitt. John Pertwee's portrayal of the jaded horror star Paul Henderson in "The Cloak" segment, however, is arguably the most memorable performance in the film. "At heart he's pure gothic," one of the segment's other characters remarks of the cantankerous thespian as Henderson continually grouses about the dismal state of horror movies in general and the chintzy, low-budget production he is contracted to

This poster for the omnibus horror film *The House That Dripped Blood* (1971) illustrates some of the terrors that await in every room of the haunt.

act in in particular. Bloch's literate, frequently tongue in cheek screenplay references the works of classic horror writers, including E.T.A. Hoffmann, Bram Stoker and Montague Summers.

In this case the haunted house provides a framework for Bloch's collection of weird tales, but the house itself is not the primary focus of the myriad narratives. The exterior of the haunt is not particularly gothic-looking, but the interior sets, shot at Shepperton Studios, contains the requisite cobwebs, along with odd-looking statuary and a library stocked with many a quaint and curious volume of forgotten lore. Art director Tony Curtis and cinematographers Dick Bush and Alan Hume lend the house a claustrophobic and menacing ambience that sustains itself through all four (actually five, counting the framing story) tales of terror. Despite the title, little blood is shown dripping in the house, in contrast to the bleeding walls in evidence in the "House of the Seven Gables" episode of *Twice Told Tales*. While there are no ghosts in the house, the most interesting aspect of the haunt lies in the real estate brokers claim that it "reflects the personality of whoever lives in it and treats them accordingly," a motif that would recur in *The House Next Door* (2002).

Veteran screenwriter Richard Matheson, who had scripted Corman's *House of Usher* (1960), adapted his own haunted house novel, *Hell House*, for the screen under the title *The Legend of Hell House* (1973). The haunt in question is the Belasco House, dubbed the "Mount Everest of Haunted Houses," was formerly owned by the nefarious millionaire Emeric Belasco, who was dubbed the "Roaring Giant," and was reputedly the site of numerous evil transgressions, including "drug addiction, alcoholism, sadism, bestiality, mutilation, murder, vampirism, necrophilia, cannibalism, not to mention a gamut of sexual goodies." As the film opens, aged millionaire Rudolph Deutsch (Roland Culver), hoping to unravel the enigma of life after death, recruits physicist Dr. Lionel Barrett (Clive Revill) to explore the secrets of Belasco House and gives the scientist one week to obtain answers about the afterlife and thereby earn a reward of 100,000 pounds sterling.

Dr. Barrett hires a couple of psychics to assist him on his paranormal quest. Florence Tanner (Pamela Franklin) is a "mental medium," who can reputedly communicate with the spirits of the dead, while Benjamin Fischer (Roddy McDowell) is a "physical medium" with the ability to exude a ghostly substance called "ectoplasm" that can interact with the physical environment. Ben is the sole survivor of another experiment gone wrong in Hell House twenty years earlier. Also along for the ride is Barrett's wife Ann (Gayle Hunnicutt). The scientist promptly installs a high-tech machine inside the house that he believes will eliminate the electromagnetic energies that he theorizes are the true cause of the ghostly disturbances.

Belasco House is shrouded in fog outside and dark and threating inside. It is stocked with all manner of weird statuary, especially in a room called the Chapel, the "unholy heart of the house" which is described as "a church in hell," that is dominated by a demonic figure of a crucified Christ. Predictably, it isn't long before the paranormal forces inside the haunt manifest themselves as poltergeist phenomena and other disturbances assail the party. During a séance Florence materializes strands of gossamer-like ectoplasm that emanate from inside her body and speaks in strange voices. Worst of all, both Florence and Ann descend into an uncharacteristic promiscuity, causing emotional problems between Barrett and his wife.

As Barrett prepares to activate his ghostbusting machine, Florence attempts to destroy it, believing that it will have a negative effect on the spirits in the house, but the physicist prevents her from accomplishing this. Florence then enters the Chapel intending to warn the ghosts about Barrett's intentions, but she is killed when the grotesque crucifix falls on top of her. Barrett switches his machine on, which at first seems to exorcise the spirits, but a flood of psychic energies returns and kills the physicist. In response, Fischer and Ann defy the forces within the house and the medium uses his power to shatter a stained-glass panel in the Chapel, revealing a hidden door. Behind the door they discover the preserved corpse of Emeric Belasco (Michael Gough) inside a lead-lined room designed to shield the chamber from electromagnetic radiation. They find that Belasco had his legs amputated and replaced with prosthetic limbs that augmented his height in order to transform him into the Roaring Giant. Fischer and Ann leave the room wide open and re-activate the machine as they exit Hell House, hoping that the device will exorcise the unquiet spirits within.

Director Peter Hough and screenwriter Richard Matheson's talents work in synergy to produce a superior haunted house thriller, but the film is not without its faults. Matheson's basic plotline, in which a scientist attempts to unravel the mysteries of a notorious haunt accompanied by three others, two of whom are psychic, derives from Robert Wise's *The Haunting* (1963) and the Shirley Jackson novel on which it is based. Star Roddy McDowell delivers an uneven performance in which he merely looks perplexed during most of the film, only to explode into scenery-chewing histrionics in the final reel, while co-star Clive Revill, playing the part of a coldly logical scientist, exudes enough British reserve to generate little in the way of audience sympathy. On the other hand, Pamela Franklin, who had played the ghost-obsessed girl in Jack Clayton's *The Innocents* (1961), delivers a knockout portrayal of an otherworldly medium, and glam actress Gayle Hunnicutt also shines in her role as a chaste wife forced into humiliating erotic obsessions under the malignant supernatural influences of the house. All in all, however, *The Legend of Hell House* lacks the depth of dramatic involvement between the characters in comparison with *The Haunting*.

Hough, working with cinematographer Alan Hume, invests Hell House with a memorably ghostly ambience through the use of expressionist lighting, extreme facial close-ups, distorted imagery and unusual camera angles. Composers Delia Derbyshire and Brian Hodgson contributed an eerily effective electronic music score. Exteriors of the Belasco haunt were filmed on location at Wykehurst Park in West Sussex where the fogbound atmosphere was natural and not the product of studio fog machines. The film connects the haunted house with the quasi-religious phenomenon of spiritualism and mediumship, in which psychic sensitives are thought to be able to communicate and interact with the dead. No apparitions of "ghosts visible" are seen in Belasco House; instead, the unquiet spirits manifest themselves in poltergeist disturbances, mediumistic trances, bodily mutilation, and, in one case, through a demonic black cat. The film is prefaced with a quotation from an individual named Tom Corbett, who claims to be a "clairvoyant and psychic consultant to European royalty," which states, "Although the story of this film is fictitious, the events depicted involving psychic phenomena are not only very much within the bounds of possibility, but could well be true."

Producer/director Dan Curtis, who had a fascination with the gothic, was the creative force behind the popular supernatural soap opera *Dark Shadows* and the vampire TV movie *The Night Stalker* and its sequel, *The Night Strangler*, among a number of other efforts. Curtis brought this gothic sensibility to the big screen in the haunted house thriller *Burnt Offerings* (1976). British actor Oliver Reed stars as New Yorker Ben Rolf, who rents a manor house in Long Island for his family, which includes his wife Marian (Karen Black), son Davy (Lee H. Montgomery) and his elderly aunt Elizabeth (Bette Davis). Oddly, the owners, Arnold Allardyce (Burgess Meredith) and his sister Roz (Eileen Heckart), insist on the odd proviso that their elderly mother, who lives a hermit-like existence in an attic room, must be left alone and provided with three meals a day that are to be placed outside her door. The Rolfs agree to these terms and happily move into their spacious summer rental.

Marian seems to be especially taken with the old house and volunteers to prepare and serve Mrs. Allardyce her meals, although she notes that the food goes mostly uneaten. She begins to wear the antique clothing she finds in Mrs. Allardyce's suite, and becomes obsessed with the old woman's collection of photographs depicting the former inhabitants of the house. As Marian comes under the spell of the place, it begins to have an effect on the other members of the family as well. While playing with his son in the swimming pool, Ben inexplicably tries to drown Danny, and one night the boy is nearly asphyxiated by a gas heater when the windows in his room are found tightly closed and Aunt Elizabeth is implicated in the incident. In addition, Ben begins to have frightening visions of a grinning phantom hearse driver (Anthony James). Finally, Aunt Elizabeth suddenly dies from a heart attack and Marian refuses to attend the funeral.

After several more travails, Ben realizes that it is time for the family to leave. They are all packed up and ready to go when Marian insists on going back inside to tell Mrs. Allardyce they are leaving. Ben gets antsy when she fails to return and goes back in the house to look for her. When he can't find her anywhere, he enters the forbidden room of Mrs. Allardyce and is horrified to find that Marian has become the old woman. Ben comes hurtling out of the attic window to land on the windshield of the family car, and Danny runs into the house's collapsing chimney and is killed. In the aftermath, Arnold and Roz are heard gushing over their house, which has somehow restored itself, and the framed portraits of Ben, Danny and Aunt Elizabeth, the latest victims of the haunt, are now part of Mrs. Allardyce's picture gallery.

Despite a fine cast, competent direction and decent production values, *Burnt Offerings* fails to offer much in the way of spook house chills. The main problem is the screenplay, adapted by Curtis and William F. Nolan from a novel by Robert Marasco, that devolves into a series of tepid episodes that lack a central coherence. Principals Oliver Reed and Karen Black plod through the mediocre material to the best of their abilities with dubious results. Oscar winning veteran Bette Davis gets a reprieve from the unpleasant parts she had played in the "hagsploitation" movies such as *Whatever Happened to Baby Jane?* (1962) and this time is cast in a sympathetic role as Aunt Elizabeth, and character actor Burgess Meredith delivers a small but amusing performance as the eccentric Arnold Allardyce.

Despite its flaws, *Burnt Offerings* is significant as the first film to revolve around the narrative of a family assaulted by the supernatural forces of a haunt, plot elements that would later be replicated in films like *The Amityville Horror*, *Poltergeist* and *The Shining* and would provide a template for many of the haunted house flicks of the 21st century. The gothic plotline has affinities with *Psycho*, with its secret room inhabited by an elderly homicidal woman who possesses a younger living person, and the ending in which those who died in the house appear in photographs might have been cribbed by Stanley Kubrick for the final scene in *The Shining*.

While the film supposedly takes place in Suffolk County in Long Island, it was actually shot at Dunsmuir House in Oakland, California, a house with a curious history. Built in 1899 by coal magnate Alexander Dunsmuir, the neo-classical mansion was supposed to be a wedding gift for his new bride, but he died during his honeymoon and never got to live in it. His widow inherited the manor and lived there for two years before passing away in 1901. The City of Oakland eventually purchased the property, whereupon it attained historic landmark status. The Dunsmuir House was later used as a location for the filming of the horror sleeper *Phantasm* (1979) and a number of other films.

Polish-born director Roman Polanski, who had lensed *Rosemary's Baby*, brought forth another tale of terror set inside a haunted apartment in *The Tenant* (*Le Locaitaire*, 1976). Polanski cast himself as the film's protagonist, a shy and retiring Eastern European émigré file clerk named Trelkovsky, who rents a run-down Paris flat from the cantankerous Monsieur Zy (Melvyn Douglas). Inquiring about the apartment's previous tenant, Trelkovsky is told that it was a female Egyptologist named Simone Choule and that the place became vacant after she attempted suicide by throwing herself out of the apartment window. She is clinging to life at a local hospital, but is not expected to survive.

Trelkovsky decides to pay the unfortunate woman a visit at the hospital, where he runs into her friend Stella (Isabel Adjani) at her bedside. Choule's head is completely swathed in bandages except for her mouth and one eye, and she doesn't seem to recognize Stella but seems to know Trelkovsky and lets out an anguished scream. After the aborted visit, the two of them enter into an impulsive and somewhat strained love affair. Trelkovsky's severe lack of assertiveness causes him to be humiliated and bullied by his co-workers, by the building's unpleasant concierge (Shelley Winters), and by the other tenants in the apartment complex. The environment of the drab, cheerless flat causes him to become more and more withdrawn and delusional, and he begins to suffer from bouts of paranoia in which he thinks the tenants are plotting against him. He keeps seeing them watching him in a threatening manner while they stand in the hallway toilet.

Sinking deeper into delusion and psychosis, Trelkovsky starts to assume the identity of the dead woman, buying a wig and dressing in her clothes as his identity blurs. He makes the grim discovery of one of Choule's teeth hidden inside a hole in the apartment wall, and begins to see his own doppelganger watching him. In the film's most eerie sequence, he sees an apparition of Choule's ghost standing in the toilet as she unwraps the bandages from her head to reveal a hideously grinning visage. Finally, he has the delusion that the complex's tenants are cheering for him to defenestrate himself, and still dressed in Choule's clothes, he hurls himself out of the window. He awakens in the hospital swathed in bandages, watching himself and Stella visiting him and utters the same anguished cry as the identity transference comes full circle.

Like *Rosemary's Baby*, *The Tenant* takes place within the confining space of an apartment, but it is most similar to the first film in his "apartment trilogy," *Repulsion* (1965), in which Catherine Deneuve portrays a young, mentally unstable woman who descends into murder and madness when left alone in her sister's London flat for a weekend. Unlike the other two films in the trilogy, however, *The Tenant* is slow-moving, unfocused and overlong, thanks to a complex screenplay adapted from Roland Topor's novel *Le locataire chimerique* by Polanski and Gerard Brach. As an actor, though, Polanski manages to carry the film and elicit sympathy for the hapless Trelkovsky character, who is caught in a grim web of fate from which he cannot escape. The film does have its spooky moments, such as the sight of Simone Choule unwrapping her bandages to reveal the grinning face of a ghost.

There are affinities with *Psycho*, in which a dead woman takes possession of a living man and compels him to cross-dress while assuming his identity. And, like *Psycho*, *The Tenant* evokes the notion of the doppelganger, or double, an ancient mythical belief sometimes described as "the ghost of one's self." It is always considered a bad omen to encounter one's doppelganger, as it is in this case. Trelkovsky's drab little apartment, still adorned with the dead woman's accoutrements, is a particularly claustrophobic haunt, although all of the spooky goings-on occur in the common areas of the complex. The film never makes it clear whether Trelkovsky's visions are entirely psychological or are the result of a supernatural agency. Paris locations enliven the action, and the haunted apartment was a real flat located at no. 39 Rue la Bruyere.

Writer Peter Straub is arguably the most acclaimed exponent of the American ghostly tale, and is best known for his novel *Ghost Story*, which was filmed in 1981. The first screen adaptation of his work, however, was based on his earlier novel *Julia*, entitled *The Haunting of Julia* (1976). *Rosemary's Baby*'s Mia Farrow stars as the titular character Julia Lofting, a wealthy British woman who is emotionally shattered after her daughter Katie (Sophie Ward) chokes during a meal and dies when Julia attempts to perform an emergency tracheotomy. The tragedy causes Julia to separate from her domineering husband Magnus (Kier Dullea) and buy a townhouse in a posh section of London. Upon moving in, she finds a long-unused nursery room containing a child's toys and other possessions. She also experiences a number of odd but minor poltergeist disturbances.

The bereaved woman gravitates to a children's playground in nearby Holland Park, where she watches the children. She notices a little girl playing in the sandbox, but when she approaches her the child seems to vanish and Julia finds she has mutilated a tortoise with a knife. Things get even stranger when Julia allows Magnus' sister Lily (Jill Bennett) to conduct a séance in the house, and the medium, Mrs. Flood (Anna Wing) gets frightened and warns Julia that she should leave the house immediately. The next day, while Julia is out, Magnus gains entrance and is drawn into the building's basement, where he falls down a flight of stairs and is killed when his throat is slit on a broken piece of glass and he bleeds to death.

Seeking answers, Julia visits Mrs. Flood and the medium tells her that while in her trance state she saw a little boy bleeding to death in Holland Park. She does some research and finds that a boy was murdered in the park in 1938, and that a vagrant was executed for the crime. Visiting the boy's mother (Mary Morris), she learns that the boy was really killed by several neighborhood children who had fallen under the influence of a wicked little girl, Olivia Rudge, who had once lived in the house Julia bought. Continuing her investigation, Julia visits two of the grown-up children who were involved in the affair, both of whom suddenly come up dead in freak accidents. Finally, she goes to see Olivia Rudge's mother, who is in an insane asylum in Wales, and Mrs. Rudge reveals that she murdered her daughter because she was evil, and after Julia leaves the old woman dies of a sudden heart attack. Returning to her London home, Julia is confronted with the apparition of Olivia Rudge's ghost, who looks just like Katie, and tries to embrace her, but the film's final images show that Julia has had her throat slit and has bled to death at the hands of the evil spirit child.

An unhappy confluence of indifferent direction by Richard Longcraine, a highly flawed screenplay adaptation by scenarists Harry Bromley Davenport and David Humphries and the drab cinematography of Peter Hannan combine to doom this British/Canadian production to filmic obscurity. There's hardly any attempt by the filmmakers to establish a spooky vibe in the visuals, while the leaden narrative plods along to a downbeat conclusion. One of the film's major flaws lies in the alteration of the Magnus character, who in the novel is an imposing, dominating barrister and authority figure. Kier Dullea, best known for his role as one of the astronauts in Stanley Kubrick's *2001* (1968), is woefully miscast in the part, and his character is killed off early in the film, whereas in the novel he is possibly involved in a plot to gaslight Julia for her money by staging an ersatz haunt. Only Mia Farrow's intense performance as the film's tormented heroine Julia, which is reminiscent of a similar portrayal in *Rosemary's Baby*, shines above the mediocrity. The film's haunted London townhouse is depicted as an entirely normal domestic dwelling, but many of the horrific scenes, however, take place outside the house. There are similarities with the Japanese horror film *The Grudge* (2004) in that both films feature vengeful ghosts that emanate from a haunt to cause a series of violent deaths among the film's doomed characters.

An unusual take on the haunted house theme was offered in the British production of *The Legacy* (1979). The film stars Katherine Ross as Los Angeles architect Maggie Walsh, who is offered a job in England and travels to London with her boyfriend, Pete Danner (Sam Elliott). While touring the English countryside on Pete's motorcycle, the couple is involved in a collision with a limousine on a backcountry road. The limo's passenger, the aristocratic British gentleman Jason Montolive (John Standing) graciously invites them to his manor house named Ravenhurst while Pete's cycle is being repaired. Deprived of any means of transportation, Pete and Maggie have no choice but to accept Montolive's offer of hospitality.

Arriving at Ravenhurst, the couple is conducted inside the palatial estate while Montolive, who seems to have suddenly aged, enters separately. After they become acquainted with the manor, five other guests arrive at Ravenhurst to meet with Montolive, Karl Liebnecht (Charles Gray), Maria Gabrieli (Marianne Broome), Barbara Kirstenberg (Hildegard Neil), Clive Jackson (Roger Daltrey) and Jacques Grandier (Lee Montague), all of whom are highly successful in their various careers. The five guests, along with Maggie, are ushered into a high-tech hospital facility in the manor for an audience with Montolive, who speaks to them while hidden behind a curtain. Calling Maggie to his bedside, he reaches out with a deformed hand and places a signet ring bearing the Mountolive family crest upon her finger, which she is subsequently unable to remove.

In the aftermath of this curious ritual the five guests begin to die one by one in inexplicable ways. First, Maria encounters an invisible barrier that traps her under the water of the manor's indoor swimming pool and drowns. Next, Jackson chokes on a chicken bone and dies when an emergency tracheotomy is performed by Ravenhurst's resident nurse (Margaret Tyzak). Liebnecht is burned to death by a freak burst of flame that emerges from the fireplace, and Barbara is killed when the mirror in her room explodes and she suffers the death of a thousand cuts. Finally, Jacques dies while he is shooting at Pete with a shotgun from the roof of the mansion and the weapon explodes in his face. Maggie and Pete try to flee from the scene of the carnage by stealing Montolive's limo, but they keep getting lost and all roads always lead them back to Ravenhurst.

Exploring the manor, Maggie discovers an oil painting of the family matriarch Lady Margaret Walshingham, who is her exact double. She eventually learns that Lady Margaret was tried for witchcraft and burned at the stake during the reign of Queen Elizabeth I, and that her son Jason inherited the estate. Jason Montolive has been kept alive for centuries by black magic, and the five dead guests were his acolytes, who were sacrificed to the devil as part of the ritual of passing his powers on to his descendent, Maggie. As he dies, Mountolive makes Maggie his heir as she assumes control of Ravenhurst and becomes a powerful witch. Her first act is to make Pete into her willing supplicant and consort as he comes under the spell of her newly acquired magic.

While *The Legacy* was produced by Universal, the U.K. locale and mostly British cast give it the ambience of an Amicus production. The screenplay, co-scripted by Hammer veteran Jimmy Sangster, is highly original and contains equal parts of horror, suspense and mystery. Director Richard Marquand, while not providing a lot of intense visual atmospherics, manages to sustain the narrative admirably. Marquand would later go on to direct the crowd-pleasing *Star Wars* sequel *Return of the Jedi* (1983). The two American leads contrast nicely with the cultured English thesps as Katherine Ross and Sam Elliott's spirited performances easily carry the film. Ross' role recalls her earlier portrayal of a vulnerable heroine in the sci-fi thriller *The Stepford Wives* (1975). Roger Daltrey, lead singer for the rock band The Who, acquits himself well as an actor before choking on a chicken bone, and Margaret Tyzack has a creepy supporting part as the evil, nun-like Nurse Adams.

The Ravenhurst mansion locale was filmed at Losely House, a Tudor-era manor in Guildfore, Surrey. Unlike many cinema haunts, the film was shot in both the exterior and interior of the house. The mansion's dark, wood paneled walls adorned with paintings and odd-looking tapestries and the elegant rooms filled with antique furniture and *objects d'art* stand in contrast to Montolive's hi-tech hospital facility, which has a science fiction look. While there are no ghosts in evidence at Ravenhurst, the haunt is inhabited by devil worshippers in the manner of *Seven Footprints to Satan* and the 1934 version of *The Black Cat*. Like a number of films including *The Ghost Breakers* and *The Haunted Palace*, *The Legacy* involves the concept of the doppelganger which is linked to a painting of a reincarnated ancestor.

The doppelganger was also central to the plot of *The Changeling* (1980). In Celtic folklore a *changeling* is a fairy child exchanged for a human baby by the little people. Oscar winner George C. Scott stars as New York composer John Russell, whose life is shattered by the loss of his wife and daughter in a tragic car accident. Seeking to recover from the emotional shock of the deaths, he relocates across the country to Seattle, where he rents a vacant mansion in a quiet, secluded area of the city from real estate agent Claire Norman

Recovering composer John Russell (George C. Scott) confers with real estate agent Claire Norman (Trish Van Devere) in front of the haunted Seattle mansion in Peter Medak's stylish ghost story *The Changeling* (1980).

(Trish Van Devere), where he hopes he can continue his work. Claire, who also works at the city's historical society, informs him that the property has been vacant for twelve years.

Soon after he moves into the enormous old house, he is confronted by threatening paranormal phenomena. Doors open and shut by themselves, water faucets turn themselves on and off, strange sounds are heard and glass shatters. Exploring the house, Russell discovers a hidden room in the attic containing a child's toys, an antique wheelchair and a music box that plays a melody that is identical in key and tempo to one he has been composing. Most hauntingly, he catches a glimpse of the face of a drowned boy in a bathtub in the attic. Seeking to understand the paranormal forces at work in the house, he invites medium Leah Harmon (Helen Burns) to conduct a séance there. In an eerie sequence, the psychic goes into a trance and keeps repeating phrases like "What is your name?" and "Did you die in this house?" Listening to an audio recording of the séance on a tape recorder that he kept running during the event, he later hears the ghost reply that his name is Joseph and that he died around the turn of the century.

Seeking to unravel the mystery of the haunting, Russell becomes obsessed with finding out the identity of the dead child. With Claire's help, he searches through old municipal records and finally manages to locate Joseph's remains on another property where his ghost has also been seen. Russell obtains permission to excavate at the site and discovers a child's bones along with a golden religious medallion. His investigations lead him to the grim realization that the boy, Joseph Carmichael, was a sickly child confined to a wheelchair who was kept isolated in the house's attic room. Fearing that the family would lose its inheritance if the child did not reach his 21st birthday, his father Richard murdered the boy in 1906 and concealed the remains elsewhere. The father then adopted a boy of the same age and similar appearance and sent him off to Europe for a few years, after which he brought him back and passed him off as his own son.

After leading a life of wealth and privilege, the bogus Joseph Carmichael (who is the changeling of the title) is now a powerful U.S. senator (Melvyn Douglas) who still has an identical gold medallion in his possession. Russell confronts Senator Carmichael with the results of his research, and shows him the medallion he exhumed from the boy's grave, whereupon the Senator goes into a paroxysm of guilt over the revelations. In the meantime, Claire has returned to the house looking for Russell and is terrified as the dead boy's wheelchair chases her down the main staircase. As Russell enters the mansion, the whole house begins to shake and the composer watches as Carmichael's ghostly doppelganger mounts the stairs to the attic room and the stairway bursts into flames. Fires engulf the entire house as Russell and Claire escape and the haunt is destroyed in a fiery conflagration.

This superior haunted house story is distinguished by the fine performance of Oscar winner George C. Scott, whose electric screen presence dominates the film. Director Peter Medak and cinematographer John Coquillon utilize highly fluid camera movements that glide through the haunted spaces of the mansion like a disembodied spirit. Characters are frequently filmed in extreme long shots that make them seem lost inside the vastness of the haunt. Wide angle lenses distort the mansion's rooms to make them look larger and subtly off-kilter. As in *The Haunting*, spooky sound effects are used to heighten the tension. The protagonist is a composer and music plays a big part in the film, especially in the use of a haunting music box theme that echoes similar motifs in *The Innocents* and *The Ghost*. Russell Hunter's original screenplay contains a number of gothic tropes, including a secret room that conceals a forbidden relative and the doppelganger, or "changeling." The plot follows the haunted house story template wherein a vacant house with a dubious reputation suddenly becomes inhabited, spooky goings-on are detected, and the mystery is investigated. This, in turn, leads to the revelation of a secret death on the premises, the resolution of the haunting and the exorcism of the haunt's resident ghost.

Produced by a Canadian film unit for a modest $600,000, the movie utilized locations in Toronto, Vancouver, Seattle and New York. The interiors and exteriors of the haunt, however, were both built-up sets. On the outside, the mansion is a creepy-looking old house set in the middle of the woods, although it's supposed to be situated in an urban environment in the city of Seattle. The interior walls are paneled in dark wood, with the bare spaces of wall painted a ghastly yellow-green color that would be more appropriate for a mental hospital or other institution. This color scheme emphasizes the decrepit dreariness and unpleasant environment of the long-vacant house that, as one character describes, "doesn't want people." The huge multistory dwelling is a maze of stairways, corridors, rooms and secret passageways.

Trish Van Devere and George C. Scott are trapped by the fiery vengeance of a ghost in this poster for *The Changeling* (1980).

Although ad copy for *The Changeling* didn't claim that it was "based on a true story" (as are the films to be discussed in the following chapter), scripter Russell Hunter later revealed that his plot was inspired by his stay in a real-life haunt. The house in question was the Henry Treat Rogers mansion located at 1739 East 13th Avenue in the Cheesman Park section of Denver. The mansion was built on the former site of the Prospect Hill Cemetery, which was sold to the city in the late 1800s. When construction began on the house in 1893, workers dug up the graves, hacked the bodies into pieces and loaded them up into child-sized caskets. Some of the graves were also looted of any valuable personal effects that had been buried with the dead.

In 1969, Hunter, who had been a musical arranger for CBS-TV in New York, relocated to Denver and rented the mansion at a reduced rate (always a bad sign) because "nobody wanted to live there." Shortly after moving in, Hunter began to be plagued by loud banging and crashing sounds, faucets turning themselves on and off, doors opening by themselves and other paranormal activities. Hunter and an architect friend reportedly discovered a hidden staircase leading to a third-floor room containing a child's schoolbooks and the journal of a disabled boy who had been kept sequestered in the room. A medium conducted a séance in the mansion, and while in a trance revealed that when the sickly child became seriously ill, his parents worried that if he died his inheritance would pass to a different branch of the family. When their son passed away, the parents secretly buried the body in another location and adopted a boy from a local orphanage to replace him. Guided by the dead child's voice, Hunter dug up the boy's remains from under a house on South Dahlia Street and found a gold medallion inscribed with his name. All of this sleuthing failed to soothe the unquiet spirits in the house, however, and Hunter was obliged to find other lodgings. These purported events became the basis for the plot of *The Changeling*, but subsequent investigations have failed to corroborate most of Hunter's story. The Henry Treat Rogers mansion was demolished in the 1970s to make way for a high-rise apartment building, and during the construction one of its walls collapsed, killing a bulldozer operator.

The mystery house thriller of the 1920s and 30s made a comeback with *House of the Long Shadows* (1983). Based on a novel by Earl Derr Biggers, the creator of Charlie Chan and its stage adaptation by George M. Cohan, the film features American horror stars John Carradine and Vincent Price together with Hammer icons Peter Cushing and Christopher Lee. The movie's protagonist is Kenneth Magee (Desi Arnaz, Jr.), a popular writer who makes a $20,000 bet with his publisher Sam Allyson (Richard Todd) that he can produce a literary quality novel in 24 hours. Allyson suggests that Magee do his scribbling at a manor house in Wales named Bllyddpaeter in Welsh dialect, which translates as "Baldpate" in plain English. Baldpate has been vacant for 40 years and has no electricity, but Magee accepts the wager, thinking that the gothic mansion will spark his imagination.

Arriving at the dark and gloomy manor, Magee sets up his typewriter in one of Baldpate's rooms and gets to work, but soon finds he is not alone. He is confronted by the elderly Lord Grisbane (Carradine) and his middle-aged daughter Victoria (Sheila Kieth), who have been maintaining the property for decades. Soon they are joined by Grisbane's sons Sebastian (Cushing) and Lionel (Price), along with Mr. Corrigan (Lee), a prospective buyer of the estate, and Allyson's secretary, Mary Norton (Julie Peasgood). The Grisbane sons reveal that they have returned to Baldpate to free their insane brother Roderick, "a raving thing" who has been confined in an upstairs room for the last 40 years. When he was 14 years old, Roderick seduced a village girl and made her pregnant, then lured her back to the mansion and killed her. The Grisbane clan took the law into their own hands and kept Roderick locked up, but after 40 years they have decided to release him.

When they open Roderick's room, however, they find it empty, and soon afterward the family members start coming up dead one by one. Lord Brisbane dies of a heart attack, Victoria is discovered strangled to death and Sebastian is found hanged. Two other victims are Andrew and Diane Caulder (Richard Todd and Louise English), an unfortunate couple who happen to wander into the mansion. Diane dies after accidentally splashing acid in her face, and Andrew succumbs to a poisoned glass of wine. Magee's and Corrigan's cars are found to have been rendered inoperative, stranding everyone at Baldpate. All of this is the work of the mad Roderick, who is revealed to be Corrigan. Roderick explains that he escaped from his confinement long ago and has periodically returned to Baldpate to make the family think he was still imprisoned. Now, on the fortieth anniversary of his crime, he is seeking to revenge himself on all of his family members. He then proceeds to brutally hack Lionel to death with a battle axe and then goes after Magee and Mary, but Magee knocks Roderick down a flight of stairs and he is accidentally killed when he is impaled upon the axe. From there, the film proceeds to a surprising, but rather silly denouement.

While it's entitled *House of the Long Shadows*, the main problem with the film is that (at least in its current DVD release) the lighting setups are so dark that in many scenes nothing at all can be seen on the screen. Lacking electricity, Baldpate can supposedly only be lit by candlelight, but a competent cinematographer could provide enough illumination to at least get basic exposure, and hopefully could even use the limited light to create a dark atmosphere, none of which is accomplished by director of photography Norman Langley. The viewer is frequently left squinting at a black screen, trying to ascertain what's going on.

Director Pete Walker moves the action along briskly and does a decent job of putting the film's talented cast through their paces. While the film's nominal star, Desi Arnaz, Jr., comes across as a nonentity, the main draw is watching the four "titans of terror" interact. Both Cushing and Carradine seem old, weak and debilitated, while Price and Lee are in fine form. Price seems to have been afforded the best lines, as he rattles on about "the stench of decay" in the "cursed place" in his dulcet, stentorian tones. The plot is reminiscent of that of James Whale's 30s classic *The Old Dark House*, in which a group of family members and trapped guests are menaced by an insane relative who escapes from a long confinement within a secret room and wreaks havoc. Most of the action takes place inside the house's ornate dining room, an immobility that accentuates the film's theatrical origins. Exteriors and interiors were shot at an estate at Rotherfield Park, East Tisted, Alton, Hampshire, England, but the mansion is only seen in daylight in a couple of brief long shots, imparting an indistinct sense of place upon the proceedings.

Something that becomes apparent from a survey of haunted house films from these decades is that the majority of them were produced outside of Hollywood. In addition to entries originating on the Continent and Canada such as *The Ghost*, *Kill, Baby, Kill*, *The Tenant* and *The Changeling*, there was a preponderance of films produced or shot in England, a list that includes *A Place of Our Own*, *Three Cases of Murder*, *The House That Dripped Blood*, *The Legend of Hell House*, *The Haunting of Julia*, *The Legacy* and *House of the Long Shadows*. Perhaps the haunted house tale could only blossom outside of the strictures of rationalist America, and had to return to its British roots. Of the American entries, 1976's *Burnt Offerings* offered a seminal narrative framework for many haunted house films to come. Works by critically acclaimed horrormeisters such as Mario Bava, Roger Corman and Roman Polanski contributed greatly to the sub-genre.

In the following chapter haunted house films that claim to be based on cases of real-life hauntings will be examined, both in terms of their cinematic quality and their factual adherence to the paranormal incidents that inspired them. Is truth stranger than fiction? You be the judge.

Chapter Six

"Based on a True Story"

While the vast majority of haunted house films are based on works of fiction, there are a few that claim to be based on true life accounts of actual hauntings and advertise this alleged fact up front. Oddly a number of the best films in the subgenre, namely *The Innocents*, *The Exorcist* and *The Changeling* were all reputedly inspired by actual events that serve to give them a certain verisimilitude, but the filmmakers did not claim that they had any basis in fact. The "based on a true story" trope, however, lends an edge of the uncanny to the proceedings and evokes a wondering belief in the reality of the supernatural that translates into more receipts at the box office.

The scientific study of ghosts and hauntings dates back to the 19th century with the formation of the Society for Psychical Research (SPR) in England in 1882. Founding members of the SPR included scientists and celebrities such as physicists Sir Oliver Lodge and Sir William Crookes, Cambridge philosopher Henry Sidgwick, psychologist Fredrick Myers, Nobel Prize–winning physiologist Charles Richet, the acclaimed poet William Butler Yeats and Sir Arthur Conan Doyle, the creator of Sherlock Holmes. This was followed by the formation of an American offshoot, the American Society for Psychical Research, or ASPR, in Boston in 1885. During the early 20th century, scientist J.B. Rhine founded the Parapsychology Laboratory at Duke University that investigated poltergeist hauntings.

As the century wore on, however, research into ghostly phenomena and haunted houses was conducted by amateurs such as Harry Price, who conducted investigations of Borely Rectory ("the most haunted house in England") and Guy Playfair, who investigated the Enfield Poltergeist, the subject of the fiction film *The Conjuring 2* (2016). Ghost hunting had escaped from the laboratory and had passed into the hands of amateurs who brought all manner of hi-tech paraphernalia into haunted locations to record documentary evidence of the existence of ghosts. A very different approach has been taken by self-styled "demonologists" Ed and Lorraine Warren, who consider hauntings and poltergeists the work of the devil and his minions and who actively try to exorcise unclean spirits.

The Warrens founded the New England Society for Psychical Research (NESPR) in 1952 to investigate hauntings and related phenomena, and claim to have investigated over 10,000 cases of the paranormal, including such high-profile events as the Amityville haunting in Long Island and the Enfield Poltergeist in London. Ed Warren died in 2006, but Lorraine continues to maintain their Occult Museum in their home in Monroe, Connecticut, that contains mementos of their psychic exploits. Lorraine claimed to be a gifted medium, while Ed was the occult scholar. To the Warrens, haunted houses and poltergeists were invariably ascribed to being the work of demons conjured by black magic rather than ghosts or spirits. In recent years the Warrens have become the central characters in a number of horror films claiming to be based on their supernatural exploits and are portrayed by actors Patrick Wilson and Vera Farmiga. These films include *The Conjuring* (2013), *The Conjuring 2* (2016) and *The Nun* (2018), while the Warrens' case files also provided material for *Annabelle* (2014) and *Annabelle: Creation* (2017).

The Amityville Horror (1979) was adapted from an allegedly nonfiction book by Jay Anson concerning the Lutz family of Long Island, who moved into a house in which the murder of an entire family had taken place in 1974. The film stars James Brolin and Margot Kidder as newly-marrieds George and Cathy Lutz, who purchase a Dutch Colonial home in Amityville, Long Island, at a bargain price (always a bad sign) in which Ronald DeFeo, Jr., had slaughtered his entire family during the previous year. Undeterred by the house's unwholesome history, the Lutzes move in with their three children, Greg (K.C. Martel), Matt (Meeno Peluce) and Amy (Natasha Ryan), and it isn't long before a series of supernatural events begin to assail the family. The house's telephone malfunctions, cold spots appear and a black goop fills the toilet. When local priest Father Delaney (Rod Steiger) arrives to bless the house he is lured into an upstairs room where he is beset by a plague of flies that cause him to sicken and wound his hand.

Predictably, matters go from bad to worse as Amy acquires a strange imaginary friend named Jody, a large sum of cash goes missing and the children's babysitter is locked in a bedroom closet by an unseen force. Then Father Delaney is seriously injured in an accident when his car mysteriously malfunctions and he loses his sight, while the family dog starts digging up something unholy in the cellar. These supernatural events cause George to become sullen and withdrawn as his land surveying business suffers and he spends a lot of time chopping wood for fires to warm the house's cold spots. In the meantime, Kathy does some research at the local library where she learns that the house was built on top of a Shinnecock Indian burial ground and that a notorious devil worshipper named John Ketchum had also lived on the land.

Things come to a head one stormy night when George comes under the domination of the demonic forces within the house and goes after the children, who are locked in a bedroom, with his woodcutter's axe. As he is in the process of chopping the door down, Kathy arrives in time to avert a tragedy and bring George to his senses. As he is rescuing their dog from the hellish cellar, George is covered in a black slime that drips down the walls, and the family flees for their lives from the haunt as an end title informs us, "George and Kathleen Lutz and their family never reclaimed their house or their personal belongings. Today they live in another state." The Lutz's supernatural ordeal had lasted for only 28 days.

Director Stuart Rosenberg manages to move the action along nicely while putting the cast through their paces, but invests little in the way of lighting, composition or other visuals to establish a proper spooky ambience for his haunted house chiller. Obliged to follow the narrative of Jay Anson's "true story," scripter Sandor Stern constructs a plot that seems more like a series of single episodes than a unified whole. Stars James Brolin and Margot Kidder do a workmanlike job with this episodic and occasionally silly material, but Rod Steiger's over-the-top performance as the stricken priest dominates in the acting department as he spews immortal lines of dialogue like "I can tell the difference between the supernatural and a bad clam" and fights off swarms of evil Satanic flies. Oddly, Steiger's scenes are shot so that he has no interplay with Brolin or Kidder at all, and at times seems to be acting in a different movie.

Most critics decried the film's numerous flaws, but despite the bad press *The Amityville Horror* was an enormous popular success for independent studio American International, and proved to be the second highest-grossing film of 1979. Horror luminary Stephen King ascribes the film's success to its easily digestible haunted house story and its emphasis on the picture's subtext of contemporaneous economic unease, particularly in the scene in which George Lutz loses track of fifteen hundred dollars, which has presumably been spirited away by the house's mischievous spooks. He refers to it as an "economic horror story" and quipped, "The movie might as well have been subtitled *The Horror of the Shrinking Bank Account*."[1]

The ghostly goings-on and poltergeist manifestations at the haunt are attributed to the work of demons, the haunt being a kind of gateway between our world and the infernal regions. Apart from the Bates Mansion in the *Psycho* series of films, the Amityville French Colonial is the second most iconic haunted house in screen history, its windowed façade presenting an anthropomorphic, face-like appearance. The actual haunt is located at 112 Ocean Avenue in Amityville, Long Island, but the film's exteriors were shot at a private residence at 18 Brooks Road in Toms River, New Jersey, where a superstructure was erected around the outside of the house to make it resemble the Lutz home. Interiors were filmed at an MGM studio lot in Los Angeles.

Like *Psycho* and *Poltergeist*, *The Amityville Horror* struck a chord with movie audiences and led to a series of sequels. *Amityville II: The Possession* (1982) was an execrable prequel that purported to tell the story of the mass-murder of the DeFeo family by Robert DeFeo, Jr., in 1974, who was allegedly possessed by evil spirits within the house. In the third entry, *Amityville 3-D* (1983), a new owner of the haunt encounters a reanimated corpse and a fire-breathing monster. *Amityville 4: The Evil Escapes* (1989) involves a lamp from the Amityville house that is transported to California, where it becomes the vehicle for more supernatural mayhem. Similarly, *Amityville 92: It's About Time* (1992) featured a 15th century clock formerly owned by a French sorcerer that is taken from Long Island to San Gabriel, California, where it quite predictably unleashes the forces of the nether-

James Brolin and Margot Kidder pose in front of the photogenic Amityville haunt in this publicity still for *The Amityville Horror* **(1979).**

world. Finally, the original film was remade in an unnecessary and inferior version as *The Amityville Horror* in 2005. Additionally, the film apparently influenced *The Shining*, in which a father falls under the influence of a haunted house and attempts to attack his family with an axe, and the sub-plot in *Poltergeist* in which a family home is built on top of a former cemetery.

The fact that the movie was based on an allegedly true story probably added a certain edge to the film's appeal, but almost every aspect of the Anson book and the film versions has been the subject of controversy and debate, and many of the "facts" of the haunting have been disproven by skeptics. While it is true that Ronald "Butch" DeFeo, Jr., murdered his family on the night of November 13, 1974, and claimed he heard voices in his head directing him to commit the killings, he later admitted that this was part of his lawyer's defense strategy during his trial that was designed to allow him to cop an insanity plea, and that he had actually committed the crimes while high on alcohol and heroin. The priest involved in the case was revealed to be Father Ralph Pecoraro, who did not encounter a plague of flies at the house and later claimed he didn't see anything strange during his visit. Amy Lutz did indeed have an imaginary friend, but so do a lot of other children. The Shinnecock tribe did not reside in Amityville, but had lived some distance away.

The Amityville haunting received wide coverage from the local media, and a news outlet contacted the Warrens, who descended on the house along with a gaggle of reporters and paranormal investigators. Twenty days after the Lutzes had fled their home, the Warrens and their crew conducted a "psychic pajama party" at the haunt and claimed to detect a demonic presence there. Ed Warren claimed that a supernatural force threw him to the floor, and Lorraine and the other psychics supposedly had perceptions of the evil forces within the house. A photographer snapped a creepy-looking picture of what is purportedly the ghost of one of the DeFeo children using infrared film that was widely circulated in the media. A highly fanciful version of the "party" events appears in the opening sequence of the 2016 film *The Conjuring 2*.

In the wake of the publication of the Anson book and the 1979 movie a court battle ensued between the Lutzes and lawyer William Weber, who had negotiated the initial book contract. During the litigation claims and counterclaims, Weber insisted that the entire story was a hoax concocted by Weber, Anson and the Lutzes, and the facts that emerged during the trial tended to corroborate Weber's version of events. Eventually all claims and counterclaims were settled, but the facts brought forth during the trial, along with numerous inconsistencies in the Lutz's narrative, tend to uphold the notion that the haunting was indeed a hoax. What is incontrovertible is that the Lutzes reaped (and continue to reap) substantial monetary gains from the *Amityville Horror* story. In 1977 the home at 112 Ocean Avenue was purchased by another family and has been inhabited ever since by a succession of owners, none of whom have reported any ghostly manifestations.

A more obscure series of paranormal events that were much better documented inspired the paranormal thriller *The Entity* (1983). The film stars Barbara Hershey as Carlotta (Carla) Moran, a single mom struggling to make ends meet in Los Angeles, who is plagued by an invisible being that causes objects to move and subjects her to violent sexual assaults. At first only Carla experiences these phenomena, and fearing for her sanity, she consults Dr. Sneiderman (Ron Silver), a psychiatrist at a local clinic. Sneiderman's diagnosis is that she is suffering from mental delusions, and he dismisses bruises on various parts of

Carla Moran (Barbara Hershey) begins to psychologically disintegrate under the psychic onslaught of a malicious poltergeist in *The Entity* **(1983).**

her body as being self-inflicted. Unfortunately, the attacks continue as the entity causes her to lose mechanical control of her car and manifests itself by causing rampant destruction at the home of her best friend Cindy Nash (Margaret Blye).

One day while Carla and Cindy are perusing books in the occult section of an L.A. bookstore, they overhear two men discussing paranormal matters and introduce themselves. The men turn out to be UCLA parapsychologists Gene Kraft (Richard Brestoff) and Joe Meehan (Raymond Singer), who become intrigued by her situation and wind up visiting her home, where they observe strange odors, cold spots and electrical disturbances. The scientists set up recording instruments in Carla's home, and record evidence of "classic poltergeist activity" that convinces the head of the parapsychology unit, Dr. Jean Cooley (Jacqueline Brooks), to investigate the case more fully. Dr. Cooley devises a plan to trap the entity under laboratory conditions in order to prove its existence. A full-scale simulacrum of Carla's house is constructed in the college gym without ceilings, and a device that sprays liquid helium is installed that is designed to freeze the being into molecular immobility. Carla is to be the bait in the trap and is supposed to run to a "safe room" where she will be protected from the liquid helium when the entity appears.

Dr. Sneiderman is appalled by the experiment and tries to have the university administration shut it down, but lacks the political clout to do so. Once Carla enters the mock-up, it isn't long before the entity manifests itself and takes control of the hi-tech equipment, then tries to kill her with streams of the ultra-cold fluid. Sneiderman rushes in to save her, and the being is trapped when the helium tanks explode and bathe it in the freezing liquid, but even the molecular deep freeze can't hold the entity for long as it bursts out of its frozen prison and vanishes. In the aftermath, Carla packs up her children and moves out of state, and a postscript informs us, "The film you have just seen is a fictionalized account of a true incident which took place in Los Angeles, California in October, 1976. It is considered by psychic researchers to be one of the most extraordinary cases in the history of parapsychology. The real Carla Moran is today living in Texas with her children. The attacks, though decreased in both frequency and intensity, continue."

Released a year after the big-budget special effects extravaganza *Poltergeist*, *The Entity* is a more modest, but a more daring and controversial R-rated treatment of the theme that has a basis in real events. Barbara Hershey's intense and dignified performance as an ordinary woman who comes under assault by a paranormal force beyond human comprehension dominates the film, with an able assist from Ron Silver as the arch-skeptic psychiatrist Dr. Sneiderman. Sidney J. Furie's direction deftly weaves a tale that he considered a supernatural suspense thriller rather than a straight-up horror picture. The movie gets down to business within the first seven minutes as the psychic force within the Moran household goes on the attack. Furie uses time-honored techniques such as skewed camera angles, fluid camera movements and the evocative use of light and shadow to build cinematic tension. Sound is used to great effect as spooky winds howl through the haunt, bolts of electrical energy hiss and a loud, jarring noise accompanies the film's horrific rape scenes. Composer Charles Bernstein contributes an eerie electronic score that effectively complements the film's dark mood.

The Entity's screenplay was penned by Frank DeFelitta from his novel of the same name. In novelizing the poltergeist case on which the film was based. DeFelitta created the Dr. Sneiderman character out of whole cloth in order to create a rationalistic viewpoint that provides a dramatic *frisson* between science and the paranormal. The film's unusual subject matter involved Hershey performing in the nude, including a scene involving full-frontal nudity and another in which the entity's invisible hands palpate her naked breasts. A number of critics thought that the film's R-rated scenes were exploitative and even misogynistic, but they are not presented in a prurient manner. The talented Ms. Hershey would later appear in a supporting role in the haunted house thriller *Insidious* (2012).

Carla's haunted house is a modest, single-story Los Angeles dwelling that comports with the type of home in the actual case. The interiors are painted in a dull, pale yellow color that accentuates the drab surroundings and also serves to create an atmosphere of psychic oppression. Building a copy of Carla's house in order to lure the spook inside so it can be studied is a novel idea, although this did not happen in real life and no parapsychology lab in history has ever had the resources to attempt such an expensive and extensive project. In any event, poltergeist activity is not limited to the confines of a haunt, but, as the film correctly shows, follows the person who is the focus of the activity from place to place,

The DVD release includes a short documentary special feature about the actual incident that inspired both the novel and the movie entitled "The Entity Files" which is narrated by former UCLA parapsychologist Barry Taff, the lead investigator on the case. Dr. Taff, who served as technical advisor on the film, was working as a research assistant at the Neuropsychiatric Institute at UCLA under the direction of Dr. Thelma Moss in 1974 when he accidentally met a woman named Doris Bither in a Los Angeles bookstore after she overheard him discussing psychic phenomena with a colleague, Kerry Gaynor. When Ms. Bither remarked that her house was haunted, the two parapsychologists later paid her a visit at 27547 Braddock Street in the Culver City suburb of L.A. Taff describes the place as a rundown property that had been condemned by the city where Bither and her children were living illegally. Once inside, however, they perceived odd smells and a cold spot, and witnessed a closet door open by itself and a frying pan eject onto the floor. On the basis of this initial visit, Taff was assigned to head up a full-scale investigation by the UCLA team.

Bither claimed that she had been sexually assaulted on several occasions by an unseen entity and had endured malicious poltergeist attacks such as the house's fuse box being ripped out of the wall and thrown at her. The spook had also attacked her children, who reported being slapped, bitten and scratched by an unseen being. A group of about 30 investigators set up cameras and other equipment in the Bither home to document the phenomena and managed to get pictures of anomalous orbs of light leaving arcing trails inside a darkened room. Many of them simultaneously witnessed the bizarre apparition of a male torso sculpted in light that gradually dissipated, but this event did not show up on photographs. When Bither moved away, houses adjacent to her new home also experienced poltergeist manifestations. Writer Frank DeFelitta heard about the strange goings-on and befriended Bither, who gave him information that he incorporated into his novelization of the case, and later into his screenplay for the film. Of course, the sequences involving the attempt to trap the being in liquid hydrogen are pure fiction, but the rest of the plot was grounded in fact. While erotic encounters with discarnate entities are rare, they have been reported from time to time in the annals of parapsychology.

A famous haunting from the early 19th century called the "Bell Witch" case provided the basis for the costume melodrama *An American Haunting* (2005). The story takes place in 1817 on the rural farm of John Bell in Robertson County, Tennessee, where Bell (Donald Sutherland) becomes embroiled in a land and debt dispute with his neighbor, Kate Batts (Gaye Brown). When the local church council rules in favor of Bell despite the fact that he has charged her usurious rates of interest on a loan, Batts, who is reputed to be a witch, curses him, proclaiming, "Darkness will fall upon you, and your precious daughter, too."

Soon afterward Bell's adolescent daughter Betsy (Rachel Hurd) begins to hear strange sounds in her bedroom that quickly escalate into a full-blown poltergeist manifestation as doors open and close by themselves, pages are ripped out of the family Bible and fly around the room, and Betsy herself is physically attacked by an unseen force. The Bell family is horrified when they watch helplessly as Betsy is lifted up by her hair and slapped in the face while suspended in midair by the unseen entity. These psychic assaults cause negative behavioral changes in Betsy that come to the attention of her teacher, Richard Powell (James D'Arcy), who is skeptical when he hears about the haunting and goes to the Bell house to investigate. He is forced to change his view, however, when he witnesses the strange phenomena with his own eyes.

The Bells and Richard attempt to exorcise the supernatural force using prayer and religious observances, to no avail. Betsy's mother Lucy (Sissy Spacek) is horrified by the family's plight and is plunged further into despair when a sack of clothes previously pilfered by Kate Batts is returned to the Bell farm, indicating that the witch has used their personal garments to cast her spell upon them. John Bell visits the witch's farm and begs her to remove the curse, but is told, "I didn't curse you, you cursed yourself." Things go from bad to worse as the entity begins to speak to the family in a spooky chorus of voices and apparitions of ghosts appear. Betsy goes into a comatose state while the evil spirit visits its afflictions upon John, who becomes seriously ill. The underlying reason for the haunting is finally revealed when Lucy suddenly remembers catching John in the act of sexually abusing Betsy. She then allows her daughter to administer a spoonful of poison to her father in retribution, and with his death the supernatural manifestations cease.

Written and directed by Courtney Solomon and "based on the terrifying true story" of the Bell Witch, *An American Haunting* seems to echo themes from *The Entity* in its depiction of a young woman who is subjected to a series of brutal assaults at the hands of an invisible being. The spook is even referred to as "the Entity" at various times in the script. The setting inside the early 19th century rural Tennessee farmhouse is atmospheric, and the director has a fine eye for period detail in this historical melodrama. Stars Donald Sutherland and Sissy Spacek turn in dignified, restrained performances acting through this potentially exploitative material, while newbie Rachel Hurd-Wood has her work cut out for her in the movie's scream queen role and Gaye Brown does a fine job in her portrayal of the witch Kate Batts. Director of Photography Adrian Biddle's fluid camerawork darts and swoops through the Bell house in a fashion that suggests he is capturing the point of view of the discarnate entity plaguing the family.

The main problem with the film is Solomon's screenplay that can't seem to decide on the underlying cause of the supernatural disturbances. Based on the 1995 novel *The Bell Witch: An American Haunting* by Brent Monahan, the film posits multiple and seemingly contradictory explanations for the haunting. One suggestion is that Kate Batts stole the Bell's clothes and used them to put a hex on the family, but this is belied by the witch's statement to John Bell, "You cursed yourself." Another hypothesis is that Bell caused the haunting by having incestuous sexual relations with his daughter, but this explanation is also unclear. And why are apparitions of ghosts being seen by the Bells, and what is their connection to the poltergeist? There's also the matter of a fierce black dog or wolf that attacks family members on the property. The seemingly endless cascade of scenes in which a screaming Betsy is subjected to the savage attacks of the entity quickly becomes tiresome, and the film sometimes becomes hallucinatory to the point of incoherence.

Filmed in Canada and Romania, the film's haunt is an isolated farmhouse located in the middle of a misty landscape where most of the action plays out. The interiors are drab and darkly lit by candlelight in a realistic 19th century fashion that creates an ambience of confinement. The haunter of the Bell house is surely a poltergeist rather than a traditional ghost. The manifestations center around a girl in young adulthood, the being causes disruptions to the physical environment and is shown performing typical poltergeist tricks like pulling the covers from the sleeping Betsy and profaning the family Bible (they are notoriously sacrilegious).

The saga of the Bell Witch was first recounted in a book entitled *Our Family Trouble* written by family member Richard Williams Bell in 1846. Although it was written decades after the events, it is the only eyewitness account of the haunting extant. In 1894 a newspaperman named Martin Van Buren Ingram penned *An Authenticated History of the Bell Witch of Tennessee* that has become the primary source for historical information about the legend, even though it was written 60 years after the fact. Some historians consider Ingram's book a work of historical fiction that embellished many details of the haunting. According to these accounts the haunting of the Bell house began in 1817 with knocking sounds heard along the doors and walls, which quickly escalated into the growling of invisible dogs and the noise of chains dragging across the floor. The Bell children, especially Betsy, experienced sheets being pulled from their beds, had their hair pulled and were scratched, slapped, pinched and stuck with pins by an invisible agency.

The entity even began to speak and respond to questions. When asked, "Who are you and what do you want?" a voice replied, "I am a spirit. I was once very happy but have been disturbed." As the voice became more prolix it became a source of amusement to the local community, who flocked to hear it display knowledge of distant events and reveal juicy tidbits of private gossip. The being appeared to have telepathic and clairvoyant abilities that enabled it to read people's thoughts and perceive events that happened at a distance. Some versions of the legend claim that future president Andrew Jackson visited the Bell home to witness the phenomenon, but there is no documentary evidence for this ever having occurred. There is likewise no documentation for the film's contention that John Bell's death was based on "true events validated by the State of Tennessee as the only case in U.S. history where a spirit has caused the death of a human being." The attribution of the phenomenon to incestuous acts committed by Bell upon his daughter is derived from Monahan's novel and does not appear in any source material on the case. While *An American Haunting* contains much in the way of exaggeration and hyperbole, the film does depict many events enshrined in the legend of the Bell Witch and is consistent with many aspects of the poltergeist phenomenon as reported by psychic researchers.

Another case of allegedly true ghostly manifestations that centered around an American family was chronicled in *The Haunting in Connecticut* (2009). The film takes place in 1987, as Sara Campbell (Virginia Madsen) is obliged to drive her ailing son Matt (Kyle Gallner) from their home in upstate New York to a hospital in Connecticut for frequent cancer treatments. Looking for a rental property closer to the hospital in order to spare Matt from the ordeal of these long trips, Sara finds a large house for rent at very reasonable rates (always a bad sign) and moves in with her young son Billy (Ty Wood) and their cousins Wendy (Amanda Crew) and Mary (Sophi Knight) while her husband Peter (Martin Donovan), who is struggling with alcoholism, stays behind at their family home in New York. Although it's a large house, Matt decides to sleep in a room in the basement where the temperature is cooler that is adjacent to a mysterious locked enclosure.

Soon after the move, Matt begins to experience terrifying visions of a strange bearded man, a boy about his age, and corpses with strange symbols covering their entire bodies. When Matt manages to gain entrance to the locked basement room, he discovers an embalming table and a full suite of mortician's tools, revealing that their house was formerly a funeral home, which is the reason that the rent is so cheap. Matt continues to have bizarre hallucinations that are perceived only by him, and he begins to wonder if these are actually ghostly apparitions or a side effect of his cancer treatments. While undergoing a medical procedure at the hospital he meets a fellow patient, Nicholas Popescu (Elias Koteas), a reverend who is suffering from the same illness, and Matt bonds with the clergyman, who seems to possess an inner strength and wisdom that arise from his deep religious faith.

Matt's visions continue to grow in strangeness and intensity, and his bizarre behavior begins to weigh upon the other family members. One day the children discover a box in the attic containing photographs of dead people, along with a picture of the ghostly boy Matt has been seeing with a weird substance protruding from his mouth. They also find a smaller box containing objects that look like dried leaves. Wendy does some research at the local library and finds out that the funeral parlor was owned by a man named Ramsey Aikman (John Bluethner), who conducted séances at the mortuary using his son Jonah (Erik Berg) as the medium. After one of the séances, Aikman and four others were found dead and Jonah had disappeared. With no one else to turn to, Matt invites Nicholas over to the house to examine the evidence. The Reverend surmises that Aikman was practicing necromancy, a type of magic that involves the manipulation of the dead. The leaf-like objects in the box are dried human eyelids cut from the corpses as part of a ritual and the bodies covered with symbols are designed "to bind the spirits" to the house. The strange substance emerging from Jonah's mouth is ectoplasm, the ghostly stuff exuded by mediums that interacts with the physical world.

Psychic forces within the house become more and more malevolent as the entire family is subjected to anomalous electrical effects and flocks of phantom birds seen only as shadows. Matt experiences more vivid visions of Jonah's ghost, and as his health fails the dead boy, who was burned to death in the mortuary's crematorium in the aftermath of the séance, becomes a kind of doppelganger. Reverend Nicholas and Matt start to have simultaneous visions of the ghosts wherein they learn that Aikman was robbing graves from a local cemetery for his necromantic rituals and that the bodies are still concealed within the house. Taking an axe to the walls, Matt uncovers piles of corpses stacked up inside like mummies that tumble to the floor in piles. He sets the bodies on fire and nearly dies in the conflagration until Sarah arrives to pull him from the burning building. A postscript states that in the wake of the ordeal Matt's cancer went into remission and the house was later rebuilt and cleansed of the evils within.

While it's an effective horror flick, *The Haunting in Connecticut* frequently goes over the top with its macabre depictions of grim mortuary scenes and piles of corpses that tend to horrify rather than terrify. Director Peter Cornwell, working from a screenplay by Adam Simon and Tim Metcalfe, crafts a supernatural thriller set against the backdrop of the dramatic situation of a mother struggling to care for her terminally ill son. Much of the action takes place within the subjective viewpoint of Matt's visions, which lends the film an unreal, hallucinatory quality and an excessive visual morbidity. Like many haunted house movies of the period, it's constructed as a series of ghastly episodes, but the intricate script manages to tie them all together into a coherent whole. While it's not an actor's film, the cast turns in competent performances, but Virginia Madsen's intense portrayal of the mother of a dying son provides the film's dramatic grit, and character actor Elias Koteas, who had played sinister roles in horror noir thrillers like *Fallen* (1998) and *Shutter Island* (2010), delivers a restrained, dignified portrait of the cancer-ridden ghost expert Reverend Nicholas. An uneasy sense of life's tenuous mortality lurks just below the film's grim horror movie façade.

The film's haunt is a conventional suburban house on the outside, but the interior walls are painted in drab grays and browns that accentuate a feeling of claustrophobia, and the mortician's workshop, with its embalming table and weird-looking tools, is especially creepy. Its ghostly apparitions and lurking shadows are typical of the phenomena of a traditional haunted house, but the film melds these narrative elements with the themes of spirit mediumship and necromantic black magic. The bodies inscribed with magical characters was probably derived from Masaki Kobayashi's classic Japanese ghost story *Kwaidan* (1965), in which a Buddhist acolyte's entire body is covered in magical characters in order to protect him from malevolent ghosts.

The film was based on the 1992 novel *In a Dark Place: The Story of a True Haunting* by Ray Garton, a chronicle of the alleged paranormal experiences of the Snedecker family. In 1996, the Snedeckers moved into a house at 208 Meriden Avenue in Southington, Connecticut, because of its proximity to the hospital where their son Phillip was undergoing treatment for Hodgkin's Lymphoma. After moving in they found out that the place had formerly been a mortuary called the Hallahan Funeral Home, and the family discovered an embalming room, mortuary equipment and eerie photographs of dead people inside the house. Before long the Snedeckers claimed that they began to experience paranormal activity in the haunt, which included seeing apparitions of dead people, hearing strange voices and smelling the scent of rotting flesh. Anomalous electrical phenomena were observed. Family members were subjected to being slapped, beaten, pushed and even sexually assaulted by unseen entities. Phillip, who was undergoing radiation treatments, began to hear voices in his head, was diagnosed with schizophrenia and taken to a mental hospital after he attempted to rape his cousin.

In desperation, the Snedeckers called in celebrity ghost breakers Ed and Lorraine Warren (who you gonna call?), along with psychic researcher John Zaffis. After the Warrens had experienced the ghostly phenomena for themselves, they contended that a member of the funeral home staff had committed necrophilia, but this was never proven. They conducted a full-scale exorcism of the premises, which seemed to ameliorate the spooky happenings, and Phillip's cancer went into remission. In the aftermath, the Warrens called in novelist Ray Garton, who was contracted to write the "true story" of the haunting, but embellished his narrative with many fictions. There were no piles of corpses concealed within the house's walls, and the character of Reverend Nicholas is likewise fictive. The ectoplasm that plays such a crucial role in the story, and was also featured in the séance scene in *The Legend of Hell House*, was proven to be a fraudulent device exposed by Harry Houdini and other spiritualist debunkers in the early 20th century. The reported "ectoplasm" was invariably found to be made of cheesecloth or some other pliant substance that was concealed on the medium's body and later brought forth as the purported proof of spirit activity. As in the Amityville case, subsequent residents of the house have reported no such phenomena, which the current owner ascribes to "Hollywood foolishness." Although it's hard to say what actually might have occurred, many skeptics consider the entire case to be a hoax. A sequel in name only, entitled *The Haunting in Connecticut 2: Ghosts of Georgia* (2013), chronicled the haunting of a family at a farmhouse in rural Georgia, but has nothing to do with the original movie.

Horror director James Wan's *The Conjuring* (2013) introduced ghostbusters Ed and Lorraine Warren as characters in a haunted house movie about their demonological exploits. They are introduced with the dubious claim that they are "the world's most renowned paranormal investigators. Lorraine is a gifted clairvoyant, while Ed is the only non-ordained demonologist recognized by the Catholic Church." As the film opens, Ed (Patrick Wilson) and Lorraine (Vera Farmiga) are shown in action exorcising a demon-possessed doll in the "Annabelle" case and discussing their supernatural exploits during a college lecture. The narrative then shifts to Roger and Carolyn Perron (Ron Livingston and Lili Taylor), who are moving into a large but rundown farmhouse in Harrisville, Rhode Island, with their five daughters, Andrea (Shanley Caswell), Nancy (Hayley McFarland), Christine (Joey King), Cindy (Mackenzie Foy) and April (Kyla Deaver).

The haunting begins a few nights after they move in. All clocks in the house stop at precisely the same time, knocking sounds are heard, pictures are torn from walls and the family dog is found dead. Cindy begins to have sleepwalking spells, the other girls are attacked by unseen spirit entities and unexplained bruises appear all over Christine's body. As the family struggles to deal with these unearthly manifestations, Christine takes it upon herself to approach Ed and Lorraine after their lecture at a nearby college and enlists their aid. The Warrens visit the farmhouse, where they set up video and audio equipment to record the anomalies, while Lorraine has a vision of a woman hanging from a tree in the yard. Their research soon reveals that the house formerly belonged to a woman named Bathsheba Sherman, who had been accused of witchcraft and was related to the Salem witches. Bathsheba sacrificed her newborn baby to the devil and hung herself, cursing all who would possess the land, and subsequently a string of murders and suicides occurred on the property.

The Warrens conclude that the house must be exorcised and approach the Church for permission to have a priest conduct the ritual, but while their request is going through channels the supernatural forces within the house mount an attack. Carolyn becomes possessed by the spirit of Bathsheba and Ed decides that her peril is so great that he must perform the exorcism himself. She is tied to a chair in the cellar and covered with a sheet as she rages, biting through the sheet with bloody lips as the chair levitates and flocks of birds attack the house. Fortunately the spiritual powers of the Warrens prevail, the evil spirits are routed and the house is purified as the curse of Bathsheba is lifted.

Director Wan throws everything but the proverbial kitchen sink into this supernatural mish-mosh as the dynamic duo of Ed and Lorraine do battle with the dread forces of darkness. There's lots of screaming and prowling around in dark spaces, and Wan's liberal use of hand-held camera, presumably to lend a documentary look to the film, becomes both irritating and self-referential. The screenplay by Chad Hayes and Carey W. Hayes throws ghosts, witchcraft, spirit possession, exorcism, infanticide and somnambulism, along with the demonic Annabelle doll into a heady brew as the supernatural thrills just keep on coming. This was the film that introduced the Warrens, "the world's most renowned paranormal investigators," to movie audiences, and Patrick Wilson and Vera Farmiga come off as a couple of pious twits who believe "God brought us together for a reason" and seem to be part of a religious crusade against their demonic foes. The rest of the cast turn in workmanlike performances, but Lili Taylor, who had played the part of Eleanor in the 1999 remake of *The Haunting* (see Chapter Eight), has a juicy role as the spirit-possessed Carolyn Perron.

Critical response to the film was mixed, with some critics noting derivative resemblances with *Poltergeist* and *The Exorcist*. The theme of a witch who sacrificed her baby to Satan and yet was descended from one of the unfortunate innocents hanged during the Salem witch trials turned some critics off. Despite any flaws, however, *The Conjuring* was wildly successful at the box office, grossing nearly $320 million worldwide against production costs of only $20 million. The film was shot primarily at Screen Gems Studios in California and at various locations around Wilmington, North Carolina. The bucolic farmhouse appears pleasant and rustic on the outside, but the interior walls are painted a ghastly shade of brown that serves to set the proper mood, although it seems unlikely that a family would choose to live in such drab and depressing surroundings without repainting the premises.

The real-life Perron family lived in the 14-room Rhode Island farmhouse from 1971 to 1980, where they claim to have numerous paranormal experiences. During the first few months of their tenancy the behavior of the ghosts was benign. The girls reported that a friendly spook that smelled like flowers and fruit would tuck them into their beds and kiss their foreheads at night. As time went by, however, the ghosts reportedly became malignant, attacking the children and even possessing Carolyn Perron during a séance conducted by the Warrens, making her speak in a voice not her own, levitating her chair and throwing her across the room. The family detected the smell of rotting flesh in the house, and disembodied voices told the girls that dead soldiers were buried within the house's walls. A spirit named Bathsheba proclaimed herself the mistress of the house and visited her anger upon Carolyn. There was however, no history of witchcraft or child sacrifice associated with the haunt, and Carolyn's dramatic exorcism by Ed Warren never took place. Lorraine Warren acted as a consultant on the film and appeared in promotional spots with the Perron family prior to the film's release and even had a cameo appearance in the movie. Like the Amityville affair, there's nothing except the family's testimony to corroborate the strange events, and subsequent tenants reported no further paranormal activity. It's perhaps telling that the Perrons remained in the house for nine years despite the allegedly dire events of the haunting. After the film's release, the current owners of the home sued James Wan and the other producers, charging that their house has been repeatedly vandalized by Satanic cult members.

The "Annabelle" case is woven into the movie's narrative, and a film based on the Warren's investigation of this incident in 1970, entitled *Annabelle*, was directed by Wan and released in 2014. The allegedly demon-possessed doll is an example of a haunted object rather than a haunted house and is similar to the occult "dybbuk box" in *The Possession* (2012) and the bewitched mirror in *Oculus* (2013). Note that the doll used in the films is grotesque and resembles the evil-looking clown doll in *Poltergeist*, but the actual Annabelle was a plain vanilla Raggedy Ann doll. Skeptics point to a 1963 episode of TV's *The Twilight Zone* entitled "Living Doll," in which a malevolent talking doll is given to a little girl by her mother, whose name happens to be Annabelle.

One of the most notorious and extensively investigated paranormal events, England's "Enfield Poltergeist," formed the basis for the next film version of the Warren's exploits in *The Conjuring 2* (2016). As previously mentioned, the movie opens with the Warrens (Patrick Wilson and Vera Farmiga reprising their roles) conducting a séance at the Amityville house in 1976, where Lorraine goes into a trance and relives the murders of the DeFeo family. The action then shifts to the Hodgson family home in the London suburb on Enfield in 1977, where single mom Peggy Hodgson (Frances O'Connor) is struggling to raise her four children, Margaret, 13 (Lauren Esposito), Janet, 12 (Madison Wolfe), Johnny, 11 (Patrick McAuley) and Billy, seven (Benjamin Haigh), in government housing. After Janet and Margaret get caught playing with a homemade Ouija Board by their mum, Janet begins sleepwalking and having nightmares about an elderly man. Then a series of strange sounds and knockings is heard around the house. One night, responding to a ruckus in the children's bedroom, Peggy witnesses a heavy chest of drawers moving by itself and calls the police. When a couple of bobbies arrive, they watch a chair move across the floor, but can offer no further assistance and promptly leave.

On the other side of the pond, Ed Warren has painted a grotesque picture of a ghostly nun that seems to be taking on a life of its own. Lorraine goes into one of her trances and perceives that the name "Valak" is associated with the nun and writes the name in her Bible. Meanwhile. back in Enfield, the paranormal phenomena continue to increase in intensity as Janet becomes possessed by the spirit of an old man named Bill Wilkins, who had lived in the house before the Hodgsons moved in and had died there. Janet begins speaking in the elderly man's eerie, gravelly voice and curses the current inhabitants of "his" house. The strange goings-on attract the attention of the press, some of whom witness the effects of the poltergeist firsthand, and parapsychologists Maurice Grosse (Simon McBurney) and Anita Gregory (Franka Potente) are called in to investigate. Results are mixed, as Grosse becomes convinced that the phenomena are genuine, while Gregory is completely skeptical.

As the haunting continues unabated it comes to the attention of the Catholic Church, and Ed and Lorraine are dispatched to Enfield to sort things out. Confronted with the evidence, including a videotape of Janet deliberately trashing the family's kitchen to simulate poltergeist activity, the Warrens conclude that the case is a hoax and are on the point of returning to the States when Lorraine suddenly realizes that her psychic abilities have been blocked by the powers of the demonic nun, and the Warrens hastily return to the Hodgsons' house. They arrive just in time to save Janet from committing suicide while in a possessed state, while Lorraine confronts the demon Valak and sends it back to Hell. The evil in the

Ghostbuster Lorraine Warren (Vera Farmiga) attempts to exorcise the Enfield Poltergeist in *The Conjuring 2* **(2016).**

house having been exorcised, the family can continue living a normal life and the Warrens return to Connecticut after a job well done, but they anticipate meeting Valak in the future (thereby setting up the 2018 sequel, entitled *The Nun*).

The Conjuring 2 offers the usual heady brew of religion, demonology and family drama as the intrepid ghostbusting team goes *mano a mano* with their evil adversaries once again in this haunted house thriller. Some of the events of the Enfield affair are depicted accurately, which lend the film a measure of verisimilitude, but the screenplay by Chad Hayes and Carey W. Hayes subsumes the Hodgson's supernatural plight in favor of the Warren's entirely fictitious battle with the demonic nun. Director Wan, along with production designer Julie Berghoff, do a good job in recreating the drab environment of the family's "council-owned" U.K. government housing, but cinematographer Don Burgess shoots using dim lighting setups that render the house's environs in dull, muddy colors that are uninteresting to the eye. Acting by the predominately British cast is straightforward and believable, and young actress Madison Wolfe's sincere portrayal of the possessed Janet Hodgson carries much of the film. Patrick Wilson and Vera Farmiga, reprising their roles as the Warrens, portray their annoyingly pious characters once again, and Wilson takes time off from his strenuous ghostbusting duties to strum a guitar and render his version of Elvis' hit song "I Can't Help Falling in Love with You." Whatever its faults, however, *The Conjuring 2* struck box-office gold, grossing over $320 million worldwide to become the second highest-grossing horror film of all time behind *The Exorcist*.

Exterior shots of the haunt were filmed on location near the Hodgsons' former residence at 284 Green Street in the north London suburb of Enfield. The house is a three-bedroom, two-story semi-detached dwelling built during the 1920s that lies in the middle of a typical middle-class neighborhood of the city. A replica of the Green Street house was built at the Warner Brothers sound stage four in their Burbank studio that was designed to be slightly larger than the original in order to accommodate the cameras and sound equipment used in the filming. Due to some reported paranormal activity on the set, a priest from the Roman Catholic Archdiocese of Santa Fe was reportedly brought in to bless the soundstage, but this is probably just studio hype.

The Enfield case was extensively investigated by the press, government officials and psychic investigators, and is one of the most well documented hauntings on record. It was a complex affair that began as a poltergeist infestation and developed into Janet Hodgson's apparent possession by the deceased former residence of the house. The principal investigators were Maurice Grosse of the Society for Psychical Research and ghost hunter Guy Playfair, who documented the case in his 1980 book *This House Is Haunted: An Investigation of the Enfield Poltergeist*. Sound recordings of Janet speaking in the dead man's voice and photos of the girls supposedly levitating in their bedroom were examined by experts. The phenomena were witnessed by neighbors, policemen, professional photographers and the psychic investigators. In addition to moving objects, the poltergeist also was observed to make small fires break out, cause anomalous pools of water to form and to teleport objects through walls.

The reality of the haunting was called into question when Janet was caught throwing objects about and faking the poltergeist's actions. This type of behavior from the usually adolescent foci of the phenomenon is not uncommon, and has been noted in other cases. It is judged to be either a ploy to halt the investigation or a way to mimic the spook's effect when unable to demonstrate it on demand. The haunting lasted for about two years, and during that time the Hodgson house was visited by a parade of mediums, psychics and ghost breakers, including the Warrens. Contrary to the narrative of *The Conjuring 2*, the Warrens were only peripherally involved in the investigation, and the demon-nun "Valak" is likewise pure invention. While not centering on the overblown ghostbusting activities of the Warrens, however, the film does depict some of the phenomena in an accurate fashion. A special feature documentary included in the DVD version entitled "The Enfield Poltergeist: Living the Horror" provides eyewitness accounts by members of the Hodgson family and others, as well as further information about this complex and fascinating case.

Nestled in the middle of San Jose's urban sprawl in California's Silicon Valley is one of America's premier haunted attractions, the Winchester Mystery House. This sprawling structure is a labyrinth that contains 161 rooms, including 40 bedrooms, 2 ballrooms, 47 fireplaces, 17 chimneys, three elevators and over 10,000 panes of glass. Now a tourist attraction, the house was built in 1884 by Sarah Winchester, heiress to the Winchester armaments company, and has long had a reputation for being haunted. Some of the alleged mysteries surrounding the Mystery House were the subject of the haunted house melodrama *Winchester* (2018).

The film begins in 1906 San Francisco, where physician Eric Price (Jason Clarke) is recruited by the Winchester Repeating Arms Company to evaluate the sanity of its major shareholder, Sarah Winchester. Mrs. Winchester (Helen Mirren), an elderly widow who has inherited a large fortune after the death of her husband, William Wirt Winchester, manufacturer of the Winchester repeating rifle, the so-called "gun that won the West." A strong-willed, eccentric woman, Sarah has been involved for ten years in the seemingly endless construction of her mansion in San Jose, which has caused the company bigwigs to doubt her sanity. Dr. Price, who has become a reprobate after the tragic death of his wife Ruby (Laura Brent), is addicted to laudanum (tincture of opium). He accepts the assignment, though, because he is heavily in debt.

Price arrives at the Winchester mansion and is greeted by Sarah's niece Marian Marriott (Sarah Snook), who shows him around parts of the maze-like dwelling and introduces him to her son Henry (Finn Scicluna-O'Prey). Marian is recently widowed, and Henry has become afflicted with bouts of sleepwalking after the premature death of his father. At dinner, the doctor is introduced to Sarah, who presents a spectral appearance wearing a veil and black mourning clothes. Soon after his arrival, Price starts seeing apparitions, but chalks this up to the hallucinatory effect of the drugs. He takes to snooping around the mansion at night and prevents Henry from killing himself by catching him after he hurls himself off a roof in one of his somnambulistic trances. On another occasion, he observes Sarah in a seemingly possessed state drawing up a plan for a new room.

During an extensive series of interviews, Dr. Price learns that Sarah is suffering from severe guilt and anxiety stemming from her belief that she is being haunted by the ghosts of people killed by the Winchester rifle. She keeps detailed records of all the victims in a series of bound volumes, and knows that Price was shot and nearly killed by his wife with one of the rifles. Price has kept the bullet, which is inscribed with the words "together forever" as a memento. Further probing reveals that Sarah believes that the mansion is "the house that spirits built" and that she is being guided by the ghosts to first trap them inside rooms in the house in order to finally liberate them. Each spirit is imprisoned by a wooden bar across the door secured by thirteen nails.

Drug-addicted physician Eric Price (Jason Clarke) is haunted by the ghost of his dead wife Ruby (Laura Brent) in *Winchester* (2018).

One spook, however, has become so malevolent that it is threatening her family because it cannot be contained. It is revealed to be the ghost of Benjamin Block (Eamon Farren), a Confederate soldier whose two brothers were killed by Winchester rifles during the Civil War. In retribution, Benjamin invaded a Winchester office and massacred the staff before being shot dead by police, and it is his malignant ghost that has been possessing Henry. A paranormal firestorm erupts as Benjamin attacks during the devastating earthquake that struck the San Francisco Bay Area in 1906 that causes extensive damage to the haunt, and in the film's climactic scene Benjamin's spirit is dispatched to the netherworld when Price shoots it with his "together forever" bullet fired from a Winchester rifle. In the aftermath, Price, who has witnessed the ghostly activities with his own eyes, certifies Sarah's sanity as she contemplates the rebuilding of her dream house.

Lensed by the Australian director/producer/screenplay team of twin brothers Peter and Michael Spierig, *Winchester* is an old-fashioned haunted house thriller that eschews CGI special effects in favor of acting, camerawork and setting to achieve a mood of ghostly dread. The film displays exquisite period detail in its costuming by Wendy Cork and set design by Matthew Putland, while cinematographer Ben Nott uses hazy lighting effects to achieve a mood of supernatural tension. The performance of acclaimed actress Helen Mirren as Sarah Winchester is the most memorable in the film, while Jason Clarke's portrayal of her foil, Dr. Price, is correspondingly weak in comparison. The main problem with *Winchester*, however, is in its screenplay, co-authored by Tom Vaughn and the Spierigs, which is completely fabricated and lacks narrative cohesion. There are too many talky scenes of a seemingly endless series of interviews between Sarah and Dr. Price that tend to detract from the horrors of the situation, and the sub-plot involving Price and his deceased wife blunt the general thrust of the story. Amid all the spooky goings-on, however is a portrait of a haunted, yet strong-willed and intelligent woman brought to vivid life by Ms. Mirren.

The house itself is one of the main characters, and the exteriors of the haunt were shot at the actual Mystery House, a Queen Anne–style Victorian structure located at 525 South Winchester Boulevard in San Jose. For the interiors, many of the exquisite rooms of the mansion were painstakingly recreated on soundstages in Melbourne, Australia. The maze-like structure has been compared to the haunted labyrinth of Hill House in *The Haunting* and to the spatial anomalies of the house in Mark Z. Danielewski's novel *House of Leaves*. It also reportedly inspired the titular mansion in the Stephen King miniseries *Rose Red*, as well as the Haunted Mansion Disney attraction. The house as depicted in the film is replete with wood paneled walls that give it a warm, lived-in feeling, but the film's hazy lighting setups impart a sense of unreality and mystery to these rooms. In some shots the house is shown sporting an imposing seven story tower that was destroyed in the 1906 earthquake and never rebuilt.

The legend behind the Winchester mansion states that after the deaths of her husband and baby daughter, who died shortly after childbirth of a rare disease called marasmus, Sarah believed her family was cursed and consulted a Boston medium named Adam Coons to ascertain the cause. She was told she was being haunted by the ghosts of those who had been killed by Winchester rifles, most of whom were Native Americans who had been decimated during the Indian Wars. The only solution was to build a house that was a maze designed to confuse the avenging ghosts and prevent them from finding their way to her. She was also told that she would live as long as the house was under construction. Accordingly, Sarah moved to San Jose, where she purchased an eight-room farmhouse and kept adding to it until her death in 1922.

Unfortunately for the legend, stories about Sarah's spiritualist beliefs have no basis in fact and were concocted by tabloid newspapers of the time. According to those who had intimate knowledge of the heiress, Sarah was an intelligent, level-headed woman whose

The Winchester mansion, prior to the great San Francisco earthquake of 1906, is depicted in this still from *Winchester* (2018).

wealth enabled her to indulge her eccentricities. She was a skilled architect who designed most of the house herself and invented devices like the "annunciator," an intercom system used to communicate throughout the many areas of the vast house. The mythology of the haunting was extended and amplified after Sarah's death, when the house was purchased by entertainment entrepreneur John H. Brown and turned into a tourist attraction. As to the plot of *Winchester*, this was entirely the fictional product of the screenwriters. The Winchester Company never sought to certify Sarah's sanity, and contrary to one of the movie's plot points, the Winchester rifle was not purchased for use by the Union army during the Civil War and was not responsible for the wholesale slaughter of Confederate soldiers. The film's contention in an end title that "the house remains one of the most haunted mansions in America" is likewise a total exaggeration, as little in the way of ghostly activity has been recorded there over past decades.

Although a horror film can be an effective thriller even if the plot is totally makebelieve, the notion that it is "based on a true story" can add a measure of supernatural dread that amps up its fear factor. All of the films discussed have some basis in actual events, but all of them have embellished the recorded facts of these cases to make them more sensational in typical Hollywood fashion. Some of these, such as *The Amityville Horror* and *Winchester*, are entirely fictional. On the other hand, both *The Entity* and *The Conjuring 2* depict aspects of hauntings that were intensively investigated and documented by teams of reputable parapsychologists. All of the others fall somewhere in between these two polarities. The best that can be said about all of them is that, to varying degrees, they do reflect, however imperfectly, upon the existence of core supernatural phenomena that provide inspiration for tales of ghosts, poltergeists and haunted houses throughout the ages.

Chapter Seven

Haunted Houses for a New Millennium

The haunted house film reached new heights of popularity in the 21st century, during a period when the horror genre in general was undergoing a revival. In the hi-tech environment of the new millennium, horror represented a throwback to the atavistic past, but at the same time, advances in film technology enabled the use of computed-generated special effects capable of conjuring all manner of fantastic visions. The popular success of M. Night Shyamalan's ghost story *The Sixth Sense* (1999) would lead to a revival of the supernatural horror film. Another factor was the importation of Japanese horror films (sometimes referred to as J-horror) like *Ringu* (1998), *One Missed Call* (2003) and *Ju-On: The Grudge* (2003) into the American market. These films brought a new and exotic sensibility to the genre, and a number of them were remade in English-language versions with American actors. In addition, paranormal-themed reality TV shows such as *Ghost Hunters, Ghost Whisperer, The Haunted, Most Haunted USA, Paranormal Files, Paranormal Witness* and others served to popularize the notion of hauntings as real-world phenomena. Haunted house films such as *The Others* (2001) and the American version of *The Grudge* (2004) took off with movie audiences, but the big box-office champ was *Paranormal Activity* (2007). Shot in seven days with a home video camera inside a suburban home on a minuscule budget, the film was purchased by Paramount for a mere $350,000. It wound up grossing $193 million worldwide, making it the most profitable film in history in terms of return on investment.

Unlike science fiction or superhero extravaganzas, which required mega-million-dollar budgets for special effects, haunted house films could be made cheaply and were therefore highly profitable. *The Conjuring 2* (2016), for instance, was made for about $20 million and made a total of $320 million in American and International markets. The hour of the haunted house thriller had come at last. Like a harbinger of things to come, the cusp of the new millennium was graced with modern remakes of the black and white classics *The Haunting, House on Haunted Hill* and *Thirteen Ghosts.*

In the update of *The Haunting* (1999), psychologist Dr. David Marrow (Liam Neeson) is doing research into the psychology of fear and has concocted an experiment in which subjects will be placed in the environment of the notoriously haunted Hill House in order to study their reactions. He recruits his guinea pigs under the guise of an "insomnia study" that hides his true intentions. One of these unfortunates is Eleanor (Nell) Vance (Lili Taylor), a vulnerable young woman who has been turned out of her home by her venal relatives and has nowhere else to go. Arriving at Hill House, she meets the study's two other participants, the worldly Theodora (Catherine Zeta-Jones) and the youthful Luke Sanderson (Owen Wilson). In order to trap his subjects in a web of terror, Dr. Marrow instructs the caretakers, Mr. and Mrs. Dudley (Bruce Dern and Marian Seldes) to lock the front gate every night. In the meantime, Nell and Theo go off exploring the enormous mansion, including a bizarre room with a slowly revolving floor and mirrored walls. Hill House is filled with eerie statuary and vaulted stained-glass windows that make it seem more like a medieval cathedral than a house.

After dinner that night Dr. Marrow relates the history of the haunt, which was built by the eccentric textile tycoon Hugh Crain in the 19th century. He explains that Crain built the enormous mansion to house a large family, but all of his children died in childbirth and his wife subsequently committed suicide. In the aftermath, Crain was engulfed in the dread silence of the house and became a recluse, and a large, forbidding portrait of him hangs in one of Hill House's central halls. Later that night, Nell and Theo are frightened by hearing an invisible force trying to enter their room, and Crain's portrait is found defaced with the words "Welcome Home Eleanor" written in large, bloody letters, while the face in the picture has morphed into a skull.

On the following night Nell finds a trail of bloody footprints on the hallway floor and follows them into the library, where she discovers a hidden room containing Hugh Crain's papers. Going through his notebooks, she learns that Crain took children from his cotton mills, murdered them and burned their bodies within Hill House. She also finds out that he had another wife, Carolyn, from whom Nell is descended, and that she is Crain's great-granddaughter. Nell sees apparitions of the dead children and is also menaced by Crain's ghost, who seals up the house, trapping everyone inside. A series of terrifying events ensue as a statue comes alive and tries to drown Dr. Marrow and Crain's malevolent spook decapitates Luke. Rather than flee the accursed haunt, Nell chooses to exorcise Crain's ghost but dies in the process as the ghosts of the children are freed and they escort Nell's discarnate spirit up to heaven.

Arguably one of the worst remakes in screen history, *The Haunting* was the work of cinematographer turned director Jan de Bont, who had lensed the crowd-pleasers *Speed* and *Twister*. One major problem lies in the film's overall approach to its source material. The filmmakers opted for an expensive, "big picture" treatment that concentrated primarily on elaborate, outsized sets and digital special effects to the detriment of story and characterization. Much of the blame for the film's failure lies with the screenplay by David Self and Michael Tolkin, which dispenses with the core dramatic tensions that enliven both Shirley Jackson's novel and Robert Wise's screen version by altering the plot and characters almost beyond recognition. Another major problem is in casting Lili Taylor in the lead role of Eleanor Vance, whose insipid performance pales in comparison to Julie Harris' electric portrayal in Wise's original. Catherine Zeta-Jones and Owen Wilson are similarly bland in supporting roles, while only Liam Neeson projects a strong screen presence. The film's happy, sappy ending, in which Eleanor ascends into heaven accompanied by the ghosts of Hill House's children, is particularly ludicrous. All in all, this version of *The Haunting* is one of the least frightening haunted house flicks ever made, but despite the film's obvious shortcomings and poor critical reviews, the film went on to make $177 million at the box office.

The most interesting thing about the remake is Hill House itself. The creation of production designer Eugenio Zanetti, it is one of the most impressive haunts ever to appear on the big screen. The films budget of $90 million allowed for the construction of monumental sets built inside the enormous hanger that once housed Howard Hughes' gigantic "Spruce Goose" airplane in Long Beach, California. Hill House's main hall is dominated by an imposing stairway flanked by huge columns and ornamental griffins that make it resemble a pagan temple. The idea was to create an environment in which the human characters are swallowed up inside the haunt's vast spaces like lost souls, and the visual effect of a house that goes on forever is stunning at times. Among the myriad rooms and antechambers are Hugh Crain's enormous library, the aforementioned room with spinning floor sections and mirrored walls, a decrepit greenhouse overgrown with mold and weeds, and Theo and Nell's sumptuous, ornate bedrooms. Moroccan, Indian, Gothic, Neo-Classical, Romanesque and Baroque designs are interwoven into Hill House's variegated architecture, where they are melded into an impressive whole. The house's exterior shots were filmed at the suitably creepy Harlaxton Manor in Nottinghamshire, England.

The haunted house film revival continued with the remake of William Castle's 1959 B&W classic *House on Haunted Hill* (1999). The film begins with a prelude set in 1931 at the Vannacutt Institute for the Criminally Insane, where the sadistic Dr. Richard Vannacutt (Jeffrey Combs) is conducting unorthodox experiments on his patients. These tortured victims rebel against this inhuman treatment and set the hospital afire, killing Vannacutt, the patients, and all but five of the staff. Cut to 1999, where amusement park tycoon Steven Price (Geoffrey Rush) leases the restored building at the insistence of his estranged wife Evelyn (Famke Janssen), ostensibly to celebrate her birthday. The unhappy couple has a hateful, poisonous relationship in which they both contemplate killing each other. Five guests arrive at the former nuthouse for the party, Eddie Baker (Taye Diggs), Sara Wolfe (Ali Larter), Melissa Marr (Bridgette Wilson), Dr. Donald Blackburn (Peter Gallagher) and the building's owner, Watson Pritchett (Chris Kattan). Mysteriously, none of them are the people that Price had invited.

Undeterred by this, Price proceeds with this macabre birthday party, offering the guests $1 million each if they are able to survive in the house until dawn. All of the guests accept the arrangement, and a security mechanism is tripped to lock the place down for the night. Everyone is provided with their own handgun from miniature coffin-shaped boxes, and the game is on. While the guests wander through the decrepit corridors of the old hospital seeking a way out, they are confronted with seemingly paranormal occurrences. Sara encounters a doppelganger of Eddie, who jumps into a vat of blood and nearly drowns her before she is rescued by the real Eddie. Melissa disappears while exploring the basement, leaving nothing but a trail of bloodstains behind. Some of these events seem to be orchestrated by Price's assistant Schecter (Max Perlich), who is arranging illusions from a hidden room, but Pritchett warns of a ghostly spirit of darkness that dwells within the house that can destroy them all.

As the night progresses the film's complex plot unravels as one by one the guests trapped inside the house are killed or vanish. Are ghosts responsible or is Price secretly manipulating illusions of dread from behind the scenes? When Price and Evelyn are seemingly killed, are they really dead or is it part of a twisted double homicide scheme? The narrative takes several unexpected turns before its final climax as the dark spirit within the house finally emerges in all its phantasmagoric, computer-generated glory, and resolution comes with the dawn.

(Left to right) Steven Price (Geoffrey Rush) and his wife Evelyn (Famke Janssen) play a deadly party game with their guests (Ali Larter, Taye Diggs, Chris Kattan) in the update of *House on Haunted Hill* (1999).

This was the first release from fledgling production company Dark Castle Entertainment, who specialized in remakes of classic horror flicks. Compared with William Castle's juvenile original, the remake is awash in blood, gore, decapitated heads, pickled anatomical specimens and all manner of ghoulish nastiness. Computer generated imagery depicting the Darkness entity was provided by KNB effects, and ace makeup artist Dick Smith designed some of the ghostly apparitions. William Malone's direction keeps the action flowing along briskly, but there are too many repetitious scenes of the hapless victims wandering around inside the ruined hospital facility as they encounter various supernatural menaces accompanied by enough strobing lights to induce seizures in susceptible viewers and a chorus of spectral moans and groans on the soundtrack.

Geoffrey Rush's performance as Steven Price carries much of the film as he does a fine job of channeling the original's star Vincent Price's florid mannerisms. He is ably supported by Famke Janssen playing his homicidal wife Evelyn, as the two marital enemies engage in a war of wits with exchanges of deliciously wicked dialogue. One major problem with the screenplay by Robb White and Dick Beebe, however, is that it's long on plot twists but short on character development. While concentrating on the war between the Prices, the five "birthday guests" are poorly-drawn, two-dimensional characters that fail to engage the audience's sympathies as they fall victim to the human and inhuman evils within the house.

The remake replicates the procession of hearses scene in the beginning of the original film, but this time they drive up to the exterior of Griffith Park Observatory in Los Angeles. Special effects added a featureless vertical structure that towers into the air like a cross between a futuristic fortress and a skyscraper. Restored areas of the building feature stained glass windows and art-deco style interiors, while the older sections of the mental hospital, where much of the action takes place, are suitably grungy and gothic. Scenes of the mad Dr. Vannacutt's hideous surgeries and the victim's revolt may have been inspired by similar antics in the classic horror film *Island of Lost Souls* (1933). The ghosts in the haunt take various forms, including Eddie's doppelganger, apparitions of the hospital staff and the slithering Darkness, which was reportedly inspired by the polymorphous creatures that populate the fiction of H.P. Lovecraft.

Dark Castle's next project was the remake of another William Castle classic *Thirteen Ghosts* (2001), spelled as *Thir13een Ghosts* in ad copy. The film opens in an auto graveyard, where wealthy ghost hunter Cyrus Kritikos (F. Murray Abraham) and his assistant Dennis Rafkin (Matthew Lillard) head up a team that is stalking the ghost of the notorious serial killer Horace "Breaker" Mahoney, a.k.a. "The Juggernaut" (John DeSantis). Cyrus is killed during the mission, but the Juggernaut is captured by the team and his spirit is confined within a metal and glass containment unit and carted off.

A short time later attorney Ben Ross (J.R. Bourne) visits Cyrus' nephew Arthur (Tony Shaloub) to inform him that upon his uncle's death he has inherited Cyrus' mansion and estate. A recent widower who is struggling financially, Arthur decides to move in with his daughter Kathy (Shannon Elizabeth), son Bobby (Alec Roberts) and the family cook Maggie Bess (Rah Digga). They find that the mansion is an eccentric structure built entirely of glass and steel, a clockwork funhouse with obscure Latin phrases inscribed in red on the transparent walls. Soon after their move in, Dennis shows up at the house disguised as a power company inspector, along with Ross the lawyer, but both men are secretly looking for a cache of Cyrus' cash hidden somewhere inside the manor, and Dennis, who has psychic abilities, hopes to find the money first. Instead, his paranormal vision makes him realize that Cyrus has been collecting ghosts and that there are twelve angry spirits confined inside the house by magical spells. When Ross enters the basement and attempts to make off with a valise containing the missing cash, he unwittingly activates a mechanism that kills him while he tries to escape, seals off the house trapping everyone inside, and releases the ghosts from their psychic confinement.

Their first victim is Bobby, who is rendered unconscious by one of the spooks and dragged out of sight. In the meantime, Dennis finds a pair of special glasses that augment his psychic vision and allow him to see the ghosts. While looking for Bobby, Kathy and Arthur are attacked by one of the ghosts and are rescued by the sudden appearance of Kalina Oretzia (Embeth Davitz), a mysterious intruder who claims to be a ghostbuster trying to free the house's spirits. She explains that the house is a psychic machine in which Cyrus has trapped a "Black Zodiac" of twelve ghosts, and that a thirteenth ghost is needed to fully activate the house and open up a supernatural "Ocularus," or "Eye of Hell" that will enable its user to perceive the past, present and future. It turns out that Cyrus is still alive and is working with Kalina to activate the machine by making Arthur the thirteenth ghost, but the Kriticos family members unite and work together to destroy the machine and exorcise the ghosts.

Arthur Kritikos (Tony Shaloub) explores a haunted clockwork funhouse in the remake of *Thirteen Ghosts* (2001).

Like the *House on Haunted Hill* remake, the update of *Thirteen Ghosts* took William Castle's whimsical original and turned it into an explicitly bloody gore-fest. The individual ghosts of the Black Zodiac are grotesque apparitions such as "The Jackal," a maniac with his head encased within a metal cage, "The Juggernaut," whose body is covered in bleeding bullet wounds, and "The Torso," an armless, legless spook whose decapitated head lies gibbering on the floor. Once again plotting and characterization take a backseat to eye candy visuals and special effects. Director Steve Beck, working from a weak screenplay by Robb White, Neal Marshall Stevens and Richard D'Ovidio, fails to generate much in the way of suspense or terror, while veteran actor F. Murray Abraham and Tony Shaloub (future star of TV's *Monk* detective series) struggle valiantly with the thin material.

But, like the remake of *The Haunting*, the most interesting aspect of the *Thirteen Ghosts* retread is the haunt itself. Making the house into "a machine built by the Devil and powered by the dead" instead of the standard gothic mansion was a novel concept. A marvel of steel and glass construction, the haunted clockwork funhouse was the brainchild of production designer Sean Hargreaves, who based his design on the architecture of the New York Science Museum. The Kriticos Mansion took three months to build and utilized 8,500 cubic feet of glass welded together with five tons of tempered steel. During filming, production crews were obliged to wear black garments in order to reduce unwanted reflections in the glass. The house was supposedly designed by the 15th century astrologer Basileus, who drew up the plans in a book called "The Arcanum" while in a state of demonic possession, and it was meant to function as an occult machine fueled by the psychic energies of captive ghosts.

All three of these big-budget, effects-laden Hollywood haunted house movies made money, but the sub-genre was poised to move into new and innovative territory at the

The ghostly Stewart family mansion is pictured in this atmospheric still from Alejandro Amenabar's *The Others* (2001).

hands of foreign filmmakers, beginning with Spanish writer/director Alejandro Amenabar's *The Others* (*Los Otros*, 2001). Set in an old manor house on Britain's Channel Islands (located between England and France) after World War II, the film stars Nicole Kidman as Grace Stewart, who is caring for her children Anne (Alakita Mann) and Nicholas (James Bentley) while waiting for her husband to be demobilized from the army and return home. The children suffer from a rare disorder called Xeroderma Pigmentosa that renders them highly sensitive to sunlight, and accordingly they must be kept in darkened rooms within the gloomy mansion.

Grace hires three servants, the middle-aged Bertha Mills (Fionulla Flanagan), the elderly Edmund Tuttle (Eric Sykes) and a mute young woman named Lydia (Elaine Cassidy) to help her maintain the estate. The house has no electricity or telephone service, and the rooms are illuminated only by candles and lamplight. Strange sounds are heard throughout the house, locked doors mysteriously open and the children report seeing ghosts who proclaim "the house is theirs." At first Grace refuses to believe the house is haunted until she hears their piano playing by itself, whereupon she resolves to bring the village priest in to bless the house, but she loses her way in the perpetual fog that surrounds the estate and unexpectedly encounters her husband Charles (Christopher Eccleston) returning from the war. Charles is emotionally distant from his family, however, and declares that he has just come back to say goodbye, and soon disappears after a short stay.

The hauntings continue, as the children claim to see a little boy named Victor and a weird old woman who they think is a witch. In the film's most frightening episode, Grace comes upon Anne playing by candlelight in a darkened room, her face and body transformed into those of a withered crone. "What have you done to my daughter?" she exclaims in horror, to which the apparition replies, "But mummy, I *am* your daughter," whereupon Grace attacks the apparition, who promptly transforms back into Anne. One day the children wake up to find the blackout curtains removed from the windows and unfamiliar furniture in the rooms. That night the family witnesses a séance being conducted in the parlor by the "ghosts," as they gradually perceive the truth that the three servants are ghosts and that Grace murdered her children during a fit of madness during the war and then committed suicide. Not knowing they were dead, the family continued to inhabit the house, and now Bertha Mills tells her, "We must all learn to live together, the living and the dead." After the séance the new family flees from the haunted manor, which now has a "For Sale" sign posted on the front gate.

Writer/director Alejandro Amenabar (who also composed the film's eerie musical score) crafts a tour-de-force classic of the modern ghost story and brought a European artistic sensibility to the haunted house film that had been absent since the days of Ricardo Freda and Mario Bava in the 1960s. Eschewing high-budget production values and Hollywood-style special effects, Amenabar, in his English-language film debut, renders a chilling supernatural mystery story solely through the use of gothic atmosphere, dramatic understatement and misdirection, finely-drawn characterizations and a beautifully plotted, intriguing screenplay. Powerful performances by all of the cast members contribute mightily to the film's total effect. Nicole Kidman fills out the complex leading role of the domineering, borderline psychotic Grace Stewart with both dignity and vulnerability, while Fionulla Flanagan projects wisdom and quiet strength as the grandmotherly Bertha Mills and young Alakina Mann delivers a bravura performance as the rebellious daughter Anne Stewart.

The film's haunt is one of the most memorable in horror film history. Its grounds are perpetually wreathed in overcast and fog that serves as a barrier to imprison the ghosts, and the interior of the mansion, kept in a state of perpetual gloom due to the children's illness, is a claustrophobic netherworld. Amenabar's approach to the film's haunted environment was that "light kills," and his cinematographer Javier Aguirresarobe utilizes low-key, low contrast lighting setups as a backdrop for the pale, spectral characters. Instead of the histrionics of ghostly screams and groans on the soundtracks of many haunted house films, the director instead relies on silence and whispers to conjure the suffocating aural landscape of the haunt. While M. Night Shyamalan's *The Sixth Sense* (1999) had presented a haunting from the ghost's point of view, this motif is more powerful in *The Others* because all of the film's major characters are ghosts. Exterior locations for the haunted house included the "Lime Walk" at Penshurst Place in Kent,

"But mummy, I *am* your daughter," a wizened Anne (Alakita Mann) insists to her mother (Nicole Kidman) in this tense scene from *The Others* (2001).

England, and the Palacio de los Hornillos in Las Fraguas in Northern Spain. The film was an enormous popular success, garnering over $100 million in box-office receipts against modest production costs of only $17 million, continuing the renewed popularity of the sub-genre, and is now considered one of the finest cinematic ghost stories in horror film history.

The year 2001 also saw the release of another classic haunted house thriller by a foreign director, Guillermo del Toro's *The Devil's Backbone* (*El espinazo del diablo*). Set near the end of the Spanish Civil War in 1939, the film begins as young Carlos (Fernando Tielve), whose father is a casualty of war, is brought to live at a boy's orphanage. The facility is a rundown place located in the middle of a desolate, forbidding plain that has a large, unexploded bomb embedded in the dirt in the middle of its main courtyard. The orphanage is presided over by the middle-aged headmistress Carmen (Marisa Paredes), who has an artificial leg, and her assistant and sometime lover Dr. Casares (Federico Luppi), as well as Jacinto (Eduardo Noriega), a sadistic young man who does odd jobs and keeps the boys in line.

Carlos befriends two of the younger boys, Owl (Javier Gonzalez-Sanchez) and Galvez (Adrian Lamana), but is intimidated by an older boy, Jaime (Inigo Garces), with whom he vies for dominance of the group. During his first night in the dormitory the communal water pitcher gets spilled, and Jaime dares Carlos to sneak into the kitchen and refill it. As he is fulfilling this quest, he hears a mysterious voice proclaim, "Many of you will die." The next day Jaime threatens Carlos with a knife at the school's underground water cistern, but as they struggle Jaime falls into the deep well and is rescued by Carlos. Jacinto arrives to break up the fight, but Carlos perceives that the cistern holds some special significance for him. It seems that Jacinto is actively seeking a cache of gold hidden somewhere in the orphanage by the Nationalists, its location known only to the headmistress.

In the meantime, the boys tell Carlos that the orphanage is haunted by the ghost of a boy named Santi who disappeared under mysterious circumstances on the night that the bomb was dropped. One evening Carlos goes looking for the ghost and encounters Santi (Andreas Munoz). The apparition appears as a pale little boy with a wound in his head that bleeds upward. Terrified, Carlos flees back to the dorm and hides from the ghost in a closet all night.

As enemy forces approach closer to the orphanage, Dr. Casares and Carmen decide to evacuate the children to a safer location. Upon hearing this, Jacinto demands the gold, but is chased away by Casares with a gun, but as they are preparing to leave, Jacinto ignites a cache of gasoline, causing a massive explosion that kills Carmen and many of the boys, as Santi had predicted. As the surviving boys await Jacinto's return to find the gold, Jaime relates how he and Santi had observed Jacinto trying to break open the safe, whereupon Jacinto had killed Santi to keep him quiet and then dumped his body in the cistern. When Jacinto returns and locates the gold inside Carmen's prosthetic leg, the boys attack him with improvised weapons and drive him into the well where, weighted down by the gold, he sinks under the water where Santi's ghost materializes to exact his revenge.

Combining elements of fantasy, drama and horror, *The Devil's Backbone* melds a gothic ghost story with a tragic tale of war, loss and greed. Mexican Director del Toro, who would later win a best picture Oscar for his 2017 romantic fantasy *The Shape of Water*, tells a compelling story of supernatural retribution set against the realistic backdrop of the Spanish Civil War, and del Toro considers the film a companion piece to his acclaimed *Pan's Labyrinth*, which is also set during the same historical period. The screenplay, co-written by the director, Antonio Trashorras and David Munoz, weaves a compelling and complex narrative around a quirky *dramatis personae* who are brought to vivid life by the film's talented cast. The performances of Fernando Tielve as the protagonist Carlos, Marisa Paredes as the world-weary headmistress Carmen and Federico Luppi as the noble Dr. Casares, are particularly memorable. After a couple of cinematic misfires in his previous films, del Toro claims to have found his personal style in *The Devil's Backbone*, but although the film was a critical success, in America it only played on the art house circuit and did not receive a wide release.

The film's orphanage setting makes for a unique type of haunt that is an original variation on the haunted house theme that would later be replicated in the gothic thriller *House of Voices* (2007). The dreary horizontal structure, located in the middle of a featureless plain, constitutes a kind of limbo in which the characters are caught within a grim web of war, darkness and tragedy, while the building's basement, which is the locus of the haunt's supernatural activity, is built like a catacomb with vaulted stone arches. Carlos, the film's protagonist, is a kind of medium who is able to perceive the ghost of Santi more clearly than the other children. Assigned to sleep in the dead boy's bed in the dorm, he gradually becomes a kind of doppelganger who aids the spirit in gaining its vengeance. A series of spoken titles poetically describes the concept of a ghost as "something dead which still seems to be alive/an emotion suspended in time/like a blurred photograph/like an insect trapped in amber." The film's title refers to a deformity of the spine exhibited in one of Dr. Casares' preserved fetus specimens that was thought to be diabolical by the superstitious.

Darkness (2002), another haunted house melodrama produced in Spain, revolves around an American family who relocate to a house in Barcelona that has been uninhabited for forty years. The family consists of father Mark (Iain Glen), mother Maria (Lena Olin), teenage daughter Regina (Anna Paquin) and her younger brother Paul (Stephan Enquist). The real estate deal has been arranged by Mark's father Dr. Albert Rua (Giancarlo Giannini), a physician who is treating Mark for Huntington's disease, a degenerative condition that affects his mental stability.

As the family tries to settle in to the gloomy house they experience mysterious power outages and the anomalous movement of objects. Mark experiences a medical emergency from a sudden attack of disease symptoms and is cared for by Dr. Rua, while Paul senses unseen entities in the house. Regina and her newfound friend Carlos (Fele Martinez) research the history of the house and learn that is was connected to the murder of six children four decades earlier. The two of them manage to track down Villalobos (Fermin Reixach), the architect who built the house, who reveals that its design was based on the plan of an ancient pagan temple consecrated to the powers of darkness. Delving through old newspapers and occult texts at the city library, they discover that the children's murders were connected to a group of occultists as part of a ritual human sacrifice.

Regina hurries to warn Dr. Rua, but is shocked to find that he is one of the cultists. He tells her that seven sacrificial victims were needed to complete the spell forty years ago and that the seventh was to be his own son, Mark. Rua was unable to complete the ceremony because the victims had to be killed by hands that love them, and when he realized he did not love his son he was forced to let Mark live. Now, forty years later, he has arranged for the ritual to be completed properly, which will release a demonic entity called "the darkness" into our reality during a total eclipse of the sun. Hearing this, Regina races back home to find that her father is choking on a batch of pills he swallowed during one of his attacks. She and Maria attempt to perform an emergency tracheotomy on Mark to save his life, but the operation fails and he dies at the hands of loved ones, thus completing the spell. Maria is killed as the darkness descends upon the house, but in the ambiguous ending a doppelganger of Carlos appears and drives Regina away from the house and into a darkened tunnel which is perhaps meant to represent oblivion.

This minor-key iteration of the haunted house thriller is indifferently lensed by Spanish director Jaume Balaguero and indifferently acted by a mediocre cast. The one exception is veteran Italian thesp Giancarlo Giannini, who imbues his role as Dr. Rua with a weary but effective brand of villainy. For unknown reasons, the director employs numerous shots of running water that don't add much to the film's somber mood, and several scenes take place in the pouring rain. Another major problem is the screenplay, co-scripted by Balaguero and Fernando de Felipe, which presents plot ideas that are poorly realized and relies on unpleasant notions like the serial murder of children. The film's confusing, downbeat ending does nothing to alleviate its lack of effect.

The notion of a house whose architecture is based on pagan temples and specifically designed to attract dark spiritual energies is a novel one that recalls the haunts in H.P. Lovecraft's fiction, although the exterior of the house as it appears in the film looks entirely conventional. There are thematic similarities with the Kritikos haunt in *Thirteen Ghosts*, which also featured a haunted house specifically constructed for occult purposes. Filmed in Barcelona and other locations in Catalonia, the movie makes effective use of the city's subway in one tense scene. Although the children's ghosts do appear from time to time, the plot revolves around devil worshippers who have imbued the house with its evil. *Darkness* should not be confused with a later film similarly titled *The Darkness* (2016), which is not a remake or sequel, but a variation on the theme of the "haunted object."

Back in America, the haunted house parade continued with the thriller *Cold Creek Manor* (2002). Dennis Quaid and Sharon Stone star as Cooper and Leah Tilson, a New York City couple who get fed up with the dangers of the urban jungle and decide to quit their jobs and leave the Big Apple behind. They obtain a too-good-to-be-true deal on a fixer-upper in the upstate New York town of Bellingham and move in with their teenage daughter Kristen (Kristen Stewart) and young son Jessie (Ryan Wilson). The sprawling estate is called Cold Creek Manor and is still filled with all the possessions left behind by the previous owners, the Massie family, and Cooper, who is a documentary filmmaker, decides to make a film archiving the house's history using the family's photographs, artifacts, writings and other materials.

Events take an ominous turn when Dale Massie (Stephen Dorff), one of the house's previous owners, shows up on the property looking for work after having just gotten out of prison and Cooper hires him, thinking Dale's intimate knowledge of the place will help with the home's renovations. It proves to be a poor choice, however, as it soon becomes obvious that Dale harbors resentment towards the Tilson's ownership of the manor as he displays an arrogant and menacing attitude toward the family. More alarmingly, a truck tries to run Cooper off the road, their pet horse is found dead in the swimming pool and the house is invaded by poisonous snakes. Cooper suspects Dale of being behind these events and fires him, but later Dale humiliates Cooper in front of the unsympathetic townsfolk and Dale's lowlife girlfriend Ruby (Julitte Lewis).

Looking to find out more about the manor's history, Cooper visits Dale's aged father Theodore (Christopher Plummer) in a nursing home, where the addled and obnoxious old man inadvertently reveals that Dale was responsible for the murder of his wife and children, who had mysteriously disappeared several years earlier. He later finds a dental appliance belonging to one of the Massie family members on the estate. Hoping to find evidence of these crimes that will send Dale back to prison, Cooper scours the 1200 acres of the property, and using some of his hi-tech video gear, discovers three corpses hidden in the Devil's Throat, a deep well in a wooded area. When Dale learns about Cooper's visit to his father, he kills the old man out of spite and heads to the Manor to exact his revenge. In the final reel, Cooper and Leah are forced into a desperate last stand with the psychotic Dale on the roof of the house during a raging lightning storm that ends in death.

Cold Creek Manor is a slick, competently made Hollywood thriller that is smoothly paced, nicely shot and well-acted by A-listers Dennis Quaid, Sharon Stone and Christopher Plummer, with an able assist from Stephen Dorff, who steals every scene he's in. Director Mike Figgis moves the action along briskly and DeClan Quinn's cinematography renders some colorful visuals, but many critics opined that Richard Jefferies' screenplay was too clichéd and predictable. The film's plot follows the narrative template first laid out in Dan Curtis' 1976 haunted house thriller *Burnt Offerings*, in which an urban family relocates to a mansion in a rural area where they are placed in mortal peril.

Cold Creek Manor house is an imposing, maze-like structure that, like the haunt in *Psycho*, is menaced not by ghosts but by a homicidal psychopath. The film was shot at Cruickston Park Manor, a Victorian manor house located in Cambridge, Ontario, near Toronto that was also used in the films *The Handmaid's Tale* and *Red*. In the interior sequences, cinematographer Quinn shoots using a fluid moving camera and wide-angle lenses that distort perspective inside the house, making it seem larger and oddly off-kilter, a technique that had previously been used in Robert Wise's *The Haunting* and Peter Medak's *The Changeling*. The theme of a documentarian investigating the malign history of a house while poring over photos and videos would be revisited in the horror thriller *Sinister* (2012).

In the early 2000s Japanese horror films began to find a niche in the American market. Japan has a rich folk tradition of ghost stories, or *kaidan*, that stretches back many centuries and is reflected in their literature and their Noh and Kabuki theaters. Modern works of J-horror bring these traditional elements into a 21st century technological milieu to create an exotic meld of science and the supernatural set in the contemporary world. Some of the more popular J-horror movies involve the idea of a deadly curse that is passed from person to person like a contagion. In *Ringu* (1998) an accursed videotape will kill anyone who watches it within seven days, while in *One Missed Call* (2003) mysterious cell phone messages from the future predict the deaths of those who answer the calls. Takashi Shimizu's *Ju-On: The Grudge* (2002) offered a variation on the theme that featured a contagious curse that emanated from a haunted house. Under the tutelage of American horror producer/director Sam Raimi, Shimizu directed an English-language version entitled *The Grudge* (2004) and a sequel, *The Grudge 2* (2006), that comprises a two-part unified narrative.

A house in Tokyo is the scene of the brutal murders of the Saeki family by husband and father Takeo Saeki (Takashi Matsuyama), who kills his wife Kayako (Takako Fuji) in a fit of rage when he discovers that she has fallen in love with her college professor Peter Kirk (Bill Pullman) after reading her diary. For good measure he also murders his young son Toshio (Yuya Ozeki) and even the family's black cat, Mar. In the aftermath, the ghost of Kayako becomes an *onryo*, or vengeful spirit. who in turn kills Takeo for revenge, and a supernatural curse is laid upon the house that destroys anyone who crosses its threshold. The haunt's first victim is Peter Kirk, who enters the house looking for Kayako, but discovers her corpse instead and subsequently hurls himself from a tall building to his death.

Several years later American businessman Matt Williams (William Mapother) relocates to Tokyo with his wife Jennifer (Clea DuVall) and elderly mother Emma (Grace Zabriskie) who move into the house with no knowledge of its stigma. Emma suffers from dementia and is being cared for by social workers, but when one of them, Yoko (Yoko Maki) fails to report back to the office, her supervisor Alex Jones (Ted Raimi) dispatches Karen Davis (*Buffy the Vampire Slayer*'s Sarah Michelle Gellar) to the Williams home to find out what's going on. At the house, Karen discovers Emma in a comatose state and encounters the ghosts of Toshio and Mar, causing her to panic and summon Alex to the house. He arrives to find Emma dead and Karen in a state of shock after witnessing the apparitions and notifies the police. Detective Nakagawa (Ryo Ishibashi) and his partner Igarashi (Hiroshi Matsunaga) arrive at the house to investigate, and find the bodies of Matt and Jennifer in an upstairs room, along with a severed human lower jaw.

The curse moves into high gear as it begins to spread its influence outside the house. Matt's sister Susan Williams (KaDee Strickland) is spirited away by Kayako's ghost in her apartment in an ultra-modern high-rise building, while Alex is killed by Yuko's jawless corpse that has been re-animated by the ghosts. Karen begins to sense the presence of the revenants and researches the history of the haunt along with her boyfriend Doug McCarthy (Jason Behr), an exchange student at Tokyo University. In the meantime, Detective Nakagawa has been investigating Susan's disappearance and watches a security camera video of the apartment hallway that shows eerie images of Kayako's ghost. When Karen confronts him about the

Social worker Karen Davis (Sarah Michelle Gellar) explores the Saeki murder house in *The Grudge* (2004).

supernatural events, he reveals that three of his colleagues who had entered the house to investigate the Saeki killings all died subsequently, victims of the ghostly curse.

Knowing that he is doomed, Nakagawa brings several cans of gasoline into the house that night with the intention of burning it down, but he is killed by Takeo's ghost before he can ignite the fuel. The next day Karen is horrified to learn that Doug has gone to the house looking for her and hurries there to prevent him from entering, but is too late. Once inside, she finds Doug petrified with fear and tries to get him to leave, but he is killed by Kayako. As the vengeful spirit is about to kill her, she spies the gas cans and ignites them, causing the house to erupt in a fiery conflagration. In the aftermath, Karen wakes up in a hospital, only to be told that the haunt was not destroyed in the fire as she anticipates the curse that will eventually claim her.

This cinematic *kaidan* is a directorial tour-de-force that constitutes one of the most artistic and frighteningly effective haunted house thrillers in the history of the horror film. Director Takashi Shimizu builds a palpable atmosphere of suspense and dread around the haunt and the inevitable dire fates of the people unlucky enough to enter there. Shimizu employs a particularly effective technique wherein the apparitions are shown to the audience but not seen by the characters. During a scene in which Susan is ascending to her floor in the hi-rise complex inside a glass walled elevator, for instance, Toshio's ghost is seen standing on every level she passes, and in another Toshio's reflection appears in the window of a bus motoring through the city as if the ghost is watching Karen and Doug. These images convey to the audience that the characters are surrounded by supernatural forces that are invisible to them. As in other J-horror films, ghosts are able to infiltrate technology, which is most clearly depicted in the scene in which Detective Nakagawa watches Kayako's ghost materialize on the grainy black and white apartment security video. Location shooting in Tokyo adds an exotic backdrop to the proceedings, and a mixed cast of Japanese and American actors perform flawlessly together without a trace of culture shock. Stephen Susco's screenplay presents the events of the haunting in a non-linear fashion that jumps back and forth in time, a narrative technique that was possibly inspired by Quentin Tarantino's *Pulp Fiction* (1994). Like *The Others*, *The Grudge* was a monster hit, raking in over $110 million in the United States and $187 million worldwide against production costs of less than $10 million, numbers that encouraged the making of similarly-themed haunted house films.

The movie's haunt is an unremarkable multi-story structure located in the middle of Tokyo's urban sprawl. On the inside, however, loose papers and junk litter the floors, indicating a loss of order and reason within the accursed domain. The house's curse quickly spreads beyond its threshold as the ghosts pursue their missions of vengeance against their victims at various locations in the city. *The Grudge* reflects Japanese ideas about the spiritually polluting nature of death and the notion that those who die violently or in the grip of strong emotions return as *onryos*, or dangerous, vengeful spirits is a mythic theme that has also been part of their literature and folklore for centuries. The appearance of Kayako's ghost is derived from the iconography of these apparitions as depicted in traditional Kabuki theater and art, the phantom woman appearing as a pale figure with long black, unkempt hair dressed in a white kimono. Another traditional feature of Japanese horror appearing in the film is the *bakeneko*, a ghostly black cat who exacts vengeance upon its victims that is represented by Toshio's cat Mar.

Shimizu followed up with an English language sequel, *The Grudge 2* (2006), that picks up where the first movie left off, and like *The Grudge* its narrative also unfolds in a non-linear fashion. The film begins in 2006, two years after the events of the first movie, with three teenage girls who attend the International High School in Tokyo, where the socially awkward Allison Fleming (Arielle Kebbel) is making a pathetic attempt to ingratiate herself with two of the more popular students, Miyuki (Misako Uno) and Vanessa (Teresa Palmer). The two mean girls play a trick on Allison by luring her into the haunted Saeki residence, where they lock her inside a closet for fun. Allison notices a weird-looking book that turns out to be the diary of Kayako Saeki just before Kayako's ghost materializes to terrify the girl as her two companions flee in terror, and the panic-stricken Allison manages to escape from her confinement and runs screaming from the haunt.

Takako Fuji as Kayako, the vengeful ghost in Takashi Shimizu's *The Grudge* (2004).

The action then reverts to Pasadena, California, in 2004, shortly after the events of the first movie, where Karen's worried mother (Joanna Cassidy) dispatches her other daughter Aubrey Davis (Amber Tamblyn) to Tokyo to check on Karen because she is too ill to make the journey herself. Arriving in Tokyo, Aubrey manages to find her way to the hospital where Karen is being treated and is befriended by a journalist, Eason (Edison Chen), who saved Karen from the house fire at the end of *The Grudge*. Using Eason as an interpreter, Aubrey gets to see Karen (Sarah Michelle Gellar), who is in a state of extreme agitation anticipating the coming vengeance of the ghosts. After her visitors leave, Karen escapes from her restraints and is stalked through the hospital by Kayako. She makes her way to the building's roof seeking refuge, but the ghost reappears and hurls her to her death right in front of Aubrey and Eason as they are leaving the hospital.

The film then shifts to a third narrative thread in 2006 Chicago, where youngster Jake Kimble (Matthew Knight) watches as a mysterious hooded stranger is moved into an apartment down the hall in their brownstone building. An inquisitive Jake observes the new arrival lining the apartment windows with newspapers for some unknown reason, and he secretly watches as the strange, forlorn figure roams through the building's hallways and basement areas at night. In the wake of the stranger's arrival, marital tensions begin to boil over between Jake's father Bill (Christopher Cousins) and his new wife Trish (Jennifer Beals) for no discernable reason.

Back in 2006 Tokyo, the curse begins to stalk Allison, Vanessa and Miyuki. Its first victim is Miyuki, who checks into a "love hotel" with her boyfriend, where she is attacked by Kayako and pulled inside the room's mirror into oblivion. After the disappearance, Allison and Vanessa are called before the school administrator, Ms. Dale, and when Vanessa is left alone in the office the ghost comes after her and pursues her into the street, where she is engulfed in a web of Kayako's black hair inside a telephone booth and transported to the netherworld.

Meanwhile in 2004 Tokyo, Eason, who has been researching the phenomena in the Saeki house for three years, joins forces with Aubrey as they continue the investigation. They return to the haunt where Eason retrieves Kayako's creepy diary as Aubrey is pulled inside by Toshio's ghost. Deciphering the arcane symbols in the diary, they learn that Kayako's mother was an *itako*, or exorcist, who drew evil spirits out of people and "fed" them to her daughter as part of a Shinto religious ritual. That night Eason is killed by Kayako, who emerges from one of his photographs, and Aubrey flees his apartment when she discovers his corpse. Thinking that Kayako's mother Mrs. Kawamata (Kim Miyori) may have the power to dispel the curse, Aubrey travels to her home in a rural area of Japan, where she converses with the elderly *itaku*. The exorcist cannot help her, but Kayako's ghost has followed Aubrey and chokes her mother to death before Aubrey's horrified eyes.

In 2006 Chicago, Jake's family all fall victim to the curse, dying in various horrific ways. A terrified Jake discovers that the mysterious hooded figure is Allison, who suffered a mental breakdown from the haunting events in Tokyo and was returned to Chicago by her parents, while back in 2004 Aubrey returns to the Saeki house to confront the evil spirits, with predictable results. The threads of the two narratives then merge as the curse claims its final victims in its inevitable fashion.

Critical response to the sequel was largely negative, and it was not nearly as popular with audiences as the first film. The primary reason cited was the fragmented narrative structure of Stephen Susco's screenplay that jumped around in time and space and was

(Left to right) Tokyo schoolgirls Vanessa (Teresa Palmer), Allison (Arielle Kebbel) and Miyuki (Misako Uno) prepare to enter the accursed Saeki house in *The Grudge 2* (2006).

difficult to follow. However flawed, *The Grudge 2*, under Shimizu's masterful direction, has its high points, including Kayako's materialization in front of Allison in the Saeki house, again in the high school shower room as she stalks Vanessa, and her emergence from a photograph to kill Eason under the baleful red light of a developing lamp. There's also a scary scene in which Eason detects the image of Kayako in a freeze frame of a video interview of Detective Nakagawa from the first movie. The coming of the ghosts is always announced by an eerie creaking noise that sets the nerves on edge, while Christopher Young's musical score provides a disturbing yet understated aural backdrop to the hauntings. Amber Tamblyn carries much of the film in her protagonist's role as Aubrey Davis, but Arielle Kebbel delivers a knockout performance as Allison Fleming, who morphs from shy schoolgirl to haunted burnout during the course of the film and conveys the sheer terror of the supernatural in a most convincing fashion.

The blackened, fire-scarred Saeki residence, dubbed "one of the most haunted houses in all of Japan," by one of the characters in the film, is even more forbidding than it was in *The Grudge*. A series of titles appearing right after the opening credits explains the dire influence of the haunt thusly: "When someone dies in the grip of a powerful rage, a curse is born/The curse gathers in the place of death/Those who encounter it will be consumed by its fury." It is intimated that the attempt to burn the house down at the end of the first movie potentiated the curse to move beyond the house and reach as far as America. The Chicago brownstone where much of the action takes place constitutes an ancillary haunt, its walls painted in a ghastly green hue that creates a spectral mood of gloom through which the doomed characters move as if in a nightmare. A follow-up, *The Grudge 3* (2009), had little to do with the previous films and was not directed by Shimizu.

Hideo Nataka, who had directed one of the first international J-horror hits, *The Ring* (*Ringu*, 1998), directed another contemporary *kaidan*, *Dark Water* (*Honogurai Mizu no soko kara*, 2002). It tells the story of single mother Yoshimi Matsubara (Hitomi Kuroki), who is struggling through a contentious divorce and moves into a dilapidated Tokyo apartment with her daughter Ikuko (Rio Kanno). Yoshimi enrolls Ikuko in a kindergarten at the local school and manages to land a position as a proofreader despite being out of the job market for many years. The family's main problem becomes the apartment, which has a leaky ceiling that the superintendent will not fix. In addition, Ikuko finds a child's red bag emblazoned with the image of a cartoon bunny that keeps showing up no matter how often they try to get rid of it, while Yoshimi catches glimpses of a mysterious little girl in a yellow raincoat.

The leak continues to worsen, leaving a spreading blotch of discoloration on the ceiling. During the divorce proceedings it is revealed that Yoshimi has had a history of mental instability and may be having hallucinations. She keeps seeing apparitions of the girl in the yellow raincoat in the building's corridors and on the roof, and learns that a girl named Mitsuko Kawai who lived in the apartment directly above them disappeared a year ago and was never found. As the haunting continues, Ikuko begins acting strangely, and when she disappears one night, Yoshini finds her in the apartment upstairs, which is flooded because the water taps have been opened.

Yoshimi starts to become unhinged as the hauntings continue with black hair found in the building's drinking water as Ikuko becomes ill. Following some vague intuition, she is drawn to the roof, where she has a vision of the ghost of Mitsuko (Mirei Oguchi) climbing up to the top of the building's water tank. She watches as the phantom child accidentally drops the red bag into the water and falls in when she tries to retrieve it and drowns. In the meantime, Ikuko turns on the bathtub faucet but is unable to turn it off, whereupon Mitsuko's ghost emerges from the murky water and nearly drowns the child before Yukiko arrives to rescue her. In order to save her daughter, Yukiko embraces the ghost and becomes Mitsuko's surrogate mother as she is engulfed in the dark water, and in a postscript, Ikuko learns that her mother's ghost continues to protect her in the afterlife.

Like the *Grudge* films, the plot of *Dark Water* revolves around the destructive actions of a vengeful ghost. Adapted from a story by Koji Suzuki by screenwriters Yoshihiro Nakamura and Kenichi Suzuki, the otherworldly events are set against the dramatic conflict of a single mother desperately trying to maintain custody of her daughter while shielding her from the supernatural assaults of the *onryo*. Mitsuko's ghost, played by six-year-old Mirei Oguchi, is a particularly disturbing kind of spook whose visage is never shown to the audience. Set during the Japanese rainy season, or *tsuyu*, that occurs every year during the early summer months, cinematographer Junichiro Hayashi shoots many scenes in the pouring rain and paints Tokyo in grey, subdued tones that shroud it in perpetual overcast. Director Nakata builds tension slowly and inexorably toward the inevitable tragedy and shoots this *kaidan* in a mostly naturalistic style that makes the weird events of the narrative seem utterly believable. A fine Japanese cast headed by Hitomi Kuroki as Yoshimi and Rio Kanno as Ikuko deliver understated yet powerful performances in this unusual and haunting story.

Dark Water, like Polanski's *The Tenant*, is set within the claustrophobic confines of a haunted apartment house rather than a spacious home or mansion. The apartment and the hallways are painted in drab grey colors that accentuate the worn-out, despairing nature of the place. Watery imagery pervades the film, as flowing water is thought to be a portal through which souls could travel to the world of the dead in Japanese folklore. The ghost's control of water also recalls cases of "water poltergeists" recorded in the annals of parapsychology. Nakata's previous *kaidan, Ringu,* also featured the ghost of a "dead wet girl" who emerges from a well to menace the living. By the end of *Dark Water* Mitsuko has become Ikuko's doppelganger and a substitute daughter to Yoshimi. The film was remade

This Japanese poster for *Dark Water* (2002) features Mirei Oguchi as the ghostly child Mitsuko (left) and Rio Kanno as Ikuko.

in America under the same title in 2005 starring Jennifer Connelly and Tim Roth in an inferior version set on New York's Roosevelt Island.

J-horror aficionados have pointed out similarities between the plot of *Dark Water* and a real-life mysterious incident. In January of 2013, 21-year-old Canadian student Elisa Lam checked into the Cecil Hotel in downtown Los Angeles while vacationing in the city. When her parents hadn't heard from her after three weeks, they contacted the LAPD who launched an investigation. They conducted an extensive search of the hotel using police dogs but were unable to find a trace of her. Their only clue was a surveillance video showing Ms. Lam going in and out of an elevator while apparently talking and gesturing to someone who can't be seen in the recording. Several weeks later guests at the Cecil complained about dirty "black" water coming from their showers and faucets, and when a maintenance crew inspected the water tower on the hotel's roof they discovered the cause of the water problem—Elisa Lam's naked body. Whether Ms. Lam's strange and tragic death was a homicide or a suicide has never been ascertained.

Back in America, Louisiana bayou country was the setting for the southern gothic thriller *The Skeleton Key* (2005). Kate Hudson stars as Caroline Ellis, a New Orleans hospice worker who decides to quit her job and take a position as a personal caretaker for a terminally ill man at an isolated backwater plantation. Her patient is Ben Devereaux (John Hurt), who has recently suffered a stroke that has rendered him mute and confined to a wheelchair. He lives with his sister Violet (Gena Rowlands) in the gloomy 30-room mansion, and Violet gives Caroline a skeleton key that will open any door in the house in order to facilitate her access. Also on hand is the cynical Devereaux family lawyer, Luke Marshall (Peter Sarsgaard), who is preparing Ben's last will and testament.

Violet warns Caroline that she must avoid going up to the mansion's attic, and informs her that mirrors are forbidden anywhere in the house for some odd reason. Ignoring the stricture, Caroline investigates the forbidden room and finds it is filled with weird magical paraphernalia. When she confronts Violet about the objects in the attic, she is told that it was formerly inhabited by two African American servants, Mama Cecile (Jeryl Prescott Sales) and Papa Justify (Ronald McCall), who were the leaders of a local Hoodoo cult, and whose ghosts can still be seen in mirror reflections inside the house. The couple was lynched 90 years ago by the original owners of the house, and Violet reveals that Ben suffered his stroke while he was in the attic. Intrigued, Caroline returns to the attic, where she pilfers a phonograph recording of Papa Justify reciting a Hoodoo ritual called "Conjure of Sacrifice." Thinking that Ben's condition may be psychosomatic, she consults her friend Jill (Joy Bryant) about Hoodoo and learns of a secret shop in New Orleans, where she purchases magical objects and instructions for casting a spell. She conducts a ritual designed to cure Ben, who temporarily regains enough power of speech to beg for her help.

Caroline begins to suspect that Violet is acting out of some sinister motive toward her brother and herself. Coming to believe in the powers of Hoodoo, she learns from practitioners that the Conjure of Sacrifice spell is intended to keep one from dying by stealing another person's remaining years of life. Her fears are realized when she confronts Violet, who is unable to cross a line of brick dust she has placed on the floor, proving that Violet is involved in the cult. Caroline attempts to flee the mansion with Ben but is unable to, so she hides him on the property and goes to Luke's office seeking his help, but is taken prisoner by the lawyer and driven back to the Devereaux plantation instead. The film ends with a

Hospice worker Caroline Ellis (Kate Hudson) performs a hoodoo ceremony in a Louisiana haunt in *The Skeleton Key* (2005).

nasty plot twist in which the spirits of Mama Cecile and Papa Justify ultimately have the last laugh.

This atmospheric thriller is competently directed by Iain Softley and moodily photographed by Dan Mindel on location in Louisiana bayou country. Oddly, like *Dark Water*, many scenes take place during torrential downpours that serve to isolate the characters indoors and emphasize an uneasiness engendered by wetness. Kate Hudson exhibits a lot of pluck as well as compassion in her role as Caroline, while Oscar-winner John Hurt turns in a fine acting job using only facial expressions as the dying Ben. Gena Rowlands, however, steals the show with her portrayal of the sinister, acid-tongued Violet Devereaux. Ehren Kruger's screenplay hangs together well and builds toward an unusual and unforeseen climax. The film's soundtrack utilizes a meld of New Orleans musical traditions, including Dixieland, Delta Blues and Gospel (as well as the enigmatic pop hit "Iko-Iko" by the Dixie Cups) in a manner similar to Alan Parker's NOLA-based horror noir thriller *Angel Heart* (1987).

The film's haunted plantation was filmed on location in the exteriors and interiors of the historic Felicity Plantation in Saint James Parish, Louisiana, while additional scenes were shot at Evergreen Plantation in Wallace, Louisiana. Like the 1939 version of *The Cat and the Canary* and *The Haunted Mansion*, *The Skeleton Key* partakes of Southern Gothic atmosphere, with its swampy bayous, waving strands of Spanish moss and semi-tropical decay. And like another Southern Gothic thriller, *Midnight in the Garden of Good and Evil* (1997), it explores the African American realm of Hoodoo. Unlike Voodoo, which is a polytheistic religion brought to the Caribbean by African slaves that involves ecstatic drumming and ritual possession, Hoodoo is a folk magic practice that derives from Christianity and utilizes herbs, magic potions and spells to manipulate fate and reality.

The American South was also the setting for a very different take on the haunted house theme in *The House Next Door* (2006). The film takes place in a cozy, upscale suburb of Atlanta, where thirty-something couple Col and Walker Kennedy (Lara Flynn Boyle and Colin Ferguson) are appalled when a house is constructed in a vacant lot next to their home. Wunderkind architect Kim Dougherty (Mark-Paul Gosselaar) designs an imposing, ultra-modern structure described as being "magical" and "a little piece of heaven" that is the envy of the neighborhood once it is completed, but Kim is an aloof, quasi-mysterious character, and Col has an intuition that there is something off-kilter about the house next door.

Lawyer Buddy Harrelson (Stephen Amell) and his pregnant wife Pie (Charlotte Sullivan) move in and appear to be a loving, upwardly mobile couple that the Kennedys immediately take to, but things start to go awry immediately as dead animals are found on the new house's property, including Pie's puppy. Then, during the Harrelson's housewarming party, Buddy inexplicably pushes his wife down the cellar stairs, causing her to miscarry, and in the aftermath the marriage is ended and the couple moves out. The house is put back on the market and is sold to another couple, Buck and Anita Sheehan (Aidan Devine and Julie Stewart), who have lost their son Toby while he was serving as a helicopter pilot in Iraq. It soon becomes evident that Anita has not psychologically accepted Toby's death when she momentarily mistakes a pizza delivery man for her son. Then she begins to receive mysterious phone calls that she believes are coming from Toby. When a TV set is installed in the home, images of Toby's helicopter exploding appear on the screen that cause Anita to have a mental breakdown, but Col witnesses this with her own eyes and later learns that no war movies were scheduled to be shown that day. Shortly afterward Col enters the house to find Anita watching static on the TV set and discovers Buck making love to her friend Virginia (Heidi von Palleske), and the infidelity causes Anita to hang herself in the house's living room, and in the aftermath the property is put up for sale once more.

By now Col is entirely convinced that the house is haunted "in a unique and terrible way" that "finds some weakness in us" and "destroys what you love." The evil of the house reaches out to the Kennedys one night when Kim returns and takes Col into the empty house, where they fall into each other's arms and start making love. Unfortunately, Walker sees this and attacks Col with a knife intending to murder her before coming to his senses. This incident finally convinces a skeptical Walker that something is indeed horribly wrong with the house that Kim has put there. "It's not the house, it's him," she opines, and Walter is forced to agree.

While they are deciding what to do, a third couple moves into the house, Norman and Suzannah Greene (Noam Jenkins and Emma Campbell), along with their young daughter Belinda (Niamh Wilson). It doesn't take long for the haunt to exert its wicked influence on Norman, an obsessive control freak who cruelly abuses his wife. When the Greenes hold a housewarming party for the neighborhood, Norman explodes when most of the guests fail to show up because Suzannah has failed to mail the invitations and humiliates her in front of the Kennedys and the few other couples in attendance. After the guests have left, Norman continues to berate his wife until she snaps and shoots him dead with his own pistol.

After this last debacle the Kennedys resolve that the haunted house next door must be burned down and the ground sown with salt, theorizing that Kim has invested some perverse part of his being into the haunt. When Kim returns unexpectedly from a European trip and announces that he has bought the house, they decide they must act. Gaining entrance to the building, they open all the gas jets as Kim arrives to intervene, but during the struggle the house explodes, killing Kim while Col and Walker survive. The house is destroyed and cannot be rebuilt on the site, but a postscript shows a young couple perusing home designs with an architect who shows them Kim's design, implying that they intend to resurrect the evil house next door for someone else.

Produced for the Lifetime cable TV channel, this adaptation of Anne Rivers Siddons' highly original take on the haunted house novel by scenarist Suzette Couture is faithful to its source material, although the book's plot has been somewhat compressed to fit a 90-minute TV-movie format. Canadian director Jeff Woolnough, who has worked mostly in the television medium, elevates the film beyond the usual telefilm standards to craft a well-paced, well-acted supernatural thriller that is a cut above the usual bland TV fare. Lara Flynn Boyle's performance as protagonist Col Kennedy dominates the film, and she is aided by a competent cast of Canadian actors who make the unusual story feel natural and believable. The film, like the novel, is told from a distinctly feminine point of view as Col intuitively unlocks the secrets of the house by using her intuition. The film's quotidian suburban setting provides a disarmingly normal backdrop against which the weird events unfold that is a far cry from the gothic environments prevalent in most films of this type.

Like Hill House in *The Haunting*, the film's haunt is a house that is born bad from its very inception, and like the haunted house in the *Grudge* films there is a contagion effect. In this case the house curses those who enter with a destructive corruption of their libidos that leads to sexual excess, although this concept is drawn more clearly in the novel. The house's contemporary design recalls the unusual architecture of the Bauhaus fortress in the 1934 version of *The Black Cat*, as well as Frank Lloyd Wright's modernist Ennis House as it appears in the 1958 version of *House on Haunted Hill*.

Another contemporary suburban structure was turned into a haunted house in the 2007 mega-hit *Paranormal Activity*. San Diego couple Katie (Katie Featherston) and Micah (Micah Sloat) are experiencing anomalous phenomena such as knocking sounds, flickering lights and water taps being turned on in their home. Because these events usually happen while they are sleeping, Micah purchases some hi-tech equipment with the aim of capturing this activity on audio and video. They also invite psychic researcher Dr. Fredrichs (Mark Fredrichs) into their home to advise them how to deal with the anomalous situation. Katie reveals that these kinds of paranormal events have plagued her ever since she was a child and have followed her to her new home. On the basis of this, Fredrichs explains that they are not dealing with a traditional haunting, but attributes the phenomena to the work of a demon that will follow her wherever she goes. He also warns them not to attempt to communicate with the entity.

Micah sets up his equipment and records a number of weird happenings, including the bedroom door moving, odd noises and flickering lights, but the phenomenon gradually escalates into demonic screeching and their chandelier moving by itself. One night the camera records Katie getting up and standing beside the bed for hours in a somnambulistic trance, but when she awakens, she has no memory of the event. Discounting Dr. Fredrichs' advice not to attempt to communicate with the entity, Micah buys a Ouija board and leaves it in front of the running camera, which records the planchette moving around by itself before spontaneously combusting.

Katie becomes highly upset by all these ghostly happenings, but Micah seems obsessed with recording them. The paranormal activities begin to ramp up, leaving strange footprints in powder sprinkled on the bedroom floor, slamming the bedroom door, pulling the sheets off the bed and other intimidating tactics. One night, Katie is bodily pulled out of bed by an unseen force, hauled out of the bedroom and bitten on parts of her body. She begins to show symptoms of spirit possession, but strangely resists leaving their home, proclaiming, "It's not the house, it's me" while realizing that the entity will follow her wherever she goes. Things come to a head one night when Katie sleepwalks out of bed, goes downstairs and kills Micah when he follows her, hurling his body at the camera while grinning demonically. An end title informs the audience that Micah's corpse was found in the house by police while Katie has disappeared.

Paranormal Activity was reportedly filmed using home video equipment on a seven-day shooting schedule with a budget of $15,000 by writer/producer/director triple threat Oren Peli in his own home, and considering these factors it's a remarkable achievement. While the film purports to be "found footage" of actual events recorded on video, a format made popular by the 1999 horror hit *The Blair Witch Project*, the images have obviously been subjected to extensive editing, including numerous fades and dissolves between shots and accelerated time code. As befits a non-professional production, the sound often has too much reverb and the camera is frequently hand-held, while the camera's wide-angle lens distorts perspective. All of this, however, adds to the creepy intimacy of the haunting

San Diego couple Katie (Katie Featherston) and Micah (Micah Sloat) record video of a supernatural force in *Paranormal Activity* (2007).

by adding an element of non-studio realism that approximates the way one might experience a ghostly poltergeist infestation in actuality. In contrast to a big budget extravaganza like *Poltergeist*, the film's special effects are minimal but actually more effective. Many of the film's climactic scenes take place in the couple's bedroom as Micah's camera records supernatural phenomena that are unseen by the characters in stark black and white. Audiences shrieked in terror when the entity slammed the bedroom door shut, pulled the covers off the sleepers or cast a fleeting black shadow over the room's threshold. Katie Featherston delivers a dynamic performance as the doomed victim of the demon who suffers a mental breakdown and slowly sinks into a state of possession. The cast acted without a script, and were only given an outline of the action to be filmed, an improvisation technique known as "retroscripting," that enhanced the film's sense of realism.

Peli reportedly conceived the film after being subjected to the normal night-time noises of his house settling and imagined they were due to ghosts. In preparation for filming, he extensively studied paranormal phenomena to familiarize himself with various aspects of the supernatural. The strange events depicted are attributed to a demonic influence rather than ghosts, and while the term "poltergeist" is never used, it is closest to describing the activities shown in the film, although there are many similarities and overlaps between the poltergeist phenomenon and so-called "demonic possession." The film's haunt is an ordinary Southern California tract home that is transformed into a place of dread by the unusual goings-on, but it is Katie, not the house that is the focus of the evil entity. While poltergeist activity is sometimes captured in still photos or videos, for the most part the phenomenon tends to be camera shy and avoids being imaged by photographic devices. In many cases poltergeist actions are more numerous and dramatic than could be shown given the film's limited budget. This crowd pleaser and box-office sensation led to several sequels, including *Paranormal Activity 2* (2010), *Paranormal Activity 3* (2011), *Paranormal Activity 4* (2012) and *Paranormal Activity: The Ghost Dimension* (2015).

Asian filmmaking siblings Danny and Oxide Pang brought another slice of J-horror to the West in the Canadian/American offering *The Messengers* (2007), which was executive-produced by Sam Raimi and Ghost House Pictures, who had adapted the English-language versions of *The Grudge* and its sequels. The action is set in an isolated farm house in North Dakota, where a brief prologue shows a mother and her young son being brutally slaughtered by an unseen assailant. Five years later the Solomon family from Chicago moves into the farmhouse seeking a new life. The family consists of father Roy (Dylan McDermott), wife Denise (Penelope Ann Miller), teenage daughter Jess (*Twilight*'s Kristen Stewart) and son Ben (Evan and Theodore Turner). Ben has been rendered mute after being in a car accident when Jess was driving, and Roy hopes that the bucolic setting will heal the family's wounds.

Roy busies himself with raising a crop of sunflowers while the rest of the family tries to adjust to their bucolic existence. Jess has a particularly hard time with the move, being cut off from her former school and social life, but she manages to befriend a schoolmate, Bobby (Dustin Milligan). As the Solomons try to settle in to the gloomy old place, Ben begins to have visions of the ghosts of the murdered mother and child scuttling around the rooms, but does not communicate anything about the phantoms to the family. One night when Jess and Ben are left alone in the house the ghosts manifest themselves and attack the children. Jess calls 911, but when the police arrive the house is mysteriously put back into order and her emotional stability is called into question, but in the aftermath of this event the apparitions continue to appear to her.

Another problem plaguing the family consists of flocks of crows that infest the farm and threaten the crops. One day Roy is aggressively attacked by the birds until a stranger suddenly appears to drive them off. The man is John Rollins (John Corbett), who is looking for work and seems to be knowledgeable about sunflower farming, so Roy takes him on as a hired hand. While John seems a bit rough around the edges, he proves to be a hard worker as the farm's crops ripen for harvest. The supernatural manifestations continue, however, as Jess is attacked by the boy's ghost and hospitalized, but her wounds are thought to be self-inflicted, and afterward Jess and Bobby begin to research the history of the house. They find out that farmhand John Burwell is in reality John Rollins, the man who murdered his wife and son in the house five years ago, and they race back to Jess' home to inform her parents.

Back on the farm Denise is dismayed by a bloody-looking stain on the wall that she can't seem to clean, but as she watches the grotesque ghost of the murdered woman, Mary Rollins (Shirley McQueen) emerges from the stain. Terrified, she attempts to flee with Ben, but John, who has suffered a mental breakdown after being attacked by the crows, now thinks Denise is Mary and attempts to kill her and Ben. Jess and Bobby arrive in time to avert the tragedy, and John winds up being pulled down into a mud pit to his death by the spirits of his murdered family. In the wake of these climactic events Ben regains the power of speech, the crows cease attacking the farmhouse, and the Solomon family is able to live in harmony.

Despite their J-horror expertise, directors Danny and Oxide Pang turn out a mediocre and derivative haunted house thriller that fails to generate much in the way of ghostly

The haunted North Dakota farmhouse in *The Messengers* (2007).

thrills. One major problem is Mark Wheaton's formulaic screenplay, which borrows elements from *Burnt Offerings*, *Cold Creek Manor* and *The Grudge* as well as *The Sixth Sense* and Hitchcock's *The Birds*. It is unclear, for instance, why the crows (presumably the messengers of the title) are plaguing the farm, and why the film's ghosts desist from taking vengeance upon their murderer until the very last reel. The film attempts to combine the terrors of a supernatural haunting with the menace of a crazed serial killer and comes up deuces on both counts. The cast of mostly unknown actors turn in workmanlike but uninspired performances, including future vampire lover Kristen Stewart, who plays the film's obligatory insouciant teenage daughter. The haunted farmhouse, a ramshackle building located in the Qu'Appelle Valley, near Abernethy, Saskatchewan, Canada, is a typically grungy haunt, while the film's creepy revenants and shambling creatures are familiar to aficionados of Japanese horror movie fare.

The French-Romanian haunted house chiller *House of Voices* (a.k.a. *Saint Ange*, 2007) is set in the Saint Ange orphanage in the French Alps in 1958. As the film opens Alex (Martin Chouquet), a little orphan boy, gets up in the middle of the night to use the communal lavatory where he sees something in a large mirror over a tub and climbs up to take a better look. Whatever he sees frightens him and he falls backward to the floor and is killed. The child's mysterious death causes the evacuation of the orphans from Saint Ange just as housekeeper Anna Jurin (Virginie Ledoyen) arrives to take up her new position. The stern director of the facility, Madam Francard (Catriona MacColl) departs with the children, leaving Anna alone at the orphanage with the middle-aged cook Helenka (Dorina Lazar) and Judith (Lou Doillon), an adult orphan who has mental problems and has been there since 1946.

Anna is pregnant after being raped by her former employer and is taking pains to conceal the fact. Soon after her arrival she begins to have nightmares, hear strange sounds at night, and finds children's toys and drawings in odd places around the empty building. Seeking answers, she begins snooping around the orphanage and its grounds, where she discovers a cache of children's records concealed within a ruined chapel and starts to suspect that something terrible happened at the orphanage in the aftermath of World War II. Anna befriends Judith, who is heavily medicated and lives in a fantasy world as she begins to slip into unreality herself. She comes to believe that hundreds of orphans were killed or allowed to die of neglect because they could not be cared for.

Judith and Anna slip into a psychological relationship that is called *folie a deux*, a delusional state that is shared by two people. One night, Judith leads her into the communal bathroom where Alex died, which she believes is the nexus of the haunting, and when Anna sees a child's face on the other side of the mirror, she shatters it. Anna crawls through the opening into a dark area where she finds decrepit toys, broken furniture and ruined equipment, but she insists on exploring further despite Judith's protestations. She fits herself inside a functioning dumbwaiter elevator and descends through this netherworld to a strange and terrible fate.

In his feature film debut, writer/director Pascal Laugier constructs an arty but tepid ghost story lacking in suspense or horror movie chills. Laugier's screenplay owes much to del Toro's *The Devil's Backbone*, lensed just a few years earlier, in its orphanage setting, war-related angst and child ghosts that are connected with water. These specters hardly appear until the very end of the film, and are not used to create fear or tension as in most haunted house movies. The performances of the actresses in the four leading roles is adequate, but not particularly inspired, although Lou Doillon's portrayal of the reality-challenged, child-like Judith stands out. Rather than depicting a supernatural haunting, the film is really a psychological study of Anna's descent into madness, and it is marred by a downbeat, grotesque denouement.

The haunted orphanage in *House of Voices* is a much grander affair than the cramped, gritty locale of *The Devil's Backbone*, sporting an imposing marble stairway and a lofty ceiling with palatial windows in its main area. Many of the interior scenes were shot at Castel Studios in Bucharest, Romania, where the sets were given a distressed look to simulate the decaying rooms and corridors of the aging building. Saint Ange seems to have been built in a location in which thunderstorms are frequent because they occur with regularity and cause light fixtures to strobe dramatically during key sequences. This is an example of an institutional haunt, and in addition to orphanages, a number of former prisons, hospitals and mental institutions have a reputation for being haunted due to the severe human suffering experienced within their walls.

A short story by horror luminary Stephen King was the basis for a very different cinematic haunt in *1408* (2007). The film stars John Cusack as Mike Enslin, a failing author who specializes in writing books about haunted locations throughout America. His books include *10 Haunted Graveyards*, *10 Haunted Lighthouses* and *10 Haunted Hotels*, but Enslin is a cynical skeptic who has never actually encountered a ghost. His preoccupation with the afterlife is due in part to the untimely death of his daughter Katie (Jasmine Jessica Anthony) from a childhood illness that has led to the breakup of his marriage to his ex-wife Lily (Mary McCormack).

Enslin lives a carefree existence in the seaside community of Hermosa Beach, California, where he visits the local post office and receives an anonymous postcard depicting the Dolphin Hotel in New York City inscribed with the cryptic message "Don't Enter 1408." Intrigued, he decides to visit the Dolphin as part of his research for another book. The hotel's manager, Gerald Olin (Samuel L. Jackson), tries hard to persuade him not to stay in the room, claiming that 56 guests have committed suicide or died of natural causes while staying in the room, and that no one can stay there longer than a single hour. He even gives Enslin a book containing gory post-mortem photos of the room's victims, but the ghost-busting author will not be persuaded and is reluctantly checked into 1408. The room is only accessible using an antique brass key that turns a mechanical lock because electronics don't work there.

At first Enslin is appalled by the banality of his supposedly accursed accommodations (actually a suite of rooms rather than a single room), taunting the spooks to "show me the rivers of blood." He doesn't have long to wait before the supernatural manifestations begin as the clock radio suddenly turns itself on and a couple of complimentary hotel candies appear on his pillow. The psychokinetic events continue as a faulty thermostat suddenly malfunctions and overheats the suite, and a window forcefully slides shut, painfully wounding his hand. The former skeptic is turned into a terrified believer as he witnesses apparitions of the dead guests as well as the ghosts of his father (Len Cariou) and daughter Katie. Enslin is unable to unlock the door when the key breaks inside the lock, and he then tries to escape through the ventilation system but somehow finds himself back in 1408. The same thing happens when he attempts to walk the building's outside ledge to an adjacent window.

Seven. Haunted Houses for a New Millennium

Arch-skeptic Mike Enslin (John Cusack) is trapped in a haunted hotel room in *1408* (2007).

The malignancy within the room seems to have omnipotent powers as a wall cracks open and drips blood and the place is plunged into sub-zero temperatures. At one point, Enslin thinks he has contacted his wife Lily, who lives in New York, on his laptop and pleads with her to call the police, but soon learns that the entity has taken control of the device and is mocking him. When Enslin hurls a chair at a painting of a ship at sea, the wall cracks open and the room is inundated with water. He wakes up back on Hermosa Beach after nearly drowning during a surfing accident and is taken to a hospital where he reunites with Lily. Thinking that his experience inside 1408 was only a vivid nightmare he tries to get on with his life, but little by little perceives that he is still held captive inside the haunted room. In a final act of desperation, he manages to set 1408 on fire and the room is destroyed in an explosion. Enslin survives and wakes up in a hospital with Lily at his bedside in a repeat of the previous scene, but is this real or just another illusion, and will he ultimately find that he is still trapped inside 1408?

Widely considered one of the best screen adaptations of Stephen King's works by critics, *1408* is a chilling exercise in terror that eschews the shock and gore of many contemporary horror movies in favor of a more measured psychological approach. The film plays with the uncertainty as to whether the psychokinetic events Enslin is witnessing are real or just an illusion planted in his mind by the malign force that haunts the room. It unfolds like an extended dream or hallucination, and the screenplay by Matt Greenberg, Scott Alexander and Larry Karaszewski touches on the enigmatic phenomenon of lucid dreaming. This is a dreaming state in which the dreamer perceives that they are awake inside the dream and can even experience "false awakenings" in which they think they are awake but are still inside the dream. In the film Enslin refers to his experience as a "lucid nightmare" at one point, and he also appears to awaken and then goes back into the realm of illusion inside 1408. Director Mikael Hafstrom keeps the supernatural action moving along briskly while investing the unusual events with a requisite dose of believability. John

Cusack is alone on the screen most of the time and does a fine job of portraying the film's jaded ghostbreaker as he fearfully contends with the uncanny, while Samuel L. Jackson has a small but memorable role as the suave but vaguely sinister hotel manager.

The film *1408* is frequently compared with King's other haunted hotel opus, *The Shining*. The two films offer a study in contrasts of this theme, as the Overlook Hotel in *The Shining* is an enormous maze that seems to swallow up the characters in its innards, while *1408* offers the claustrophobic terrors of "infinite horrors in a little room" (to paraphrase the Bard). In any event, Enslin muses "hotels are naturally creepy places." in which all manner of strange behaviors take place in anonymity. Note that the protagonists in both films are struggling writers. The film's opening scenes poke fun at the proliferation of "spook house" attractions that are "selling the mystique" of being haunted, such as the Stanley Hotel where King conceived *The Shining*. No explanation is offered as to why an evil presence resides in only one room in the Dolphin Hotel and no others, or the reason why the room came to be haunted in the first place. There are similarities between *1408* and the short story "The Spiders" by German horror writer Hanns Heinz Ewers, in which a hotel room in Paris is haunted by a mysterious entity that compels those who stay there to commit suicide. The entity inside room 1408 is not a conventional ghost or poltergeist, but seems to be an unseen force capable of manipulating the mind. Exteriors of the Dolphin were filmed at the venerable Roosevelt Hotel in New York, while the lobby scenes were shot at the elegant Reform Club in London.

A novel take on the haunted house theme was offered in supernatural thriller *The New Daughter* (2009). Kevin Costner stars as John James, a novelist who moves with his daughter Louisa (Ivana Baquero) and son Sam (Gattlin Griffith) to a large Plantation-style house in rural Mercy, South Carolina. The family is suffering through the aftermath of a bitter divorce that has alienated Louisa from her father. During the move-in a trail of dusty footprints is found leading to the window in Louisa's upstairs bedroom, and that night a dark form is seen scurrying over the house's roof.

The next day the children are exploring the grounds of the estate when they discover a large, earthen mound on the property, which Louisa is oddly attracted to. In the meantime, John learns from the townsfolk that the last owner of the house disappeared under mysterious circumstances. As Louisa has a hard time fitting in to her new environment and tensions mount between father and daughter, John turns to her teacher, Cassandra Parker (Samantha Mathis) for aid and comfort. Louisa, however, becomes more and more withdrawn from her family and starts to spend a lot of time perched atop the mound listening to eerie sounds emanating from within while in a trance state. One night, John finds her walking in her sleep and when he guides her back into bed he notices she is holding a crude doll made of straw. When he examines it more closely, he finds a tiny box inside containing a live spider.

As Louisa continues to fall under the sway of the forces within the mound, she acquires a series of strange scars on her body. After her worried father consults with Cassandra at a restaurant one evening, while driving home in his car he observes a shadowy figure running through the woods that breaks one of the car windows with a thrown stone. The next day John summons his real estate agent (Martin Thompson) to the house to answer questions about the previous owners, the Wayne family. He learns that Sarah Wayne locked her daughter Emily in a room inside the house before disappearing, and that Emily was rescued by her grandfather Roger, who took her to live with him in Charleston and that the girl subsequently died in a house fire.

Seeking clues to the enigma, John arranges to have middle-aged babysitter Mrs. Amworth (Sandra Ellis Lafferty) mind Louisa and Sam while he travels to the Wayne home in a suburb of Charleston. While exploring the burned-out house he finds a "nest" made of branches and twigs inside a closet along, with a picture of the mound inscribed with the word "home." He is startled to encounter a distraught Roger Wayne (James Gammon), who explains that his granddaughter Emily had changed until she hardly seemed human any more, and that he deliberately burned her alive inside his house. Wayne advises John to do the same, explaining that "a father will do anything for his daughter, even the worst thing." Meanwhile, Louisa returns from a visit to the mound, and when Mrs. Amworth steps outside for a smoke she finds the front door locked as she is brutally attacked by an unseen creature. When John returns home he calls the police, who search the grounds but can find no trace of the woman.

The next day John finds a nest similar to the one in Roger Wayne's house which makes him realize that Louisa is undergoing a similar transformation, and that the mound must be destroyed. He arranges to have it demolished by a local crew, but Professor Evan White (Noah Taylor), an archeologist from the local university arrives to persuade him to preserve it. The professor explains that these mounds were burial sites for godlike beings called "mound walkers" who periodically seek to mate with mortal women in order to perpetuate their race. John remains unmoved by the savant's pleas and orders the demolition to continue, whereupon a tractor unearths the mutilated body of Mrs. Amworth. John is taken in for questioning by the local police while Cassandra looks after the children, but as he is being driven home that night by officer Ed Lowry (Erik Palladino), the police car is attacked by a grotesque humanoid creature that pulls Lowry from the car to his death. When John commandeers the car and arrives home, he finds the house besieged by the inhuman mound walkers and must fend them off while he races to destroy the mound and rescue Louisa.

While the film's plot follows a well-worn haunted house template previously used in horror thrillers like *Cold Creek Manor* and *The Messengers*, a major difference lies in the approach of Spanish director Luis Berdejo to the material. *The New Daughter* has affinities with the classic horror films of Val Lewton such as *Cat People* (1941) that convey horror via what is unseen or almost seen rather than the explicit gore and grotesquerie so prevalent in the modern era. For instance, the scene in which Mrs. Amworth is killed by one of the mound walkers behind a locked door bears a striking resemblance to a similar sequence in Lewton's *The Leopard Man* (1942). Director Berjedo, in his first feature, brings a cultured, European sensibility to this haunted house tale, building a mood of unease and tension inexorably to a terrifying climax, although some critics groused about the film's ambiguous ending.

Scenarist John Travis adapted Irish writer John Connolly's short story to feature film length by developing a subtext involving a troubled father struggling to deal with changes in his adolescent daughter and a family suffering through their abandonment by an unfaithful wife and mother. John James is faced with the heartbreaking dilemma of being forced to do the "worst thing" to protect his daughter from a horrible fate. Oscar winner Kevin Costner crafts a sensitive portrait of a father confronting an impossible dilemma, while

Pan's Labyrinth's Ivana Baquero lends her talents to the portrayal of another confused adolescent drawn into a terrifying alternate reality. The film is beautifully photographed by cinematographer Checco Varese, who uses wide angle lenses, shadows and silhouettes to build a subtle atmosphere of tension and dread. Despite these strong points, the movie received mixed reviews and died at the box office due to a non-existent marketing strategy, and has fallen into an undeserved obscurity.

Like *The Skeleton Key, The New Daughter* is an exercise in Southern Gothic, the locale having been shifted from England in Connolly's original story to the American South. It was shot on location at the Wedge Plantation, a Federal-style clapboard structure built by rice planter William Lucas sometime around 1826. The real haunt, however is the mound in the woods, a burial site that serves as a womb for a race of monsters. Mysterious Pre-Columbian mounds built by the Hopewell and Adena Native American peoples in the American mid-west and the Mississipian cultures of the South have long held a fascination for archaeologists and laymen alike. The film's fictional "mound walkers" are creepy-looking humanoids that are never clearly seen by the audience, and are a major departure from the myriad entities that are usually responsible for haunting houses.

Horror director James Wan, who had given the world the seminal torture porn flick *Saw* (2004), and who would go on to direct *The Conjuring* (2013), and *The Conjuring 2* (2016), took another stab at horror with *Insidious* (2010). As the film opens, the Lambert family is settling into their new home in a suburban neighborhood in Los Angeles. The family consists of father Josh (Patrick Wilson), his wife Renai (Rose Byrne) and young sons Dalton (Ty Simpkins), Foster (Andrew Astor) and their baby Cali (Madison Bowie). One night, as Dalton is exploring the house's attic, he is startled by seeing a fleeting shadow and falls down the ladder. At first the boy seems fine, but the next day he lapses into a strange coma that baffles his doctors.

Three months later he is still in a coma and his parents decide to care for him at home, where he is ensconced in his bedroom surrounded by medical equipment. Soon afterward, the household is plagued by a series of frightening, inexplicable events. Renai hears a guttural voice transmitted over Cali's baby monitor when no one is in the room, the house's burglar alarm system goes off for no apparent reason and a bloody handprint is found on Dalton's bed. When Renai is attacked by a demonic apparition, she insists that she can no longer live in the house and persuades Josh to move.

Moving the family to new digs does nothing to alleviate their problems, as the spooks follow them into their new home. Enter Josh's mother Lorraine (*The Entity*'s Barbara Hershey), who convinces Josh to bring in demonologist Elise Reiner (Lin Shaye) along with her team of goofy parapsychologists Specs (Leigh Whannell, the film's screenwriter) and Tucker (Angus Sampson). Elise reveals that "it's not the house that's haunted" and that their son Dalton is a "traveler" born with the ability to travel on the astral plane. In his comatose state he has become lost in "the Further," a dark realm filled with the tortured souls of the dead and cannot return to his body. Their only hope is to have Josh, who also has the ability to travel outside his body, to venture into the Further and bring back Dalton's spirit.

Elise conducts a séance in which the demon who is haunting the family is identified as "the man with the fire on his face," who dwells behind a red door, but during the ceremony Dalton becomes possessed by the demonic parasite and rises up to wreak havoc in the

Seven. Haunted Houses for a New Millennium

room. She then puts Josh in a hypnotic trance that allows his spirit to leave his body and enter the Further, a realm of darkness where he encounters a number of weird ghosts before finding his way to the red door and the room where Dalton is imprisoned. Josh does battle with the demon, manages to free his son and bring him back from the netherworld, but in the end is it really Josh who has returned?

Insidious has some decent atmospherics and a few shocks, but its major problem is Leigh Whannell's screenplay, which borrows heavily from *The Exorcist* and especially from *Poltergeist*. As in *Poltergeist*, there is a child in danger who has been captured by an evil entity and transported to a supernatural realm, and it also features a team of amateur ghost-busters and a quirky female medium who is all-knowing concerning psychic phenomena and assists in the rescue of the child. Director Wan utilizes techniques like wide angle shots, skewed angles and low-key lighting to build tension and avoids the violence, blood and gore he had employed in *Saw*, but the movie ultimately comes up short as an exercise in horror cinema. The film is competently acted and it's a treat to see veteran Barbara Hershey registering abject fear of the uncanny once more. Many critics felt that the buildup of the first half of the film was effective, but that it went off the rails in the second half. The demonic realm of "the Further" is disappointingly nothing more than a darkened corridor, for instance, and during the séance sequence Elise dons a silly-looking gas mask for no particular reason. Perhaps the most horrifying thing in the film is the use of Tiny Tim's novelty hit "Tiptoe Through the Tulips," as the singer's eerie falsetto warbling truly sends a chill down one's spine.

As in a number of haunted house thrillers, the film begins with a family moving into a new home. While the movie's tag line reads, "it's not the house that's haunted," the plot

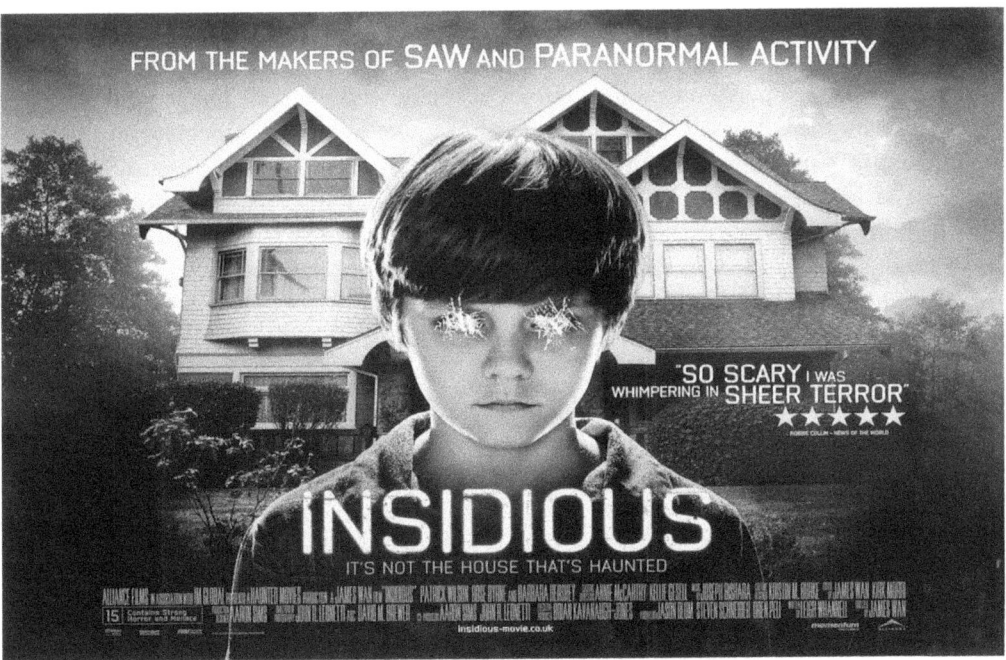

Possessed child Dalton Lambert (Ty Simpkins) stands in front of his L.A. home in this poster for James Wan's *Insidious* (2010).

proceeds from the family's move-in, although it's unclear why Dalton's out of body experiences are stimulated by the move to their new home. The film's hodgepodge of supernatural menaces includes apparitions, demons, spirit possession and poltergeist phenomena that all emanate from the astral realm of the Further. Exteriors of the first Lambert home were shot at 4350 Victoria Park Drive, a single family house in Los Angeles built in 1909, while other scenes were filmed at the historic Herald Examiner Building in L.A.'s downtown area. Colors inside both houses are pale and muted, giving the film a monochromatic look. *Insidious* made $97 million worldwide against production costs of only $13 million and its profitability inspired the sequels *Insidious Chapter 2* (2013), and the prequels *Insidious Chapter 3* (2015) and *The Last Key* (2018).

Continuing in the vein of one word ominous titles, the horror thriller *Sinister* (2012) stars Ethan Hawke as Ellison Oswalt, a true crime writer who has (once again) relocated his family into a new home in suburban King County, Pennsylvania. This time however, Oswalt, author of lurid bestsellers like *Kentucky Blood*, is chasing down leads for a new book based on the murder of four members of the house's former inhabitants, the Stevenson family. A fifth family member, the Stevenson's ten year-old daughter Stephanie, mysteriously disappeared after the tragedy. Once installed at the murder site, Oswalt's young son Trevor (Michael Hall D'Addario) starts to suffer from night terrors and his little girl Ashley (Clair Foley) begins painting weird images on the walls of her room, but Oswalt keeps his wife Tracy (Juliet Rylance) in the dark about the place's sordid history.

Oswalt's research gets a major boost when he discovers a box in the attic containing a Super 8mm projector and several cans of film containing what are supposedly home movies, but when he runs them through the projector he finds that they are actually homemade snuff films. The first reel shows the four murdered members of the Stevenson family being hung by an invisible force in the home's back yard. Other "home movies" depict different families being drowned, immolated and having their throats cut, all while being filmed by an unseen person. Oswalt becomes obsessed with the eerie images and comes to believe that all the killings are linked together in a grand homicidal scheme. He enlists the aid of the town's sympathetic deputy sheriff, who he refers to as "Deputy So-and-So" (James Ransone), who has access to law enforcement databases, to help him unlock the mystery.

It soon becomes apparent that the Stevenson murders are linked to family homicides in St. Louis, Sacramento and other cities going back decades. Oswalt digitizes the Super 8 footage, which enables him to enhance the film quality, and discovers an occult symbol left at the murder scenes, along with blurry images of a ghostly figure. Consulting with occult forensics expert Professor Jonas (Vincent D'Onofrio), he learns that the symbol represents an obscure Babylonian deity named Bughuul, dubbed the "eater of children," who needs to consume the souls of children to survive. Oswalt begins seeing apparitions of Bughuul in the home's backyard, but stubbornly refuses to give up on his project because "this could be my *In Cold Blood*."

Things finally come to a head one night when he finds the projector running the film by itself and the demon appears to him up close and personal. Terrified, he burns the film and the projector and moves the family back to their former home. As they are moving back in he gets a call from the deputy, who informs him that all of the previous families had been murdered right after they had moved into a new residence, meaning that he has now placed his family in greater danger. Even worse, in the attic he discovers another pro-

True crime writer Ellison Oswalt (Ethan Hawke) discovers a mysterious box of home movies in his new home's attic in *Sinister* (2012).

jector and a reel of film labelled "Extended Cut Endings." The film shows the possessed child killers committing their murders in greater detail, but as he is watching he collapses into unconsciousness after drinking a cup of drugged coffee. He awakens to find himself and his family bound up as his daughter Ashley, now possessed by Bughuul, prepares to dispatch them with an axe while filming the killings.

Screenwriter C. Robert Cargill reportedly conceived the idea for the film in a nightmare he had after seeing the horror film *The Ring*, in which he discovered a film in his attic depicting the hanging deaths of a family. Enlarging on this dream material, Cargill added a child-snatching boogie man, the Bughuul, as the film's terrifying supernatural menace. Like the *Paranormal Activity* series, *Sinister* utilizes what is purportedly found footage to elicit chills, and there are also similarities with Michael Mann's 1986 crime thriller *Manhunter*, in which a detective becomes obsessed with watching the 8mm home movies of murdered families while seeking the identity of an elusive serial killer. Scott Derrickson directs this spook show with a fine sense of the macabre as he builds tension inexorably to a horrifying climax. The director frequently positions the actors in the middle of the frame surrounded by blackness, as if forces of the dark are closing in around them. Ethan Hawke's intense performance as the morally challenged crime writer is riveting, while James Ransone provides some quirky comic relief as Deputy So-and-So. Christopher Young contributes an effective, brooding musical score that provides an eerie counterpoint to the ghastly goings-on.

Like many other haunted house films of the period, *Sinister* combines the notion of ghosts with that of a powerful demonic entity. The Bughuul is a figure of dread that is never clearly seen by the viewer, and as in *The Grudge* the supernatural beings are sometimes seen only by the audience and not shown to the characters. In one memorable scene, Oswalt has a grainy image of the demon's face freeze-framed on his laptop screen that turns to regard him for a moment before turning back to its original position without being seen. Instead of being localized, the haunt moves from house to house like a strange viral infection. Oswalt's house is an unremarkable single-story tract home typical of Long Island, where the film was shot. Once again the haunted house thriller proved to be box-office gold, as the film's cumulative worldwide gross totaled nearly $88 million against production costs of only $3 million and its profitability led to a sequel, *Sinister 2* (2015).

Susan Hill's 1983 gothic ghost story *The Woman in Black* was adapted for the London stage in 1989 and again as a British telefilm in the same year. It was adapted once more by England's resurrected Hammer studios in a 2012 feature film version starring *Harry Potter*'s Daniel Radcliffe. The film begins with a prelude in the rural English village of Crythin Gifford in the year 1889, where three little girls having a tea party are seized by an unseen force that compels them to leap out of a window to their deaths. Cut to London in 1910, where solicitor Arthur Kipps (Radcliffe) is assigned to travel to Crythin Gifford to settle the estate of the recently deceased Alice Drablow pursuant to the sale of Eel Marsh House, the dead woman's property. Kipps is tortured by the death of his wife Stella (Sophie Stuckey) four years earlier in childbirth, and must leave his son Joseph (Misha Handley) at home during the journey.

Arriving at the village, Kipps is given a cool reception by its inhabitants, except for wealthy landowner Samuel Daily (Ciaran Hinds), who takes him under his wing and offers him lodging. Kipps travels to Eel Marsh House, a decrepit mansion that can only be reached via the Nine Lives Causeway and is cut off from the village during high tide. While exploring the creepy old place he hears odd sounds and spies a ghostly figure through a window dressed in black that vanishes before his eyes. As he is waiting for the carriage to take him back to town he hears the sounds of an accident and the screams of a child out in the marshes, but nothing seems amiss. He reports this to the village constable, who is skeptical of his story, but at that moment a young girl (Alexia Osborne) who has ingested lye is brought to the station by her brothers. The child dies before his horrified eyes, and the villagers hold Kipps responsible for stirring things up at Eel Marsh House.

During dinner at the Daily home that night Kipps is introduced to Daily's wife Elizabeth (Janet McTeer), who has suffered a mental breakdown after the drowning death of her son and has embraced spiritualism as a way to communicate with the dead child. Kipps returns to Eel Marsh House the next day and finds correspondence between Alice Drablow and her sister Jennet Humfrye (Liz White) that indicate that Jennet's son Nathaniel was taken away from her by the Drablows because they deemed her unfit to care for the child. When Nathaniel died in a carriage accident on the marsh, Jennet accused her sister of leaving him to die while saving herself, and Jennet subsequently hanged herself in despair. Holed up inside the haunt during a lightning storm, Kipps witnesses the ghosts of dead children and a frightening apparition of Jennet hanging herself.

Kipps comes to realize that Jennet is the Woman in Black, a ghost who is exacting revenge on the children of the village for losing her own child by compelling them to commit suicide. He believes that her spirit will be pacified if she is reunited with her dead son, so he and Daily venture into the marsh and pull Nathaniel's body out of the muck. They lay the boy's corpse out inside the house to attract the ghost, which arrives in due course but intimates that she still will not lift the curse. Nathaniel's body is given a proper burial, but Kipps suddenly realizes that his son Joseph is due to arrive at the village train station that evening and hurries there hoping against hope to save him from being the next victim of the Woman in Black.

The first Hammer Films production in several decades, the film harks back to the studio's glory days while eschewing its signature gore, violence and sex in favor of a subtle, atmospheric approach that recalls classic haunted house thrillers like *The Uninvited*, *The Haunting* and *The Innocents*. The deft direction of James Watkins, working from Jane Goldman's screenplay, crafts a superior gothic chiller that is effective in its understatement by building suspense and mood to a fever pitch of terror. The spectral Woman in Black is shown fleetingly rather than in ghastly close-up, a dread figure dressed in funereal "bride of grief" clothes with her features obscured by a black veil. A 22 year-old Daniel Radcliffe, taking a sabbatical from Hogwarts

Liz White cuts a spectral figure in this poster as *The Woman in Black* (2012).

School, fills out the lead role wonderfully and is ably assisted by a fine British cast, including Ciaran Hinds as the simpatico village elder, Janet McTeer as his hysterical, perpetually grieving wife, and Liz White as the titular phantom lady. Production designer Kave Quinn imbues the film with a lush Edwardian Period ambience and conjures the gothic shadows of the haunt with set design laid out in rich, degraded colors, while cinematographer Tim Maurice-Jones' camera perfectly captures the film's ghostly imagery.

As in all memorable haunted house thrillers, the house itself is a major character, and Eel Marsh House is one of the most beautifully realized haunts in horror film history. The forbidding, fog-shrouded house, set in the middle of a desolate marsh, is as creepy as it gets. Following in the Hammer tradition of using rustic English locations to create gothic atmospherics, exteriors of the house were shot at Cotterstock Hall near Peterborough in central England, although the production crew distressed the house's façade to make it look more decrepit and degraded and made the grounds more sinister-looking using prop shrubberies and ominous lawn statuary. The marsh scenes were filmed at an actual causeway at Osea Island in Essex, while the fictional village of Crythin Gifford was shot at the township of Halton Gills in the Yorkshire Dales. Studio interiors of the gothic haunt are honeycombed with darkened hallways, ominous, disused rooms and creaky staircases, and highly effective use is made of evil-looking dolls and toys that are filmed in disturbing close-ups. Like the Bughuul creature in *Sinister*, which was released in the same year, the film's Woman in Black is a supernatural entity that harvests the souls of children. The film was a critical and popular success, earning the biggest U.S. opening at the American box office in Hammer history and went on to gross $127 million worldwide. An inferior sequel, entitled *The Woman in Black: Angel of Death*, was released in 2015 without the involvement of Radcliffe or the original movies screenwriter or director.

A family moves from the city to an old mansion in the country in the wake of an unpleasant episode hoping to heal their wounds, but finds that their new home is haunted. If this storyline seems overly familiar, it's because it has been used in a number of haunted house flicks such as *Burnt Offerings, Cold Creek Manor, The Messengers* and *The New Daughter*, among others. In *The Disappointments Room* (2016), Kate Beckinsale plays Dana Barrow, an architect who relocates from Brooklyn to rural North Carolina with her husband David (Mel Raido) and son Lucas (Duncan Joiner) after the accidental death of their infant daughter Caroline and her subsequent mental breakdown. Their new home is the Blacker Estate, a run-down 19th century southern manse that has been uninhabited for many years that Dana hopes to refurbish during her emotional recovery.

Soon after moving in, Dana begins to hear strange sounds emanating from somewhere inside the house and experiences disturbing dreams. After awakening from such a dream one night, she steps outside to have a smoke and sees a light turn on in an attic window. Intrigued, she finds a locked room in the attic that is not on the house's floor plan. Locating a key, she enters the room alone and is trapped inside when the door shuts by itself and locks her in, where she is horrified to witness a vision of a young girl being tormented by a grim-looking older man. Puzzled, she consults the town's eccentric historian, Miss Judith (Marcia DeRousse), who tells her that she has found a "disappointments room," a secret chamber that housed the disabled or disfigured children of rich parents who wanted to keep them away from the rest of the world because their families were ashamed of them. She realizes that Judge Blacker, the previous owner of the house, must have kept such a child in the disappointments room she has discovered in the Blacker mansion.

Dana realizes she has seen the ghosts of the Judge and his daughter while trapped in the forbidden room. She also begins to be hounded by a phantom dog, a large black German shepherd that prowls around the grounds. These visions and apparitions start to affect Dana's sanity to the point that she can no longer distinguish between reality and fantasy. After witnessing a scene from the past in the disappointments room in which Judge Blacker (Gerald McRaney) brutally murders his disfigured daughter Laura (Ella Jones) with a hammer, she is attacked by the Judge's dog and kills it. The Judge's ghost then goes after Lucas, but Dana picks up the hammer and comes to her son's rescue, smashing the Judge's head to a bloody pulp wielding the same hammer he had used to kill his daughter. At this point David arrives as the scene vanishes into illusion and he realizes that his wife's mental health has taken a turn for the worse. It is revealed that the underlying problem is that Dana accidentally smothered her infant daughter to death and has been suffering from an overwhelming grief and guilt ever since. The next day, as the family packs up and leaves the Blacker house, Dana looks back to see the specter of the Judge watching her depart.

A weak screenplay, lukewarm direction and indifferent acting combine to make *The Disappointments Room* into a mediocre exercise in horror cinema. Scripter Wentworth

Miller's screenplay is the prime culprit for the film's failure as it incorporates many derivative elements from other haunted house flicks without adding anything original. Director D.J. Caruso, who also co-wrote, fails to generate much in the way of atmosphere, suspense, mystery or terror as the sometimes confusing plot unfolds. There are similarities with *The Haunting of Julia* (1976), in which a woman suffering from severe guilt over her role in her daughter's death starts seeing the ghost of a female child. The ambiguity over whether the apparitions are real or imagined further compromises the film's dramatic impact. Star Kate Beckinsale has little to do except look puzzled or frightened and the rest of the cast turn in similarly lackluster performances. Even Gerald McRaney's malign screen presence as the ghostly Judge Blacker fails to horrify, while the scariest actor of the piece is the Judge's menacing black dog. In addition, although the film attempts to come off as a restrained haunted house tale, it descends into blood and gore during the scene where Dana graphically bashes the Judge's head in. Completed in 2014, the film was not released until 2016, when it was panned by critics and performed poorly at the box-office.

The Disappointments Room, however, is more interesting for its thematics than its execution. These rooms were in widespread use from the 19th century onward, when the practice was looked upon as an alternative to committing family members with special needs to hospitals or asylums where they would not receive the same level of care. This convention was the origin of the motif of the "secret room" that housed an insane or mysterious character in gothic literature, the most famous example of which occurs in Emily Brontë's seminal novel *Jane Eyre*, where Mr. Rochester imprisons his mentally ill wife in a secret wing of his Thornfield Hall estate. In a sort of in joke, the scene where Orson Welles reveals his crazy wife in her disappointments room in the 1944 screen version of the novel is shown playing on the family's television in the film. The secret room motif is a feature of some of the most spirited haunted house thrillers, including *I Walked with a Zombie*, *Psycho* and *The Changeling*. Another interesting facet of the film is the ghostly black dog that constitutes the haunt's most menacing specter. A folklore belief in phantom black dogs has been widespread in the British Isles for centuries, and was the inspiration for Arthur Conan Doyle's most memorable Sherlock Holmes novel, *The Hound of the Baskervilles*.

The film's plot was reportedly based on the experiences of Laurie Dumas, who purchased a colonial house named the Casey B. Tyler House in West Warwick, Rhode Island and discovered it had a disappointments room in the attic. Research revealed that the house was previously inhabited by Judge Job Smith Carpenter and his wife in the late 1800s, who kept their daughter Ruth secluded in the room until her death at age five. The attic room had a doorknob and a deadbolt only on the outside of the door in order to prevent anyone from getting outside. Despite this tragic oddity, the house was never reputed to be haunted. The film was shot at the Adamsleigh Mansion in Greensboro, North Carolina, where filming took place in both the exterior and interior of the house, which contained an elaborate spiral staircase that was used for dramatic effect. During production the cast and crew thought that the Adamsleigh place was haunted, but this may just be studio hype.

In Islamic countries there is a belief in beings called *djinns*, spirit entities believed to be somewhere between humankind and angels in the hierarchy of creation. In the Koran djinns are said to have been created from "smokeless fire" or "essential fire," and some of them are beneficent and others evil. The best known djinn (rendered as "genie" in English translation) appears in *The Arabian Nights* in the story of Alladin and the magic lamp, and they also appear in the tale entitled "Ali the Cairene and the Haunted House in Baghdad," in which a benevolent djinn helps the title character to find a treasure hidden inside an abandoned house. The Farsi language production of *Under the Shadow* (2017) features an evil djinn who haunts an apartment complex in Tehran.

The story takes place in 1988, during the final year of the seemingly interminable Iran-Iraq war that has dragged on for almost a decade. During this phase of the conflict, termed the "war of the cities," the two combatants are hurling missiles and flying air raids back and forth between Tehran and Baghdad, raining terror from the skies upon their helpless inhabitants. As the film opens, Iranian medical student Shideh (Narges Rashidi) is dismissed by the medical school she attends because of her political views, crushing her dreams of becoming a doctor. Returning to her Tehran apartment, she discards all of her course books except for a medical text given to her by her deceased mother.

When Shideh's physician husband Iraj (Bobby Naderi) is drafted to serve as a medical officer on the front, she is left alone to care for her daughter Dorsa (Avin Manshadi). Iraj insists that Shideh and Dorsa go to live with his parents in a safer part of the countryside, but she elects to remain in Tehran for the time being. The city is a dangerous place with Iraqi missiles and bombs exploding on a daily basis that force the apartment dwellers to take shelter in the building's basement. Amid the carnage Dorsa befriends Mehdi (Karam Rashayda), a little boy who has been rendered mute after seeing his parents killed in an air raid, yet who somehow communicates stories about djinns to Dorsa, much to the chagrin of Shideh, who senses something uncanny about the mute child.

One day a dud missile strikes the apartment building and makes a large hole in the roof. During the confusion Dorsa loses her doll Kimia and insists that someone took it. In the aftermath of the missile strike Shideh begins to have disturbing nightmares and hears weird noises in the apartment. Mrs. Ebrahimi (Aram Ghasemy) expresses the opinion that the missile has brought a djinn along with it. She explains that djinns travel on the wind until they find someone to possess and mark their victims by stealing one of their most cherished personal belongings. Intrigued, Shideh gets hold of a book about djinns entitled "The People of the Air" that explains how the evil spirits thrive on human fear and anxiety.

As the other tenants leave the complex for safer locations, Shideh and Dorsa are left alone in the building. One night Shideh awakens in the middle of the night to see a strange man in the apartment who disappears into a crack in the ceiling. Then she finds that her mother's medical text is missing from inside a locked drawer. The haunting intensifies as Shideh sees an apparition of the djinn that appears as a female form wrapped in a billowing *chador* garment that moves with blinding speed. Shideh realizes that she must leave Tehran to protect her daughter, but Dorsa refuses to go until she can find her missing doll. Panicking because she knows that the djinn now possesses her textbook and Dorsa's doll, personal objects that can allow it to link to them, she looks everywhere before finding Kimia in a dismembered state inside the locked drawer where she had kept her textbook.

After she reassembles the doll, the two of them are free to leave, but this proves to be a difficult matter when the djinn blocks their way as they flee down the stairs. She is separated from Dorsa when the spirit conjures a double of her daughter that leads her astray, but she eventually manages to overcome the djinn and reach the garage. As they drive away from Tehran into safety from the war, it is revealed that the doll's head and Shideh's medical textbook have been left behind at the apartment and have presumably been taken by the djinn, with the implication that the evil spirit will follow them wherever they go.

Iranian writer/director Babak Anvari fashions an exquisite exercise in horror set against the drama and tragedy of genocidal warfare. The film's early scenes depicting the family's struggle for sanity and survival have the look of documentary realism, but in its second half it imperceptibly transforms into a nightmare environment of visions and apparitions where nothing seems real. Anvari does not resort to using expressionist shadows, skewed angles or other hallmarks of the horror film, but instead frames the paranormal goings-on using a naturalistic style. The war enfolds the characters in a web of doom that is constantly punctuated by distant (and not so distant) explosions, the blaring of patriotic songs on the radio and propaganda speeches on TV. There are similarities with *The Devil's Backbone* wherein the haunting is framed against the myriad tragedies of war, and both films feature the motif of unexploded ordinance bringing the phantoms into the haunt. There are also affinities with *Dark Water*, in that both films center around a mother striving to protect her daughter from the depredations of a supernatural being. Narges Rashidi's dynamic performance as a mother terrorized by both the forces of a tyrannical state and an otherworldly djinn enlivens the film, and she is ably assisted by child actors Avin Manshadi as her vulnerable daughter and Karam Rashayda as the odd mute boy Mehdi.

Like *The Tenant* and *Dark Water*, the film's haunting takes place within the claustrophobic confines of an apartment. Location shooting took place in Amman, Jordan by an international production team from Jordan, Qatar and the UK. The film's evil djinn is a truly terrifying spook, an ethereal creature of the wind that assumes a human-like form while wrapped in the flowing robes of the *chador*. It moves at a blinding speed that accentuates its otherworldliness and accentuates its menace. The apparition is accompanied by a subliminal, low-frequency rumbling noise, provided by the film's sound designer Alex Joseph, that serves to accentuate the dread and anxiety being experienced by the characters and, by extension, the audience.

The 21st century has proven to be a golden age of the haunted house movie. Driven by the enormous profitability of films like *The Others*, *Paranormal Activity* and *The Woman in Black* the sub-genre has emerged as one of the dominant modes of the modern horror film. At a time of mega-budget GCI extravaganzas, the haunted house film offers a crowd-pleasing entertainment alternative for a mere fraction of the big blockbuster's production costs, proving that it doesn't take elaborate special effects to give audiences a good scare. Many of these films inspired sequels and franchises, and in addition to the movies discussed here, titles from other chapters made during this time frame can be added, including *An American Haunting* (2005), *The Haunting in Connecticut* (2009), *The Conjuring* (2013), *Crimson Peak* (2015), *The Conjuring 2* (2016), and *Winchester* (2018), as well as remakes of *The Amityville Horror* (2005) and *Poltergeist* (2015). It's possible that the mass appeal of the haunted house film may have already peaked, but it's more likely that spooks will continue to run wild for decades to come.

Conclusion: The Haunted Screen

While ghost stories and tales of haunted houses have beguiled humankind since ancient times, these themes did not immediately translate well into the novel medium of the cinema. During the expressionist period in Germany, in which all manner of supernatural creatures such as golems, somnambulists, devils, doppelgangers and vampires lurked on Weimar movie screens, haunts were conspicuous by their absence. Horror pictures in America were similarly devoid of spooks during the silent era. Haunted houses were relegated to the realm of comedy in films such as Harold Lloyd's *Haunted Spooks* (1920) and Buster Keaton's *A Haunted House* (1921). In the late 1920s and early 30s the mystery house thriller predominated in popular features like *The Bat* (1926), *The Cat and the Canary* (1927) and *The Terror* (1928), in which ghosts were replaced by frightening masked criminals. When Universal Studios launched the horror movie craze in the 1930s, vampires, werewolves and mummies predominated over phantoms and haunted houses. The trend toward comedy continued with films like *The Ghost Breakers* (1940), *Hold That Ghost* (1941) and *Ghost Catchers* (1944), where the haunts were populated by gangsters and spies. Thus, the supernatural haunted house film languished in oblivion during the formative decades of the horror film.

There were several reasons for this dearth of specters. Germany and America were predominantly Protestant countries whose religious doctrine believed in only heaven and hell as abodes of the dead in the afterlife, meaning that there were no other realms such as limbo and purgatory in which ghosts could exist. As horror film historian Carlos Clarens has pointed out, the Hollywood studios wanted to steer clear of invoking any religious dogma concerning life after death in their commercial product so as not to offend their audiences. Additionally, Americans were a highly pragmatic people who considered tales of ghosts and hauntings to be a bunch of superstitious rubbish. This accounts for the many films in which the ghosts in a haunt turn out to be gangsters, spies or swindlers who attempt to fool the gullible by disguising themselves as bogus phantoms. Spooks and haunted houses could only be the stuff of comedy and were not to be taken seriously by level-headed Americanos. Horror films of the period featured more flesh and blood creatures of the night such as Dracula and the Wolf Man, or science fiction menaces like Dr. Jekyll and Mr. Hyde and Frankenstein's monster. The very form of the ghost story also carried its own limitations in terms of filmmaking. The typical haunted house narrative involves the protagonists solving the mystery of why the ghost inhabits the house and laying the unquiet spirit to rest in the process. Thus, unlike the Universal monsters, once the spook departed for the netherworld there was no bringing it back for an endless succession of sequels.

The Uninvited (1944) and *A Place of our Own* (1945) were the first haunted house movies that featured supernatural ghosts, but they were one-offs that did not immediately impact the thematic trajectory of horror cinema. By the early 1960s, however, a number of factors combined to make the haunted house film commercially viable, including a renewed interest in ESP and psychic phenomena, a decline of religiosity in American culture, and a relaxation of Hollywood censorship rules. A quartet of exceptional films by talented directors, namely Alfred Hitchcock's *Psycho* (1960), Roger Corman's *House of Usher* (1960), Jack Clayton's *The Innocents* (1961) and Robert Wise's *The Haunting* (1963) finally put the haunted house thriller firmly on the map. These films would clear the way for a number of memorable horror movies on the theme, including *The Haunted Palace* (1963), *The Ghost* (1963), *Kill, Baby, Kill* (1965), *Rosemary's Baby* (1968), *The Exorcist* (1972), *The Legend of Hell House* (1973), *Burnt Offerings* (1976) and *The Legacy* (1979).

By the 1980s the haunted house film had hit its stride with crowd pleasers and critical successes such as *The Shining* (1980), *The Changeling* (1980), and *Poltergeist* (1982). Comedy continued to mix with spook house chills in *House* (1986), *Haunted Honeymoon* (1986), *High Spirits* (1988), *Beetlejuice* (1988), *The Haunted Mansion* (2003), and *Dark Shadows* (2012). The real triumph of the sub-genre, however, would commence in the 2000s, when the haunted house movie started to turn big profits against low production costs. Movies like *The Others* (2001), *The Grudge* (2004), *Paranormal Activity* (2007), *Insidious* (2010), *Sinister* (2012), *The Woman in Black* (2012) and *The Conjuring* (2013) were highly profitable and most of them inspired sequels and even multi-film franchises. The new millennium has also produced well-made and critically acclaimed fare such as *The Devil's Backbone* (2001), *The Skeleton Key* (2005), *The House Next Door* (2006), *The New Daughter* (2009), *Crimson Peak* (2015), and *Under the Shadow* (2017), while Japanese haunts invaded American movie screens with J-horrors like *Dark Water* (2002), *The Grudge* (2004) and *The Grudge 2* (2006).

Haunted houses are a real-world phenomenon that has fascinated the human imagination for centuries, and a number of films have sought to pierce the veil of the supernatural by re-creating allegedly true hauntings on the big screen. *The Amityville Horror* (1979) recounted details of the highly dubious circumstances connected with the haunting of the Lutz family in Amityville, Long Island, while *The Entity* (1982) re-enacted the bizarre poltergeist manifestations experienced by Los Angeles mom Doris Bither during the 1970s in a much more convincing fashion. *An American Haunting* (2005) drew upon history and legend to tell the story of the notorious "Bell Witch" poltergeist that haunted the Bell family during the early 19th century. Paranormal activity directed at the Snedecker family was chronicled (and exaggerated) in *The Haunting in Connecticut* (2009), and the alleged haunting of the Perron family was the subject of *The Conjuring* (2013). The famous case of the Enfield Poltergeist was examined in *The Conjuring 2* (2016), while the building of the allegedly haunted Winchester House by eccentric heiress Sarah Winchester was re-enacted in *Winchester* (2018). All of these films exaggerated the reported facts of these cases to a greater or lesser degree in order to enhance their entertainment value, but they all drew their inspiration from reports of paranormal events, some of which were investigated by parapsychologists. Additionally, there were a number of films derived from fictional sources that were inspired by real-world events, including *The Innocents* (1961), *The Exorcist* (1972) and *The Changeling* (1980).

While haunted houses are typically thought to be inhabited by ghosts, movie haunts are populated by a surprising variety of tenants, both human and inhuman. The list includes grotesque masked criminals (*The Bat, The Cat and the Canary, The Terror*), devil worshippers (*Seven Footprints to Satan, The Black Cat, Rosemary's Baby, The Legacy, Darkness*), poltergeists (*Poltergeist, The Entity, An American Haunting, The Conjuring 2*), gangsters (*The Haunted House, The Ghost Breakers, Hold That Ghost, Ghost Catchers*), psychopaths (*The Old Dark House, Psycho, Cold Creek Manor, The Messengers*), demons (*The Exorcist, Paranormal Activity, Sinister*), gorillas (*The Monster Walks, The Gorilla, Spook Busters, Ghost Crazy, Hillbillys in a Haunted House*), vampires (*Dracula, Dark Shadows*), Indian "mound walkers" (*The New Daughter*) and djinns (*Under the Shadow*).

While the haunted house is usually depicted as a decrepit gothic wreck in literature, movie haunts come in a wide variety of ages, shapes and sizes. Modernistic haunted houses were featured in *The Black Cat, House on Haunted Hill, Thi13teen Ghosts* and *The House Next Door*, while haunted apartments were claustrophobic haunts in *Rosemary's Baby, The Tenant, Dark Water* and *Under the Shadow*. *The Shining* and *1408* took place inside haunted hotels, and ghosts inhabited orphanages in *The Devil's Backbone* and *House of Voices*. Ancient castles were plagued by phantoms in *The Ghost Goes West, The Canterville Ghost, The Haunted Palace* and *High Spirits*, but the most recent innovation has been the haunted suburban tract house that appears in *Poltergeist, Paranormal Activity, Insidious* and *Sinister*. Still, the most iconic cinema haunts are the French Colonial home in *The Amityville Horror* (and its sequels) and the California Gingerbread Bates house in *Psycho* (and its sequels). The only film that was actually lensed at a house reputed to be haunted, however, was *Winchester*, which utilized the exterior of the mansion to film several shots.

A more traditional gothic look for the cinematic haunted house was achieved using many of the stately homes of England as exteriors. A roster of these noble houses include the Sheffield Park mansion in East Sussex in *The Innocents*, the Ettington Park mansion in Ettington, Warwickshire in *The Haunting*, Losely Manor in Guildfore, Surrey in *The Legacy*, Knebworth House, in Hertfordshire in *Haunted Honeymoon*, Wykehurst Park in West Sussex in *The Legend of Hell House*, Rotherfield Park, East Tisted, Alton, Hampshire in *The House of Long Shadows*, the "Lime Walk" at Penshurst Place in *The Others*, and Kent Cotterstock Hall, Peterborough in *The Woman in Black*. For that Southern gothic ambience, Felicity Plantation in Saint James Parish, Louisiana was used in *The Skeleton Key*, the Wedge Plantation in McClennanville, South Carolina in *The New Daughter* and the Adamsleigh Mansion in Greensboro, North Carolina in *The Disappointments Room*. Other real-world haunted locations include the Dunsmuir House in Oakland, California used in *Burnt Offerings*, the Dakota Apartments in *Rosemary's Baby*, Cruickston Park Manor in Cambridge, Ontario in *Cold Creek Manor* and the Georgetown town house in *The Exorcist*. Filmmakers often resort to creating elaborate haunts completely inside the studio, as was the case in *Rebecca, House of Usher, The Changeling*, the 1999 version of *The Haunting, Thirteen Ghosts* (2001), *The Haunted Mansion, The Conjuring 2* and *Crimson Peak*.

Some of the most memorable haunted house films were adapted from the works of acclaimed literary talents and horror writers. Novelists Emily Brontë's *Jane Eyre*, Charlotte Brontë's *Wuthering Heights* and Daphne Du Maurier's *Rebecca* brought gothic romance to the big screen in Academy Award-winning, big budget Hollywood productions. Henry James' *The Turn of the Screw*, widely considered the greatest ghost story in the English language, was brought to vivid life in *The Innocents*. Edgar Allan Poe's gothic classic "The Fall of the House of Usher" became the first haunted house in color and widescreen in *House of Usher,* and was followed by the adaptation of Nathaniel Hawthorne's novel *House of the Seven Gables* as a segment of the Hawthorne omnibus film *Twice-Told Tales*. Several of early 20th century horror writer H.P. Lovecraft's works were melded into the screenplay for *The Haunted Palace* under a Poe title.

More recent writers specializing in the uncanny whose works were adapted for the screen include Robert Bloch's *Psycho*, Shirley Jackson's *The Haunting of Hill House* (filmed twice as *The Haunting*), Ira Levin's *Rosemary's Baby*, Richard Matheson's *Hell House* (filmed as *The Legend of Hell House*), Stephen King's *The Shining*, William Peter Blatty's *The Exorcist*, Peter Straub's *Julia* (filmed as *The Haunting of Julia*), Anne Morrow Siddons' *The House Next Door* and Susan Hill's *The Woman in Black*.

Haunted house films constitute some of the finest works of horror cinema and were the product of some of film's most talented directors. This list includes D.W. Griffith (*One Exciting Night*), Paul Leni (*The Cat and the Canary*), Todd Browning (*Dracula*), James Whale (*The Old Dark House*), Edgar G. Ulmer (*The Black Cat*), William Wyler (*Wuthering Heights*), Alfred Hitchcock (*Rebecca, Psycho*), Joseph L. Mankiewicz (*Dragonwyck*), Jacques Tourneur (*I Walked with a Zombie*), Roger Corman (*House of Usher*), Robert Wise (*The Haunting*), Jack Clayton (*The Innocents*), Ricardo Freda (*The Ghost*), Mario Bava (*Kill, Baby, Kill*). Roman Polanski (*Rosemary's Baby, The Tenant*), William Friedkin (*The Exorcist*), Stanley Kubrick (*The Shining*), Tobe Hooper (*Poltergeist*) Tim Burton (*Beetlejuice, Dark Shadows*) and Guillermo del Toro (*The Devil's Backbone, Crimson Peak*). As to actors, the undisputed king of the haunted house melodrama is Vincent Price, whose crowning achievements include his villainous roles in *Dragonwyck, House of Usher, Twice Told Tales, The Haunted Palace, House on Haunted Hill, The Bat* and *House of the Long Shadows*, while the queen of the haunts is surely Gale Sondegaard, whose spooky screen presence enlivened such classics as *The Cat and the Canary, The Black Cat* and *The Time of Their Lives*.

The haunted house film has played as mystery (*The Cat and the Canary, The Bat Whispers, The Secret of the Blue Room*), as comedy (*The Ghost Breakers, The Haunted Mansion, Dark Shadows*) and as romance (*Wuthering Heights, Dragonwyck, The Ghost and Mrs. Muir*), but it plays best as supernatural horror. In recent years the fear factor has been ramped up in eerie thrillers such as *The Others, Dark Water, The Grudge, Paranormal Activity, The Conjuring, The Haunting in Connecticut, 1408, The New Daughter, Insidious, Sinister* and *The Woman in Black*. At long last the haunted house movie has taken its rightful place as one of the most potent modalities of the horror film, and this trend is likely to continue for the foreseeable future.

Filmography

An American Haunting (2005) Director/Screenplay: Courtney Solomon. Producers: Christopher Milburn, Courtney Solomon André Rouleau. Cast: Donald Sutherland, Sissy Spacek, James D'Arcy, Rachel Hurd-Wood. Canada (Freestyle). Color. 90m. DVD: Lionsgate.

The Amityville Horror (1979) Director: Stuart Rosenberg. Producers: Ronald Saland. Screenplay: Sandor Stern. Cast: James Brolin, Margot Kidder, Rod Steiger, Murray Hamilton, Helen Shaver. USA (American-International). Color. 117m. DVD: MGM Home Entertainment.

The Bat (1926) Director/Producer: Roland West. Screenplay: Julien Josephson. Cast: Emily Fitzroy, Louise Fazienda, Eddie Gribbon, Robert McKim, Arthur Houseman, Tullio Carminati. USA (United Artists). B&W. Silent. 86m. DVD: Sinister Cinema.

The Bat (1959) Director/Screenplay: Crane Wilbur. Producer: C.J. Tevlin. Cast: Vincent Price, Agnes Morehead, Darla Hood, Gavin Gordon, Lenita Lane. USA (Allied Artists). B&W. 80m. DVD: Alpha Video.

The Bat Whispers (1930) Director/Producer/Screenplay: Roland West. Cast: Chester Morris, Una Merkel, Grayce Hampton, William Bakewell, Gustav von Seyffertitz. USA (United Artists). B&W. DVD: The Milestone Collection.

Beetlejuice (1988) Director: Tim Burton. Producers: Michael Bender, Larry Wilson, Richard Hashimoto. Screenplay: Michael McDowell, Warren Skaaren. Cast: Alec Baldwin, Geena Davis, Michael Keaton, Wynona Ryder, Jeffrey Jones, Catherine O'Hara, Sylvia Sydney. USA (Warner Bros.). Color. 92m. DVD: Warner Home Video.

The Black Cat (1934) Director: Edgar G. Ulmer. Producer: Carl Laemmle, Jr.. Screenplay: Peter Ruric, Edward G. Ulmer. Cast: Boris Karloff, Bela Lugosi, David Manners, Jacqueline Wells, Harry Cording. USA (Universal). B&W. 66m. DVD: Universal Home Video.

The Black Cat (1941) Director: Alan S. Rogell. Producer: Burt Kelly. Screenplay: Robert Lees, Fred Rinalso, Eric Taylor, Robert Neville. Cast: Basil Rathbone, Broderick Crawford, Bela Lugosi, Hugh Herbert, Anne Gwynne, Gladys Cooper, Alan Ladd. USA (Universal). B&W. 71m. DVD: Universal Home Video.

Burnt Offerings (1976) Director/Producer: Dan Curtis. Screenplay: William F. Nolan, Dan Curtis. Cast: Oliver Reed, Karen Black, Bette Davis, Burgess Meredith. USA (United Artists). Color. 115m. DVD: Kino Lorber Studio Classics.

The Canterville Ghost (1944) Director: Jules Dassin. Producer: Arthur L. Fields. Screenplay: Edwin Harvey Blum. Cast: Charles Laughton, Robert Young, Margaret O'Brian, William Gargan, Una O'Connor, Reginald Owen. USA (MGM). B&W. 96m. DVD: Turner Entertainment.

Castle of Blood (a.k.a. *Danse Macabre*,1964) Director: Antonio Margheriti. Producers: Frank Belty, Walter Sarch. Screenplay: Jean Grimaud. Cast: George Riviere, Barbara Steele, Margrete Robsahm, Henry Kruger, Montgomery Glenn, Sylvia Sorente. France/Italy (Globe International). B&W.85m. DVD: Synapse Films.

The Cat and the Canary (1927) Director: Paul Leni. Producer: Carl Laemmle, Jr. Screenplay: Robert F. Hill, Alfred A. Cohn. Cast: Laura La Plante, Creighton Hale, Arthur Edmund Carewe, Gertrude Astor, Martha Mattox. USA (Universal). B&W. Silent. 74m. DVD: Kino International.

The Cat and the Canary (1939) Director: Elliot Nugent. Producer: Arthur Hornblow, Jr. Screenplay: Walter De Leon, Lynn Starling. Cast: Bob Hope, Paulette Goddard, John Beal, Gale Sondergaard, George Zucco. USA (Paramount). B&W. 75m. DVD: Universal Home Video.

The Cat Creeps (1930) Director: Rupert Julian. Producer: Carl Laemmle, Jr. Screenplay: Gladys Lehman, William Hulbert. Cast: Helen Twelvetrees, Neil Hamilton, Jean Hersholt, Montague Love. USA (Universal). B&W. DVD: Unavailable.

The Changeling (1980) Director: Peter Medak. Producer: Joel B. Michaels, Garth H. Drabinsky. Screenplay: Russell Hunter, William Gray, Diana Maddox. Cast: George C. Scott, Trish Van Devere, Melvyn Douglas, John Colicos, Jean Marsh, Helen Burns. Canada. (Associated Film Distributors). Color. 107m. DVD: HBO Home Video.

Cold Creek Manor (2003) Director: Mike Figgis. Producers: Mike Figgis, Annie Stewart. Screenplay: Richard Jeffries. Cast: Dennis Quaid, Sharon Stone, Stephen Dorff, Juliette Lewis. USA (Buena Vista Pictures). Color. 118m. DVD: Touchstone Home Entertainment.

The Conjuring (2013) Director: James Wan. Producers: Tony DeRosa-Grund, Peter Safran, Rob Cowan. Screenplay: Chad Hayes, Carey W. Hayes. Cast: Vera Farmiga, Patrick Wilson, Lili Taylor, Ron Livingston, Stanley Caswell. USA (Warner Bros.). Color. 112m. DVD: Warner Home Video.

The Conjuring 2 (2016) Director: James Wan. Producers: Peter Safran, Rob Cowan, James Wan. Screenplay: Chad Hayes, Carey W. Hayes, James Wan, David Leslie Johnson. Cast: Vera Farmiga, Patrick Wilson, Frances O'Connor, Madison Wolfe. USA (Warner Bros.). Color. 134m. DVD: Warner Home Video.

Crimson Peak (2015) Director: Guillermo del Toro. Producers: Guillermo del Toro, Callum Greene, John Jashini, Thomas Tull. Screenplay: Guillermo del Toro, Matthew Robbins. Cast: Mia Wasikowska, Jessica Chastain, Tom Hiddleston, Charlie Hunnam, Jim Beaver. USA (Universal). Color. 119m. DVD: Universal Home Video.

Dark Shadows (2012) Director: Tim Burton. Producers: Richard D. Zanuck, Graham King, Johnny Depp, Christi Dembrowski, David Kennedy. Screenplay: Seth Grahame-Smith. Cast: Johnny Depp, Michelle Pfeiffer, Eva Green, Bella Heathcote, Helena Bonham Carter. USA (Warner Bros). Color. 113m. DVD: Warner Home Video.

Dark Water (*Honogurai Mizo no soko kara*, 2002) Director: Hideo Nakata. Producer: Takashige Ichise. Screenplay: Yoshihiro Nakamura, Kenichi Suzuki. Cast: Hitomi Kuroki, Rio Kanno, Mirei Oguchi, Asami Mizukawa, Fumiyo Kohinata. Japan (Toho). Color. 101m. DVD: ADV Films.

Darkness (2002) Director: Jaime Balaguero. Producers: Julio Fernandez, Brian Yuzna. Screenplay: Jaime Balaguero, Fernando de Felipe. Cast: Anna Paquin, Lena Olin, Iain Glen, Giancarlo Giannini. Spain/USA (Dimension Films). Color. 102m. DVD: Dimension Films.

The Devil's Backbone (2001) Director: Guillermo del Toro. Producer: Pedro Almodovar, Guillermo del Toro Screenplay: David Munoz, Antonio Trashorras, Guillermo del Toro. Cast: Fernando Tielve, Marisa Paredes, Federico Luppi, Eduardo Noriega, Berta Ojea. Spain/Mexico (Warner Sogefilms). Color. 108m. DVD: Criterion Collection.

The Disappointments Room (2016) Director: D.J. Caruso. Producers: Geyer Kosinski, Vincent Newman, Tucker Tooley. Screenplay: Wentworth Miller, D.J. Caruso. Cast: Kate Beckinsale, Mel Raido, Gerald McRaney, Lucas Till, Duncan Joiner. USA (Rogue). Color. 85m. DVD: 20th Century–Fox Home Entertainment.

Dracula (1931) Director: Tod Browning. Producer: Carl Laemmle, Jr. Screenplay: Garrett Fort.

Cast: Bela Lugosi, Dwight Frye, David Manners, Edward Van Sloan, Helen Chandler. USA (Universal). B&W. 75m. DVD: Universal Home Video.

Dragonwyck (1946) Director/Producer/Screenplay: Joseph L. Mankiewicz. Cast: Gene Tierney, Vincent Price, Walter Houston, Glenn Langan, Anne Revere, Spring Byington. USA (20th Century–Fox). B&W. 103m. DVD: 20th Century–Fox Home Entertainment.

Elephant Walk (1954) Director: William Dieterle. Producer: Irving Asher. Screenplay: John Lee Mahin. Cast: Elizabeth Taylor, Dana Andrews, Peter Finch, Abraham Sofer. USA (Paramount). Color. 103m. DVD: Warner Home Video.

The Entity (1982) Director: Sidney J. Furie. Producer: Harold Schneider. Screenplay: Frank DeFelitta. Cast: Barbara Hershey, Ron Silver, David Labiosa, Margaret Blye. USA (20th Century–Fox). Color. 125m. DVD: Starz/Anchor Bay.

The Exorcist (1972) Director: William Friedkin Producer/Screenplay: William Peter Blatty. Cast: Linda Blair, Ellen Burstyn, Jason Miller, Max Von Sydow, Lee J. Cobb. USA (Warner Bros.). Color. 132m. DVD: Warner Home Video.

1408 (2007) Director: Mikael Hafstrom. Producer: Lorenzo Di Bonaventura. Screenplay: Matt Greenberg, Scott Alexander, Larry Karaszewski. Cast: John Cusack, Samuel L. Jackson, Mary McCormack, Tony Shaloub. USA (Dimension Films). Color. 104m. DVD: Dimension Films.

The Ghost (a.k.a. *Lo Spettro,* 1963) Director: Ricardo Freda. Producers: Luigi Carpentieri, Ermanno Donati. Screenplay: Oreste Biancoli. Cast: Barbara Steele, Peter Baldwin, Elio Jotta, Harriet White. Italy (Magna Pictures). Color. 96m. DVD: Alpha Video.

The Ghost and Mr. Chicken (1966) Director: Alan Rafkin. Producer: Edward J. Montagne. Screenplay: James Fritzell, Everett Greenbaum. Cast: Don Knotts, Joan Staley, Liam Redmond, Dick Sargent, Cliff Norton. USA (Universal). Color. 90m. DVD: Universal Home Video.

The Ghost and Mrs. Muir (1947) Director: Joseph L. Mankiewicz. Producer: Fred Kohlmar. Screenplay: Philip Dunne. Cast: Gene Tierney, Rex Harrison, George Sanders, Natalie Wood, Robert Coote, Edna Best. USA (20th Century–Fox). B&W. 104m. DVD: 20th Century–Fox Home Entertainment.

The Ghost Breakers (1940) Director: George Marshall. Producer: Arthur Hornblow, Jr. Screenplay: Walter DeLeon. Cast: Bob Hope, Paulette Goddard, Richard Carlson, Anthony Quinn, Willie Best. USA (Paramount). B&W. 85m. DVD: Universal Home Video.

Ghost Catchers (1944) Director: Edward F. Cline. Producer/Screenplay: Edmund L. Hartmann. Cast: Ole Olsen, Chic Johnson, Gloria Jean, Martha O'Driscoll, Tor Johnson, Mel Torme, Lon Chaney, Jr. USA (Universal). B&W. 67m. DVD: Nostalgia Home Video.

Ghost Crazy (a.k.a. *Crazy Knights,*1944) Director: William Beaudine. Producer: Sam Katzman. Screenplay: Tim Ryan. Cast: Shemp Howard, Billy Gilbert, Maxie Rosenbloom. USA (Monogram). B&W. 63m. DVD: Reel Vault.

The Ghost Goes West (1936) Director: Rene Clair. Producer: Alexander Korda. Screenplay: Robert E. Sherwood, Geoffrey Kerr. Cast: Robert Donat, Eugene Pallette, Jean Parker, Elsa Lanchester. England (United Artists). B&W. 82m. DVD: Reel Vault.

Ghosts on the Loose (1943) Director: William Beaudine. Producer: Sam Katzman. Screenplay: Kenneth Higgins. Cast: Bela Lugosi, Leo Gorcey, Ava Gardner, Bobby Jordan, Minerva Urecal. USA (Monogram). B&W. 64m. DVD: FilmRise.

The Gorilla (1939) Director: Alan Dwan. Producers: Daryl F. Zanuck, Harry Joe Brown. Screenplay: Rian James, Sid Silvers. Cast: The Ritz Brothers, Lionel Atwill, Bela Lugosi, Patsy Kelly, Anita Louise. USA (20th Century–Fox). B&W. 66m. DVD: Desert Island Classics.

The Grudge (2004) Director: Takashi Shimizu. Producers: Sam Raimi, Robert Tapert, Ichise Takashige. Screenplay: Stephen Susco. Cast: Takashi Matsuyama, Takako Fuji, Yuya Ozeki,

Sarah Michelle Gellar, Bill Pullman. USA (Columbia). Color. 92m. DVD: Sony Pictures Home Entertainment.

The Grudge 2 (2006) Director: Takashi Shimizu. Producers: Sam Raimi, Robert Tapert, Ichise Takashige. Screenplay: Stephen Susco. Cast: Takako Fuji, Yuya Ozeki, Amber Tamblyn, Arielle Kebbel. USA (Columbia). Color. 102m. DVD: Sony Pictures Home Entertainment.

The Haunted Castle (*Le Chateau Hante,* 1896) Director/ Producer/Screenplay: George Méliès. Cast: Jehanne D'Arcy, Jules-Eugene Legris. France (Star Film). B&W. Silent. 3m. DVD: Unavailable.

The Haunted Castle (*Der Schloss Vogelod,* 1921) Director: F.W. Murnau. Screenplay: Carl Meyer, Berthold Viertel. Cast: Paul Hartmann, Olga Tschechowa, Arnold Korff, Paul Bildt. Germany (Decla-Bioscop). B&W. Silent. 75m. DVD: Kino International.

Haunted Honeymoon (1986) Director/Screenplay: Gene Wilder. Producer: Susan Ruskin. Cast: Gene Wilder, Gilda Radner, Dom DeLuise, Jonathan Pryce, Paul L. Smith. UK (Orion). Color. 82m. DVD: MGM Home Entertainment.

The Haunted House (1921) Directors/Screenplay: Edward F. Cline, Buster Keaton. Producer: Joseph M. Schenck. Cast: Buster Keaton, Virginia Fox, Joe Roberts, Edward F. Cline. USA (Metro). B&W. Silent. 21m. DVD: Kino on Video (on *The Art of Buster Keaton*).

The Haunted House (1928) Director: Benjamin Christensen. Producer: Wid Gunning. Screenplay: Richard Bee, Lajos Biro. Cast: Montague Love, Thelma Todd, Larry Kent, Chester Conklin, William V. Mong. USA (First National). Silent/Sound. DVD: Unavailable.

The Haunted Mansion (2003) Director: Rob Minkoff. Producers: Andrew Gun, Don Hahn. Screenplay: David Berenbaum. Cast: Eddie Murphy, Marsha Thomason, Aree Davis, Marc John Jeffries, Terrence Stamp, Wallace Shawn. USA (Buena Vista). Color. 86m. DVD: Buena Vista Home Entertainment.

The Haunted Palace (1963) Director/Producer: Roger Corman. Screenplay: Charles Beaumont. Cast: Vincent Price, Debra Paget, Lon Chaney, Jr., Milton Parsons, Elisha Cook, Jr. USA (American-International). Color. 85m. DVD: MGM Midnight Movies.

Haunted Spooks (1920) Directors: Alfred J. Goulding, Hal Roach. Producers: Hal Roach, Suzanne Lloyd, Robert Israel. Screenplay: H.M. Walker. Cast: Harold Lloyd, Mildred Davis, Wallace Howe, Sammy Brooks, William Gillespie. USA (Rolin Films). B&W. Silent. 25m. DVD: New Line Home Video (on *The Harold Lloyd Comedy Collection Vol. 3*).

The Haunting (1963) Director/Producer: Robert Wise. Screenplay: Nelson Gidding. Cast: Julie Harris, Claire Bloom, Richard Johnson, Russ Tamblyn. USA (MGM). B&W. 112m. DVD: Warner Home Video.

The Haunting (1999) Director: Jan de Bont. Producers: Donna Roth, Susan Arnold. Screenplay: David Self, Michael Tolkin. Cast: Liam Neeson, Lili Taylor, Catherine Zeta-Jones, Owen Wilson, Bruce Dern. USA/UK (Dreamworks). Color. 114m. DVD: Warner Home Video.

The Haunting in Connecticut (2009) Director: Peter Cornwell. Producers: Paul Brooks, Daniel Farrands, Wendy Rhodes, Andrew Trapani. Screenplay: Adam Simon, Tim Metcalfe. Cast: Amanda Crew, Martin Donovan, Ty Wood, Elias Koteas, Sophi Knight. USA (Lionsgate). Color. 102m. DVD: Lionsgate.

The Haunting of Julia (1976) Director: Richard Loncraine. Producers: Peter Fetterman, Alan Pariser. Screenplay: Dave Humphries. Cast: Mia Farrow, Kier Dullea, Jill Bennett, Tom Conti, Robin Gammell. England/Canada (Discovery). Color. 96m. DVD: Magnum Entertainment.

High Spirits (1988) Director/Screenplay: Neil Jordan. Producer: Stephen Wooley. Cast: Peter O'Toole, Steve Guttenberg, Daryl Hannah, Liam Neeson, Beverly D'Angelo. UK/Ireland/USA (Palace/Tristar). Color. 97m. DVD: MGM Home Video.

Hillbillys in a Haunted House (1967) Director: Jean Yarbrough. Producer: Bernard Woolner.

Screenplay: Duke Yelton. Cast: Joi Lansing, Merle Haggard, Ferlin Husky, Lon Chaney, Jr., Basil Rathbone, John Carradine. USA (Woolner). Color. 88m. DVD: VCI International.

Hold That Ghost (1941) Director: Arthur Lubin. Producers: Burt Kelly, Glenn Tryon. Screenplay: Robert Lees, Fred Rinaldo, John Grant. Cast: Budd Abbott, Lou Costello, Joan Davis, Evelyn Ankers, Richard Carlson. USA (Universal). B&W. 86M. DVD: Universal Home Video.

House (1986) Director: Steve Miner. Producer: Sean S. Cunningham. Screenplay: Fred Drekker. Cast: William Katt, George Wendt, Richard Moll, Kay Lenz, Mary Stavin. USA (Starmaker). Color. 93m. DVD: Anchor Bay.

The House Next Door (2006) Director: Jeff Woolnough. Producers: Wendy Gream, Philip K. Kleinbart, Noelle Volpintesta. Screenplay: Suzette Couture. Cast: Lara Flynn Boyle, Colin Ferguson, Noam Jenkins, Julie Stewart, Heather Hanson. USA (Lifetime Television). Color. 86m. DVD: Muse Entertainment.

The House of Ghosts (*La Maison Ensorcelée*, 1908) Director/Producer/Screenplay: Segundo de Chomon. France (Pathé) B&W. Silent. 6m. DVD: Unavailable.

House of Horror (1929) Director: Benjamin Christensen. Producer: Richard A. Rowland. Screenplay: Richard Bee. Cast: Thelma Todd, Louise Fazenda, Chester Conklin, William V. Mong, James Ford. USA (First National). B&W. Silent/Sound. DVD: Unavailable.

House of the Long Shadows (1983) Director: Peter Walker. Producer: Menahem Golan. Screenplay: Mitchell Armstrong. Cast: Desi Arnaz, Jr., Vincent Price, Peter Cushing, Christopher Lee, John Carradine. UK (MGM). Color. 96m. DVD: MGM Home Entertainment.

House of Usher (1960) Director/Producer: Roger Corman. Screenplay: Richard Matheson. Cast: Vincent Price, Mark Damon, Myrna Fahey, Harry Ellerbee. USA (American-International). Color. 80m. DVD: MGM Home Entertainment.

House of Voices (a.k.a *Saint Ange*, 2007) Director/Screenplay: Pascal Laugier. Producer: Christophe Gans. Cast: Virginie Ledoyen, Lou Doillon, Catriona MacColl, Dorina Lazar, Virginie Darmon. France/Romania (Arp Selection). Color. 98m. DVD: Universal Home Video.

House on Haunted Hill (1958) Director/Producer: William Castle. Screenplay: Robb White. Cast: Vincent Price, Carol Ohmart, Richard Long, Alan Marshall, Elisha Cook, Jr. USA (Warner Bros.). B&W. 75m. DVD: Warner Home Entertainment.

House on Haunted Hill (1999) Director: William Malone. Producers: Robert Zemeckis, Joel Silver, Gilbert Adler, Terry A. Castle. Screenplay: Robb White, Dick Beebe. Cast: Geoffrey Rush, Famke Janssen, Ali Larter, Brigette Wilson, Taye Diggs. USA (Warner Bros.). Color. 93m. DVD: Warner Home Entertainment.

The House That Dripped Blood (1971) Director: Peter Duffell. Producers: Max J. Rosenberg, Milton Subotsky. Screenplay: Robert Bloch. Cast: Christopher Lee, Peter Cushing, Jon Pertwee, Ingrid Pitt, Delhom Elliott. England (Amicus). Color. 101m. DVD: Henstooth Video.

I Walked with a Zombie (1943) Director: Jacques Tourneur. Producer: Val Lewton. Screenplay: Curt Siodmak, Ardel Wray. Cast: Tom Conway, Frances Dee, James Ellison, Darby Jones, Sir Lancelot, Christine Gordon. USA (RKO). B&W. 69m. DVD: Warner Home Entertainment.

The Innocents (1961) Director/Producer: Jack Clayton. Screenplay: Truman Capote, William Archibald. Cast: Deborah Kerr, Michael Redgrave, Pamela Franklin, Martin Stephens, Megs Jenkins, Peter Wyngarde. USA (20th Century–Fox). B&W. 100m. DVD: 20th Century–Fox Home Entertainment.

Insidious (2010) Director: James Wan. Producers: James Wan, Oren Peli, Steven Schneider. Screenplay: Leigh Whannell. Cast: Patrick Wilson, Rose Byrne, Barbara Hershey, Lin Shaye, Ty Simpkins. USA (Film District). Color. 102m. DVD: Sony Pictures Home Entertainment.

Jane Eyre (1944) Director: Robert Stevenson. Producer: William Goetz. Screenplay: Aldous Huxley, Robert Stevenson, John Houseman. Cast: Joan Fontaine, Orson Welles, Margaret O'Brien, Henry Daniell, Agnes Morehead. USA (20th Century–Fox). B&W. 96m. DVD: 20th Century–Fox Home Entertainment.

Kill, Baby, Kill (a.k.a. *Operazione paura; Operation Fear*, 1965) Director: Mario Bava. Producers: Luciano Catenacci, Nando Pisani. Screenplay: Mario Bava, John Hart, Romano Migliorini, Roberto Natale. Cast: Erica Blanc, Giacomo Rossi-Stuart, Fabienne Dali, Piero Lulli. Italy (Europix). Color. 86m. DVD: Diamond Entertainment.

The Legacy (1979) Director: Richard Marquand. Producer: David Foster. Screenplay: Jimmy Sangster, Patric Tilley, Paul Wheeler. Cast: Katherine Ross, Sam Elliott, John Standing, Roger Daltrey, Ian Hogg. England (Universal). Color. 100m. DVD: Universal Home Entertainment.

The Legend of Hell House (1973) Director: John Hough. Producers: Albert Fennell. Screenplay: Richard Matheson. Cast: Clive Revill, Pamela Franklin, Roddy McDowell, Gayle Hunnicut. England (20th Century–Fox). Color. 95m. DVD: 20th Century–Fox Home Entertainment.

The Messengers (2006) Directors: Danny Pang, Oxide Pang. Producers: Sam Raimi, Robert Tapert, William Sherak, Jason Shuman. Screenplay: Mark Wheaton. Cast: Kristen Stewart, Dylan McDermott, Penelope Ann Miller, John Corbett. USA/Canada (Columbia/Screen Gems/Ghost House Pictures). Color. 90m. DVD: Sony Pictures Home Entertainment.

The Monster Walks (1933) Director: Frank Stayer. Producer: Cliff Broughton. Screenplay: Robert Ellis. Cast: Mischa Auer, Rex Lease, Vera Reynolds, Martha Mattox. USA (Mayfair). B&W. 63m. DVD: Alpha Video.

The New Daughter (2009) Director: Luis Berdejo. Producer: Paul Brooks. Screenplay: John Travis. Cast: Kevin Costner, Ivana Baquero, Gattlin Griffith, Samantha Mathis, Noah Taylor. USA (Anchor Bay Entertainment). Color. 108m. DVD: Anchor Bay Entertainment.

The Old Dark House (1932) Director: James Whale. Producer: Carl Laemmle. Screenplay: Ben Levy. Cast: Boris Karloff, Melvyn Douglas, Charles Laughton, Raymond Massey. Ernest Thessiger, Gloria Stuart. USA (Universal). B&W. 71m. DVD: Kino on Video.

One Exciting Night (1922) Director/Producer: D.W. Griffith. Screenplay: Irene Sinclair. Cast: Carol Dempster, Henry Hull, Porter Strong, Morgan Wallace, Margaret Dale. USA (United Artists). B&W. Silent. 108m. DVD: Alpha Video.

The Others (2001) Director/Screenplay: Alejandro Amenabar. Producers: Fernando Bovairra, Jose Luis Cuerda, Sunmin Park. Cast: Nicole Kidman, Fionnula Flanagan, Christopher Eccleston, Elaine Cassidy, Eric Sykes. Spain/USA/France (Warner Sogefilms). Color. 104m. DVD: Lionsgate.

Paranormal Activity (2007) Director/Screenplay: Oren Peli. Producers: Oren Peli, Jason Blum. Cast: Katie Featherston, Micah Sloat, Mark Fredrichs, Amber Armstrong. USA (Paramount). Color. 86m. DVD: Dreamworks Pictures.

A Place of Our Own (1945) Director: Bernard Knowles. Producer: R.J. Minney. Screenplay: Brock Williams. Cast: James Mason, Margaret Lockwood, Barbara Mullen, Dennis Price, Ernest Thesiger. England (Gainsborough). B&W. 91m. DVD: Starry Night Video.

Poltergeist (1982) Director: Tobe Hooper. Producer: Frank Marshall. Screenplay: Steven Spielberg. Cast: Craig T. Nelson, Jo Beth Williams, Dominique Dunne, Oliver Robins, Heather O'Rourke, Beatrice Straight, Zelda Rubinstein. USA (Warner Bros.). Color. 114m. DVD: Warner Home Video.

Psycho (1960) Director/Producer: Alfred Hitchcock. Screenplay: Joseph Stefano. Cast: Anthony Perkins, Janet Leigh, John Gavin, Martin Balsam, Vera Miles, Simon Oakland. USA (Paramount). B&W. 109m. DVD: Universal Home Entertainment.

Rebecca (1940) Director: Alfred Hitchcock. Producer: David O. Selznick. Screenplay: Robert

E. Sherwood, Joan Harrison. Cast: Joan Fontaine, Laurence Olivier, George Sanders, Judith Anderson, Nigel Bruce, Leo G. Carroll. USA (Selznick Studios). B&W. 130m. DVD: MGM/UA Home Entertainment.

Return of the Terror (1934) Director: Howard Bretherson. Producer: Sam Bischoff. Screenplay: Eugene Solow, Peter Milne. Cast: Mary Astor, Lyle Talbot, Frank McHugh, Irving Pichel, J. Carrol Naish. USA (Warner Bros.). B&W. DVD: Unavailable.

Rosemary's Baby (1968) Director/Screenplay: Roman Polanski. Producer: William Castle. Cast: Mia Farrow, John Cassavetes, Ruth Gordon, Sidney Blackmer, Ralph Bellamy, Patsy Kelly, Maurice Evans. USA (Paramount). Color. 136m. DVD: Paramount Home Video.

Scared Stiff (1953) Director: George Marshall. Producer: Hal B. Wallis. Screenplay: Herbert Baker, Walter de Leon. Cast: Dean Martin, Jerry Lewis, Lizabeth Scott. USA (Paramount). B&W. 108m. DVD: Paramount (on *Dean Martin and Jerry Lewis Collection Vol. 1*)

The Secret of the Blue Room (1933) Director: Kurt Neumann. Producers: Henry Henigson, Philip Cahn. Screenplay: Rick Philippi. Cast: Lionel Atwill, Gloria Stuart, Paul Lukas, Edward Arnold, Onslow Stevens. USA (Universal). B&W. 66m. DVD: Universal Home Entertainment.

Seven Footprints to Satan (1929) Director: Benjamin Christensen. Producer: Wid Gunning. Screenplay: Richard Bee. Cast: Thelma Todd, Creighton Hale, William V, Mong, Sheldon Lewis Sojin. USA (First National). B&W. Silent. DVD: The Serial Squadron.

The Shining (1980) Director/Producer: Stanley Kubrick. Screenplay: Stanley Kubrick, Diane Johnson. Cast: Jack Nicholson, Shelly Duvall, Danny Lloyd, Scatman Crothers, Barry Nelson, Joe Turkel. USA (Warner Bros.). Color. 142m. DVD: Warner Home Video.

Sinister (2012) Director: Scott Derrickson. Producers: Jason Blum, Brian Kavanaugh-Jones. Screenplay: C. Robert Cargill, Scott Derrickson. Cast: Ethan Hawke, Juliet Rylance, Fred Thompson, James Ransome, Clare Foley. USA (Summit). Color. 109m. DVD: Summit Entertainment.

The Skeleton Key (2005) Director: Ian Softley. Producers: Michael Stamberg, Stacy Stier. Screenplay: Ehren Kruger. Cast: Kate Hudson, John Hurt, Gena Rowlands, Peter Sarsgaard, Joy Bryant. USA (Universal). Color. 104m. DVD: Universal Home Entertainment.

Spook Busters (1946) Director: William Beaudine. Producer: Jan Grippo. Screenplay: Edward Seward, Tim Ryan. Cast: Leo Gorcey, Huntz Hall, Bobby Jordan, Charles Middleton. USA (Monogram). B&W. 61m. DVD: Warner Bros. Archive Collection (on *The Bowery Boys Vol. 1*).

The Tenant (1976) Director/Screenplay: Roman Polanski. Producer: Hercules Bellville. Screenplay: Gerard Brach. Cast: Roman Polanski, Isabelle Adjani, Melvyn Douglas, Shelly Winters, Lila Kedrova. USA (Paramount). Color. 125m. DVD: Paramount Home Video.

The Terror (1928) Director: Roy del Ruth. Producer: Screenplay: Harvey Gates. Cast: May McAvoy, Louise Fazenda, Edward Everett Horton, Holmes Herbert, Matthew Best. USA (Warner Bros.). B&W. 80m. DVD: Unavailable.

Terror in the Haunted House (a.k.a. *My World Dies Screaming*, 1958) Director/Producer: William S. Edwards. Screenplay: Robert C. Dennis. Cast: Philip Tierney, Shelia Wayne, Cathy O'Donnell, Gerald Mohr, Mark Snell. USA (Woolner). B&W. 90m. DVD: Rhino Theatrical.

Thirteen Ghosts (1960) Director/Producer: William Castle. Screenplay: Robb White. Cast: Charles Herbert, Jo Morrow, Martin Milner, Rosemary De Camp, Margaret Hamilton. USA (Columbia). B&W. 84m. DVD: Columbia/Tristar Home Entertainment.

Thirteen Ghosts (2001) Director: Steve Beck. Producers: Robert Zemeckis, Joel Silver, Gilbert Adler. Screenplay: Neal Marshall Stevens, Richard D'Ovidio. Cast: Tony Shaloub, Embeth Davidtz, Matthew Lillard, Shannon Elizabeth, Alec Roberts, F. Murray Abraham. USA/Canada (Warner Bros./Columbia). Color. 91m. DVD: Warner Home Video.

Three Cases of Murder (1954) Directors: Wendy Toye, David Eady, George More O'Ferrall. Producer: Hugh Perceval. Screenplay: Ian Dalrymple, Donald Wilson, Sidney Carroll. Cast: Alan Badel, Orson Welles, Andre Morell. England (London Films). B&W. 99m. DVD: Best of British Collection.

The Time of Their Lives (1946) Director: Charles Barton. Producer: Val Burton. Screenplay: Walter De Leon, Bradford Ropes, Val Burton. Cast: Bud Abbott, Lou Costello, Marjorie Reynolds, Gale Sondegaard. USA (Universal). B&W. 82m. DVD: Universal Home Entertainment (on *The Best of Bud Abbott and Lou Costello Vol. 2*).

Twice-Told Tales (1963) Director: Sidney Salkow. Producer/Screenplay: Robert E. Kent. Cast: Vincent Price, Beverly Garland, Richard Denning, Sebastian Cabot, Mari Blanchard., Brett Halsey. USA (United Artists). Color. 119m. DVD: Kino Lorber.

Under the Shadow (2017) Director/Screenplay: Babak Anvari. Producers: Emily Leo, Oliver Roskill, Lucan Toh. Cast: Narges Rashidi, Avin Manshadi, Bobby Naderi, Ray Haratian, Arash Marandi. UK/Jordan/Qatar (XYZ/Vertical). Color. 84m. DVD: Vertical Entertainment.

The Uninvited (1944) Director: Lewis Allen. Producer: Charles Brackett. Screenplay: Frank Partos, Dodie Smith. Cast: Ray Milland, Gail Russell, Ruth Hussey, Alan Napier, Cornelia Otis Skinner. USA (Paramount). B&W. 98M. DVD: Criterion Collection.

Winchester (2018) Director/Screenplay: Michael Spierig, Peter Spierig. Producers: Brett Tomberlin, Tim McGahan. Cast: Helen Mirren, Jason Clarke, Sarah Snook, Finn Scicluna-O'Prey. Australia/USA (Lionsgate/CBS). Color. 99m. DVD: Lionsgate.

The Woman in Black (2012) Director: James Watkins. Producer: Richard Jackson. Screenplay: Jane Goldman. Cast: Daniel Radcliffe, Ciaran Hinds, Janet McTeer, Liz White, Roger Allam. USA/UK (Momentum Films). Color. 95m. DVD: Sony Pictures Home Entertainment.

Wuthering Heights (1939) Director: William Wyler. Producer: Samuel Goldwyn. Screenplay: Ben Hecht, Charles MacArthur. Cast: Laurence Olivier, Merle Oberon, David Niven, Flora Robson, Donald Crisp. USA (United Artists). B&W. 103m. DVD: Warner Home Video.

Chapter Notes

Introduction

1. Wilson, Colin, *Supernatural: Your Guide to the Unexplained, the Unearthly and the Unknown* (London: Watkins Publications, 2011), p. 211.
2. Lovecraft, H.P., "The Rats in the Walls" in *The Best of H.P. Lovecraft* (New York: Del Rey Books, 1982), p. 15.
3. King, Stephen, *Danse Macabre* (New York: Berkley Books, 1983), p. 266.
4. Ibid., p. 272.

Chapter Four

1. Clarens, Carlos, *An Illustrated History of the Horror Film* (New York: Capricorn Books, 1967), p. 116.
2. King, Stephen, *Danse Macabre*, p. 112.

Chapter Five

1. Clarens, Carlos, *An Illustrated History of the Horror Film*, p. 156.

Chapter Six

1. King, Stephen, *Danse Macabre*, p. 143.

Bibliography

Butler, Ivan. *Horror in the Cinema.* New York: A.S. Barnes, 1970.

Clarens, Carlos. *An Illustrated History of the Horror Film.* New York: Capricorn Books, 1967.

Clarke, Roger. *Ghosts: A Natural History: 500 Years of Searching for Proof.* New York: St. Martin's Press, 2012.

Curtis, Barry. *Dark Places: The Haunted House in Film.* London: Reaktion Books, 2008.

Davisson, Zack. *Yurei: The Japanese Ghost.* Seattle: Chin Music Press, 2015.

Dickey, Colin. *Ghostland: An American History in Haunted Places.* New York: Viking, 2016.

Dyson, Jeremy. *Bright Darkness: The Lost Art of the Supernatural Horror Film.* London: Cassell, 1997.

Everson, William K. *More Classics of the Horror Film.* Secaucus: Citadel Press, 1986.

Jackson, Shirley. *Shirley Jackson: Novels and Stories.* New York: Library of America, 2010.

Kerr, Margaret. *Scream: Chilling Adventures in the Science of Fear.* Philadelphia: Public Affairs Books, 2015.

King, Stephen. *Danse Macabre.* New York: Berkley Books, 1983.

Lovecraft, H.P. *The Best of H.P. Lovecraft.* New York: Del Rey Books, 1982

Murguia, Salvador, ed. *The Encyclopedia of Japanese Horror Films.* Lanham, MD: Rowan & Littlefield, 2016.

Siddons, Anne Rivers. *The House Next Door.* New York: Pocket Books, 1978.

Spencer, John, and Tony Wells. *Ghost Watching: The Ghosthunters' Handbook.* London: Virgin Books, 1994.

Stanley, John. *Creature Features: The Science Fiction, Fantasy and Horror Movie Guide.* New York: Boulevard, 1997.

Thurston, Herbert. *Ghosts and Poltergeists.* Whitefish, MT: Kessinger, 2010.

Weldon, Michael. *The Psychotronic Encyclopedia of Film.* New York: Ballantine, 1983.

Westbie, Constance, and Harold Cameron. *Night Stalks the Mansion: A True Story of One Family's Ghostly Adventure.* New York: Bantam Books, 1978.

Wilson, Colin. *Supernatural: Your Guide to the Unexplained, the Unearthly and the Unknown.* London: Watkins Publications, 2011.

Index

Abbott, Bud 14, 16, 44–45, 48–49, 64
Abraham, F. Murray 162, 163
"Ali the Cairene and the Haunted House in Baghdad" 196
Amenabar, Alejandro 164, 165
An American Haunting 8, 13, 145–147, 197, 199, 200
American International Studios 89, 111, 141
Amicus Studios 126, 133
Amityville 4: The Evil Escapes 141
The Amityville Horror (1978) 5, 7, 8, 13, 15, 110, 130, 140–142, 157, 197, 199, 200
The Amityville Horror (2005) 142
Amityville 92: It's About Time 141
Amityville 3-D 141
Amityville II: The Possession 141
Anderson, Judith 25, 49, 68, 69, 88
Angel Heart 177
Annabelle 140, 151
Annabelle II: Creation 140
Anvadi, Babak 197
Arnaz, Desi, Jr. 137–138
Around the World in 80 Days 23
Athenodorus 5
Atwill, Lionel 32–33, 39–40
The Avenging Conscience 22

Badel, Alan 112–113
Baquero, Ivana 186–188
The Bat (1926) 14, 22–24, 26, 29, 35, 39, 200, 201
The Bat (1959) 24, 35
The Bat (play) 21, 22
The Bat Whispers 24, 29–31
Bates House 91–94, 99, 110, 200
Bava, Mario 89, 120, 121, 123–124, 125, 138, 165, 201
Beckinsale, Kate 194–195
Beetlejuice 9, 14, 15, 56–59, 60, 61, 63, 64, 199, 201
The Bell Witch 8, 145–147, 199
Bentley, James 164
Berdejo, Luis 187
Best, Willie 34, 42–43, 44, 50
Biggers, Earl Derr 137
The Birds 183
The Birth of a Nation 21
Bither, Doris 145, 199

The Black Cat (1934) 8, 13, 14, 84–86, 102, 115, 134, 179, 200
The Black Cat (1941) 45–46, 49, 201
Black Friday 84
Black Sunday 89
Blade Runner 115
Blair, Linda 102–103
The Blair Witch Project 180
Blatty, William Peter 13, 103, 201
Bloch, Robert 92, 110, 126–127, 201
Bloom, Claire 97, 99
The Body Snatcher 96
Boyle, Lara Flynn 178–179
Brent, Laura 154, 155
Brolin, James 140–141
Brontë, Charlotte 9, 65, 66, 67, 200
Brontë, Emily 65, 71, 72, 195, 200
Burnt Offerings 8, 129–130, 138, 169, 183, 194, 199, 200
Burstyn, Ellen 102–103
Burton, Tim 15, 56, 57–59, 60, 62, 63, 201

The Cabinet of Dr. Caligari 14, 20
The Canterville Ghost 39, 47–48, 49, 64, 72, 200
Carradine, John 53, 54, 64, 137, 138
La Casa Sfuggita 11
The Case of Charles Dexter Ward 116
Cassavetes, John 99, 101
Castle, William 32, 35, 51, 102, 111, 113, 114, 160, 161, 162, 163
Castle of Blood 124–126
The Castle of Otronto 9
The Cat and the Canary (1927) 14, 24–26, 28, 34, 35, 39, 42, 47, 55, 75, 200, 201
The Cat and the Canary (1939) 14, 35, 40–42, 49, 61, 64, 177, 201
The Cat and the Canary (play) 21, 22
The Cat Creeps 26, 29, 42
Cat People 96, 99, 187
Chaney, Lon, Jr. 47, 53, 54, 64, 116, 117
Chaney, Lon, Sr. 20, 29
The Changeling 13, 134–137, 138, 139, 169, 195, 199, 200
Christensen, Benjamin 27, 28

Citizen Kane 68, 74, 95
Clair, Rene 39, 48
Clarens, Carlos 82, 121, 198
Clarke, Jason 154, 155
Clayton, Jack 11, 15, 80, 94, 95, 96, 110, 129, 199, 201
Cock Lane Ghost 8
Cold Creek Manor 168–169, 183, 187, 194, 200
Conan Doyle, Sir Arthur 139, 195
The Conjuring 9, 15, 140, 149–150, 188, 197, 199, 201
The Conjuring 2 8, 13, 139, 140, 142, 151–153, 154, 157, 158, 188, 197, 199, 200
Conway, Tom 72
Cook, Elisha, Jr. 100, 113, 115
Corman, Roger 9, 15, 75, 89, 90, 110, 116, 117, 118, 120, 128, 138, 199, 201
Costello, Lou 14, 36, 44–45, 48–49, 64
Costner, Kevin 186–187
Crazy House 47
Crazy Knights see *Ghost Crazy*
Crimson Peak 5, 13, 15, 65, 79–81, 197, 199, 200, 201
Crosby, Floyd 90, 117
Crowley, Aliester 85
The Curse of Frankenstein 89
Curtis, Dan 62, 129, 169
Cusack, John 184–186
Cushing, Peter 126–127, 137, 138

Damon, Mark 89–91
Danielewski, Mark Z. 13, 156
Danse Macabre see *Castle of Blood*
Dante's Inferno 28
Dark Shadows (film) 13, 59, 62–63, 64, 199, 200, 201
Dark Shadows (TV) 62, 129
Dark Water (2002) 13, 174–176, 177, 197, 199, 200, 201
Dark Water (2005) 176
Darkness 8, 14, 167–168, 200
The Darkness 168
Davis, Bette 129, 130
Dead of Night 112
Dee, Frances 72–73
Del Toro, Guillermo 79, 80, 81, 88, 166, 167, 183, 184, 197, 199, 200, 201

Index

Depp, Johnny 36, 62–63, 64
The Devil's Backbone 5, 13, 15, 81, 166–167, 183, 184, 197, 199, 200, 201
Dickens, Charles 15
Dieterle, William 78, 79, 81
The Disappointments Room 8, 194–195, 200
Disney Studios 60, 61, 72
Disney's Haunted Mansion 5, 16
Djinns 195–196
Doctor Jekyll and Mr. Hyde 35, 82
Doctor X 35
Donat, Robert 38–39
D'Onofrio, Vincent 190
doppelgangers 44, 61, 62, 120, 122, 131, 134, 135, 136, 148, 160, 162, 167, 168, 175, 198
Douglas, Melvyn 31, 130, 135
Dracula (film) 29, 31, 32, 82, 83–84, 86
Dracula (novel) 11, 13, 20, 82–83, 84, 101, 200, 201
Dragonwyck 13, 65, 74–76, 201
Dullea, Kier 12, 132
Du Maurier, Daphne 13, 65, 74–76, 201
Dunsmuir House 130, 200
Duvall, Shelly 105–106

The East Side Kids 46
Elephant Walk 13, 14, 65, 77–79, 81, 212
Elliott, Sam 133
The Enfield Poltergeist 139, 151, 153–154, 199
Ennis-Brown House 13, 86, 115, 179
The Entity 8, 13, 142–144, 146, 157, 188, 199, 200
E.T.: The Extraterrestrial 110
Ewers, Hanns Heinz 186
The Exorcist 5, 8, 13, 15, 102–104, 110, 116, 139, 150, 153, 189, 199, 200, 201

Fahey, Myrna 89–91
"The Fall of the House of Usher" 9, 201
Fallen 148
Farmiga, Vera 140, 149–153
Farrow, Mia 12, 99–101, 132
Featherston, Katie 179–180, 200, 201
Ferguson, Colin 178
Film Blanc 77
The Fly 34
Fontaine, Joan 10, 68–70, 71–72, 81
1408 108, 184–186, 200, 201
Frankenstein 14, 31, 32, 82, 84
Frankenstein Meets the Wolf Man 86
Franklin, Pamela 94, 95, 128, 129
Freaks 35, 82
Freda, Ricardo 89, 120, 121, 124, 125, 165, 201
Freund, Karl 84
Friedkin, William 8, 15, 103, 110, 201
Frye, Dwight 83
Fuji, Takako 169, 172

Gallner, Kyle 147
Garland, Beverley 118–119
Gellar, Sarah Michelle 170, 172
The Ghost 89, 120–121, 201
The Ghost and Mrs. Muir 13, 65, 76–77, 81, 201
The Ghost Breaker (1914) 20, 36, 38
The Ghost Breaker (1922) 36
The Ghost Breakers 14, 34, 36, 42–44, 47, 50, 56, 61, 64, 134, 198, 200, 201
Ghost Catchers 47
Ghost Crazy 47, 64, 200
The Ghost Goes West 38–39, 48, 49, 60, 64, 200
Ghosts on the Loose 46
Giannini, Giancarlo 167, 168
Goddard, Paulette 35, 41, 42, 43, 50
The Golem 86
Gone with the Wind 23, 70
Gordon, Ruth 100, 101
The Gorilla 39–40, 64, 200
Der Graa Dame 20
Griffith, D.W. 21, 22, 201
Grosse, Maurice 152, 153
The Grudge 5, 13, 15, 132, 158, 169–172, 174, 175, 181, 183, 192, 199, 201
The Grudge 2 169, 172–174, 199
The Grudge 3 174

Hall, Charles D. 83, 84, 86
Haller, Daniel 90, 118
Halloween 92
Hammer Studios 89, 111, 120, 126, 127, 133, 137, 192, 193, 194
The Handmaid's Tale 169
Harris, Julie 97–99, 159
Harrison, Rex 76–77
Haunted Attractions 5, 16, 108, 120, 154
The Haunted Bedroom 20
The Haunted Castle (*Le Chateau Hante*, 1896) 19, 36
The Haunted Castle (*Der Schloss Vogelod* (1921) 20
Haunted Honeymoon 55–56, 64, 199, 200
The Haunted Mansion 42, 60–61, 64, 177, 199, 200, 201
The Haunted Palace 13, 116–118, 134, 199, 200, 201
Haunted Spooks 14, 36–37, 38, 64, 198
The Haunting (1963) 5, 9, 12, 13, 14, 15, 80, 88, 90, 96–99, 103, 107, 129, 135, 156, 169, 179, 193, 199, 200, 201
The Haunting (1999) 15, 150, 158–160, 163, 200, 201
The Haunting in Connecticut 8, 9, 13, 15, 147–149, 197, 199, 201
The Haunting in Connecticut 2: Ghosts of Georgia 149
The Haunting of Cecil P. Gould 20
The Haunting of Hill House 12, 96, 201
The Haunting of Julia 9, 12, 132, 138, 195, 201

Hawke, Ethan 190–191
Hawthorne, Nathaniel 10, 118, 119, 120, 201
Hell House 128
Hellzapoppin 47
Henry Treat Rogers Mansion 136, 137
Hershey, Barbara 143–144, 188, 189
Hiddleston, Tom 79, 80
High Spirits 58, 59–60, 64, 199, 200
Hill, Susan 13, 192, 201
Hillbillys in a Haunted House 53–54, 200
Hitchcock, Alfred 15, 26, 39, 49, 68, 69, 72, 81, 90, 92, 110, 113, 183, 199, 201
Hoffmann, E.T.A. 9, 127
Hold That Ghost 14, 44–45, 56, 64, 198, 200
Hoodoo 176, 177–178
Hooper, Tobe 108, 109, 110, 201
Hope, Bob 14, 26, 34, 35, 36, 40–44, 50, 64
The Horrible Dr. Hitchcock 120
Horror Hospital 56
Horror of Dracula 39
The Horror Show 55
The Hound of the Baskervilles 195
House 54–55
House IV: Home Deadly Home 55
The House Next Door (film) 5, 13, 14, 15, 127, 178–179, 199, 200
The House Next Door (novel) 12, 13, 16–17, 201
House of Dracula 14
House of Frankenstein 14
The House of Ghosts (*La Maison Ensorcelée*, 1908) 19–20, 36
House of Horror 28–29
House of Leaves 13, 108, 156
House of the Long Shadows 137–138, 201
House of the Seven Gables 5, 10
The House of the Seven Gables 10, 13, 118–120
House of Usher 13, 15, 75, 89–91, 95, 98, 99, 117, 120, 128, 199, 200, 201
House of Voices 13, 167, 183–184, 200
House on Haunted Hill (1959) 13, 14, 86, 113–115, 163, 179, 200
House on Haunted Hill (1999) 14, 15, 102, 158, 160–162, 200
The House That Dripped Blood 126–127, 138
House II: The Second Story 55
Howard, Shemp 45, 47, 64
Hudson, Kate 176, 177
Hull, Henry 21
The Hunchback of Notre Dame 20
Hurt, John 176, 177

I Am Legend 90
I Married a Witch 39
I Walked with a Zombie 72–74, 78, 81, 86, 195, 201
The Incredible Shrinking Man 90

Index

The Innocents 5, 11, 13, 15, 80, 94–96, 98, 99, 123, 129, 135, 139, 193, 199, 200, 201
Insidious 144, 188–190, 199, 200, 201
Intolerance 21
The Invisible Ray 84
Island of Lost Souls 35, 82, 162
It Conquered the World 120

Jackson, Samuel L. 184, 186
Jackson, Shirley 12, 96, 97, 98, 110, 129, 159, 201
James, Henry 10, 13, 94, 96, 110, 200
Jane Eyre (film) 10, 13, 14, 32, 65, 71–72, 80
Jane Eyre (novel) 10, 65, 72, 74, 78, 81, 195, 200
Janssen, Famke 160, 161
The Jazz Singer 26, 27, 29
Jones, Darby 73
Jotta, Elio 120
Julia 12, 132
Ju-On: The Grudge 138, 169
Jurassic Park 60

Kaidan 169, 171, 174, 175
Kanno, Rio 174, 175
Karloff, Boris 31, 32, 33, 84–85
Keaton, Buster 14, 37–38, 64, 198
Keaton, Michael 57–58
Kebbel, Arielle 172–174
Kerr, Deborah 94–95
Kidder, Margot 140–141
Kidman, Nicole 164–165
Kill, Baby, Kill 121–124, 138, 199, 201
King, Stephen 1, 8, 12, 13, 15, 16, 99, 104–106, 110, 141, 156, 184, 185, 201
Knotts, Don 36, 52–53, 64
Koteas, Elias 147, 148
Kronos 34
Kubrick, Stanley 12, 15, 104–106, 108, 110, 130, 132, 201
Kuroki, Hitomi 174, 175
Kwaidan 149

Laemmle, Carl, Jr. 26
Lair of the White Worm 56
Lam, Elisa 176
Lang, Fritz 1, 84
The Last Laugh 84
The Last Warning 26
Laughton, Charles 31, 33, 47–48, 64
Laura 74
LaVey, Anton 1–2
Ledoyen, Virginie 183
Lee, Christopher 126–127, 137–138
The Legacy 133–134, 138, 199, 200
The Legend of Hell House 9, 13, 15, 128–129, 138, 149, 199, 200, 201
Leigh, Janet 90, 92
Lemp Mansion 5, 16
Leni, Paul 24, 26, 34, 35, 42, 55, 201
The Leopard Man 187
Levin, Ira 12, 101, 201
Lewis, Jerry 36, 44, 50, 64
Lewton, Val 72, 73, 74, 86, 88, 96, 99, 187

The Lights of New York 29
Lives of the Noble Greeks and Romans 6
Lloyd, Harold 14, 36–37, 64, 190
Lockwood, Margaret 111
Lodge, Oliver 8
London After Midnight 20
Lovecraft, H.P. 11, 116, 117, 162, 168, 201
Lucid Dreaming 185
Lugosi, Bela 11, 39, 40, 45, 46, 64, 83, 84–85

Madsen, Virginia 147, 148
Magnifilm Format 30
Magritte, Rene 103
Das Majorat 9
Manhunter 191
Mankiewicz, Joseph L. 74–75, 76, 77, 81, 201
Mann, Alikita
Manners, David 84
Manshadi, Avin 196, 197
Manson, Charles 2, 7, 102
Margheriti, Antonio 124, 125
Mark of the Vampire 82
Marquand, Richard 133
Marshall, George 43, 44, 50
Martin, Dean 36, 49, 50–51
The Mask of Fu Manchu 35
Mason, James 111–112
Matheson, Richard 98, 128, 201
McDowell, Roddy 128, 129
Medak, Peter 134, 135, 169
Méliès, George 19
Menzies, William Cameron 23, 30, 70
The Messengers 181–183, 187, 194, 200
Metropolis 1, 84
MGM Studios 35, 47, 48, 65, 82, 99 141
Midnight in the Garden of Good and Evil 177
Milland, Ray 86–88
Miller, Jason 102, 103, 104
Mirren, Helen 154, 155, 156
The Monster Walks 34, 40, 200
Morehead, Agnes 35, 71, 72
Mostellaria 6, 36
The Murders in the Rue Morgue 34–35
Murnau, F.W. 20, 84
Murphy, Eddie 36, 42, 60–61
My World Dies Screaming see *Terror in the Haunted House*
The Mysteries of Udolpho 9
Mystery of the Wax Museum 35, 82

Nataka, Hideo 174
Neeson, Liam 59, 60, 158–159
Nelson, Craig T. 108–109
The New Daughter 186–188, 194, 199, 200, 201
The New England Society for Psychical Research 139
Nicholson, Jack 12, 105–107
The Night Stalker 129

Night Stalks the Mansion 7–8
The Night Strangler 129
Nosferatu 14, 29
Not of this Earth 180
The Nun 140, 153

Oberon, Merle 10, 66, 67
O'Brien, Margaret 47, 48, 71, 72
O'Connor, Frances 151
The Old Dark House (1931) 5, 31–32, 33, 34, 35, 112, 138, 200, 201
The Old Dark House (1963) 35
Olivier, Laurence 10, 65–67, 69, 81
One Exciting Night 21–22, 38, 201
One Missed Call 158
Operation Fear see *Kill, Baby, Kill*
The Others 5, 9, 14, 15, 158, 164–166, 171, 197, 199, 200, 201
O'Toole, Peter 59, 60, 64

Paget, Debra 116, 117
Pan's Labyrinth 167, 188
Paquin, Anna 167
Paramount Studios 14, 35, 44, 77, 82, 86, 88, 101, 158
Paranormal Activity 8, 15, 158, 179–181, 191, 197, 199, 200, 201
Paranormal Activity 2 181
Paranormal Activity 3 181
Paranormal Activity 4 181
Paranormal Activity: The Ghost Dimension 181
Paranormal TV Programs 16, 158
Peli, Oren 180
"Pepper's Ghost" 15
Perkins, Anthony 90–93
Pertwee, John 126, 127
Phantasmagoria 13, 16
The Phantom of the Opera 20
A Place of Our Own 111–112
Plautus 6, 36
Playfair, Guy 139, 153
Pliny the Elder 5, 6
Plummer, Christopher 169
Plutarch 61
Polanski, Roman 130–131, 138, 175, 201
Poltergeist (1982) 5, 9, 13, 14, 15, 88, 108–110, 130, 141, 142, 144, 146, 150, 151, 181, 189 197, 199, 200, 201
Poltergeist (2015) 110
Poltergeist II: The Other Side 110
Poltergeist III 110
poltergeists 3, 8, 13, 15, 19, 81, 90, 97, 102, 103, 104, 108–110, 119, 120, 128, 129, 132, 139 141, 143, 144, 145, 146, 147, 151–154, 157, 175, 181, 186, 190, 199, 200
Price, Harry 139
Price, Vincent 24, 35, 74–75, 81, 89–90, 113–115, 116–119, 137, 138, 161, 201
Psycho 5, 15, 55, 90–94, 99, 126, 130, 131, 141, 169, 195, 199, 200, 201
Psycho II 93
Psycho III 93

Psycho IV: The Beginning 93
Pullman, Bill 169
Pulp Fiction 171
Puritan Passions 28

Quaid, Dennis 168–169

Radcliffe, Anne 9
Radcliffe, Daniel 192–193, 194
Radner, Gilda 55
Raiders of the Lost Ark 88
Rashidi, Narges 196–197
Rathbone, Basil 45, 46, 53, 54, 64
"The Rats in the Walls" 11
The Raven 84
Ready Player One 108
Rebecca 13, 14, 26, 49, 65, 68–70, 71, 72, 77, 78, 79, 80, 81, 86, 88, 93, 115, 200, 201
Red 169
Redgrave, Michael 94, 95
Reed, Oliver 129, 130
Repulsion 102, 131
Return of the Jedi 133
Return of the Terror 35
Revill, Clive 128, 129
Rinehart, Mary Roberts 21, 22
Ringu 158, 169, 174, 175
The Ritz Brothers 39–40
Riviere, Georges 124, 125
Rose Red 13, 156
Rosemary's Baby 2, 5, 8, 12, 13, 15, 40, 99–102, 104, 110, 130, 131, 132, 100, 200, 201
Ross, Katherine 133–134
Rossi-Stuart, Giacommo 122, 123
Rowlands, Geena 176–177
Rush, Geoffrey 160, 161
Russell, Gail 86, 88

Saint Ange see *House of Voices*
Sangster, Jimmy 183
Scared Stiff 36, 44, 50–51, 64
Scott, George C. 134–136
Scream 92
The Secret of the Blue Room 32–34, 201
Selznick, David O. 68, 69, 70
Seven Footprints to Satan 8, 28, 102, 134, 200
Shaloub, Tony 162–163
The Shape of Water 81, 166
Shimizu, Takashi 169, 171, 172, 174
The Shining (film) 5, 9, 13, 15, 16, 104–108, 130, 142, 186, 199, 200, 201
The Shining (novel) 8, 12, 104
The Shunned House 11
Shutter Island 148
Shyamalan, M. Night 158, 165
Siddons, Anne Morrow 12, 16–17, 179
Silver, Ron 142, 144
Simpkins, Ty 188, 189
Sinister 169, 190–192, 194, 199, 200, 201
Siodmak, Carl 72

The Sixth Sense 158, 165, 183
The Skeleton Key 176–178, 188, 199, 200
Sloat, Micah 179–180
Society for Psychical Research 139, 153
Sondegaard, Gale 35, 42, 45, 46, 49, 52, 64, 88, 201
The Sorrows of Satan 28
Spacek, Sissy 145, 146
"The Spiders" 186
Spielberg, Steven 108, 110
spiritualism 9, 129, 192
Spook Busters 46–47, 200
Stambovsky v. Ackley 7
Stanley Hotel 12, 16, 104, 108, 186
Steele, Barbara 120–121, 124–125
Steiger, Rod 140
The Stepford Wives 134
Stephens, Martin 94, 95–96
Stewart, Kristen 168, 181–183
stigma 7
Stoker, Bram 11, 20, 82, 83, 84, 101, 127
Stone, Sharon 168–169
Straub, Peter 12, 96, 131, 201
The Student of Prague 14
Supernatural 35
Sutherland, Donald 145–146
Svengali 35

Taff, Barry 8, 144, 145
Tamblyn, Amber 172, 174
Tamblyn, Russ 97
Taylor, Elizabeth 72, 77–79, 81
Taylor, Lili 150, 158–159
The Tenant 13, 15, 102, 130–131, 138, 175, 197, 200, 201
The Terror 14, 21, 29, 35, 198, 200
Terror in the Haunted House (a.k.a. *My World Dies Screaming*) 115–116
The Texas Chainsaw Massacre 92
Thesiger, Ernest 31, 32, 112
Thirteen Ghosts (1960) 51–52, 102, 158
Thirteen Ghosts (2001) 13, 14, 15, 162–163, 168, 200
The Thirty-Nine Steps 39
Three Cases of Murder 112–113, 138
Tielve, Fernando 166, 167
Tierney, Gene 74–77, 81
The Time of Their Lives 14, 45, 48–49, 64, 201
Toland, Greg 67, 68, 95
Tourneur, Jacques 72, 81, 201
Turkel, Joe 106, 107
The Turn of the Screw 10, 11, 13, 94, 96, 200
Twice Told Tales 118–120, 127, 201
The Twilight Zone 90, 110, 113, 117, 151
2001: A Space Odyssey 105, 132

Ulmer, Edgar G. 85, 86, 110, 201
Under the Shadow 196–197, 199, 200
The Unholy Three 34

The Uninvited 5, 8, 14, 82–88, 112, 193, 199
Universal Studios 16, 22, 26, 29, 31, 32, 33, 34, 44, 45, 46, 53, 54, 72, 82, 83, 84, 86, 89, 92, 133, 198
The Unseen 88

vampires 3, 11, 19, 20, 35, 46, 62, 63, 64, 82, 83, 126, 129, 190, 193, 198, 200
Van Devere, Trish 134–135, 136
Village of the Damned 96
Von Sydow, Max 102, 103, 104

Wallace, Edgar 21, 29
Walpole, Horace 9
Wan, James 149, 151, 188, 189
Warner Bros. Studios 26, 27, 29, 35, 82, 158
Warren, Ed 9, 139, 140, 142, 149, 150, 151, 152, 153, 154
Warren, Lorraine 9, 139, 140, 142, 149, 150, 151, 152, 153, 154
Wasikowska, Mia 79–80
Waxworks 24
Welles, Orson 10, 68, 71–72, 74, 81, 112, 195
Wells, Jacqueline 84
The Werewolf of London 22
West, Roland 22, 23, 29–30, 35
Whale, James 31, 32, 35, 84, 138, 201
Whatever Happened to Baby Jane? 130
White, Liz 192, 193
Wilde, Oscar 39, 47, 48
Wilder, Gene 36, 55–56, 64
Willard, John 21, 24
Williams, JoBeth 108–109
Wilson, Patrick 140–149, 153, 188
Winchester 154–156
Winchester, Sarah 154, 155, 156–157
Winchester Mystery House 1, 108, 154, 156
Winters, Shelley 131
Wise, Robert 12, 15, 80, 88, 96, 97, 98, 110, 129, 159, 199, 200
Witchcraft Through the Ages 27
Wolfe, Madison 151, 163
The Woman in Black (film) 13, 192–194, 197, 199, 200, 201
The Woman in Black (novel) 5, 13, 15, 192
Wright, Frank Lloyd 13, 86, 115, 179
Wuthering Heights (film) 13, 14, 65–68, 71, 81, 200, 201
Wuthering Heights (novel) 9, 65, 200
Wyler, William 65, 66, 67, 81, 201

Young Frankenstein 55

Zanuck, Daryl F. 75
Zeta-Jones, Catherine 159
Zucco, George 35, 41, 42, 64

www.ingramcontent.com/pod-product-compliance
Ingram Content Group UK Ltd.
Pitfield, Milton Keynes, MK11 3LW, UK
UKHW050528150426
5217IPUK00026B/1847